COIMISIÚN LÁIMHSCRÍBHINNÍ NA hÉIREANN
IRISH MANUSCRIPTS COMMISSION

REGISTRY OF DEEDS DUBLIN

ABSTRACTS OF WILLS

VOL. II

1746-85

EDITED BY
P. BERYL EUSTACE

CLEARFIELD

Originally published
Dublin, 1954

Reprinted for
Clearfield Company, Inc. by
Genealogical Publishing Co., Inc.
Baltimore, Maryland
1996

ISBN: 978-0-8063-5509-2

Made in the United States of America

INTRODUCTION

The Act setting up the Registry of Deeds in Ireland included provision for the registering of all Wills and devises in writing where " the devisor or testatrix shall die after the said 25th March 1708." Nevertheless, there are, in this volume of Abstracts, several instances of testators who took the unusual step of recording their own Wills, as, for example, John Gaynor.(1) He was so angry with his two undutiful daughters for not visiting him during his long illness that he drew up a Will leaving them one shilling each, and registered it himself.

The Registry of Deeds is indeed a mine of information, and, from the genealogical point of view in particular, much can be learnt from the vast mass of material available—not only from the Wills but from marriage settlements, leases, and recorded Deeds of all kinds.(2) The Wills at the Registry of Deeds have now a special importance because they replace some of those destroyed in the Record Office in 1922, when virtually all the original Irish Prerogative and Consistorial Wills perished.(3) As explained more fully in the

---

(1) See Abstract 721.

(2) Research must be undertaken personally or through an agent. The organisation and rules of the Department preclude the transaction of such business by correspondence.

(3) Before 1857 Wills were proved in the Consistorial Court, that is the Court of the Bishop or Ordinary within whose diocese or jurisdiction the testator dwelt; but if there were effects to the value of £5 in two or more dioceses the Will had to be proved in the Prerogative Court of the Archbishop of Armagh, Primate of All Ireland, which was the Supreme Court in matters of which the ecclesiastical jurisdiction had cognisance. The jurisdiction of the Ecclesiastical Courts was abolished and transferred to the Probate Court by the Court of Probate Act 1857 (20 and 21 Vict., c. 79).
Sir William Betham, Ulster King of Arms, compiled his valuable Will Pedigrees from all the Prerogative Wills up to the year 1800. His volumes of these pedigrees, now at the Genealogical Office, Dublin Castle, have been used in checking many doubtful points met with in the Wills recorded at the Registry of Deeds. I am indebted to Dr. Edward MacLysaght, Keeper of Manuscripts, National Library, and Chief Herald, for enabling me to consult these and other MSS.

Introduction to Vol. I *Abstracts of Wills at the Registry of Deeds 1708–45* Wills were recorded at the Registry in one of three ways which, for the sake of brevity, I have termed " Full," " Narrate " and " Précis." A Will described as " Full " in the following abstracts is one which was registered in the testator's own words, a " Narrate " is a Will recorded in the third person singular, while a " Précis " is a brief statement showing to whom a testator assigned his real estate. Transcripts of the memorials of the Wills and all other forms of Deeds are bound into large Books and may be inspected at the Registry of Deeds, on payment of a small fee. The original memorials, signed and sealed by the person registering the Will or Deed, are stored in a fireproof vault. These documents should always be examined if there is any doubt as to the accuracy of the copies in the Books of Transcripts.

Method adopted in making abstracts

The Abstracts were made from the transcripts of the Wills, many doubtful points having been checked with the original memorials. The Abstracts are numbered in chronological order of registration. Following the *name and address* of the testator is his *occupation,* if mentioned in the Will. After the *date of signing* the Will comes the description of *how it is recorded* at the Registry of Deeds (that is, whether in " full," " narrate " or " précis " form), *the length of* the transcript of the memorial and the *date of registration. The relatives* are listed next as they are described by the testator. Ambiguous descriptions are, unfortunately, often used, particularly in the case of Wills recorded in the third person singular. In order to give every possible clue to the correct identity of the persons named all surnames have been copied. Following the relatives come the names and addresses of all other *legatees, trustees, executors,* etc., and any outstanding legacy of general interest. Less important legacies to charities have been omitted from the Abstracts, but bequests to churches are included as this information is sometimes helpful to the research worker. *The lands* detailed by the testator are then listed. The names of grantors are given, especially in cases where the exact localities of the lands are either not mentioned at all by the testator or are not clearly stated([1]). The *names of the witnesses* to the signing of the Will are next shown, followed by the

([1]) A search under the names of these grantors in the Names Index of Grantors at the Registry of Deeds would probably bring further facts to light.

names of *those who witness the registration* of the memorial after the testator's death. One of these, usually an executor named in the Will, signs and seals the memorial. By quoting the *number of the Book, page and memorial,* which are given at the end of each abstract, a certified copy of the memorial of the Will from which the Abstract was made can be obtained from the Assistant Registrar of Deeds, Registry of Deeds, Henrietta Street, Dublin(1).

The dates given in the Abstracts are exactly as found, that is, following the official Old Style year before 1752. In the Old Style year the new year commenced on Lady Day 25th March. This accounts for dates which would at first glance seem to imply that a Will was registered before it was written by the testator. In such cases the date of registration has been amended(2). Scotland adopted New Style in 1600 but in England and Ireland Old Style continued until 1752 when eleven days in September were dropped out of the Calendar for that year.

Indexing of personal and place names in the abstracts

In the index of personal names I have assigned surnames to persons such as sons and daughters mentioned by testators by their christian names only. The fact, therefore, that a surname appears in the Index of Persons does not imply that it should be read into the Abstract. Married daughters are indexed under both their maiden and their married surnames whether the maiden surname appears in the Will or not. The words "my sister" (or "my brother," "my mother" etc.) are often used incorrectly. Great care must be exercised in deciding on exact relationships, especially when either "sister-in-law" or "step-sister" could be inferred. Because of these possibilities I have seldom added a maiden surname to the Index as a cross reference.

Place names are often difficult to index in cases where the testator or person registering the Will had not indicated county or barony. Where it has been possible to ascertain the precise location of any particular place the county has been inserted in

---

(1) The Office can supply certified copies of memorials of given Deeds or Wills but cannot undertake research work on behalf of correspondents.

(2) For example Abstract 44, Herbert Price's Will dated 22 Dec. 1748, registered 24 Jan. 1748—this second date is amended to 1748/9.

square brackets in the Abstracts. Similarly place names which seemed particularly unusual in sound or spelling are followed by corrections—as suggestions—within square brackets([1]).

I am again indebted to the Registrar of Deeds, Mr. J. M. O'Byrne, B.L., for permission to make these Abstracts, and to the successive Assistant Registrars under whose authority I worked. The task of handling the heavy Books of transcripts and of examining memorials in the vaults was made easier for me by the willing help of the staff, to whom I return my best thanks. Finally I must again thank Prof. J. Otway Ruthven for her advice.

Dec. 1953. P. BERYL EUSTACE

([1]) Modern spellings, taken from the Topographical Index, Census of Ireland 1901, are shown within square brackets. Square brackets also enclose fresh pedigree information from MS. sources—usually taken from Betham's Will Pedigrees. I have also checked many points with statements in such authorities as *The Complete Peerage* by G.E.C., printed and MS. indices of Wills, *Reports of the Deputy Keeper of the Records, Ireland, Alumni Dublinenses* by Burtchaell and Sadleir, etc.

REGISTRY OF DEEDS
DUBLIN

ABSTRACTS OF WILLS

VOL. II
1746-1785

1 BOND, JOHN, Woodfort, Co. Cork, Esq.

29 April 1741. Codicil 10 Jan. 1745. Narrate 3 pp. 2 May 1
His wife Sarah Bond, exor. John Bond, eldest son of his ι
Harmer Bond deceased. Geo. Bond, another son of said Ha
Bond. His niece Mary Spires Gabbett, daughter of Spires Gab
His cousin Harmer Delahoide.

John Raymond, Greenhill, Co. Cork, Esq., and Robert H
Cork, Esq., trustees. Robert Travers, Ballycurreen and Th
Spires Gabbett, Arraglin, trustees of Will and codicil in place of
John Raymond and Robert Hoare.

Lands of Carrickdownan, Ballinhalisk and Lisnago[o]rneen
all other his real estate in Barony Fermoy, Co. Cork. House
lands of Woodfort otherwise Killvelliton [? Kilvealaton], Co. (
which he held from Geo. Foot. Lands of Rebogue, in liberti
city of Limerick (mentioned in Will, and as sold in codicil).

Witnesses: Harmer Delahoide, Cork, merchant, John Dow
Cork, hatter, Robert Wallis, Cork, notary public.

Witnesses to codicil: Rev. Boyle Davies, Dawnybrook, C
city of Cork, clerk, Robert Hoare, Cork, Esq., Hans Ber
Mountgomery, Cork, chirurgeon.

Memorial witnessed by: John Dowman, Hans Bernard M
gomery.

119, 475, 83294 Sarah Bond (seal)

2 DAWSON, JOHN, Greenane, Co. Tipperary, Esq.

16 Jan. 1743. Narrate ½ p. 16 May 1746.

His wife Eleanor Dawson otherwise Southcote, exor. His kinsman John Jephson, Esq., exor.

Sir Wm. Osborne, Bart., exor., the Hon. Arthur Blenerhassett, Judge of Court of King's Bench, exor.

Lands of Greenane and other lands in Co. Tipperary purchased by him from the Earl of Arran. Lands of Borrisnafarney, Barony Ikerrin, Co. Tipperary. His estate of East and West Kiele, Co. Tipperary. To Incorporated Society for Erecting Charity Schools in Ireland and their successors, for ever, for educating poor children in the Protestant religion, the lands of Currighbane and Curroghiglass, Barony Lower Ormond, Co. Tipperary.

Witnesses: Nicholas Nash, Dublin, Esq., deceased, Jos. Robbins and Jas. Pierse, both of Dublin.

Memorial witnessed by: Jos. Robbins, Wm. Jephson, Dublin, gent.

119, 507, 83420 John Jephson (seal)

3 KEOUGH, DENIS, James Street, brewer.

9 May 1743. Précis ¼ p. 27 May 1746.

All his worldly substance to his wife Jane Keough, extx.

Witnesses: Patt. FitzGerald, victualler, Owen Mitchell, clerk to said Jane Keough, Thomas Barnes, ribbon weaver, all of Dublin.

Memorial witnessed by: Owen Mitchell, Wm. Hall, clerk to James Saunders, Dublin, gent.

122, 177, 83479 Jane Keough (seal)

4 COOKE, THOMAS, Youghall, Co. Cork, gent.

21 Aug. 1745. Narrate 1 p. 13 June 1746.

His cousin Thomas Cooke, Arnasack in liberties of Youghal, Co. Cork, exor. Testator's sister Mable Harrison otherwise Cooke.

Ballyhay and lands of Ardra, Co. Cork, and all other his estate in Co. Cork or elsewhere which belonged to the testator in right of his mother Margaret Cooke otherwise Tynte.

Witnesses: Samuel Luther, Youghall, merchant, Geo. Mannix, Youghall, gent., Thos. Gimlet, Youghall, merchant.

Memorial witnessed by: Samuel Luther, Thos. Gimlet.

124, 16, 83604 ([1]) Thos. Cooke (seal)

5 SMITH, JAMES, Dublin, Esq.

12 June 1746. Narrate 1 p. 9 July 1746.

His wife Ruth Smith, extx. His eldest son John Smith. His son Edward. Rev. Richd. Ratcliffe, clerk, trustee.

His lands etc. in Co. of Tipperary and Waterford. His lands and premises in Co. Antrim to such of his children as his said wife shall think fit. His houses in Ross Lane and Kennedys Lane, Dublin.

Witnesses: Redmd. Boate, Dublin, chirurgeon, Jos. Kathrens, Dublin, gent., Timothy Green, Dublin, yeoman.

Memorial witnessed by: Timothy Green, Jos. Kathrens.

124, 72, 83831 R. Radcliffe (seal)

Ruth Smith (seal)

6 HOWISON, JOHN, Dublin, gent.

17 Dec. 1744. Narrate 2 pp. 19 Aug. 1746.

An annuity payable to his mother. His father, deceased. His brother Thos. Howison. His brother George Howison. His brother Richd. Howison. His sister Hannah Howison, exor. His sister Elizth. Howison. His sister Sarah Howison. His sister Frances Howison. His uncle Charles Howison and his sister Hannah Howison exors. and guardians to such of his brothers and sisters as should be minors at his death. Henry Mitchell and Frederick Falkiner, Dublin, Esqrs., trustees.

([1]) Pages 17 and 18 in Book 124 are missing. The names of the witnesses to the registration of the memorial have been taken from the original memorial.

His lands in Co. Longford. Ground in Patrick Street, Dublin. Ground and houses in Rosemary Lane and Lazers Hill, High Street, Dublin.

Witnesses: Thos. Hall, gent., Richard Brown Bamber, Esq., Hugh Ker, merchant, all of Dublin.

Memorial witnessed by: Elizabeth Howison, Dublin, spinster, George Donovan, Dublin, gent.

123, 159, 84046 Hannah Ker (seal)

Hannah Ker otherwise Howison, one of the devisees and exors. named in said Will, since intermarried with the above Hugh Ker.

7 MOORE, JAMES, Mollaghmore, parish of Aghalow, Co. Tyrone. 23 May 1746. Narrate ¾ p. 13 Oct. 1746.

His wife Sarah Moore. His children. His daughter Sarah Moore. His daughter Mary Horner.

James Moore, Tulleybrick, Co. Armagh, and Richd. Bryson, Garron, parish of Clownish, Co. Monaghan, exors. His house, estate and lands in Mologhmore.

Witnesses: Robt. Hussie and Wm. Henderson, both of Mollaghmore, Co. Tyrone, farmers, Arthur McGinnis, English schoolmaster.

Memorial witnessed by: Arthur McGinnis, John Erwin, Glasslough, Co. Monaghan, apothecary.

125, 79, 84272 Sarah Moore (seal)
her mark

8 BARNES, GEORGE, Donore otherwise Donover, Barony Kells, Co. Meath, gent. 6 Oct. 1732. Narrate ¾ p. 6 Nov. 1746.

His wife Alice Barnes. His brother Thos. Barnes of city of Kilkenny, alderman. His nephew Thos. Barnes, junr., eldest son of said Thos. Barnes.

His estate of Donore otherwise Donover. Concerns in Ross, Co. Waterford, and in Co. Kilkenny.

Witnesses: John Hatch, Belair, Co. Meath, gent., James Adjore, Alexr. Nowlan, testator's menservants.

Memorial witnessed by: Joseph Robbins, Dublin, Esq., Samuel Crone, Dublin.

123, 235, 84373 Thos. Barnes (seal)
(Thos. Barnes, junr.)

9 AGAR, HENRY, Gowran, Co. Kilkenny, Esq.

20 Sept. 1743. Narrate 1 p. 29 Nov. 1746.

His wife Anne Agar, extx., guardian to his sons. His eldest son James Agar (married). His second son Welbore Ellis Agar. His third son Charles Agar.

Lands held from the Rector and Vicar of Gowran. Leasehold lands adjoining testator's deer park, and leases held from John Bayly of Gowran, Esq. His estate of Gowran. Lands of Lowgrange, Barony Gowran, Co. Kilkenny. Lands of Drakeland within the liberties of city of Kilkenny, part of lands and houses in possession of the testator's sister Ellice Lady Mayo. Lisnewhinshion, Co. Kilkenny. Ballynebouly, Barony Gowran, Co. Kilkenny.

Witnesses: Frances Allen and Ann Bushe, Dublin, widows, Joyce Forster, Dublin, spinster.

Memorial witnessed by: Ann Bushe, Charles Doyle, Clonconey, Co. Carlow, Esq.

121, 556, 84616 Anne Agar (seal)

10 KELLY, WILLIAM, Mucklo[o]n, Co. Galway, gent.

12 July 1746. Codicil 13 July 1746. Narrate 1½ p. 2 Dec. 1746.

His eldest son Daniel Kelly. His 2nd son Ledwith Kelly (under 21 years). His 3rd son Dennis Kelly. His 4th son Bryan Kelly. His eldest daughter Elinor Kelly. His 2nd daughter Elizabeth (unmarried and under 21 years), his 3rd daughter Katherine (ditto). Ross Mahon, Castlegare, Co. Galway, Esq., and James Mahon, Castlegare, gent., trustees and exors. His real estate.

Witnesses: Edmd. Glinan, innkeeper and William McHugo, gent., both of Mucklo[o]n, John Gately, Ahaskra, Co. Galway, miller.

Codicil witnessed by: Mary Glinan, wife of said Edmond, Michael Bourke of Ahaskra aforesaid, Peter Gready, servant to said Ross Mahon.

Memorial witnessed by: Peter Gready, Robt. Stafford, Dublin, gent.

123, 296, 84641 Ross Mahon (seal)

11 LAWLESS, DENNIS, Newstreet, Co. Dublin, gardener.

27 Jan. 1746. Narrate ¾ p. 31 Jan. 1746.

His wife Mary Lawless, exor. His son Peter, under age, unmarried. His daughter Christian Lawless. His daughter Dunn's two sons Dennis and James. 5/– to said daughter Dunn. His daughter Ellinor Fyance (1) wife to Robert Fyance, her two children Lawless and Esther.

Rev. Richard Lincoln. Edmund Kelly, Grangegorman Lane, gardener, exor. His holding in New Street.

Witnesses: John Moran, weaver and Bartholomew Ward, carpenter, both of New Street.

Memorial witnessed by: Michael Argent, gent., and Wm. Hall, both of Dublin.

123, 375, 85020 Mary Lawless her mark (seal)
Peter Lawless (seal)

12 DEYOS, ROGER, Melville, Co. Kilkenny, Esq.

2 March 1746. Narrate ½ p. 13 March 1746.

His wife Ann Deyos, exor. Cornelius Bolton, Waterford, Esq., trustee. Edward Lee, Waterford, Esq., exor.

Lands of Melville, Ballyhomuck, Gaulswood, Farnoge called Barnegelough, Ballyvilloge, Rathard and BallyMcGibbon, all in Co. Kilkenny. Houses in cities of Waterford and Kilkenny.

---

(1) The Will of Ellinor Fyans, Thomas Street, widow, 1758, is listed in *Index of Dublin Grants and Wills* 26th Report of Deputy Keeper of the Records.

Witnesses: John Allen and Oliver Keating, Waterford, gents., Mary Swiney wife of John Swiney, Kilkenny, gent.

Memorial witnessed by: Oliver Keating, Mary Swiney.

122, 549, 85347 Ann Deyos (seal)

13 LASALLE, ANTHONY, Portarlington, then of Dublin, tailor.

26 Feb. 1746. Narrate ½ p. 19 March 1746.

His son Isaac Lasalle, Dublin, grocer, exor. His daughter Easter Horrell, Portarlington. His daughter Gabriel Duff.

A plot of ground in Portarlington left to testator by his uncle Lewis Cevario then late of Portarlington.

Witnesses: Chrisr. Pazey, Dublin, gent., Chas. Walker, Dublin, grocer, John Ward, Dublin, baker.

Memorial witnessed by: John Kathrens, Dublin, public notary, Henry Steevens Reily his clerk.

125, 363, 85375 Isaac Lasalle (seal)

14 JUDGE, PETER, Ballysheil, King's Co., Esq.

15 Oct. 1745. Full 4 pp. 8 April 1747.

My wife Mary Judge. My eldest son Arthur Judge. My second son John Judge. My third son Daniel Judge. To my daughter Ellinor £500 when 21 or day of marriage, to my daughter Mary Judge £800, and to my daughter Elizabeth(1) £400, in like manner. My daughter Catherine Lauder. My daughter Rebecca Lauder. My son Saml. Judge (under 14 years). My nephew Poyntz Judge.

Danl. Toler, Graig, Co. Tipperary, Esq., and Thos. Fetherston, Ardagh, Co. Longford, trustees. Town and lands of Ballyshiel, Knoggas, Buoy and Cush in King's Co., and all other my real estate.

Witnesses: Philip Langton, Birr, King's Co., merchant, Thos. Mullegan, Ferbane, merchant, Edmd. Lowrey, Cush, yeoman.

Memorial witnessed by: Edmd. Lowrey, Peter Scott, servant to Arthur Judge, Esq.

123, 492, 85501 Mary Judge. (seal)

(1) Betham's abstract of this Will at the Genealogical Office does not mention a daughter Elizabeth.

15 YARNER, ABRAHAM, late of London, gent., now in Dublin. 21st June 1744. Full ½ p. 10 April 1747.

My mother Katharine Yarner. All my estate real and personal.

Witnesses: Robt. Marshall, Dublin, Esq., Michl. Mockler, Dublin, yeoman, Job Burnett, Dublin, upholsterer.

Memorial witnessed by: Job Burnett. Alexr. Castell, Dublin, gent.

125, 407, 85511 Cath. Yarner (seal)

16 BUTLER, BUCKLY, Kilkenny, Esq.

30 Jan. 1736. Narrate ¾ p. 21 May 1747.

His wife Elizabeth Butler, guardian of his daughters. His son John Butler, his daughter Sarah Butler, and his daughter Elizabeth Butler (unmarried and under age). His brother Thomas Butler, Kilkenny, surgeon.

Pooley Mollyneux, Esq., Wm. Warring, Esq., and said Thos. Butler, exors. His real and personal estate.

Witnesses: Wm. Austin, Kilkenny, gent., Robt. Harrison, Dublin, gent., Henry Walsh, Kilkenny, gent.

Memorial witnessed by: Robt. Harrison, Henry Walsh and John Birch, Kilkenny, gents.

127, 52, 85848 Eliz. Butler (seal)
widow of testator

17 HEYWOOD, ANN, Drogheda, widow and relict of Benjamin Heywood late of said town, merchant. 25 May 1747. Full 3¼ pp. 30 June 1747.

My brother the Hon. Brigadier Genl. Wm. Graham, trustee. My eldest son and heir Arthur Heywood. My second son Benjamin Heywood. My third son Nathaniel Heywood. My grandson Benjamin Caldwell. My daughter Elizabeth Caldwell. My son-in-law Chas. Caldwell. My father Mr. Arthur Graham deceased. My six younger children . . . . my sons Benjn. and Nathaniel and my daughters Elizabeth, Mary, Isabella and Ann. My daughter Mary Stewart. My daughter Isabella Heywood. My daughter Ann Heywood. My sister Elizth. Johnston, her daughter my niece Ann Johnston. My sister-in-law Mrs. Elizabeth Heywood of Liverpool.

"Lands of Carnaghtowne otherwise Carlintown, Ballymakenny and Succlets Hamletts and all other my estate of inheritance in the liberty of the county of the town of Drogheda." A lease I held under Ald. John Godfrey of Drogheda deceased. A lease which I hold from the Corporation of Drogheda.

Witnesses: Chas. Moore, Dublin, Esq., Barrister at law, George Maconchy of the same city, Esq., Doctor of Physick, and Richard Moore, Fishamble Street, Dublin, gent.

Memorial witnessed by: Richd. Moore, Robt. Bonham, clerk to Chas. Caldwell, Dublin, Esq.

129, 32, 86168 A. Heywood (seal)

Arthur Heywood of Liverpool, merchant, eldest son of testatrix.

18 CULBRATH, JOHN, Corkiran, parish of Aughnamullen, Co. Monaghan. 9 May 1747. Précis ½ p. 2 July 1747.

His sister Mary Culbrath. His nephew James Johnston, his son James Johnston.

Mr. Brabs. Noble, attorney, said James Johnston his nephew, and Mr. Robert Wallace, Anny, overseers.

The house he then dwelt in, the farm and stock thereon. All his estate and mortgages.

Witnesses: Revd. Robt. Cuming, clerk, James Stennous, sexton and George Kerr, yeoman, all of Aughnamullen.

Memorial witnessed by: George Kerr, Henry Chritchly, Dublin, gent.

124, 534, 86190 Js. Johnston (seal)

19 FITZGERALD, THOMAS, Moyhinnah, Co. Mayo, Esq.

9 July 1747. Précis ½ p. 18 July 1747.

His wife Henrietta FitzGerald, sole extx. His second son Nicholas FitzGerald. His younger children.

Lands of Ballyvary and Tuormore, Co. Mayo. His estate in Co. Roscommon.

Witnesses: Hugh Maguire, Roger Palmer, Peter Daly, all of Dublin, Esqrs.

Memorial witnessed by: Hugh Heaney, Dublin, victualler, James Dillon, Dublin, gent.

124, 541, 86318 Nic. FitzGerald (seal)

20 FARRELL, IGNATIUS, Dublin, wigmaker.

4 May 1741. Narrate ½ p. 18 July 1747.

Being minded to travel abroad. John Mahon his brother-in-law. Said brother-in-law J. Mahon and Paul Mahon both of city of Dublin, merchants, exors.

Witnesses: Luke Armstrong, Dublin, victualler, Thos. Robertson, Dublin, butcher.

Memorial witnessed by: Patk. Currin, Robt. Stafford, both Dublin, gents.

128, 135, 86324 John Mahon (seal)

21 CHAMBERLAIN, JOSEPH, Knockfynn, Queen's Co.

16 Sept. 1744. Narrate ¾ p. 10 Aug. 1747.

His sons John Chamberlain and Joseph Chamberlain. His farm, house, etc. at Knockfynn.

Witnesses: Robert Baldwin, Coolkerry, Queen's Co., gent., Joseph Palmer, now of Durrow, Co. Kilkenny, gent., John Emson, Munage, Queen's Co., farmer.

Memorial witnessed by: Joseph Palmer, Richd. Hoey, Abyleix, Queen's Co., farmer.

128, 162, 86662 Joseph Chamberlain (seal)

22 FISHER, HENRY, [? of Killeny].

5 April 1747. Précis ½ p. 4 Nov. 1747.

To Frances Fisher his wife £30 per year out of lands he held from Mr. Dawson in Killeny. Profits of the Brickfields to his children share and share alike but £12 a year to Dr. Jemmett for life.

Witnesses: Arthur Fisher, Jas. Fisher, Kryian Dullany, all of Killeny aforesaid.

Memorial witnessed by: Said Jas. Fisher, Killeny, Queen's Co., farmer, Wm. Bolger, Dublin, gent.

129, 290, 87099 Frances Fisher (seal)

23 BRAY, ROBERT, Portanure, Co. Longford, Esq.

19 May 1747. Précis ½ p. 15 Dec. 1747.

His daughters Elinor, Jane and Mary; Elinor and Mary exors. The issue of his daughter Catherine deceased.

His estate of Portanure, Co. Longford. His real estate in county of city of Limerick, namely the lands of Conohie and Garanhea.

Witnesses: Nathan Forth, Mala, Co. Tipperary, Lieut. in H.M.'s service, Jas. Williams, Longford, Co. Longford, gent., Joseph Luggad, Mala, yeoman.

Memorial witnessed by: James Dillon, Dublin, gent., Richard Broughton, Dublin, gent.

126, 319, 87287 Elinor Forth (seal)
said Elinor now married to Saml. Forth, Esq.
Mary Kelly (seal)
said Mary married to Dennis Kelly, Esq.

24 LEWIS, ELINOR, alias SCOTT alias LABAN, wife of Henry Lewis, Aughmacart, Queen's Co., gent. 25 March 1746. Full 4 pp. 15 Dec. 1747.

Henry Lewis my husband, exor. Marriage settlement 9 July 1734 executed by me (by name of Ellinor Scott alias Laban, widow of William Scott, late of Fisherstown, Queen's Co., gent.) on intermarriage with Henry Lewis of Aughmacart, Queen's Co., gent.; Wm. Laban, Newmarket, Co. Dublin, tanner, and Wm. Scott of Monycoughlin, Queen's Co., gent., the elder, parties to said settlement.

My brother Joseph Laban. My niece Margt. Laban, daughter of my brother Joseph Laban. My sister Anderson. My niece Mary Palmer. My nephew Wm. Laban, son of my brother Jon. Laban. My brother Wm. Laban, exor., and his two sons. My daughter Hannah Palmer and my daughter Sarah Hutton. My nephew Thos. Laban and my niece Jane Newbold. My nephew Thos. Anderson and my niece Jane Baily alias Anderson. My brother Joseph [Laban's] children. My nephew Samuel Laban, son of my brother Wm. Laban. My nephew Nehemiah, son of my brother Samuel Laban, deceased. My niece Margaret French als. Laban. My daughter Mary Lewis. My son Daniel Lewis. Daniel Lewis of Aughmacart and Samuel Laban my nephew, merchant in Dublin, overseers of Will.

Sarah Mullin. James Cowan. Ellinor How alias Cowan. Elizabeth Bennett alias Cowan. Steven Ray my old servant. Elizabeth Tinan my old servant. Our servant John Fletcher.

Lands of Rickardstown and Ballyshanduff, [? Queen's Co.]

Witnesses: John Gordon, John Doughan, servant to said Henry Lewis, Mary Magachie, wife to Rev. Stephen Magachie, Kilnacourt, Queen's Co., clerk.

Memorial witnessed by: Robert Hutton, currier, Robt. Stafford, gent., both of Dublin.

127, 407, 87288 Saml. Laban (seal)

25 ARREL, ROBERT, Cabrach, parish of Termoneeny, Barony Lo[u]ghinsholin, Co. Londonderry. 21 Oct. 1747. Codicil 23 Oct. 1747. Narrate 1 p. 18 Dec. 1747.

Left his sister Jane Arrel land " during her widowhood "; her two sons John and William. To his dear beloved brothers John and Henry each 13 pence to disinherit them. Robin Mills. William Downing, exor.

His holding in Cabrach, William Downing [? tenant], Benjamin Crocker and David Miller, tenants.

Witnesses: Adam Averel, Lurgangoose, parish of Termoneny, Barony Loughinsholling, Co. Londonderry, gent., William Downing, the elder, Cabrach, Joseph Meas, Toberhead, said parish and barony, gent.

Memorial witnessed by: Adam Averel, William Downing.

126, 320, 87325 Jane Arrel her mark (seal)

26 CATHERWOOD, JOHN, Ballyvester, Barony Ards, Co. Down. 14 March 1739. Narrate ½ p. 15 June 1747.

His wife Phillis Catherwood. His sons John, Robert and Andrew. His daughters Elizabeth, Margt., Ellin, Phillis, Mary, Jane, Charity, Martha. To his son William all his lands etc.

Witnesses: Thomas Crooks, John Faires, John Baird, all of Donaghadee, Co. Down.

Memorial witnessed by: John Faires, Hugh Boyd, Donaghadee.

128, 423, 87445 Phillis Catherwood (seal)

27 BARRINGTON, MARK, Bristol, England, formerly of Ballycogly, Co. Wexford, gent. 28 June 1738. Full ½ p. 10 Feb. 1747.

My brother Nichs. Barrington, Ballycogly, Barony Forth, Co. Wexford, exor. Lands of Ballycogly.

Witnesses: Charles Cruoly then of Bristol, mariner, mate of the ship called *The Hobhouse* then belonging to the city of Bristol and bound on a voyage to the coast of Guinea in Africa, John Burrows, then of the same, mariner and gunner of said ship, Valentine Broder, Knockingall, Co. Wexford, farmer.

Memorial witnessed by: Valentine Broder, Henry Hatton, Wexford, Esq.

126, 362, 87692 Anne Barrington (seal)
widow and extx. of said Nicholas
Barrington since deceased.

28 MIDLETON, ALAN VISCOUNT

1 Feb. 1744. Précis ½ p. 15 Feb. 1747.

All real and personal estate to his wife Mary now Lady Viscountess Dowager Midleton, extx.

Witnesses: Edwd. Garthwaite, Eashing, Surrey, Rev. John Warner, clerk and Francis Eliot, gent., both of Goldalming, Surrey.

Memorial witnessed by: Chas. Powell, New Burlington Street, parish of St. James, Westminster, gent., Wm. Ick, of same place, servant to said Lady Midleton.

130, 39, 87728 M. Midleton (seal)
Mary Viscountess Dowager Midleton

29 PEPPARD, JACOB, Dublin, Esq.

13 March 1724. Narrate 1¼ p. 19 March 1747.

His wife Jane Peppard. His son Robt. Peppard, exor. Edwd. Hunt, Dublin, Esq., and Thos. Gonne, Dublin, gent., trustees. His daughter Dianna Peppard (unmarried). His daughter Elizth. Barlow. His grandson James Barlow. His son-in-law Wm. Barlow, exor. with testator's son Robert Peppard and said Edward Hunt who is since deceased.

House in Hoyes Alley wherein he dwelt. Town and lands of Kerdiffstowne, Co. Kildare. Houses and gardens in James Street, Dublin. Lands of Raffin, Dowdstowne and part of Fletcherstowne in Co. Meath. Premises held under him by Wm. Paine [situation not mentioned] and all his estate in and about the town of Swords, Co. Dublin. Reversion of lands of Ballymacad, Ballynegangy [Ballynagranshy], Tobrid [? Tubbrid], Rossilla [1] and part of Rathmea in Co. Meath then in lease to John Leigh, Esq. His estate of inheritance in the town of Wicklow. Houses on Ormond Quay and in Aron Street, city of Dublin. His lease of Ardellis, King's Co. [? Co. Kildare], Ballybeg, Co. Kildare. Lenihrim, King's Co.

Witnesses: John Stoyte, Dublin, alderman, deceased, George More, then clerk to Thos. Cooke, junr., public notary, Dublin, and said Thos. Cooke.

---

(1) Possibly Ross in parish of Killeagh. The townlands of Ballymacad and Tubbrid are in the same parish.

Memorial witnessed by: Geo. More, John Nolan, servant to said Thos. Gonne.

129, 487, 87930 Thos. Gonne (seal)

30 RAKESTROW, JOHN, Newry, Co. Down, distiller.

30 Jan. 1747. Narrate ½ p. 9 April 1748.

His wife Jane Rakestrow. His nephew Wm. Davis, son of John Davis of High Street, Newry. John Corbett, Dublin, attorney.

House and tenement which he dwelt in in Newry, leased from Robt. Needham, Esq. His malt kiln and tenement in High Street, Newry.

Witnesses: Chas. Laurant, John Davis and George Walker, all of Newry.

Memorial witnessed by: John Davis, Hugh Bigger, Dublin, joiner.

128, 555, 88131 John Corbett (seal)

31 CARR, GEORGE, Stonehouse, Co. Waterford, gent.

20 May 1745. Précis part in full, ¾ p. 2 May 1748.

My son Thomas Carr, exor. My friend Alderman Thos. Baker of Dublin. My friend Geo. Backus.

My farm of Stonehouse. My houses in Little Patrick Street, Waterford.

Witnesses: Ignatius Flyming, John Burton, both of city of Waterford, John Douse, Ballyduff, Co. Waterford, gent.

Memorial witnessed by: Ignatius Flyming, Richd. Hinde of said city, gent.

131, 102, 88266 Thos. Carr (seal)

32 BURNSIDE, JOHN, Corcreevy, Co. Tyrone.
27 Feb. 1747. Narrate ½ p. 12 May 1748.

His brother Charles Burnside, exor. His brother Anthony Burnside. John Thompson, Coothill, exor.

His estate known and called by the name of Corcreevy, and also his house and tenement in Fivemiletown, Co. Tyrone.

Witnesses: Rev. Thomas Higginbotham, Fivemiletown, clerk, Mathew Caldwell, Cron, Co. Fermanagh, farmer, Joseph Johnston, Corcreevey, Co. Tyrone, blacksmith and James Reed, Cavanaleek, Co. Fermanagh, merchant.

Memorial witnessed by: George Livingston, Caldrum, Co. Tyrone' gent., James Wadsworth, Miletown, Co. Monaghan, gent.

132, 64, 88411 Charr. Burnside (seal)

33 BAYLY, DOROTHY DAME, Dublin, widow.

12 May 1744. Full ¾ p. 14 May 1748.

My son Lambert Bayly, exor. My son Edward Bayly. My son Charles Bayly. My grand-daughter Dorothy Bayly, daughter of said son Edward Bayly. My three daughters Dorothea Bayly, Arabella Bayly and Lucinda Bayly.

My houses, lands, tenements and hereditaments called Barbican in or near city of London, and lands etc. in Kent, England. £40 to the poorest creditors of Sir Edward Bayly, Bart., late of Tiney Park, Co. Wicklow, my late husband, as live near Tiney Park (said son Lambert and James Rooney to distribute this).

Witnesses: Richd. Sumner, Dublin, confectioner, Henry Stearn, clerk to Wm. Sumner, Dublin, public notary, and by said Wm. Sumner.

Memorial witnessed by: Henry Stearn now clerk to Christopher Dalton, Dublin, public notary, James Rooney, Dublin, gent.

132, 78, 88454 Elizth. Bayly (seal)
widow and extx. of said Lambert Bayly.

34 CORKER, EDWARD, Ballymaloe, Co. Cork, Esq.

14 Oct. 1725. Narrate ¾ p. 18 May 1748.

His brother Chambre. Robert Corker, eldest son of said Chambre, Thomas Corker, second son of said Chambre, Edward Corker, third son of said Chambre. His brother Thos. His nephew Stephen Wright. Richard Bolton, Bazill Bolton.

Lands of Mentrim, Co. Meath to his mother for life. Lands of Cornelstown, Co. Meath.

Witnesses: John Pierce and Wm. Simmins heretofore clerks to Robert Wallis late of city of Cork and now of city of Dublin, public notary, and by said Robt. Wallis.

Memorial witnessed by: Michael McCarthy and John Staples, clerks to said Robt. Wallis.

131, 154, 88490 Thos. Corker (seal)

35 BIGG, RICHARD, son of Boleyn Bigg of Clonmel, Esq. 23 April 1748. Précis three lines, 27 June 1748.

All his real estate to his father said Boleyn Bigg, Esq.

Witnesses: John Staples and Michael McCarthy, clerks to Robert Wallis, Dublin, notary public, and by said Robt. Wallis.

Memorial witnessed by: Jno. Connor, Clonmel, Co. Tipperary, gent., Darby Lonergan, Redmondstown, Co. Tipperary, farmer.

126, 545, 88861 Boleyn Bigg (seal)

36 SCROGGS, THOMAS, Athlone, Lieut. in Gen. Blygh's Regt. of Dragoons. [Date not recorded]. Narrate ½ p. 15 July 1748.

His wife Abigal Scroggs alias Graves. To his daughter (unmarried and under 21 years) Elizabeth Scroggs £1,000 deposited in hands of Capt. Theophilus Debrizay being the purchase of his commission. His said wife and Elizabeth Scroggs of Berkshire guardians of his daughter and exors. His real and personal estate.

Witnesses: Rev. Wm. Tisdall, Athlone, Co. Westmeath, clerk, Rev. Elias Handcock of same, clerk, Mathew McNemara, Athlone, Co. Roscommon, apothecary.

Memorial witnessed by: Robert Handcock, Athlone, Co. Westmeath, Esq., John Quartermain of same, gent.

131, 274, 89023 Abigail Scroggs (seal)

37 EGMONT, JOHN EARL OF, who died on or about 1 May 1748 in the parish of St. James, Westminster, Co. Middlesex. 6 March 1744. Narrate 1½ p. 15 July 1748.

His wife Catherine Countess of Egmont. A settlement made on the marriage of his son John Lord Viscount Perceval with the Lady Catherine Cecil. Testator's brother Philip Perceval. Testator's daughter Lady Catherine Hanmer.

His wife's woman Bridget Wheatley. Sir Francis Clerke, Baronet. £300 to Protestant Charity Schools in Ireland. All his lands, tenements, etc. in Ireland.

Witnesses: Samuel Seddon, said parish of St. James, gent., John Newton and William Lambe of same, gents.

Memorial witnessed by: Samuel Seddon, William Lambe.

126, 574, 89026 Catherine Egmont (seal)

38 TRAIL, JAMES, Marybrook, Co. Down, gent.

7 March 1742. Narrate 1¼ p. 3 Aug. 1748.

His wife Mary Trail. His uncle Hugh Hamilton to continue to lodge with testator's wife or to have an annuity of £10 per annum. His eldest son Hamilton Trail. Exors. his wife, said Hugh Hamilton, William Bruce, Dublin, gent. and Charles Johnston, Ballee, gent.

His townland of Drummaticonner, Co. Down. Releagh, parish Kilmore, Co. Down. Lease of Armillan, Co. Down.

Witnesses: James Crawford, Crawfordsburn, James Bruce, Killeleagh, both Co. Down, gents., Samuel Bruce, Dublin, gent.

Memorial witnessed by: Saml. Bruce, Hamilton McClure, Dublin, gent.

134, 11, 89176 William Bruce (seal)

39 WALSH, CHRISTOPHER, Oldcourt, Co. Wicklow, gent.

18 Feb. 1746. Précis ¾ p. 13 Aug. 1748.

His wife Ann. His three sons Robt., David and Chas. His daughter Mary. His daughter Jane. His daughter Dorcas. Exors. his wife Ann and sons Robt. and Chas. His lease of Oldcourt.

Witnesses: Jon. Heally, Francis Keanan, both of Oldcourt, farmers, Joshua Richardson, Blessingtown, Co. Wicklow, parish clerk.

Memorial witnessed by: John Jameson, merchant, Wm. Hall, clerk to James Saunders, both of Dublin.

130, 322, 89234 Charles Walsh (seal)

40 BROWNE, ELINOR, New Markett Lane, Co. Dublin, widow of Bernard Browne, Esq., late of same place. 2 Jan. 1747. Codicil 16 Jan. 1747. Narrate 1½ p. 22 Oct. 1748.

Her late husband Bernard Browne by Will dated 5 July 1716 devised his houses etc. in liberty of Thomas Court and Donore to said Elinor his wife and his son Thomas Browne by his first wife equally. Testator in 1733 conveyed her share to Newcomen L'Estrange, Moistown, King's Co., Esq. Mary Atkinson alias L'Estrange is heir at law of said Newcomen L'Estrange.

Witnesses: Rev. Phillip Cooley, Dublin, clerk, Wm. Milton, Truck Street, liberty of Thomas Court and Donore, gent., Wm. Devall, Dublin, public notary.

Memorial witnessed by: Philip Cooley, Thomas Mulock, Dublin, public notary.

132, 339, 89522 Ber Browne (seal)
Bernard Browne son of textatrix

41 LUNEMAN, SIMON, Dublin, gent.
24 Sept. 1748. Précis ¼ p. 25 Oct. 1748.

His mother. Mrs. Susanna Tramasse, wife of Michl. Tramasse, Dublin, merchant, extx.

Testator was entitled to a remainder in fee, after the death of his mother, in lands of Lower Killeen, Barony Granard, Co. Longford.

Witnesses: Jane Dugan, Mary Welsh and Jane Dugan the younger.

Memorial witnessed by: Mary Welsh, Henry Hawkins, both of Dublin.

134, 63, 89536 Su Tramasse (seal)

42 MINCHIN, HUMPHREY, Inchmore, Co. Kilkenny, gent.
22 Sept. 1748. Full 1¼ p. 7 Nov. 1748.

Sister Penelope Carey otherwise Minchin. My sister Jane Stotesbury otherwise Minchin, her children by her first husband Henry Stotesbury deceased. My sister Mary Lewis otherwise Minchin. My brother-in-law Peter Carey, gent., husband to my said sister Penelope, trustee and exor. My nephew Wm. Minchin (under 31 years) son of my sister Penelope by her first husband Thos. Minchin deceased. My nephew John Minchin, son of my brother Boyle Minchin. My nephew John Minchin son of my brother Chas. Minchin deceased. My real and personal estate.

Witnesses: David Harborne, Dublin, gent., Catherine Carey, Dublin, spinster, Joseph Deane, Dublin, gent.

Memorial witnessed by: Henry Chritchly, Robt. Stafford, Dublin, gents.

132, 354, 89580 Peter Carey (seal)

43 MILLEY, REV. NICHOLAS, Graiguenamanagh, Co. Kilkenny, clerk. 1 Jan. 1748. Narrate 1½ p. 24 Jan. 1748.

His wife Catherine Milley, extx. His son Rev. John Milley, clerk, exor. Testator's daughters Lucy Milley, Elizabeth Doyle and Mary Harman. His daughter Ann Beauchamp. George Dunbar, Esq., trustee.

Lands of Knockbrack and Knockbarragh, Barony Forth, Co. Catherlogh. Townlands of Cappaghwater, Clashadarragh, Barony Forth, Co. Catherlogh.

Witnesses: Rev. Wm. Darby, Dublin, clerk, Wm. Dale, town of Catherlogh, apothecary, Solomon Delane and Theophilus Perkins, both of Dublin, gents.

Memorial witnessed by: Theophilus Perkins, Solomon Delane.

132, 523, 90253 John Milley (seal)

44 PRICE, HERBERT, Mullingar, Co. Westmeath, Esq.
22 Dec. 1748. Full 1 p. 24 Jan. 1748/9.

To be privately buried at Mullingar. My sister Dudley Jervis. My grand-daughter Ann Ambrose. My grand-daughter Elinor

Williamson. My son-in-law Anthony Lennon, exor. My son-in-law Henry Guyon. My daughter Sabina Lennon. My daughter Catherine Lennon. My daughter Margt. Guyon.(1) Her two children by her first husband, viz. Jno. Wilson and Margaret Wilson, to have an equal share in a legacy with " her other children."

My leases from George Earl of Granard in the Manor of Mullingar. Rest of real and personal estate.

Witnesses: Stephen Bootle, Newtown, Co. Westmeath, clerk, Charles Coghlan, Mullingar, Doctor of Physick, Anthony Fearns.

Memorial witnessed by: Anthony Fearns, Mullingar, Doctor of Physick, John Saule, Dublin, gent.

133, 195, 90254 Anthony Lennon (seal)

45 MINCHIN, HUMPHREY, Inchmore, Co. Kilkenny.

7 Oct. 1748. Précis ½ p. 1 March 1748/9.

His brother Boyle Minchin. Exors. said brother Boyle Minchin, and Michael Lewis. Lands of Inchmore, Co. Kilkenny.

Witnesses: Mathias Archdekin, Kilkenny, merchant, Robert Stotesbury, Three Castles, Co. Kilkenny, gent., Henry Walsh, Kilkenny, gent.

Memorial witnessed by: Francis Duggan, Dublin, Esq., Joseph Duggan, Dublin, gent.

134, 310, 90639 Boyle Minchin (seal)

46 WILKINSON, SAMUEL, Antrim town, weaver.

2 March 1743. Narrate ¾ p. 6 April 1749.

His brother Thos. Wilkinson. His brother Josh. Wilkinson. His brother Isiah Wilkinson. Jacob Baxter.

His lands and tenements in town and parish of Antrim which his father had formerly mortgaged to Wm. Hartson, clerk, then held by

(1) These three daughters Sabina Lennon, Catherine Lennon and Margt. Guyon are each to get one third of testator's estate. It is not clear which daughter was wife to Anthony Lennon.

Wm. McConchy and Wm. Holmes or in tenancy to John Maxwell and Robert Harlow and others.

Witnesses: Saml. Stewart, Robt. Mewha, Jas. Camron.

Memorial witnessed by: Saml. Stewart, Antrim, blacksmith, Robt. Mewha and Jas. Camron, both of Antrim, weavers, Nathl. Holmes, Antrim, merchant.

134, 247, 90826 Thos. Wilkinson (seal)

47 SCOTT, JONATHAN, Kishavany, Co. Kildare, farmer.
20 March 1742. Narrate 1 p. 9 May 1749.

His wife Mary Scott. His sons Henry, Richard, William, Nathaniel and Jonathan Scott. His daughter Isabella. His daughters Elizabeth and Rachell Scott alias Jephson. His lease of lives in Kishavany [Kishawanny].

Witnesses: Wm. Bleayds, Connyberry, King's Co., woollen weaver, Robt. Frith, Dublin, linen weaver, Robt. Gavin, Kishavany, tanner.

Memorial witnessed by: William Bleayds, Robt. Gavin.

136, 222, 91153 Mary Scott (seal)

48 READ, PAUL, clerk, rector of parish of Leckpatrick, Co. Tyrone. 23 Feb. 1739. Narrate 1½ p. 18 May 1749.

Settlement 21 Nov. 1732 made before his intermarriage. His wife Elizabeth, guardian of children (said wife since intermarried with John Ferguson late of Arabane, Co. Tyrone, apothecary, deceased). His eldest daughter Mary, his youngest daughter Ann (both under 15 years). His son Francis (under 21 years). His brother Isaac Read. " His brothers and sisters Walter, Thomas, Elizabeth, Mary and Sarah " (Walter Read, Thomas Read, Elizabeth Read, Sarah Macartney). " His sister Edie."(1) Alexander McAulay, Dublin, Esq. and Francis Hamilton, Stewartstown, trustees, and also exors. with testator's wife, and Rev. Paul Read, Fellow of Trinity College, Dublin. Lands of Longfield [situation not mentioned].

(1) Betham's abstract of this will at the Genealogical Office omits the testator's son Francis and shows " my sister Edie " as Mary wife of . . . . Edie.

Witnesses: Rev. John Hamilton, Charlestown, clerk, Rev. William Hamilton, clerk, and Thos. Gillaghan, then servant to testator but since deceased, both of Strabane.

Memorial witnessed by: Wm. Hamilton, Edward Morris, Strabane, gent.

133, 311, 91241 Elizth. Ferguson (seal)
Elizabeth Ferguson otherwise Read
widow of testator

49 MARSH, HENRY, Moyally, King's Co., Esq.

26 Aug. 1748. Précis ½ p. 22 May 1749.

His brother Peter Marsh guardian to testator's daughter Mary Marsh.

All his lands etc. in King's Co., Co. of Westmeath, Co. of Galway and elsewhere.

Witnesses: Thos. Darragh and Eusebius Low, both of Pill Lane, Dublin, merchants, Thos. Mulock, Dublin, public notary.

Memorial witnessed by: Thos. Mulock, Christopher Deey his clerk.

136, 251, 91252 Peter Marsh (seal)

50 KELLY, JOSEPH, Kellymount, Co. Kilkenny, Esq.

2 Feb. 1748. Narrate 1½ p. 22 May 1749.

An indenture made previous to his intermarriage with Dorothea Molyneaux. His wife, sole extx. His dau. Elizabeth Kelly. His sister Elizabeth Kelly. His cousin Jno. Kelly of Middle Temple, London, Esq. His uncle Chas. Monck, Esq. His cousin Henry Monck. His cousin Thos. Monck. His uncle Wm. Monck. Jno. Stanley Monck, son to said William.

Trustees: Isaac Holroyd, Saml. Card, Dublin, Esqrs.

All his lands, tenements and hereditaments. A sum of £1,000 secured to him on estate of late Robt. Oliver, Esq.

Witnesses: John Rose, Dublin, Doctor of Physick, Rev. Kene Percivall, Powerscourt, Co. Wicklow, Wm. Clarke, servant to Henry Monck, Esq.

Memorial witnessed by: John Rose, Edwd. Cullen, clerk to Geo. Moore, public notary.

134, 345, 91259 Dorothea Kelly (seal)

51 GORE, DAME JANE alias WORTH, wife of Sir Arthur Gore of Newtowngore, Co. Mayo, Bart. 14 Oct. 1747. Narrate 3½ pp. 23 May 1749.

Reciting indenture quadrupartite of 12 March 1730 made between (1) Sir Arthur Gore of Newtown Gore, Co. Mayo, Bart., and Arthur Gore, Esq., eldest son and heir apparent of said Sir Arthur, (2) Dame Jane Gore by the name of Jane Worth widow, sole daughter and heiress of Richard Saunders late of Saundersgrove, Co. Wexford, Esq., deceased, (3) Sir Henry King, Boyle, Co. Roscommon, Bart., and Whitfield Doyne, Dublin, Esq., (4) the Rt. Hon. James Tynte, P.C., Arthur French, Frenchpark, Co. Roscommon, and Isaac Dobson, Dublin, Esq., whereby in consideration of a marriage intended between said Arthur Gore and said Jane Worth the said Jane Worth granted to said Sir Henry King and Whitfield Doyne, as trustees, the towns, lands, etc. of Ballynecarrigg, Keile, Poledarrigg, Ballyneslany, Kereaght and part of Newtown, Redmondstowne, Coolenaboy, Coolenemaine, Oyle, Raheale (Rahealy) and Coolkip, Davidstown, Tin(n)ecrossy, Kildennis and part of Ballymony (Barrmoney) Mackmain and Killeragh, Ballyhines and part Rowstown, Ballysillagh, Newcastle, Killowen alias Killwin, Ballymacshonin, Killmallock, Rudenagh, Cornwall, Garrywilliam and parts of Garryclarry, Ballydonagan, Ballyshane (Ballyshean), Killbride, Barmony, part of Ballincash in the possession of Thos. Bannisterd and Thos. Goodall, another part of Ballincash now in possession of John Rath, part of same called Ballyneroad, Killoques alias Killdish, Ballintogher, Kilmacthomas Roe alias Old Keile, part of Toghman now in possession of Thos. Batt, another part in possession of Joshua Hillary, Knockduffy (Knockduffe), Ballynebarn(e)y, Curtalogh (Curtellogh), Tinrahin, Knockue(c)lary, Killurin, Takillin (Tikillin) and Ballynecrossy, Tin(n)ekilly and Shanconlagh, Ballyhara(s)ham, Deepes, Newtown, Ballyedekin, Killnebay alias Kileene now in possession of Michael

Franey, Kilpatrick now called Saunderscourt, and Gallbally, Ballyneskagh now in possession of Wm. Roach, Ballyroe and part of Ballynagh, Blackmore and Norristown, which several lands and premises are in Co. Wexford, also Ballickmoyler, Shrogh and Cudagh in Queen's Co.(1) Snowshill (Snowhills) in parish of Staunton, Gloucestershire. Said marriage was afterwards soleminized and said Sir Arthur Gore was since dead.

Testatrix bequeathed all said lands to her husband Arthur Gore, now Sir Arthur Gore, exor.

Witnesses: Jacob Jackson, Dublin, gent., Richard Magenis and Saml. Wallace, Dublin, gents.

Memorial witnessed by: Richard Magenis, Saml. Wallace.

135, 248, 91266 Arthur Gore (seal)

52 COLVILLE, ROBERT, formerly of Newtown, Co. Down, and late of parish of St. George near Hannover Square, Middlesex. Testator was son and heir at law of Hugh Colvill late of Newtown, Esq., deceased, and grandson and heir at law of Sir Robert Colvill, late of Newtown, Knt., deceased. 4 Dec. 1746. Narrate 2¼ pp. 10 June 1749.

Sir Cecil Bishop, Berkeley Square, said parish of St. George, Bart., Hutchison Mure, Saxham, Suffolk, Esq., and George Draper, parish of St. Paul's, Covent Garden, apothecary, trustees. Mrs. Martha Colvill of Grosvenor Square in said parish of St. George to have care during her minority of Miss Mary Degg, daughter of Col. Wm. Degg and Catherine his wife both deceased, and grand-daughter of Catherine Meighen of Berkeley Square aforesaid, widow of Francis Meighen, gent., deceased. Said Catherine Meighan. His sister Alice Moore otherwise Colvill then wife of Stephen Moore of Killworth, Co. Cork. Hon. Wm. Ponsonby commonly called Lord Viscount Duncannon. Miss Mary Bishop, daughter of Sir Cecil Bishop. His real and personal estate.

Witnesses: Robt. Talbot, Peter Hemet, junr., and Samuel Baldwin, all of liberty of Westminster.

(1) Acreages of all above lands are given.

Memorial witnessed by: Samuel Baldwin, Richd. Clarke, Bride Street, Co. Dublin, Esq., Doctor of Laws, then of Cecil Street in the Strand, Middlesex.

134, 401, 91485

Cecil Bishop (seal)
Hutchinson Mure (seal)
Geo. Draper (seal)

53 McLAUGHLIN, LAWRENCE, Glenleary, Co. Londonderry, farmer. 2 June 1744. Précis ½ p. 21 June 1749.

To his brother Richard McLaughlin the south part of Glenleary whereon the Pattersons then dwelt.

Witnesses: Joseph Patterson and Thos. Patterson, both of Glenleary, farmers, Wm. Young, Crossgarr, Co. Londonderry, linen draper.

Memorial witnessed by: Joseph Patterson, Patrick O'Conning, Coleraine, yeoman.

131, 563, 91603 Richard McLaughlin (seal)

54 SWIFT, JAMES, Dublin, merchant.

28 April 1748. Codicil 1 Dec. 1748. Full 3½ pp. 30 June 1749.

My nephew Mr. Nathl. Priestly of North Owram, parish of Halifax, Co. York (my heir and exor.). My niece Mrs. Elizabeth Ingham of North Owran, widow. My niece Mrs. Sarah Daniel, wife of John Daniel, Leeds, York. John, Elizabeth and Hannah Priestly children of said nephew. Hannah Priestly, wife of said nephew, and Richd. Holden of Bradford, York, salter, exors. and trustees if said nephew should die before the testator. Codicil leaves £50 more to " my niece Mrs. Mary Ingham hath come over from England and hath with great care and diligence attended on me."

Sir Thos. Taylor, Bart., Mr. Sankey Dennis and Mr. John Lodge, all of Dublin, trustees. Money for mourning rings to Mary Pyddock, widow and Catherine her daughter, Geo. Grierson, Esq., the King's Printer, and Mr. Geo. Riske, Geo. Ewing and his spouse, Chas. Dennis, his spouse, his daughters Mary and Sarah, Mrs. Lydia Holden, Rev.

John Dennis, Mr. Wm. Dennis, Dr. John Leland and his spouse, Chas. Higson and Ralph Higson (both under 21 years). Patk. Attwell my servant man. Bridget Scully my servant maid. Mr. Nathl. Priestly and his spouse. Saml. Clarke of Marley near Leeds in Yorkshire (£200). 4/- per week till £50 paid to Mrs. Elizth. Worrall of Boothtown, parish of Halifax; if £50 not paid at her death residue to her child or children. Jeremiah Swift near Halifax in Yorkshire. £5 to poor Housekeepers in or about the Fould near Halifax, to poor of the Dissenting Meeting house in Halifax and to poor of Halifax church. To Dr. John Leland in Eustace Street, Dublin, £20 in consideration of his great labours in his late noble defence of the Christian religion. John Goddard and James Goddard in London. Mr. John Lodge of Dublin. Robt. Colvill, book keeper to Gleadowe and Company's Bank in Castle Street. To that diligent clerk of the said Bank Danl. Malone £10. The charity children of Eustace Street Meeting House. Sum due to me from the Bank in Castle Street kept by Arthur Dawson, Agmonm. Vesey, Geo. Cuppaidge and Wm. Dawson, Esqrs., and Thos. Gleadowe, gent.

My holding in Dirty Lane, Dublin, Mr. Newham lessee. My house and holding in Eustace Street, Dublin, Mr. Newham lessee. Three houses on Arbour Hill near Dublin, two houses on the Strand near Dublin.

Witnesses: John Richardson, late of Arbour Hill, surburbs of city of Dublin, farmer, deceased, Geo. Smith, Arbour Hill, gent., Samuel Hattanville, merchant.

Codicil witnessed by: John Lodge, Dublin, gent.
Memorial witnessed by: Samuel Hattanville, John Lodge.

137, 4, 91674 Nathl. Priestley (seal)

55 POTTER, JOHN, Killinchy, Co. Down, merchant.

10 April 1747. Narrate ¾ p. 4 Nov. 1749.

His son James Potter's marriage with Margaret Stewart, said James Potter and Margt. his wife having lately deceased leaving issue one daughter Mary Potter. His son Thomas Potter. Lands of Ringhaddy and Kinninchy devised to his son Jno. Potter, exor.

Witnesses: Alexr. Potter, Ballow, Alexander McKee, Baffry, and Saml. Harris, Ballymaccarran, all in Co. Down, farmers.

Memorial witnessed by: Alexr. Potter, Hamilton McClure, Dublin, gent.

138, 136, 92461 Jno. Potter (seal)

56 ROE, JANE, Dublin, widow of Doctor Wm. Roe, deceased.

6 Feb. 1744. Full 2 pp. 23 Nov. 1749.

My son Andrew Roe, exor. My daughter Mary Walsh. My granddaughter Jane Walsh (unmarried and under 21 years), my granddaughter Jane Cane (ditto). My daughter Jane Cane, her husband. Wm. Despard, Dublin, Esq. My sister Ann Levinge. My son-in-law Phillip Walsh, Esq., exor.

Lands of Greastown [? Graystown] and Burnchurch, Co. Tipperary.

Witnesses: John King, Dublin, Esq., Nathl. Smith, Dublin, woollen draper, deceased, Henry Duggan, Dublin, tailor.

Memorial witnessed by: John King, Rev. Jeremiah Walsh, Rathfarnham, Co. Dublin, clerk.

136. 535, 92893 Mary Walsh (seal)

57 BOYD, ALEXANDER, Waterford, Esq.

24 March 1745. Full 2½ pp. 14 Dec. 1749.

A charge on the Ballytruckle estates and Grange Upper and Lower, liberties of city of Waterford, by marriage articles with my late wife Urith Boyd alias Mason, £1,000 of this for my daughter Jane Drake's fortune. Settlement made by me on my eldest son James Boyd, deceased, on his marriage. My grandsons by him Alexr. and Thos. Boyd. My eldest son now living Robt. Boyd, Glanshaw, Co. Kilkenny. My son George Boyd, exor. My son John, exor. (under 21 years), his mother Urith Boyd my late wife. My grandchildren Alexr., Thos., and Henrietta Boyd. Marriage articles of my daughter Mary with my son-in-law Wm. Paul, merchant. My four eldest daughters Frances Ward, Ellen Elliot, Ann Winkworth and Elizth. Napper. My son-in-law Darcius Drake, exor.

Lands of Ballyno[o]ny in the [Barony] of Knocktopher, Co. Kilkenny, commonly called Campbell's Lot which I purchased from Wm. Smithwick. My estate in Dunkit[t], Co. Kilkenny which I purchased from Thos. Hillam and Jane his wife and to which Thos. Mackey is now tenant. My house which I dwell in in city of Waterford. Town and lands of Knockhouse, Co. of the city of Waterford.

Witnesses: John Burrough, Joanna Berth, Robt. Snow, all of Waterford.

Memorial witnessed by: John Burrough, Richd. Hinde, Waterford, gent.

133, 531, 93191 Robt. Boyd (seal)

58 McDERMOTT, CHARLES, otherwise DORMOND, Waterford, mariner. 27 Nov. 1749. Précis ½ p. 4 Jan. 1749/50.

His wife. Jeremiah Hurley, Waterford, innkeeper, exor. [No lands mentioned].

Witnesses: Maurice Terrill, innkeeper, Joseph Hanberry, wigg-maker, Oliver Keating, schoolmaster, all of Waterford.

Memorial witnessed by: Oliver Keating, Paul Keating, Waterford, writing clerk.

138, 312, 93333 Charles McDermott (seal)

59 MERVYN, AUDLEY, Naul, Co. Meath, Esq.

15 June 1717. Narrate 1¼ p. 29 Jan. 1749.

His wife Olivia Mervyn, extx. His son Audley Mervyn. His son James Mervyn. His son Theophilus Mervyn. His son Henry Mervyn. The daughters of the testator.

Town and lands of Raranah, Atta[g]hmore, Mulliviny Donemeney [1], Cavan, Camder[r]y, Straduffe, Golan, Cavanaca[w], Killmenan [? Killymoonan], Tallaheren [Tullyheeran], Adenafagree [Edenafogry], Tatemoney, Craney, Drumgiane, Lisglannan, Skreen, Monalboy, Moughterard[2], Mulliagh, Mullaghbane, Cloonemullin,

(1) Possibly Mullawinny in parish Donacavey.
(2) This might be Oughterard in Barony Omagh East.

Curnemucklane [Cornamucklagh], Lisnedan, Tulliclinagh [Tully-clunagh], Ranneinbeg([1]), Edenderry, Garva[g]hy, Upper Aghagallon, Lower Aghagallon called Galwelly, Arvallea, Tatakish, Crananah, Campson [Campsie], Lissnamallaho, Lisnally, Shergroome, Killmore, Bailey Park, the park and tenements then in possession of Mr. Maxwell, the park in possession of Widow Machon, the tenement and park then in possession of John Hill, Highland Hill([2]), Gretrash, the Warren park then in possession of Wm. Wilson, all in Co. Tyrone. Naul, Burringtown, Flemingtown, Moorside, Kendresstown [? Kennet-stown], Dardistown, Cloghan and Cloghiestown, Barony Duleek, Co. Meath, and all other lands, tenements and hereditaments in Co. Tyrone and Co. Meath.

Witnesses: Chidley Coote, Cootehill, Co. Roscommon, Esq., Elizth. Doughlas, servant maid to testator, Wm. Barry, Dublin, notary public.

Memorial witnessed by: Redmond Kane, Bernard Kane, both of Dublin, gents.

133, 556, 93516 James Mervyn (seal)

Ann Mervyn (seal)

James Mervyn of Castlehill, Co. Tyrone, Esq., married to Ann Mervyn one of the daughters of said testator, a devisee in said Will.

60 LAWDER, JAMES, Killmore, Co. Roscommon, Esq.

21 July 1746. Narrate ½ p. 13 Feb. 1749.

His wife Dorcas Lawder, exor. His son Jas. Lawder, exor. To his grandson Thos. Ahmuty £400 when 21 years. To his grand-daughter Deborah Constable £100 on day of marriage. His son-in-law Edwd. Constable exor. Fredk. Lawder, Esq., Arthur Lawder, Esq., and Saml. Ahmuty, Esq., overseers of Will.

Mortgage on lands of Tully, Co. Roscommon made to him by his son Jas. Lawder, Esq. Lands of Tuliscan and Moyglass, Co. Roscommon.

---

(1) Possibly Rakeeranbeg in parish Dromore.
(2) This could be the name of a tenant but has been taken as that of a townland.

Witnesses: Michl. Dougherty, Patk. Croghan, Michl. Kelly, all of Killmore, aforesaid.

Memorial witnessed by: Anty. Hamilton, Killnacarra, Co. Longford, gent., Henry Townley of same, yeoman.

101, 566, 93767 Dorcas Lawder (seal)

61 LINDSAY, SARAH, Newry, Co. Down, widow.

3 March 1748. Narrate ¾ p. 26 Feb. 1749.

Her son Samuel. To her daughter Rose the house wherein Richd. Egliston lives. Her two sons David and Wm. [Lindsay]. Her son David then in America. Her real and personal estate. Her brother John Ferguson, Moone, and said Wm. Lindsay exors.

Witnesses: Jas. Pollock, John Pollock, merchant and Josh. Catherwood, tobacconist, all of Newry, Co. Down.

Memorial witnessed by: Jas. Pollock, George Walker, Newry, public notary.

137, 427, 93928 Wm. Lindsay (seal)

62 SANDERSON, WILLIAM, Dromkeen, Co. Cavan.

26 March 1748. Précis ½ p. 27 Feb. 1749.

His uncle Capt. Robt. Sanderson of Dromkeen. Wm. Sanderson second son of Frans. Sanderson late of Annsbrook, King's Co.

Lands of Dromkeen, Drum[m]ulla[gh], and the two Drumlarks, Co. Cavan.

Witnesses: Luke Pea, Pollamore, Co. Cavan, farmer, Jas. Lockinton, Dromkeen, servant to said Robt. Sanderson, Jno. Reilly, Cavan, Co. Cavan, shopkeeper.

Memorial witnessed by: Jas. Lockinton, Patrick Brady, Dublin, gent.

138, 477, 93964 Robt. Sanderson (seal)

63 READ, RICHARD, Back Lane, Dublin, dealer.

21 June 1748. Narrate ¾ p. 3 March 1749.

Deed of settlement 1738 made on his intermarriage with Phillis Lennox otherwise Read his wife. His nephew Mathew Read son of his brother Wm. Read. His niece Katherine Read daughter of his brother Wm. Read. His niece Dina Read daughter of his brother Wm. Read. His brother James Read. The two daughters of the said James Read. His brother Wm. Read and his friend and relation Jno. Clarke, Dublin, chandler, exors. His house in Back Lane in which he then lived.

[Names of witnesses not given in transcript].

Memorial witnessed by: Murray Kathrens, Dublin, gent., Lucy Read, Dublin, spinster.

138, 484, 94008 Catherine Read (seal)
one of the legatees mentioned

64 LYNCH, MARK, Garraclune, Co. Mayo.

17 July 1749. Codicils 16 Sept. 1749, 20.Sept. 1749 (2). Narrate 3½ pp. 20 March 1749/50.

His wife Jane Lynch otherwise Kelly guardian of son James. His son James Lynch (under 15 years). Thomas Browne his son-in-law, George Blake of Killerinan, Co. Mayo, Esq., the testator's other son-in-law and Edmond Kelly, Churchborrough, Co. Roscommon, Esq., trustees, and exors. with Dominick Browne, Ashford, Co. Mayo, Esq. Ross Mahon, Castlegar, Co. Galway, Esq., trustee.

Leasehold interest in and near town of Loughrea held under Earl of Clanrickard and under said Earl in lands of Pollkeen and Carrowgarry, Co. of town of Galway. Mortgage on lands of Peak and Tigre[e]na[u]n part of the estate of Ambrose Kirvan, gent. in Co. Galway which was assigned to testator by his son-in-law Thomas Browne of Newtown, Co. Galway, Esq. Drumilly, Co. Mayo held from See of Tuam. Carrowmanagh, Co. Galway. A house commonly called Gibralter lying in that part of the town of Galway commonly called the Gutt and formerly the property of Dominick Skerrett, gent., deceased. His real estate in Co. Galway and Co. of the town of Galway. Lands of Killeen, Co. of town of Galway, George Drury tenant. His stone house in the Middle street in the town of Galway.

Witnesses: Thomas Bodkin and Thomas Joyce, both of Galway, merchants, John Davis, Tuam, Co. Galway, notary public.

First codicil witnessed by: John Davis, Stephen Deane, Cong, Co. Mayo, gent., Mary Kelly, Dublin, spinster.

Second and third codicil witnessed by: Mary Kelly, James Darcy, Tuam, Co. Galway, chirurgeon, Thomas Marshall, Garraclune, Co. Mayo, gent.

Memorial witnessed by: Thomas Joyce, Stephen Deane, Thomas Marshall.

138, 519, 94177 Jane Lynch (seal)

65 YORK, JAMES, Derrygarve, Co. Londonderry (parish of Artrea, Diocese of Armagh), gent. 14 Dec. 1748. Full 1 p. 18 April 1750.

My wife Mary. My son John York. My son Henry York. My son James York. My daughter Mary. My daughter Jane. My daughter Rachell. My grandson James York (not of age) and my grandson Thos. York sons to my son Thos. York, deceased, one English shilling each and the farm I gave to their father as a marriage portion. My two sons Jas. York and John York trustees and exors. Rev. Jas. Gordon overseer.

The house and farm of Derrygarve now in my possession.

Witnesses: Joseph Shaw, smith, John Shaw, farmer, James York the youngest all of Derrygarve.

Memorial witnessed by: John Shaw, aged upwards of 40 years, James York the youngest.

139, 350, 94446 James York (the younger) (seal)
John York (seal)

66 DALYEL(L), THOMAS, Ticknevan, Co. Kildare, Esq. 4 Sept. 1749. Précis ½ p. 5 May 1750.

Thos. Cooley, Dublin, Esq., trustee.

Town and lands of Ticknevan, Kilkeaskin, the two Drummins([1]), Up. and Lr .Ballynakill, Kilpatrick, Killena, Cushelin, Ballyshannon, Derrygough, Derrybren[n]an, Derrymiller, Coolern, in Barony Carbery, Co. Kildare, and all other his real estate in Co. Kildare or elsewhere.

Witnesses: Endymion Lawson, Nathaniel Shelton and Samuel Kyle, Dublin, gents. and belonging to the Bank of Kane and Latouche in said city.

Memorial witnessed by: Endymion Lawson, Nathaniel Shelton.

138, 533, 94592 Thos. Cooley (seal)

67 CRAWFUIRD, JAMES, Ballysavage, Co. Antrim, gent.

19 June 1736. Narrate 1 p. 12 May 1750.

His wife Margt. His son Jno. Crawfuird. His son Wm. Crawfuird. Wm. McCulloch, Piedmount, John Crawfuird of Crawfuirdsburn and Wm. Agnew, Killwaughter, trustees of lands " to the use of the said James Crawfuird [the testator] for life and after his death to the use of Patrick Crawfuird his eldest son for life." John Crawfuird his second son. Wm. Crawfuird his third son. Said Wm. McCulloch, John Crawfuird and Wm. Agnew exors, trustees and guardians of his sons during their minority.

Ballyboutrom [? Ballybought], Barony Belfast, Co. Antrim. Tythes great and small of townland of Moedom [? Moyadam], Barony and Co. Antrim. Lands of Oldmoor and Inner Birkett, parish of Dalray, Bailiry of Cunningham and Shire of Air in North Britain. Ballysavage, part of townland of Moedom, Tobergall and Ballynoe, Co. Antrim.

Witnesses: Henry Shaw, Ballytweedy, Co. Antrim, gent., Henry Blair, Blairmount, Co. Antrin, gent., Robert Robinson, Ballyclare, Co. Antrim, gent.

Memorial witnessed by: Henry Blair, Jno. Arnold, Dublin, gent.

141, 143, 94738 Will Agnew (seal)

([1]) Possibly Drummond in Kilpatrick parish.

68 GLASS, EDWARD, Athlone.

29 Jan. 1749. Précis ½ p. 15 May 1750.

His daughter Catherine Glass and his brother Loftus Glass exors.

Lands of Clonowe, Ballymullee, Bonngirder, Coxcastle and his estate all being in Co. Roscommon.

Witnesses: Robt. Handcock, Esq., Rev. Wm. Tisdall, clerk, both of Athlone, Co. Westmeath, Henry Fry, Athlone, Co. Roscommon, merchant.

Memorial witnessed by: Henry Fry, Laughlen Naghten, Thomastown, Co. Roscommon, gent.

139, 422, 94804 Loftus Glass (seal)

69 MULCAIL, THOMAS, Ballynakill, Queen's Co., gent.

28 June 1748. Précis ¼ p. 17 May 1750.

His real and personal estate to his son Nichs. Mulcail. Jas. FitzGerald, Redmondstown, Co. Westmeath and Wm. FitzGerald, Ballyroan, Queen's Co., gent., exors.

Witnesses: Arthur Jacob and Michael Jacob, both of Ballynakill aforesaid, Keadagh FitzGerald, Redmondstown, gent.

Memorial witnessed by: Keadagh FitzGerald, Paul D. Roberston.

137, 557, 94840 James FitzGerald (seal)

70 ROBINSON, ANN, Dublin, widow.

24 Feb. 1749. Précis ½ p. 21 May 1750.

Her brother John Jackson, clerk. Her cousin Rev. Daniel Jackson, clerk, and Jas. Grattan, Esq., trustees. Her sisters Jane and Frances Jackson. Sums due to Francis Evans, attorney.

Her portion of the estate of Drumloman and Markhill, and all other the estate whereof she was seized or otherwise entitled to in Co. Cavan.

Witnesses: Catherine Gunning, Dublin, spinster, Robt. Robinson, Dublin, Esq., Fras. Evans, Dublin, gent.

Memorial witnessed by: Fras. Evans, Peter Shee, Dublin, merchant.

142, 122, 94882 John Jackson (seal)

71 DELANE, DENNIS, parish of St. Martin in the Fields, Middlesex. 18 June 1747. Précis 1 p. 14 June 1750.

His wife Margaretta Delane. His estates in Co. Roscommon and Co. Galway.

Witnesses: John George Cox, then of parish of St. Martins in the Fields, gent., Alexander Crudge, parish of St. Sepulchre's, London, gent., Herbert Laurence of the parish of St. Martins in the Fields, apothecary.

Memorial witnessed by: John George Cox, now of parish of Fulham, Theodosius Forrest, York Buildings, in parish of St. Martins in the Fields, gent.

140, 341, 95149 Margtta Delane
(resides in G. Britain)

72 FRENCH, NICHOLAS, Dublin, ale draper.

29 Dec. 1749. Précis ½ p. 21 June 1750.

His wife, extx. Elizth., Catherine and Margaret [? French] his three nieces. [No lands mentioned].

Witnesses: Capt. Michael Reily, Richd. Keen, Dublin, gent.

Memorial witnessed by: Richd. Keen, Henry Stevens Reily, Dublin, brother to said Michael Reily.

139, 501, 95232 Allice French her mark (seal)

73 GERRARD, MARY otherwise MASON, Dublin, widow.

8 March 1747. Narrate 1 p. 21 July 1750.

Her son Mason Gerrard; testator had conveyed to him since the death of her husband her estates and other interests to which she was entitled in right of her father. All her nieces and nephews. Her niece Elizabeth Jenkins. Her two daughters Barbara Marsh wife of Henry Marsh, Esq., and Sarah Burton wife of John Burton. John Nixon, clothier and John Ross, apothecary, trustees.

Witnesses: Benjn. Johnston, Dublin, public notary, and Richd. Thwaites, his clerk.

Memorial witnessed by: Anthy. Hart, servant to John Burton, Dublin, Esq., Wm. Hall of same, gent.

142, 310, 95623 Sarah Burton (seal)

74 SHIELL, JAMES, Grenan, Co. Westmeath, gent.

8 Nov. 1746. Précis ½ p. 6 Sept. 1750.

His nephew Wm. Shiell, Tully, King's Co.

Lands of Muldrum and Quiganstown. Lands of Cloghlea, Killena, Brackinehern and Grenan.

Witnesses: Walter Daly, Donore, Co. Westmeath, farmer, Thady Murtaugh, Ballycomen, King's Co., farmer, Christopher Moore, Kilbegan, Co. Westmeath, gent.

Memorial witnessed by: Charles Tuckey, Dublin, gent., James Dillon, Dublin, gent., John Hopkins, clerk to said James Dillon.

140, 462, 96020 Will Shiell (seal)

75 BROWN, HUGH, Strabane, Co. Tyrone, merchant.

[Date not recorded]. Narrate ¾ p. 14 Sept. 1750.

His son Wm. Brown. His daughter Catherine Brown. His niece Elizabeth Pearson. His brother John Brown. His niece Catherine Stewart.

Archibald Cunningham, Londonderry and Robert Barclay, Strabane, Co. Tyrone, merchants, trustees and exors. £5 to poor of parish of Camus. His real and personal estate.

Witnesses: William Aughenleck, merchant, Samuel Law, Doctor of Physick, John McCollagh, merchant, all of Strabane.

Memorial witnessed by: John McCollagh, Simeon Rouse, Strabane, gent.

140, 472, 96081 Will. Brown (seal)

76 MOFFITT, JOHN, Hazelhatch, Co. Dublin, gent.

— July 1750. Narrate ¾ p. 14 Sept. 1750.

His wife Mary Moffitt. His sons-in-law George Bell and James Little trustees. His grandson John Bell. His grandson David Bell. His grandson William Little. His daughter Elizabeth Bell. His daughter Alice Little. His daughter Mary Moffitt. His daughter Ann Moffitt. His real estate.

Witnesses: James Heather, shopkeeper to George Bell, Dublin, merchant, Charles Wren, apprentice to said George Bell, Daniel Bourne, Dublin, gent.

Memorial witnessed by: Daniel Bourne, James Heather, Charles Wren.

140, 473, 96082 Geo. Bell (seal)

77 LUCAS, MATHEW, Rathdaniel, Co. Carlow, Esq.

16 Sept. 1750. Narrate 1¼ p. 27 Sept. 1750.

His eldest son John Lucas (under 21 years). His second son Francis Lucas. His youngest son Charles Lucas. His daughter Judith. His daughter Catherine. His daughters Carolina and Mary. Their mother Margt. Ennis. His sisters Judith Higginbothom and Ann Grogan. Col. Josa. Paul, Henry Byrne, Rathmore, farmer, and said John Lucas when he should be capable to transact, exors.

Witnesses: Garrett Fitzgerald, Tullow, apothecary, Wm. Fenelon, Rathdaniel, yeoman, Jon. Sexton, Killcollitrim, all Co. Carlow.

Memorial witnessed by: Michael Argent, Jeremy Healy, both of Dublin.

141, 461, 96176 Henry Byrne (seal)

78 LAYFIELD, LEWIS, Martins Lane, Dublin, gent.

4 Oct. 1750. Précis ¼ p. 19 Oct. 1750.

His wife Sarah Layfield, extx.

His lease of house etc. in Martins Lane devised to him by Wm. Wall, Esq.

Witnesses: Ann Lawrence, the daughter of testator, Wm. Holt and Wm. Carmichael, Dublin, gents.

Memorial witnessed by: Ann Lawrence, Wm. Holt, Wm. Carmichael.

142, 477, 96333 L. Layfield (seal)

79 ROGERS, BIGNELL, Dublin, gent.

29 Sept. 1747. Full ¾ p. 6 Nov. 1750.

His wife Eliz. Rogers alias Phepoe, extx.

Lands of East Curragh, parish of Hollywood, Barony Ballruddery [Balrothery], Co. Dublin, and all other his real estate.

Witnesses: Edwd. Warner, Dublin, gent., Obedia Bolton, Barry Gordon, Dublin, gent., deceased.

Memorial witnessed by: Obedia Bolton, John Wolverston, Dublin, gent.

143, 170, 96435 Elizabeth Rogers (seal)

80 FURNELL, PATRICK, Ballyclough, liberties of city of Limerick, Esq. 2 July 1748. Narrate ¾ p. 9 Nov. 1750.

His wife. Michael Scanlan, Mein, Co. Limerick, gent., Jno. FitzGibbon, Esq., Counsellor at law and Burk Furnell his brother trustees. His son Michael Furnell.

Ballynacloghy in liberties of city of Limerick. Ballyosheedy and Caherelly, Co. Limerick. " His farm or moietie of Mein called Collyroe Ballygulline as divided between him and his father [? father-in-law] Scanlan."

Witnesses: Michael Scanlan, Duckstown, Co. Limerick, gent., Laurence Scanlan, Newcastle, Co. Limerick, gent., Wm. Hannan, Ballyclogh in liberties of city of Limerick, servant to testator.

Memorial witnessed by: Wm. Hamman, Wm. Lane, Dublin, gent.

140, 522, 96513 Michl. Furnell (seal)

81 DAUNT, THOMAS, Owlpen, Gloucester, Esq.

14 Feb. 1745. Codicil same date. Full 6¼ pp. 13 Nov. 1750.

My wife Elizabeth Daunt. My son Achilles Daunt. My son Kingscote Daunt. My eldest son Thomas Daunt. My three daughters Martha, Hannah and Elizabeth. My nephew George, second son of my late brother Henry Daunt. My nephew Achilles, third son of my late brother Henry Daunt. My nephew Hungerford, fourth son of my late brother Henry Daunt. My friends Randall Roberts, Britfieldstown, Co. Cork, and Wm. Hodder, Hodderfield, Co. Cork, Esq., trustees.

Lands of Gortigrenane and Parkinnaul, Co. Cork. The manor of Owlpen and estate there. My lands of Boysestown, Ballianinig otherwise Ballenanringbeg, Gurtinnownbeg, Ballitreideen otherwise Ballintrideen, Co. Cork.

Witnesses to Will and codicil: Samuel Terrett, Owlpen, broadweaver, John Ferebee of same, tailor, Will Jones, Dursley, Co. of Gloucester, gent.

Memorial witnessed by: Thos. Daunt, Owlpen, Esq., brother of Kingscote Daunt, Will Daunt.

145, 29, 96614 Kingscote Daunt (seal)

82 BALFOUR, JOHN, Drumcrow, Co. Fermanagh.

[Date not recorded]. Narrate 1 p. 15 Nov. 1750.

Lucy Balfour an infant and daughter to Cath. Greenlees who then lived with him. Her brother John Balfour (testator's heir) son of said Cath. Greenlees. £100 to Aramintha Balfour who then lived with him but if she shall marry Wm. Graham son to Francis Graham of Coolavan, Co. Fermanagh, within three years of testator's death

1/- only. Townley, eldest son of Blaney Townley, Piedmont, Co. Louth. Jas. Forster, Drumgoone, Co. Fermanagh, Rev. John Dundass, curate of Aughlucher, exors. and trustees. His real and personal estate.

Witnesses: Wm. Elliott, Belturbet, Co. Cavan, shoemaker, Thos. Forster, Croghan, James Noble, Glassdrumond, Co. Fermanagh, gent.

Memorial witnessed by: James Noble and Murray Kathrens, Dublin, gent.

143, 228, 96711 J. Noble (seal)

83 CHARTERS, DAVID, Mullaghboy, parish of Eniskeen, Co. Meath. 2 Jan. 1747. Narrate ¾ p. 21 Nov. 1750.

His wife Sarah. His daughter Mary Charters (a minor). His brother James Charters. His nephews and nieces to wit Jane Charters daughter of George Charters, Jane Ogle daughter to Catherine Charters and Thos. Young son to Ann Charters. Josa. Gore, Mullaghboy, Robert Dyas, Bellnacloas, exors.

His lease of Mullaghboy in the parish of Eniskeen, Co. Meath.

Witnesses: William Ker, Newcastle, gent., Gart. Fleming, Raaths, farmer, Jas. Charters, Mullaghboy, farmer, all in Co. Meath.

Memorial witnessed by: Wm. Ker, Patk. Farrelly, Ballinlurgin, Co. Meath, farmer.

146, 95, 96832 Frans. Peacock (seal)
Sarah Peacock her mark (seal)
Sarah Peacock otherwise Charters wife of said Francis Peacock, and late wife of testator.

84 ROCHE, EDMOND, Cork, Esq.

21 April 1750. Narrate 1½ p. 26 Nov. 1750.

His wife Barbara then enceinte. His son or reputed son Edmond Roche. His son or reputed son Francis Roche. His son Edward Roche. Said wife Barbara, Eaton Stannard, Dublin, Esq. and Robert Travers, Cork, Esq., exors. and guardians of his son Edward Roche.

Lands of Killuntin and Glannegaul and the houses in city of Cork which he purchased from Mr. Waters.

Witnesses: Maurice Connell, Cork, Doctor in Physick, Daniel Curtin, Ballenvarrig, north liberties of city of Cork, gent., Edmond Prior, Mallow Lane, suburbs of Cork, gent.

Memorial witnessed by: Edmd. Prior, Richd. Burke, Dublin, gent.

141, 486, 96877 Ea. Stannard (seal)

85 BINGHAM, SIR JOHN, Castlebar, Co. Mayo, Bart.

13 Nov. 1750. Narrate 1¼ p. 31 Dec. 1750.

Rt. Hon. Thomas Lord Baron of Athenry and his dear mother the Lady Ann Bingham trustees. His brother Charles Bingham (under 25 years). His sister Ann Bingham. To his brother George Bingham money to purchase the Commission of a captain of Foot. His servant Patrick Kelly. John Brown, Westport, and Rev. Thomas Ellison, Castlebar, clerk, both Co. Mayo, exors.

All his real estate, as also his lease and interest for years which he held under the See of Tuam. Money borrowed from St. George Caulfield, Esq., H.M.'s Attorney General secured by mortgages and judgements affecting his real estate.

Witnesses: Thomas Ward, Dublin, cloth merchant, Wentworth Thewles, Esq., and John Thewles, gent., both of Dublin.

Memorial witnessed by: said Wentworth Thewles and John Thewles.

145, 139, 97294 Athenry (seal)
(Thomas Lord Baron of Athenry)

86 FORD, EDWARD, WOODPARK, Co. Meath.

[Date not recorded]. Précis ½ p. 28 Jan. 1750.

His wife Deborah Ford and his sister Eliz. Ford, exors. His estate of inheritance.

Witnesses: Ann Taylor, Woodpark, Denis Brian, Pierstown, carpenter, both Co. Meath, George Cooper, servant to said Edwd. Ford.

Memorial witnessed by: Wm. Crowe, Dublin, gent., and his clerk Thos. Tudor.

141, 506, 97476 Deb. Ford (seal)
Elizabeth Ford (seal)

87 GAY, WILLIAM, Wicklow town.

26 March 1747. Précis ¼ p. 5 Feb. 1750.

His wife Mary Gay, extx. His four children, that is to say Frances Hayes, wife of John Hayes, his son Thomas and his daughters Elizabeth and Lettice. His real and personal effects.

Witnesses: Solomon Williams, Wicklow, postmaster, Mary Williams his wife, Thos. Wilde, of same, gent.

Memorial witnessed by: Wm. Williams, Mark Gerrard, both clerks to Christopher Dalton, Dublin, notary public.

143, 418, 97588 Mary Gay (seal)

88 DALY, THOMAS, Kilcleagh, Co. Westmeath, Esq.

15 March 1717. Narrate 1 p. 8 Feb. 1750.

His daughter Mary Daly. His daughter Catherine Daly. His eldest son James Daly. His son Denis Daly. Felix Coghlan, King's Co., Esq., and Denis Daly, Raford, Co. Galway, trustees, and exors. with Denis Daly of Frenchbrook, Co. Mayo, Esq.

Kilcleagh, Corraghbegg, Cloonmore, Aghanvony, Tooridonnellan, Buollyconnor, Buollyharra, Clonydonnin Lower, Cloonlannane Wood, Boggaghshioge, Boggagheighteragh, Boggagh alias Boggaghfurys Orchard, Boggagh Conrane, B(r)yanaghcolmanagh, Blackoryes, Buollydoriagh and all his estate in Co. Westmeath.

Witnesses: Thos. Daly, Dublin, gent., one of the attornies of H.M. Court of Common Pleas in Ireland, Richard Eustace, Dublin, mercer, Edmd. Coghlan.

Memorial witnessed by: Wm. Mott, Laughlen Naghten the younger, both of Dublin, gents.

142, 530, 97631 Mary Daly (seal)

89 ASH, JAMES, Captain in Bury's Regiment of Foot.

17 April 1750. Full 1 p. 7 May 1751.

My wife Elizth. Ash, extx. My father-in-law and uncle Mr. Wm. Ash, his son Henry Ash. The two daughters of my late father Cairns Ash by his last wife.

My lands of Neffeeny, Co. Londonderry.

Witnesses to Will and memorial: Hamilton Benson, merchant, James Cowdon, apothecary and Robt. Lee, notary public, all of Londonderry.

149, 5, 98640 Elizth. Ash (seal)

90 WHITE, ROBERT, Raheen, Queen's Co., gent.

[Date not recorded]. Précis ¼ p. 30 May 1751.

His son Samuel White and his son Charles White exors. His freehold lands as also all other his estate.

Witnesses: William Lynch, Thomas Hutchinson and Alexander Perkinson, all of Raheen, Queen's Co., gents.

Memorial witnessed by: Wm. Lynch, John Pilkington, Dublin, Esq.

145, 397, 98963 Saml. White (seal)

91 BEWLEY, MARTHA, Edenderry, King's Co., widow.

28 Jan. 1750. Précis ½ p. 31 May 1751.

Joseph Barcroft, Dublin, her residuary legatee. Said Joseph Barcroft and Joseph Inman exors. Eliz. Gowen.

A tanyard in Dolphins Barn in Dublin to be sold by her exors.

Witnesses: Fras. Grattan, Edenderry, Doctor of Physick, Benj. Wilson, Mount Wilson, King's Co., gent., Aaron Scott, Edenderry, tanner.

Memorial witnessed by: John Pilkington, Robt. Acheson, Dublin, gent.

149, 91, 98984 Joseph Barcroft (seal)

92 BARRY, HENRY, LORD BARON SANTRY.

19 March 1749. Précis ½ p. 12 June 1751.

His mother Bridget Lady Dowager Santry and his uncle Rt. Hon. Sir Compton Domville, Bart., exors. Graham Chappell. His servant Andrew Murray. Edward Madden, Dublin.

Witnesses: Wm. Chappell, Nottingham, Great Britain, gent., Wm. Madden, Dublin, gent., Edward Madden the younger, Manor Waterhouse, Co. Fermanagh, gent.

Memorial witnessed by: Wm. Madden, Dublin, Wm. Sandford, Dublin, Esq.

140, 568, 99146 C. Domvile (seal)

93 BELL, NATHANIEL, Creve, parish of Donoghmore, Co. Tyrone.

26 May 1743. Narrate ½ p. 20 June 1751.

His eldest son George Bell, London. Wm. Scott who married his daughter Sarah. His daughter Margaret, her husband Wm. Baillie. His daughter Ellinor. His grand-daughter Sarah Scott. His daughter Mary. His son Samuel Bell exor. with George Bell of Armagh.

All his lands and tenements which he holds under the See of Armagh.

Witnesses: James McNeese, Mullaghbane, Thos. Hill, Anaghginny, David Cullon, Mullyrodan, all in Co. Tyrone, farmers.

Memorial witnessed by: David Cullon (Cullen), Thos. Corbet, Dungannon, Co. Tyrone, gent.

147, 177, 99269 Nat Bell (seal)

94 MULVEY, DANIEL, Aghabrack, parish of Granard, Co. Longford, farmer. 22 May 1750. Narrate ½ p. 2 July 1751.

His wife Catherine Mulvey otherwise Taylor, extx. His sister Margt. Reynolds otherwise Mulvey. His brother John Mulvey, Dublin, shoemaker.

His farm of Aghabrack held by lease from Wm. Blyth deceased.

Witnesses: John Biglan and John Fay, Aghabrack, farmers, Fras. Gordon, Dublin, gent.

Memorial witnessed by: Michael Argent and Wm. Hall, Dublin, gents.

149, 186, 99409 John Mulvey (seal)

95 HANKISON, RICHARD, Dublin, Esq.

16 April 1741. Précis ½ p. 20 July 1751.

His daughter Margaret Cochran, extx. To Mrs. Mary Stapleton an annuity out of his houses, concerns, etc. in Plunket Street, Dublin.

Witnesses: Abel Onge, gent., and Wm. Dixon, notary public, both of Dublin.

Memorial witnessed by: Wm. Dixon, Thos. Dixon, Dublin, hosier.

146, 543, 99641 Mary Stapleton (seal)

96 BROWN, JOHN, Tullamore, King's Co., gent.

15 April 1751. Précis ½ p. 30 July 1751.

His wife Catherine Brown otherwise Brisco (enciente) and his relation Edwd. Brisco commonly called Cornet Brisco exors. His farm and freehold of Clown, Co. Westmeath.

Witnesses: Edwd. Brisco, sadler, Wm. Hill, malster, both of Tullamore, King's Co., Andw. Nowlan, Killdangan, said county, farmer, Patrick Brisco, Killenewer, Co. Westmeath, gent.

Memorial witnessed by: Andrew Nowlan, Michael Argent, Dublin, gent.

146, 544, 99733 Catherine Brown (seal)

97 WILLIAMS, WILLIAM, Killeentierna, Co. Kerry.

21 Jan. 1742/3. Narrate ¾ p. 23 Sept. 1751.

His son Joseph Williams. His son John Williams. His son Richard Williams. His son-in-law Patrick Hore, his wife [? testator's wife] Elizabeth. His son Charles Williams. His daughter Sarah Williams otherwise Olive. To his son John Williams the gneeve of land that his brother William Williams deceased held from testator. Exors. Robert Twiss and Christopher Hovell.

Gortellay, held by lease from Col. John Blenerhasset.

Witnesses: George Twiss, William Twiss, Edmond McGuire.

Memorial witnessed by: William Twiss, Richard Meredith the third of Tierneguose, Co. Kerry.

150, 76, 100153 Robert Twiss (seal)

98 RUSSELL, HENRY, Hodgestown, Co. Kildare, farmer.

21 March 1748. Précis ½ p. 24 Oct. 1751.

His two sons Solomon and Samuel, exors. Lands of Hodgestown.

Witnesses: Caleb Eves, Baltray, Co. Kildare, farmer, Benjamin Tayle, Corebritt, Co. Kildare, farmer, William Watson, Baltray, Co. Kildare, farmer.

Memorial witnessed by: Benjamin Johnston, notary public, Richard Thwaites his clerk.

150, 122, 100344 Solomon Russell (seal)

99 WHITE, SOLOMON, Banbridge, Co. Down, Esq.

17 Sept. 1744. Précis ½ p. 11 Nov. 1751.

His nephew William Chamberlain. All his real estate in county of Down and Louth containing about fifteen thousand acres Irish measure.

Witnesses: Rev. William Rowan, rector of Seapatrick, Co. Down, John Trevor, Loughbrickland, Co. Down, gent., John Robinson, Banbridge, Co. Down, farmer.

Memorial witnessed by: Samuel White, Golden Lane, Dublin, gent., Timothy Murphy of same, yeoman.

149, 464, 100603 Wm. Chamberlain (seal)

100 SHINTON, RICHARD, Captain in Major Gen. St. George's Regiment of Dragoons. 4 June 1744. Précis ½ p. 28 Nov. 1751.

His brother-in-law John Pepper then of Waterstown, Co. Louth, Esq., exor. Ballyhoe, Carrickavegsorgy, Molloghmore, and Rathlagan, Co. Meath.

Witnesses: Rev. Charles Wye, Dromiskin, Co. Louth, clerk, Jas. Tisdall, Bawn, Co. Louth, Esq., Thos. Shekelton, Wollerstown, Co. Louth, gent.

Memorial witnessed by: John Jones, Dublin, gent., Jacob Scriven, Dublin, gent.

148, 438, 100980 John Pepper (seal)

101 CROKER, JOHN, Ballyneguard, Co. Limerick, Esq.

24 Sept. 1751. Narrate 3½ pp. 6 Dec. 1751.

His son Edward Croker, Esq., exor. Henry Croker, second son of his eldest son Edward Croker. Testator's grandson John Croker, junr., eldest son of said Edward Croker. Edward Croker, junr., third (youngest) son of said Edward. Testator's youngest son John Croker, junr. His son Rickards Croker, Esq. His grandson Edward Croker, son of his son Andrew Croker. His grand-daughter Mary Croker. His daughter Dillon's two daughters. His grandson Croker Dillon. His son Abraham Croker.

John Dillon, Quartertown, Co. Cork, Esq., and Charles Landley, Lisnamrock, Co. Tipperary, Esq., trustees. Mortgage from Henry Desterre, Esq.

Lands of Ballyneguard, Upper and Lower Rochestown, Carriggnattin and Bancanimorish, Co. Limerick. Lands of Williamstown. Ballynlahane set unto John Rice. His estate of Ballygrennan near Croom, Co. Limerick and his farm and lands of Derryallin (leasehold). His lease and farm of Richstown, Ballyneety otherwise Whitestown which testator held from John Naper. Lands and concerns of Croom, Co. Limerick, with his advowson and perpetual presentation to the several parishes of Croom, Adare, Dromin and Athlacky, Co. Limerick. Farm and lands of Luddenmore [Co. Limerick]. Carnane, Co. Limerick.

Witnesses: James Casey, Ballyneety, Co. Limerick, gent., John Boyle, Scarravahane, Co. Limerick, gent., Thomas Barry, Ballyneguard, yeoman.

Memorial witnessed by: Thos. Barry, William Leech, servant to Richard Shaw, Clonmell, Co. Tipperary, gent.

149, 476, 101068 Edwd. Croker (seal)

102 DEANE, EDWARD, Terenure, Co. Dublin, Esq.

31 July 1750. Narrate 3½ pp. 17 Dec. 1751.

His father Edward Deane, Esq., deceased. His eldest brother Amyas Deane. His second brother Joseph Deane. His sister Willemina Bowen otherwise Deane, wife of Nicholas Bowen, gent. If her male issue shall become entitled to testator's estate they shall take surname of Deane. His uncle Joseph Deane. Edward Deane, first son of said uncle Joseph Deane. Stephen, second son and Brice, third son of his said uncle Joseph Deane.

Amyas Bushe, Kilfane, Co. Kilkenny, Esq., John Bourke, Palmerstown, Co. Kildare, Esq., John Hobson, Waterford, gent., trustees and exors.

Lands of "Tyrrenure," "Cammage" and The Broads, Co. Dublin, Ballyduffe, Coolroe, Cooleramy, Coolesillagh, Powerswood, Smithstown, Ballygallane, Cappagh, Fidoneragh and Ballycocksoost all in Co. Kilkenny. Danganspadogy, Upper and Lower Ballydaw, Co. Kilkenny. Rathtore, Co. Tyrone.

Witnesses: Rev. Michael Heatly, Dublin, clerk, George Clark, Dublin, hosier, Gilbert Allason, Dublin, public notary.

Memorial witnessed by: Richard Barrett, Dublin, merchant, Gilbert Allason.

150, 237, 101232 Jos. Deane (seal)

103 CLARKE, THOMAS, Ardress, Co. Armagh, Esq.

7 Nov. 1751. Narrate 2 pp. 20 Dec. 1751.

His wife. His son Thos. Clarke, his son Henry Clarke (both under 21 years). His daughter Mary Clarke (if testator's estate should descend to her her husband and eldest son to take surname of Clarke). The Rev. Doctor Henry Clarke his wife Mrs. Sarah Clarke and his sister Mrs. Elizabeth Clarke exors. His good friends Edwd. Obre and Randall Donnaldson, Esq., both of Co. Armagh, trustees.

His dwelling house and outhouses etc. in Ardress. Lands of Ardress, Derrycorr, Derrycavera, Copney, Ballygassey and his lease of Loughgall, all in Co. Armagh. His third of Tullyroan, parish of Clonfeicle, Co. Armagh. His leases of Blundallsgrange from Lord Charlemount, of Annaghmore from Mr. Cope of Drummully and of part of Ardress from late Bishop of Raphoe. His leases of Cushenny, part of Deveny and the wind and water mills of the Manor of Richmount, all in Co. Armagh.

Witnesses: Thos. Downhame Clarke of Anasvry [Annasamry], Esq., Rev. Thos. Nabb, Loughgall, clerk, both in Co. Armagh, Rev. James Dobbins, Clonfeickle, Co. Tyrone, clerk.

Memorial witnessed by: Thomas Downhame Clarke, Thos. Verner, Dublin, gent.

147, 527, 101265 Hen. Clarke (seal)
(Rev. Doctor Henry Clarke)

104 SHELLY, ALEXANDER, Courstown, Co. Kildare, farmer.

24 Aug. 1734. Narrate ½ p. 20 Feb. 1752.

His wife Mary Shelly. His son Jacob Shelly. His son Alexr. Shelly. Henry Fuller and Thomas Boolk exors.

His farm being the upper part of Courstown bounded on east by Thomas Pillsworth's holding.

Witnesses: Thos. Pillsworth and Ralph Pillsworth, Milltown, Co. Kildare, gents., Thos. Weston, Meath Street, Dublin, merchant.

Memorial witnessed by: Thos. Weston, Jas. Farrell, Dublin, gent.

151, 409, 101985 Alexr. Shelly (seal)

105 WALSH, HUNT, Ballykilcavan, Queen's Co., Esq.

20 July 1751. Full 4 pp. 22 Feb. 1752.

To be buried eight feet deep in old chancel of parish church of Corkclone where my dearest wife has promised to be laid when she dies. My wife. My nephews and nieces. My nephew Captain Hunt Walsh, eldest son of my brother John deceased. My nephew Raphael Walsh, brother to said Hunt. "As for my brother Edward's descendants of which I never heard of but one son whose name was said to be Vincent Oliver and was transported for life . . . . his father believed he must be dead." My sisters' children. My eldest sister the Hon. Rebecca Caulfield deceased. Her eldest son Toby having given up all hopes of having male issue gave his own estate to his daughter in marriage. My nephew John Caulfield, second son of my sister the Hon. Rebecca Caulfield, (to take name of Walsh if he succeeds testator). My nephew Robt. Pinsent (ditto). My nephew Hunt Calcott Chambre (ditto). His mother my sister Mary Chambre. My niece Rebecca Haskins daughter of brother Raphael deceased.

My poor labouring workmen of Corkclone [Curraclone] parish. A new frieze coat each every Christmas for poor widows and decayed inhabitants of said parish. Repairs and alterations to church of Corkclone. A debt due to Rev. Doctor Baldwin, Provost of Trinity College. Rents paid by Mr. Bambrick. Exors. Rev. Doctor Baldwin, Benjamin Burton, Burton Hall, Esq., Robt. Tench, Dublin. My real estate.

Witnesses: Edwd. Brereton, Springmount, Queen's Co., Esq. Elizabeth Brereton of same his wife, Jane Brereton of same, sister of said Edward.

Memorial witnessed by: Edward Brereton, Springmount, Esq., Thomas Tench, Dublin, gent., nephew to said Ellinor Walsh.

147, 540, 102005 Ell. Walsh (seal)
(Ellinor Walsh widow of testator)

106 HORT, DR. JOSIAH, Archbishop of Tuam and Bishop of Ardagh. 15 May 1751. Narrate 1 p. 22 Feb. 1752.

His eldest son Josiah George. His eldest daughter Elizth. His son John. His brother-in-law the Hon. John Fitzmaurice otherwise Petty and his kinsman Joseph Robbins, Dublin, barrister at law, trustees, exors., and guardians of his children during their minority.

His dwellinghouse in Dawson Street; another in George's Lane. His estate of Newtown and Aghnamadain, Co. Longford purchased from Mr. Auchmuty. His estate of Clongawney, King's Co., bought of Anthony Coghlan, Esq., deceased. His estate of Castlestrange, Co. Roscommon, purchased from Mr. Gunning. Leases held under the See of Tuam by the Rev. Robert Hort, clerk(1). His estates of Moyvalley, Clonuff, Ballinderry, Bally[na]drumny and Scullog[e]stown otherwise Hortland, Co. Kildare.

Will and memorial witnessed by: Rev. William Henry, D.D., rector of Urny, Rev. Robert Hort, rector of Templemichael and Archdeacon of Armagh, Patk. Magran, Dublin, gent.

151, 415, 102009 Josh. Robbins (seal)

107 ROSS, JAMES, Cherry Lane, Dublin, victualler.

31 March 1740. Full ¾ p. 27 Feb. 1752.

To be buried in St. Michan's churchyard, Dublin. My wife Catherine Ross and my friends Patrick Horish, Dublin, chandler and Patrick White, Dublin, exors. and guardians of my daughter Anne Ross until 21 years.

My holding and concerns in Cherry Lane, Dublin which I now dwell on and hold from Mr. Sinnot.

Witnesses: Thos. Philpott, Christopher Dalton, Dublin, notary public.

Memorial witnessed by: Christopher Dalton, Dublin, notary public, Wm. Williams his clerk.

152, 362, 102123 Ann Ross (seal)

108 POWER, ANTHONY, Rathruddy, Co. Galway, Esq.

16 May 1751. Full 1 p. 28 Feb. 1752.

My body to be interred in the tomb of my ancestors in the Abby of Loughrea. My kinsman Joseph Power, Loughrea. My sister Mary Lynch otherwise Power. My niece Julian Blake. My uncle Andrew Skerrett. Miss Monica Skerrit. Mary Hopkins. My kinsman John Hopkins. My brother Richard Blake. My kinsman Pierce Power of

(1) Robert Hort, cousin to the Archbishop and father of Josiah Hort is mentioned in Betham's Will Pedigrees, vol. 250, p. 218, Genealogical Office.

Cadiz. To Patrick Power the son of Cate Flaningan £100 when 21 years. Mary Cheevers. Doctor Dillon. Doctor Dolphin. My brother Josias Browne. My nephew Joseph Browne. Nicholas Lynch. Miss Rose Dillon. My servant Thomas Paul. Lisly Fallon otherwise Power. My servant Mary Dolphin. Rev. Archdeacon Wm. Pigott and Mr. James Burke, Isercleran, exors.

My real estate in counties of Galway and Mayo.

Witnesses: Walter French, Loughrea, Co. Galway, gent., Wm. Edington, Ballycowna, Co. Galway, gent., James Tully, Loughrea, wigmaker.

Memorial witnessed by: Charles Dempsy, Cockhill, Co. Dublin, gent., one of the attornies of the Court of Exchequer, John Daniel, gent., clerk to said Charles Dempsy.

149, 522, 102137 Joseph Power (seal)

109 WHITE, ARCHIBALD, Dublin, gent.

25 Feb. 1733. Narrate 1¼ p. 14 March 1752.

His wife Jane White otherwise Smith. His three daughters Margaret, Martha and Ann. His cousin James White, exor. His cousin Timothy White, exor., brother to said James White. His cousin Archibald White son to his uncle Archibald White.

Henry Lecky, Coleraine, Co. Londonderry, Esq., and Wm. Hamilton, Dunnemanagh, Co. Tyrone, trustees. Robert Dent, Dublin, gent. Money due to him out of residuary assets of James Martin.

Town and lands of Derryfore [? Queen's Co.]. Estate of inheritance of townland of Ballypikes [? Ballypickas, Queen's Co.] might by failure of the issue of Hugh Gordon descend to testator or his heirs.

Witnesses: Law. Lawrenson, Dublin, gent., Gerald Byrne, Francis McCollagh, Dublin, yeomen.

Memorial witnessed by: Law. Lawrenson, Hugh Burnett, Dublin, gent.

151, 510, 102331 James White (seal)

110 PLUNKET, PLUNKET, Rathbeal, Co. Dublin.

13 April 1743. Précis ½ p. 6 April 1752.

His wife Ann Plunket, extx. His nephew William Cooper, gent. His estate of inheritance and leasehold interests. His leasehold interests, mills, or concerns in or near the town of Donnybrook.

Witnesses: Samuel Allason, Dublin, gent., Gilbert Allason his son, Dublin, notary public, Daniel Sheil, Dublin, merchant.

Memorial witnessed by: Gilbert Allason, Michael Swift, Dublin, gent., attorney.

151, 546, 102523 Wm. Cooper (seal)

111 HOLLAND, MARGARET, Enniskillen, Co. Fermanagh.

21 April 1747. Précis ½ p. 15 June 1752.

The tenement she then enjoyed called Crawford's tenement to her daughter Lydia Holland otherwise Corry, William Corry her husband and heirs, failing whom to the children of her daughter Ann Holland otherwise Graham.

Witnesses: John Pilkington, carpenter, deceased, Samuel Moore, tailor, Charles Stewart, glover, all of Enniskillen.

Memorial witnessed by: Charles Stewart, Hugh Gallagher, Enniskillen, servant to Rev. Wm. Duncombe.

155, 97, 103685 George Graham his mark (seal)

112 WARING, WILLIAM, Pottlerath, Co. Kilkenny, Esq.

23 Oct. 1749. Full 3½ pp. 1 July 1752.

My wife. My son-in-law William Izod, Esq., and my brother Thomas Waring trustees. My son John. My son Thomas. To my son William £900 when 21 years. To my daughter Mary £1,100 when 21 years or on marriage. My daughter Ann (under 16 years). My sister Desarroy.

My lands of Pottlerath and Killenleagh, Co. Kilkenny. My dwellinghouse in county of city of Kilkenny. Lands of Brittis, Dryland, Shortalls, Graig[u]e, and Sheepstown, Co. Kilkenny. My real estate in Queen's Co., and other real estate in county of city of Kilkenny or elsewhere. The remainder which I have in estate of Counsellor John Lyons in the Queen's Co. [situation not mentioned]. My grandmother Drysdale by her Will left to three widows of the Poor House [parish of] St. Canice the interest of £100 to be by me paid yearly (testator wishes his son Thomas to continue to pay this out of the estate in Queen's Co.). Griffith Drysdale son of said grandmother.

Witnesses: Richard Arthur, Kilkenny, merchant, Henry Neale, Kilkenny, gent., William Gregg, Cork, notary public.

Memorial witnessed by: Henry Neale, Anthony Dempsey, Dublin.

152, 539, 103895 Thos. Waring (seal)

113 McMANUS, JAMES, the younger, Maynooth, Co. Kildare, gent.

14 Feb. 1750. Précis ½ p. 4 Aug. 1752.

His cousin John Nelson of Maynooth. His uncle James McManus Esq., counsel at law, exor. The house in which he then lived and real and personal estate.

Witnesses to will and memorial: Phillip Elwis, John Kyan, Dublin, gents.

154, 444, 104398 Jas. McManus (seal)

114 GRIFFITH, LEWIS, Dublin, Esq.

12 Aug. 1752. Narrate part in full, 1½ p. 16 Sept. 1752.

Loftus Jones, Dublin, Esq., trustee. My sister Lettice Parker otherwise Griffith, extx. Her son Marlborough Parker, her son Arthur Parker, her son Philip Parker, her daughter Lettice Parker otherwise Nash. My niece Sarah Griffith, Larne, Co. Mayo, widow.

Real estate in Barony of Gallen, Co. Mayo and elsewhere in Ireland.

Witnesses: Samuel Nicholson, Dublin, James Houston, Dublin, apothecary, Thomas Mullock, notary public.

Memorial witnessed by: Samuel Nicholson, Anthony Dempsey, Dublin, gent.

149, 557, 104678 Lettice Parker (seal)

115 HARE, NICHOLAS, the elder, Moira, Co. Down, gent.

10 Nov. 1746. Narrate ½ p. 6 Nov. 1752.

His wife Catherine. His son Andrew. His son James. His son Nicholas. His sons John and William. Peter Mason and Adam Blair, both of Moira, exors. All his houses and land.

Witnesses: William Carruthers, blacksmith, James Joyce, merchant, both of Moira, Co. Down, William Gihon, Aughalee, Co. Antrim, farmer.

Memorial witnessed by: William Carruthers, Robert Donaldson, Dublin, gent.

155, 375, 105111 Andrew Hare (seal)

116 McNEILL, ARCHIBALD, Belfast, gent.

27 Aug. 1752. Narrate 1¼ p. 10 Nov. 1752.

His wife Eleanor McNeill. Archibald McNeill of Sheepland, Co. Down, Esq., James Getty and John Fivey both of Belfast, merchants, trustees.

His estate and effects in Britain and Ireland. The townlands of Ballymaconally, Gortacher, Greenogh, part of Fernogh then or lately possessed by Jno. McConnell, Neill McNeill and partners being his proportion of the territory of Killoquin, Co. Antrim, held by lease granted 1725 by Robert Colvill of Newtown, Co. Down to Laughlin McNeill, Daniel McNeill and John McNeill.

Witnesses: Ann Arbuckle, widow, John Ashmore and Samuel Ashmore, merchants, all of Belfast, Co. Antrim.

Memorial witnessed by: John Ashmore, Saml. Ashmore.

158, 149, 105292 James Getty (seal)

117 KEATING, NICHOLAS, Dublin, Esq.

[Date not recorded]. Full 4½ pp. 17 Nov. 1752.

To be buried in St. Mary's church. Hon. Arthur Dawson and William Vesey, Esq., trustees. William Trench, second son of my niece Mrs. Frances Trench otherwise Power, wife of Richard Trench of Streamstown, Co. Galway, Esq. David Trench eldest son of said niece Frances. My brother-in-law David Power, Esq. To my sister-in-law Mrs. Hester Keating £50 for mourning for herself and family. To said nephew Richard Trench all my books, globes and mathematical instruments. Lucy Allenson, dau. of my cousin John Allenson late of Chester. My aunt Ann Barrett's children. My cousin John Barrett. Thomas Keating, Dublin, carpenter, now employed by me in receiving my rents; his children. My god-daughter and grand-niece Hester Trench, her father the said Richard Trench. Mrs. Mary McDonnell and her daughter Susanna Keating now in my house. Said trustees and niece Frances and nephew Richard Trench exors.

£30 to poor of parish of St. Mary's, Dublin. £30 to Blue Coat Hospital, Dublin.

My estates in counties Dublin, Catherlogh and Kilkenny and my estate called Butterbach in the Palatinate of Chester. Every person or persons who shall be possessed of my real estate shall take the surname of Keating and transfer the same to their children. My leasehold interest in St. Mary's Abby, to wit the house I now dwell in which I hold by lease from Mr. Christopher Taylor deceased, and house held by Widow Crawford which I hold from Thomas Tilson, Esq.

Witnesses: Alexander Thompson, plumber, Thomas Gordon and Will Devall, notary public, all of Dublin.

Memorial witnessed by: James Saunders, William Hall.

157, 458, 105477 Frances Power otherwise Trench (seal)

118 ARTHURE, BENEDICT, Seafield, Co. Dublin, Esq.

10 July 1752. Full 10 pp. 22 Nov. 1752.

My wife Margt. Arthure. My eldest son John Arthure. Trustees: Richard Seacome and Richard Hatfield, Dublin, gents. Rev. Wm. Pountney, Clondalkin, Co. Dublin, clerk, and Edward Scriven, Dublin, gent., trustees for testator's wife. Mark Anthony Morgan, Dublin, Esq., and Daniel Cooke, Dublin, Esq., Aldermen of Dublin, trustees for testator's children. Daniel Arthur, Margt. Arthure and Elinor Christian Arthure (all under 21 years).

My lands etc. in city of Dublin and county of said city, in the county of Galway and all other my lands.

Witnesses: John Bradshaw, Dublin, merchant, St. John Bowden, Dublin, Esq., Jacob Scriven, Dublin, gent.

Memorial witnessed by: Jacob Scriven, Edward Scriven, Dublin, gent.

155, 495, 105565 John Arthur (seal)

119 SENIOR, BARTHOLOMEW, Maryborough, Queen's Co., farmer. 4 Jan. 1741. Narrate ¾ p. 27 Jan. 1753.

His wife Elizth. His son Bartholomew Senior. His son William Senior. His son George Senior. Mary Stoker otherwise Senior, wife to Peter Stoker of Maryborough.

The house wherein James Mosse then lived in Maryborough, lands of Clonee near said town, house wherein Thomas Maguire then lived in Maryborough known by the name of the Three Tunns, the house wherein he lived near Maryborough known by the name of the Sign of the Red Cow and lands thereunto belonging, all held by two leases from William Wall and Pierce Moore. His holdings on the green of Maryborough held by lease from the Corporation. Lands of Moneyballytyrrell [Queen's Co.] held from St. Leger Gilbert, Esq.

Witnesses: Arthur Mosse, Jacob Knowles and Richard Swords, all of Maryborough, gents.

Memorial witnessed by: Arthur Mosse, John Pilkington, Dublin, gent.

157, 556, 106389 Bar. Senior (seal)

120 PILKINGTON, RICHARD, Grange Dirpatrick, Barony Deece, Co. Meath, gent. 19 Dec. 1752. Narrate 1¼ p. 29 Jan. 1753.

His wife Eliz. Pilkington otherwise Wilson, extx. Hercules Langford Rowley, Summerhill, Co. Meath, Esq., and Thomas Wilson, Dublin, Counsellor at law, trustees. His lands of Grange Dirpatrick, Co. Meath. His lands called the Ring, Co. Westmeath held from Viscount Bellfield to said trustees for the use of testator's wife for life and after her decease to the use of his cousin Henry Pilkington, Toar, Co. Westmeath, Esq., after his decease for the use of his eldest son Abraham Pilkington. Henry Pilkington, second son of said cousin Henry Pilkington. His [testator's] wife extx. and £300 to her [brother](1) Joseph Wilson. Miss Eleanor Walsh. Humphrey Blair and his wife Eleanor Blair and their children. James Cane, Esq. Mr. John Carroll. Dr. Fergus. Richard Hindes who had been formerly married to his eldest sister. To each of his nephew and nieces by each of his sisters 5/-.

Witnesses: John Brown, Hugh Wilson and Ephraim Morton all of Dublin, gents.

Memorial witnessed by: John Brown, Thomas White, Dublin, apprentice to Humphry Blair, upholder.

156, 419, 106433 Eliz. Pilkington (seal)

121 HAMILTON, Cornet ARCHIBALD, Strabane, Co. Tyrone.

25 May 1752. Précis ½ p. 3 Feb. 1753.

Rev. William Hamilton, clerk, Robert Barclay and William Drummond, merchants, all of Strabane, and Rev. George Gowan, prebendary of parish of Inver, Diocese of Raphoe, trustees.

His dwellinghouse in town of Strabane and two parks near Strabane in parish of Urney purchased by James Millet.

Witnesses: George McGhee, clerk, John Sproule, apothecary and Simon Rousse, attorney, all of Strabane.

Memorial witnessed by: John Sproul aged upward of thirty years, John Paterson, Thos. Barclay, Strabane.

159, 201, 106549 William Hamilton(2) (seal)
Robt. Barclay (seal)
Wm. Drummond (seal)

(1) The word " brother " is left out of the transcript of the memorial.

(2) This signature is given incorrectly as William Barclay in the transcript of the memorial.

122 HORE, PHILIP, Polehore [Co. Wexford].

7 Nov. 1745. Narrate ¾ p. 14 Feb. 1753.

A settlement made on marriage of his eldest son Thos. Hore and Catherine Harvey third daughter of William Harvey of £40 per year to be issuing out of lands of Polehore, Knoctaclor, Shalgagh, the Mill Land and Muchwood [Co. Wexford] to Rev. James Harvey in trust for said Catherine for life. His son-in-law Thos. Bacon. His younger (fourth) son Christopher. His daughters Hannah and Edith. His brother-in-law Thos. Richards Esq., exor. with testator's eldest son Thos. Hore. His second son Henry Hore. His third son Caesar Hore.

Witnesses: James Richards, farmer and John Richards, Esq., both of Rahasperd, Co. Wexford, Elizth. Hewston wife of — Hewston of Thomastown, Co. Kilkenny, Esq.

Memorial witnessed by: Will. Hall, Robt. McMullen, both Dublin, gents.

158, 449, 106701 Hen. Hore (seal)
Christr. Hore (seal)

123 ST. LEGER, SIR JOHN, Knt., Second Baron of Exchequer.

24 Dec. 1741. Narrate 2 pp. 19 March 1753.

His eldest son John St. Leger. His son Arthur St. Leger. His son William St. Leger. His fourth son Anthony St. Leger. His fifth son Barry Mathew St. Leger. Rt. Hon. Robert Jocelyn, Lord High Chancellor of Ireland, Rt. Hon. Thos. Marlay, Lord Chief Baron of H.M. Court of Exchequer in Ireland, Peter Daly, Esq., Dennis Daly, Esq., Thos. Cuffe, Esq., and Philip Walsh, Esq., trustees.

Manor and lordship of Askeaton, and the advowsons and lands thereunto belonging containing 2,550 acres in Co. Limerick which he purchased from the Earl of Orrery. Lands of Racomane [? Rathcobane], Barony Duhallow, Co. Cork, Clonine and Castletown and Dranghane all in Co. Tipperary.

Witnesses: Richard Maunsell, Limerick, Esq., James Cane, Esq., one of the attorneys of H.M. Court of Common Pleas in Ireland, James Fitzgerald then servant to testator.

Memorial witnessed by: James Cane, Walter Sweetman clerk to John Dennis, gent., one of the attorneys of the Exchequer.

158, 554, 107241 Anthony St. Leger (seal)

124 FLINN, PATRICK, Cavensport, suburbs of Dublin, dealer.

24 March 1753. Précis ½ p. 13 April 1753.

His wife Margaret Flinn extx. His daughter Bridget Flinn. To his daughter Martha one shilling said Martha Flinn having received her share of her fortune.

Witnesses: Joseph Greason, Cavensport, shoemaker, William Bryan, Cavensport, dairyman.

Memorial witnessed by: Joseph Greason, Robert McMullen, Dublin, gent.

161, 52, 107541 Bridget Flinn (seal)

125 BURNSIDE, MATHEW, Corcreevy, Co. Tyrone, gent.

21 March 1753. Narrate ¾ p. 16 April 1753.

His wife and his mother. In case he died leaving issue his real and personal estate to trustees for such issue or else subject to £10 to poor of parish of Clogher in remainder to his brother Anthy. Burnside.

Lands of Corcreevy, house and tenement in Fivemiletown and his leasehold lands of Ballyvaddan and Drummackin. John Blacker, Rachan, Co. Tyrone, gent., and George Blacker of Co. Armagh, exors.

Witnesses: Francis Rutledge, Kilclay, merchant, Wm. Brattan, Augher, innkeeper, John Christell, Ballyneigurragh, gent., all in Co. Tyrone.

Memorial witnessed by: Fras. Rutledge, John Christell.

161, 59, 107571 Mathew Burnside (seal)

126 YARNER, JANE, Church Street, Dublin, spinster.

[Date not recorded]. Narrate 1¼ p. 30 April 1753.

Her sister Elizabeth Yarner and her niece Jane Hill exors. Her nephew Francis Hill. Mary Carolina Wolverston grand-daughter of her sister Wolverston. Catherine Jane Campbell (unmarried) grand-daughter of her said sister Wolverston. Her cousin Ann Keys, widow.

Her house wherein she lived in Church Street, Dublin.

Witnesses: Ann Green, spinster, Adam Sharply, inkeeper, Arthur Parker, gent., all of Dublin.

Memorial witnessed by: Arthur Parker, Ann Keys, Dublin, widow.

159, 445, 107702 Eliza. Yarner (seal)
Jane Hill (seal)

127 SLICER, EDWARD, Dublin, jeweller.

10 Feb. 1752. Narrate 1½ p. 2 May 1753.

His only son Samuel Slicer, Richard Wilson, Dublin, gent. and Arthur Weldon, Dublin, jeweller, overseers of Will, said Wilson and Weldon trustees. His daughter Anne Paine. His daughter Mary Shaw, her husband. His grand-daughter Ann Rouse daughter of said Ann Paine.

His holdings estate and interest on the Wood Quay and Lazers Hill, Dublin, and at the place called The Folly near Lazers Hill and at the corner of White Fryars Street and Golden Lane, Dublin, and in the Mills near Kilmainham, Co. Dublin, and in Rathfarnham, Co. Dublin, and in Plunkett Street, Dublin and at Tib and Tom in Cheqr. Lane and Clarendon Street, Dublin, and elsewhere. Holdings etc. in Molesworth Street, Dublin.

Witnesses: Christopher Dalton, Dublin, public notary and William Williams and Mark Gerard his clerks.

Memorial witnessed by: Christopher Dalton, William Williams.

159, 448, 107707 Mary Shaw (seal)

128 KYLE, WILLIAM, Brackey, Co. Tyrone.

22 Feb. 1753. Narrate 1 p. 12 May 1753.

To his sister's son Robert McKelvey the tenth part of the land and mill of Brackey for life and at his decease to his son Robert McKelvey junior, failing issue to the eldest son of David Kyle and his wife Elizabeth. One half of the tenth part of Brackey Mill and land which he purchased from John Boy Kyle to said David Kyle and his wife. Said Elizabeth's brother Robert McKelvey. His beloved friends Robert McKelvey, David Kyle and John Hamilton exors.

The millstone quarry in the estate of Lisline, Co. Tyrone (Mr. Johnston to have 10/- per year).

Witnesses: James Anderson, Sixmilecross, farmer, Arthur Kyle, miller of Brackey, John McSorley, Derrigwater, farmer, Wm. Early, Brackey, farmer, all in Co. Tyrone.

Memorial witnessed by: James Anderson, Andrew Carmichael clerk to Hugh Carmichael of Spawmount, Co. Tyrone, gent.

160, 380, 107930 David Kyle (seal)

129 McNAMARA, JAMES, Dublin, servant to Mrs. Eliz. Purdon, Dublin, widow.

1 March 1753. Précis $\frac{1}{4}$ p. 14 May 1753.

His goods and chattles and personal estate to his wife Jane McNamara otherwise Donnell, extx. His son John to be put to a proper trade when of proper age.

Witnesses: Francis Lodge, Dublin, gent., Mary Purdon, daughter of said Eliz.

Memorial witnessed by: Henry Chritchly, Dublin, gent., Robert McMullen, Dublin, gent.

161, 145, 107956 Jane McNamara (seal)

130 SMYTH, HUGH, late of Dunsfort, Co. Down and then of Carrickfergus, Co. Antrim, gent. 12 Feb. 1743. Full $\frac{3}{4}$ p. 27 June 1753.

My wife extx. Thomas Knox, Ardquin, Co. Down, Esq., Thomas Nevin, Marleborough, Co. Down, gent., Alex. Hamilton, Dublin, Esq., Geo. Hamilton, Tyrella, Co. Down, Esq., and James Craford, Downpatrick, gent., trustees.

My real and personal estate. Lands of Lismore[1] (the account of the representatives of Patk. Smyth on these lands to be settled).

(1) Probably Lismore, parish of Dunsfort, Co. Down.

Witnesses: George Spaight, Thomas Gunning, both of Carrickfergus, Co. Antrim, gents., John Gordon, Belfast, Co. Antrim, merchant.

Memorial witnessed by: Robt. Hamilton, Dublin, gent., John Gordon.

164, 43, 108736 Alex. Hamilton (seal)

131 PONSONBY, ELIZABETH otherwise CLARKE, wife of Chambre Brabazon Ponsonby of Ashgrove, Co. Kilkenny. 7 April 1752. Narrate 1 p. 9 July 1753.

Agreement 26 Sept. 1746 made previous to her inter-marriage with Chambre Brabazon Ponsonby. No sons but three daughters Frances, Elizabeth and Juliana Ponsonby.

Her real estate, lands, tenements and hereditaments to her husband.

Witnesses: John Lackey, Knocktopher, Co. Kilkenny, Esq., Thomas Butler, Kilkenny, Esq., John Hobson, Waterford, gent.

Memorial witnessed by: John Hobson, Barnaby Jackson, Curluddy, Co. Kilkenny, Esq.

164, 76, 108941 Chambre Brab. Ponsonby (seal)

132 ARTHUR BENEDICT, New Church Street, parish of St. Michan's, Dublin, perukemaker. 21 March 1753. Narrate ½ p. 27 July 1753.

Testator is advised that by virtue of a deed of settlement made by John Arthur of Cabragh, Co. Dublin, Esq., deceased and Michael Chamberlain, Esq., deceased, 10 May 1693 "he is the next heir at law to the estate of the said John Arthur after the death of his son Benedict who died in October last without leaving any lawful issue." His wife Margt. Arthur, extx., to hold and enjoy said estate. His kinsman the eldest son of Thomas Arthur. John Hacket, Walterstown, Co. Westmeath, Esq., William Cooper, Carlow, Esq., Rev. Dr. John Magill, curate of parish of St. Mary's, Dublin, overseers of Will.

Witnesses: William Smart, Bryan Reilly, John Courtney, all of Dublin, gents.

Memorial witnessed by: William Smart, James Harborne, Dublin, gent.

162, 206, 109209 Margarett Arthur (seal)

133 MERVYN, JAMES alias RICHARDSON ("heretofore called James Richardson"), Castlehill, Co. Tyrone, Esq. 7 April 1753. Narrate 1½ p. 14 Aug. 1753.

His wife Ann Mervyn. His daughter Letitia. Testator's three brothers St. George, Galbraith and Erskin Richardson. His kinsman David Rynd, Derryvollan, Co. Fermanagh, Esq. His kinsman David Richardson of Drum, Co. Tyrone. His kinsman Thos. Goodlett, Derrygalley, Co. Tyrone, Esq. Andrew Knox, Prehen, Co. Londonderry and Wm. Wray, Ards, Co. Donegal, Esq., trustees.

Springtown, Aughnacarry [? Aughnacarney] McKinley, Aghamintall [Aghamilkin] McKenna(1), Corgagh, Carnamucklagh Black, Carnamucklagh Murphy, Durnesiove [? Dernaseer], Derrycloony, Dernasell, Derrydruman [? Derrydrummond], Glencapog, Killridon [Kilruddan], Killycarnan, Lisgor[r]an, Cavan, Tully, Cullamore, Lisbane, Analochan, Ballygreenhill, Altnaveagh, Aghadara, Ballymacan, Corr, Calbell, Tullingar(2), Derryclea, Aghadaragh, Lungs, Mullans, Mullaghmorebuchan, Bellclagan [? Belnaclogh, parish Clogher], Statmore [? Stratigore, parish Donacavey], Tamlymore [? Tamlagh], Caldrum, the Lough, Castle and Parks of Augher and Killaney, the corn mill etc. of Augher, his moiety of the customs of Augher; rents out of Bellnageragh, Killclay and Doris [? Doras]; moiety of advowson of the church of Ballanasagart, and the reversion of Castlehill after his wife's death, in Co. Tyrone; his estate in manor of Favor Royal in said county, Oughirad [? Oughterard], Skreen, Glennon, Lisgannon [? Lisgorran], Lisnalloy, Sheergram [Sheerigrim], Gortrush, Mullaghbane, Clonemullan, Munalboy, Golan, the mill thereof, Camderry, Straduff, Cavanaca(3), Gortmore, Kilmore, Lisnamallaght [? Lisnamaghery], Highland Hill, tenement in town of Omagh formerly in possession of Rev. Mr. Maxwell, rent out of lands of Attaghmore, his moiety of mill of Omagh and the Barley Park, Co. Tyrone. Lands of Naul otherwise Snowtown, the mill of Naul, Buringtown otherwise Bodingtown, Mooresides, Kenroestown, Dardistown and Cloghan, Co. Meath. His mansion house and demesne of Castlehill and part of the lands of Carr and the lands called the Castle and castleyard thereunto adjoining.

---

(1) "McKenna" might be the townland of Mackenny, parish Kildress.

(2) Possibly Tullygare in parish of Derryloran, though the majority of the other townlands mentioned are in Clogher Barony and parish.

(3) Possibly Cavanacaw in parish of Drumragh, but note that there is a townland called Cavanacark in Clogher parish. Compare with Abstract 675.

Witnesses: Ralph Sampson, Dublin, merchant, Thomas Gledstanes, Ferdross, Co. Tyrone, Esq., Charles Davis, Dublin, gent.

Memorial witnessed by: Ralph Sampson, Bernard Kane, Dublin, gent.

163, 319, 109436 Ann Mervyn (seal)

134 DREW, MARGARET, Waterpark, Co. Cork, widow of John Drew late of Waterpark, gent. 3 June 1753. Précis ½ p. 20 Sept. 1753.

All her worldly substance etc. to her daughters Ruth Drew and Susanna Drew both of Waterpark.

Witnesses: Catherine Drew and John Croker, gent., both of Glanaboy, Co Waterford, James Crawford, Tallow, Co. Waterford, gent.

Memorial witnessed by: James Crawford, Robert Drew, Glanaboy, gent.

163, 412, 109809 Susanna Drew (seal)

135 GORE, RICHARD, Sligo, Co. Sligo, Esq.

12 Feb. 1752. Narrate 1 p. 2 Oct. 1753.

To his daughter Ann Gore and his daughter Gertrude Gore £1,000 each for marriage portions. His brother Arthur Gore of Ballygarre[tt], Co. Carlow, Esq., deceased, bequeathed a valuable estate to testator's eldest son Richard. His son Francis Gore. His three daughters Deborah Baily otherwise Gore, Ann Gore and Gertrude Gore. His kinsman and nephew Henry Gore, Dublin, gent., eldest son of his brother Col. Francis Gore, deceased, His brother Henry Gore. Sir Richard Gethin, Sligo, Bart. and Robt. French, Dublin, Esq., one of the Judges of Court of Common Pleas, exors.

Lands in Co. Monaghan. Lands of Suey and Lissaviney, Co. Sligo, and real and personal estate.

Witnesses: Mitchelburne Knox, Sligo, Esq., Thos. Knox, merchant and George Knox, Esq., both of Sligo.

Memorial witnessed by: Thos. Knox, Henry Farrell, Sligo, physician.

161, 548, 109892 Fras. Gore (seal)

136 WEST, TICHBORN, Ashwood, Co. Wexford, Esq.

14 Oct. 1750. Narrate 1 p. 2 Oct. 1753.

His grandson Richard West. His daughter-in-law Frances West. His grandson Robert West. His grandson Nicholas West. Tichborn West, eldest son of his son William deceased. His grandson William West, son of William West. His son Mordant West, exor. with testator's daughter Jane West. His son John West. His daughters Sarah Hamilton and Jane West. His grand-daughter Elizabeth West. His niece Elizabeth Ricard. His niece Dorcas Ricard.

James Harrick. John Morris, Edward Gregory, the widow Ann Gregory. William Nicholson. £10 to poor of Arklow parish. £5 to Rev. James Dickson for use of the Charter School near Arklow. Rev. John Wynn, Hacketstown, and Rev. James Dickson, Cherymount, trustees.

Lands of Ashwood otherwise Ballyteague and Ballygullen, Barony Gorey, Co. Wexford. Rents payable out of lands of Ballydonnell, Co. Down.

Witnesses: John McAllen, Glascarick, gent., Nicholas Aplen, Medophall, gent., and James Boland, Ashwood, farmer, all in Co. Wexford.

Memorial witnessed by: John McAllen, William Magin, Dublin, gent.

162, 364, 109894 Jane West (seal)

137 HOLLIDAY, ABRAHAM, Lifford, Co. Donegal.

21 Jan. 1753. Narrate ½ p. 13 Nov. 1753.

His wife Elizabeth. Abraham Holliday son of his brother John Holliday of Strabane.

His freehold called the Well acres and the field of land in the possession of James McAnulty called by the name of Tarleton's sessiagh.

Witnesses: James Adams, nailer, James Andrews, innkeeper, Charles Andrews, glover, all of Lifford, Co. Donegal.

Memorial witnessed by: Charles Andrews, Thomas Thomson, Lifford, gent.

165, 123, 110415 Elizabeth Holliday (seal)

138 YOUNG, ROBERT, Killaghy, parish Drumragh, Co. Tyrone, gent. 29 Oct. 1753. Narrate ¾ p. 13 Nov. 1753.

His wife Mary Young otherwise Crony. His only son by her George Young. His son Leatham Young. The lease of his farm of Killaghy.

Witnesses: Alexr. Kerr, Omagh, Edward Morris, Strabane, both Co. Tyrone, gents., John Moore, Omagh, merchant.

Memorial witnessed by: John Moore aged upwards of thirty years, Edwd. Morris.

165, 123, 110416 Robert Young (seal)

139 MALONE, WILLIAM, Ballybromil, Co. Carlow, farmer. 13 April 1753. Précis a few lines. 29 Nov. 1753.

To his son Wm. Malone, exor., his land in Ballybromil.

Witnesses: William Corragan, Lumcloon, farmer, Wm. Garrett, Clonafarta, Thos. Garrett, Kilgarran, farmer, all Co. Carlow.

Memorial witnessed by: Wm. Garrett, Stephen Rice, Dublin, gent.

166, 142, 110782 William Malone (seal)

140 DAVIS, MARGARET, Hacketstown, Co. Catherlogh, widow. 5 July 1744. Narrate ¾ p. 1 Dec. 1753.

To her daughter Jane Pillson the house in which Samuel Robinson then lived at the north west quarter of the old garden.

Her son Joshua. Lands of Cronescagh and Eaglehill, Co. Catherlogh, John Brownrigg of Ballynglin tenant.

Witnesses: James Bennett, Hacketstown, Co. Catherlogh, shoemaker, James Gibbins, Ballysallagh, said county, farmer, Arthur Hinch, Hacketstown, weaver.

Memorial witnessed by: Arthur Hinch, Abraham Coates, Dublin, gent.

162, 495, 110794 Joshua Davis (seal)

141 CROW, WILLIAM, Dublin, Esq.

31 Aug. 1751. Full 1 p. 13 Jan. 1754.

Ralph Blundell, Dublin, alderman, trustee and exor. Hester Spring, widow of Jno. Spring, clerk. Hester Spring, daughter of said Hester Spring and wife of Wm. Spring, Dublin, merchant. My kinswoman Grace Cuffe, her husband Denny Cuffe. My servant Robert Wogan. John Telling Allen.

My real and personal estate in city of Dublin and elsewhere. Hutton's holding from me in Patrick Street, Dublin.

Witnesses: James King, clerk, Josh. Revell, farmer, and Samuel Ingham, gent., all of Clonegall, Co. Carlow.

Memorial witnessed by: Josh. Revell, Edwd. Mathews, Dublin, Esq.

166, 209, 11274 Ralph Blundell (seal)

142 McMASTER, ROBERT, Cabragh Lane, Dublin, gent.

26 Feb. 1754. Full ¾ p. 21 March 1754.

My wife Mary McMaster. My sister Jennet Walker, widow. My sister Elizabeth Nichol. My brother Hugh. All and every other of my brothers and sisters 1/- each. My nephew Richard Barry. My niece Frances Norton.

Rev. Wm. McBeath. Mr. Robert Moore of Hammon Lane. To poor widows and reduced housekeepers of the congregation of Protestant Dissenters on Usher's Quay, Dublin, £20.

Witnesses: Wm. Bagwell, Dublin, merchant, Chr. Dalton, Dublin, public notary, Wm. Williams his clerk.

Memorial witnessed by: Chr. Dalton, Wm. Williams.

168, 177, 112152 Richd. Barry (seal)

143 SIMPSON, ELIZABETH, Dublin, widow.

7 June 1751. Narrate ½ p. 27 March 1754.

Her son Mathew Morgan, slator, exor. Her three daughters Margret Heney otherwise Simpson wife of Wm. Heney, Jane Leonard otherwise Simpson and Sarah Simpson.

Street House and premises in Proper Lane, Dublin left by the last will of her late husband Edward Simpson to her.

Witnesses: Hugh Neill, writing clerk, Wm. Yeates, combmaker, Wm. Wallace, glazier, all of Dublin.

Memorial witnessed by: Wm. Yeates, Isaac Walsh, Dublin, gent.

166, 453, 112210 Mathew Morgan (seal)
his mark

144 GAFFNEY, JOHN, Queen Street, Dublin, shoemaker.

3 Feb. 1754. Narrate ½ p. 2 April 1754.

His grand-nephew Wm. Gaffney, son of Patk. Gaffney. His step-daughter Margt. Warth otherwise Coughan; her husband. His nephew Robert Heagarty of Sligo. His nephew John Gaffney. James Booth, Cuttpurse Row, shoemaker, James Fetherston, curate of parish of St. Paul's, Dublin, exors.

House and concerns in Church Street held by testator from his nephew Andrew Gaffney.

Witnesses: George Henry and Thos. Fagan, both of Dublin, shoemakers, John Deering, Dublin, gent.

Memorial witnessed by: George Henry, Lewis Moore, Dublin, gent.

166, 469, 112270 Wm. Gaffney (seal)

145 LEE, HELENA, Limerick, widow.

25 July 1742. Narrate 2½ pp. 17 April 1754.

Her sons John Lee of Lairn, Co. Armagh, gent. and Anthony Lee, Waterford, gent. Her sons Arthur Lee, Patrick Lee and her daughters Catherine Lee, Margaret Lee and Susana Lee. Her daughter Elizabeth Dineen otherwise Lee. Alice Dineen daughter of said Elizabeth. Bridget Terry otherwise Lee. Her daughter Helena Bates.

The real estate which she is intitled unto and in possession of in right of her brother John Dowdall, Esq., deceased, and as one of his co-heiresses, that is to say her fourth part of the castle, town and lands of Cappagh, parish of Cappagh, Barony Çonneloe, Co. Limerick. Ballynamuckeymore, Ballynamuckeybegg, Killtenane in barony and county aforesaid. " The Priory cite circuite and precinct of Tanisfallen" [Innisfallen], Meulagh, Aghacurreen, the Island of Degais and Bearoure with the advowson and right of patronage of the church of " Killelly " and Kennemarree [Kenmare] with the thythes etc. therewith belonging in Baronies Magunihie and Glanarought, Co. Kerry. Coarh[a]more and Coarh[a]begg, Barony Iveragh, Co. Kerry.

Witnesses: Jane Perry, Limerick, widow, Henry Sidley, Limerick, merchant, Patk. FitzGibbon, Limerick, gent.

Memorial witnessed by: Hen. Sidley, William Fenton.

164, 594, 112389 Helena Lee (seal)

146 BAGWELL, JOHN, Clonmel, Co. Tipperary, merchant.

7 Dec. 1752. Narrate 1 p. 6 May 1754.

His daughters Mary Riall and Grace Davis. Grand-daughter Elizabeth Riall. His son-in-law William Riall. Phineas Riall.

A reversion in fee expectant on failure of issue male of his grandson John Bagwell of and in town and lands of Kilmore, Ballynegry parcel of the same, Catherclough, Garranearly, Lisronagh, Ballydoyle, Ballyduffe otherwise Rathbrown, Upper and Lower Loughkent, Co. Tipperary to his son William Bagwell for life (his son Wm. Bagwell and his then wife). The Burgagery Lands in and about town of Clonmel which he purchased from Robt. Hamerton and Robert Marshall. Lands of Garranawisty, Garranakirky and

Clashlaghor, Nichol[a]stown, Upper and Lower Derrygrath, Knockmorrisy, Fickidaira and Loghoona [? Loughourna], Gormanstown, Ballyloughan and Ballydrenan, Scartagh, Ballyloughan, Grangebeg, Suttonrath, Barnora and Ballylegan in said county. Houses and premises in town of Clonmell purchased from Josias Thompson to William Lane, Dublin, gent. to the use of John Perry, Woodroofe, Co. Tipperary and Eccles Disney, Churchtown, Co. Waterford, under certain trusts. Liskiveen, Co. Tipperary. Holdings held from Robert Marshall and the Corporation of Clonmel, all in the town of Clonmel, Co. Tipperary. Impropriate tythes of parishes of Rathronan and Kilgrant, Co. Tipperary. Milltown, Co. Tipperary.

Witnesses: Rev. Joseph Moore, clerk, Rev. Wm. Downes, clerk, John Pennefather, Esq., all of Clonmel, Co. Tipperary.

Memorial witnessed by: Simon Newport, Waterford, alderman, John Lindsay, clerk to said Wm. Lane.

167, 312, 112608 Wm. Riall (eal)
Mary Riall (seal)
Wm. Lane (seal)

147 KEARNEY, JAMES, Kearney Bay, Co. Kilkenny, gent.

29 Oct. 1744. Narrate ½ p. 9 May 1754.

His son Benjamin Kearney. James Kearney son of said Benjamin. John Kearney son of said Benjamin. Walter Kearney son of said Benjamin. Richard Kearney son of said James [the testator]. James Kearney son of said Richard. Michl. Kearney(1) son of said James [the testator]. His sons said Benjamin and Richard Kearney exors. Lands of Parkstown, Ballyvollera, Kearneys Bay and Luffany, [Co. Kilkenny].

Witnesses: Joseph Price, Michl. Ryan and Oliver Keating, all of Waterford, gents.

Memorial witnessed by: Michl. Ryan, Andrew Dobbyn, Waterford, gent.

169, 42, 112688 Richd. Kearney (seal)
son and exor. of testator

(1) A son Nicholas instead of this Michael is shown in Betham's Will Pedigrees, Genealogical Office, Vol. 237, p. 37.

148 O'HARA, LAURENCE, Greggstown, Co. Donegal([1]).

20 Feb. 1745. Narrate 1 p. 16 May 1754.

His wife. His eldest son Laurence Hara. His four daughters Francilina (eldest), Mary, Ann and Katherin Hara. His second son William Hara. His nephew Andrew Mackilwaine, attorney. Rev. John Lamp, Raphoe, Mr. John McClintock of Trontaugh, and his wife Ann Hara exors.

His fee farm lands of Killclean, parish of Urney, Edenreaugh, Angey Scrabaugh (Augheyscrabaugh) [Aghascrebagh], Bares, Angeymore (Aughamore) [Aghamore] in parish Termonamongan, Barony Omagh, Co. Tyrone. Lease of Disert, Barony Boylaugh and Bannagh, Co. Donegal, held under See of Raphoe, of Lissnaely, Damplaugh, Mountain Park, Maughraboy [Magheraboy], all in Barony Raphoe, freehold leases of Tully, Drominahaula and Carinby, Tawnalary held under Sir St. George Gore, Bart., all in parish of Donegal, Co. Donegal. Lease of Bagaugh, Four Tops and Gortanoss, parish Raphoe, Co. Donegal held under the See of Raphoe.

Witnesses: John McIlwain, Greggstown, William McClintock, Trontaugh, Daniel Boyle, Tawnalaron [Tawnlary], all in Co. Donegal,

Memorial witnessed by: William McClintock formerly of Trontaugh merchant, but now of Strabane, Simeon Rousse; Strabane, Co. Tyrone, gent.

164, 607, 112846 Fran. O'Hara (seal)

149 COLLINDER, WILLIAM, Waterford, merchant.

17 May 1754. Narrate 2 pp. 21 June 1754.

His wife Mary Collinder. To his good friends Samuel Penrose, George Penrose and James Wyse, (exors.), Waterford, merchants, an equal share or one third part of his interest in the salt works and warehouses on the New Quay, Waterford, which he purchased from Anthony Clifford. The widow and children of Thomas Williams deceased. Susanna Tyler and her children. Susanna Watkins and her children. Sarah Heney and her mother. His aunt Elizth. Dennison and her son. The widow and children of William Kelly. Benjamin Annesly. Paul Boyd. John Heney. Mathew Mason. David Lewis.

([1]) Both in Betham's Will Pedigree and in "*Index of the Prerogative Wills of Ireland*" (Vicars) the testator appears as Laurence Hara.

Elenor Brenock and her daughter-in-law. Mary Doyle an old servant. Capt. Edward Howis. George Cottam. Robert Heney. Joseph Harris. The poor of Trinity Parish. A little boy then about eight years of age called by the name of William Collinder and then living with his sister Elizth. Mackavoy alias Collinder; her husband John Mackavoy, Queen's Co., farmer; their five children then living. A sum not less than £500 for providing convenient and fit places for helpless and poor widows in Waterford.

Witnesses: Patrick Kennedy and Henry Roche, Waterford, merchants.

Memorial witnessed by: Henry Roche, Theodore Cooke, Waterford, notary public.

166, 574, 113299 Geo. Penrose (seal)

150 GREER, ROBERT, Mullalohar, parish Belturbet, Co. Cavan. 17 Jan. 1754. Précis ½ p. 27 June 1754.

His son Thos. Greer, exor. His son-in-law Thos. Sheppeard, exor. his [testator's] daughter Sarah (wife of Thos. Sheppeard).

His farm in Mullalohar and Kealough then in the possession of the following persons viz: Thos. Greer, Bryan Caddan, Robt. Magee, James Curren, Charles Caddan, and Jno. Maguire. The bogg in Clara(h).

Witnesses: Jno. Nevins, Archibald Nevins, both of Ballyvane, Co. Kildare, farmers, John Gallagher, Kilpatrick, said Co., writing master.

Memorial witnessed by: Archibald Nevins (one of the people called Quakers), Charles Lindsay, Dublin, gent.

169, 218, 113443 Thomas Shepard (seal)

151 NOBLE, MUNGO, Glassdrummond [Glassdrumman], Co. Fermanagh. 1 Nov. 1753. Narrate 2 pp. 6 July 1754.

His father-in-law Rev. Wm. Leslie, his brother James Noble of Clentiverin and his cousin Brabazon Noble of Donamoine, Co. Monaghan, exors. His wife Mary Noble otherwise Leslie. His three younger children. His eldest son James Noble. His second son Jerome Noble. His third son Wm. Noble. His youngest son Mungo Noble. All his daughters.

His lands in Shannock, Co. Fermanagh. His farm of Killhill and Crumie. His lands of Altawark and Eshmullegan([1]), all in Co. Fermanagh. His concerns of Glassdrummond. Lands of Drombrochas [? Drumbrughas], Co. Cavan.

Witnesses: Henry Evatt, Clownish, Co. Monaghan, apothecary, Thomas Armstrong and James Mack, both of same, merchants.

Memorial witnessed by: Thos. Noble, Monaghan, gent., Robt. Armstrong, Farnacorky, Co. Fermanagh, gent.

170, 147, 113567

Will. Leslie (seal)
James Noble (seal)
Brab. Noble (seal)

152 DOWNES, ROBERT, Dublin, Esq.

19 April 1749. Précis ¾ p. 12 July 1754.

To my wife Elizabeth Downes, extx., my lands of Donnebrook to raise sums to be equally divided "amongst all the children that I shall leave."

Witnesses: Wm. Dixon, Dublin, public notary, James White then clerk to Edwd. Sterling, public notary, but now of Mount Beresford, Co. Waterford, gent., Edwd. Sterling, Dublin, public notary.

Memorial witnessed by: Edward Sterling, Isaac Holroyd, Dublin, Esq.

166, 565, 113647

E. Downes (seal)

153 PURCELL, TOBY, Archersgrove, Co. Kilkenny, Esq.

10 Aug. 1742. Narrate 2½ pp. 17 July 1754.

Provision made "in case he should have but two daughters and no other younger children, or but one daughter and one younger son living at the time of his death." His wife Mary Purcell. His daughter

([1]) Townlands with the prefix Esh- are seldom to be found except in Co. Fermanagh. There is an Eshywulligan in Clones parish where Shannock is also situated.

Ann Purcell. Rev. George Warburton, Birr, King's Co., clerk and Samuel Lowe, Dublin, Esq., counsellor at law, trustees. Elizth. Morris and Ann Porter. Rev. Michael Cox, Kilkenny, clerk, but now Lord Archbishop of Cashel, and his said wife Mary Purcell exors., Mary to be guardian of his said children during minority.

Testator had recently purchased lands of Lusk, Co. Dublin, commonly called the Riglasse of Luske otherwise the Regalls otherwise the Ragulars of Luske [? Regeens or Regles in Lusk parish], with tythes etc. of town of Luske part of the estate of Maurice Keating of Narraghmore, Co. Kildare. His estate in Co. Tipperary. Mortgage due on Hinde's holding [situation not mentioned]. Money due by Frederick French, Esq.

Witnesses: Richd. Hinde, Dublin, gent., Joseph Ivie, Waterford, gent., Richard Hinde, Waterford, junr., notary public.

Memorial witnessed by: Richard Hinde, junr., Edwd. Dowling, Kilkenny, shopkeeper.

171, 42, 113711 Mary Purcell (seal)

154 DOWLEY, MARCUS, Dublin, Esq.

11 June 1754. Narrate ½ p. 26 July 1754.

His wife Abigail Dowley alias Wolfinder, extx. His eldest daughter Ann Hearn, wife of Rev. Archdeacon Daniel Hearn. His other daughter. His lands of inheritance in the kingdom of Ireland.

Witnesses: Patk. Dunn, gent., an attorney of H.M.'s Court of King's Bench in Ireland, Thos. Quin, Dublin, apothecary, Marlborough Sterling, gent., Deputy Prothonotary of H.M.'s Court of Common Pleas in Ireland.

Memorial witnessed by: Patk. Dunn, Rev. Archdeacon Daniel Hearn.

170, 241, 113854 Abigail Dowley (seal)

155 MOORE, SIR CHARLES, Dublin, Bart.

17 Sept. 1754. Full 4½ pp. 12 Oct. 1754.

John Earl of Egmont and Henry Prittie of Killboy, Co. Tipperary, Esq., trustees. My uncle Robert Moore, Esq. My sisters Catherina

Putland and Ann Moore. Willam Perceval, Esq., second son of Rev. Dean Perceval of the city of Dublin, deceased. John Putland and said William Perceval, both of city of Dublin, Esqrs., exors. £20 to poor housekeepers of the town of Clonakilty, Co. Cork, £50 to those of the town of Clonmel, Co. Tipperary.

All my lands, tenements, hereditaments, etc. in counties of Cork and Tipperary. My house in Dublin.

Witnesses: Anthony Ivers and Robert Jones, clerks to Benjamin Johnston, public notary, Dublin, and said Benjamin Johnston.

Memorial witnessed by: Robert Jones, Joseph Berkly servant to said John Putland.

171, 282, 114588 John Putland (seal)
Catherina Putland (seal)
otherwise Moore wife of said John

156 NEWSTEAD, WILLIAM, Bellgrove, Queen's Co. Esq.
20 March 1754. Narrate 1 p. 12 Nov. 1754.

His wife Helena Newstead, extx. His cousin Richard Newstead. His brother-in-law Thomas Barter. His cousin Henry Lennan. His cousin Richard Grey. His uncle Landon Newstead. His mother-in-law Margret Barter. His sister-in-law Margret Grey.

Lands of Canistown [situation not mentioned] and real and personal estate.

Witnesses: William Smith, Cork, clothier, Clement Sadlier, Cork, cooper, Stephen Gwyn, Cork, silk dyer.

Memorial witnessed by: Stephen Gwyn, Thos. Haddock, Coledaniel, Co. Cork, gent.

173, 10, 114938 Helena Newstead (seal)

157 ROBBINS, GEORGE, Newross, Co. Wexford, Esq., late of Ballyduff, Co. Kilkenny. 1 Aug. 1754. Narrate 1 p. 19 Nov. 1754.

His wife Ann Robbins alias Hopkins extx.

Lands of Plebberstown, Dysertbegg and Ardsignane, Ballyduff, Coolroe, Coolreany and Collsillagh, [Co. Kilkenny].

Witnesses: Nars. Chas. Proby, Dublin, Esq., John Alexander, Newross, Co. Wexford and George Nixon, of same, gent.

Memorial witnessed by: John Alexander, Rev. Francis Hopkins, Tallow, Co. Carlow, clerk.

173, 7, 115111 Ann Robbins (seal)

158 DILLON, RICHARD, Dillonsgrove, Co. Roscommon, Esq.

12 Dec. 1752. Codicil 4 Dec. 1753. Narrate ½ p. 3 Dec. 1754.

Articles dated 12 April 1750 made on his inter-marriage with Maria Rebecca his wife. His wife Maria Rebecca Dillon. Baron Prettyman, Esq., her [? his] father-in-law, Arabella Prettyman her mother. His brother Aylward John Dillon.

His lands of Dillonsgrove, Slevin, Mil[l]town Dillon and Carrowgarry, and all other his lands and tenements in Co. Roscommon.

Witnesses: John French, Joseph Richardson, I. Hutson, all of city of London, gents.

Codicil witnessed by: Dominick O'Connor, Edwd. McDonnell, James Chapman, Le Chevr. D. O'Connor, then of Paris, France, gent.

Memorial witnessed by: Peter Cruise, Dublin, gent., Thos. Dollard, Dublin, writing clerk.

170, 580, 115352 Maria Rebecca Dillon (seal)

159 FITZGERALD, RICHARD, Gortnecrehy, Co. Limerick, gent.

4 Sept. 1754. Narrate 1¼ p. 7 Dec. 1754.

To Robt. Felan, Cahirmoyle, Co. Limerick, gent., lands of Callahow, Gortgullikeigh, Ahadagh, Clounruske, Culelirue, Clounbridy and Ballygulleen, in Barony Connelloe, Co. Limerick. To George Felan, Tulligmacthomas, Co. Limerick, gent., lands of Tulligmacthomas, Farrendoner otherwise Monetullugh, Aghavehine, Gortnaglugin, Lissheensheely, Gortanlassa, Clouncurrippe, Clouncomeragh, Mondillyhy[1], Acreoure, Culelebue and Kells, all in Barony Connelloe, Co. Limerick,

(1) Note that there is a townland called Mondellihy in Barony Coshma.

To Daniel Felan, Kilcoleman, Co. Limerick, gent., lands of Kilcoleman. Ballybrown, Rathfrily, Killtanna, Aghaliny and Dooneencloun all in Barony Connelloe, Co. Limerick. To John Felan, Cahirmoyle, Co. Limerick, gent., lands of Lissinsky, Raghorily, Ballybeg and Ballinvranig, Barony Connelloe, Co. Limerick. To Philip Oliver of Altimira, Co. Cork, Esq., testator's lands of Clounlara, Clounknaw, Boherure, both Ballymunganes, Coulneknockane, Churchtown, Sessive, Clounniscrahane, Movidy, Upper and Lower Dromins, all in Barony Connelloe, Co. Limerick. To Theobald FitzGerald, John FitzGerald and James FitzGerald his three natural and reputed illegitimate sons rest and residue of his real and personal estate. Said John Felan, George Felan and his sons Theobald FitzGerald and John FitzGerald exors.

Witnesses: Saml. Collins, Ardagh, Co. Limerick, gent., Michael Duane, Kiltannah, Co. Limerick, farmer, Thos. Blenr. Hasset Elliot, Rathkeal, Co. Limerick, gent.

Memorial witnessed by: Michael (Mihill) Duane, James Maglin, Dublin, gent.

169, 577, 115417 John Felan (seal)

160 McQUILLIN, ROGER, Tamladuff, Co. Londonderry.

5 Sept. 1754. Narrate ¾ p. 18 Feb. 1755.

To his son Francis McQuillin two parts of his land in Tamlaghduff in the proportion of Vintners, Co. Londonderry. To his daughter Ann McQuillin the third part of his land; James Donnolly her son. Roger McQuillin son of said Francis McQuillin. To his son George McQuillin 1/1. Abraham Hamilton, Esq., and Capt. Andrew Spotswood exors.

Witnesses: William McQuillin, Killyfaddy, linen weaver, James McQuillin, Bellachy, Thomas Jennings, Tamladuff, farmer, all in the proportion of Vintners, Co. Londonderry.

Memorial witnessed by: Wm. McQuillin, Thos. Jennings.

173, 289, 116238 Francis McQuillin (seal)

161 IRVINE, CHRISTOPHER, Castle Irvine, Co. Fermanagh, Esq.

28 Feb. 1752. Narrate 1½ p. 25 Feb. 1755.

Wm. Irvine his eldest son. Henry Irvine testator's second son.

Real estate in manor of Lowther. Corran, Forthill and Coolegrane, part of Aughnascue in Barony Magherystephanagh, Aghaleige, Killigaroe, Stranmore and Lisnagorigill, being parts of Aghaleige aforesaid, Drumsaunah, Drumsaunah More, Drumsaunah Beg. Drummalee, Edenamohill, Duccrock([1]), Cargraghree [? Carrickagreany] being parts of Drumsaunah aforesaid, Secomuldoone and Barr of Tull[a]nagin[n], rent out of lands of Drumchose, Glenarne and Stranadave [? Stranadarriff], Edenaclay [Edenaclogh], Edenavocill [? Edenamohill], Mullaghnacross and Neinemore being part of Strandave [? Stranadarriff] aforesaid, all in Co. Fermanagh. His real estate in Co. Tyrone which he purchased from his brother Henry Mervyn, that is Lettergash, Derreylaghan, Deocrock and lands of Ferny and Tullyninecrin, Co. Tyrone, an annuity out of lands of Creeve, Mealtogs [Meeltogues], Drumternion, Knocknacor and Lisduff; lands purchased from Mr. Lancelot Irvine, that is Tyremacsperde, Mulaghfynchin, Tullinaluve [? Tullynaloob], Drumnamarloe and Sessogy being parts of Termacsperde [Tirmacspird] aforesaid, Collaghty, Mulebane, Ochillacartan [Óghillicartan] and Lismarn being parts of Collaghty aforesaid, Kieran otherwise Keeranbeg being part of Bracklant [Bracklin], Drumern otherwise Drumernagh being part of Monevnse [Monavreece], one half of the island of Inismakill, Lough Erne; rent out of lands of Drumkeene, Edernagh, Cahore, Killygarry, Drumkeeran, Drumbaran, Glassmullagh and Carrickthomasnisickill being parts of Drumkeene aforesaid, situate in Co. Fermanagh.

Witnesses: Francis Hethrington, Cassedy, Co. Fermanagh, gent., Samuel Anderson, Lowtherstown, Co. Fermanagh, carpenter, George Lendrum, Co. Tyrone, gent.

Memorial witnessed by: Francis Hetherington, Samuel Anderson, Lowtherstown.

173, 322, 116299 Elinor Irvine (seal)
(exor. named in said will)

([1]) Duck Island is in the same parish as Edenamohill and Carrickagreany.

162 COOPER, THOMAS, Dublin, Esq.

25 Feb. 1755. Narrate ¾ p. 7 March 1755.

His sister Elizth. Irwin, extx. His nephew Christopher Irwin. His nephew Percivall Irwin.

The great farm in Kilmainham, Co. Dublin. Two houses in James Street, Dublin, in possession of Widow Hall and her son. Freehold in New Street and Thomas Court, Dublin, another in Dolphin's Barn near Dublin. Freehold and leasehold interest in Droghedd [? Drogheda]. Houses in Gt. Brittain Street, Caple Street, Brittain Lane, Brock Lane and elsewhere in Dublin.

Witnesses: Arthur Perrin, Dublin, apothecary, James Currin, Dublin, grocer, Wm. Crowe, Dublin, gent.

Memorial witnessed by: Wm. Crowe, John Crowe, Dublin, gent.

174, 330, 116416 Elizth. Irwin (seal)

163 MADDIN, PATRICK, Whitehouse, Co. Dublin.

8 Jan. 1754. Narrate ¾ p. 10 March 1755.

His wife Mary Maddin, exor. His son John Maddin. His son Mathew Maddin. His son Christr. Martin Walsh, Dublin, exor. His lease in Whitehouse.

Witnesses: Patk. Hughes, Dublin, weaver, Thomas Walsh, Dublin, glover, Richard Walsh, Dublin, weaver.

Memorial witnessed by: Thos Walsh, Richard Walsh.

173, 340, 116441 Mary Maddin (seal)
her mark

164 DANIEL, MARY, Dublin, widow of Wm. Daniel then late of said city, orace weaver, deceased. 3 March 1755. Narrate ½ p. 26 March 1755.

Her daughter Elizabeth Shaw, extx., wife of Samuel Shaw, orace weaver. Her grand-daughter Isabella Shaw (under 21 years). Her son John Daniel. Her daughter Elinor Shaw.

Witnesses: Isaac Bently, Dublin, carpenter, Philip Brew, Dublin, watchmaker, Henry Stearne, Dublin, gent.

Memorial witnessed by: Isaac Bently, Philip Brew.

175, 165, 116586 Elizabeth Shaw (seal)

165 MURRAY, JAMES, Carrigans, Co. Monaghan, joiner.

20 March 1752. Full 1 p. 14 April 1755.

My real and personal estate to my wife Margaret Murray, extx. Sons Nathan and Robert Murray. My daughters Amy and Judeth. John Mullan and Bullingbrooke Anketell exors.

Witnesses: William Johnston, apothecary, Jas. Montgomery, English schoolmaster, both of Glaslough, Anne Stephens, Anketelles Grove, spinster, all in Co. Monaghan.

Memorial witnessed by: Anne Stephens, Francis Cooper, Glaslough, Co. Monaghan, merchant.

175, 203, 116703 Margt. Murray (seal)
her mark

166 KING, MARGARET, Kilpe[a]can, Co. Limerick, widow of George King of same place, Esq., deceased. 24 Jan. 1752. Précis ¼ p. 6 May 1755.

To Richard Villiers (exor.), Ballynabooly, Co. Kilkenny, Esq., all her lands, tenements and hereditaments in the Barony of Coonagh, Co. Limerick, which she had from her husband George King.

Witnesses: George Wallace, Limerick, surgeon, George Tuthill, Faha, Co. Limerick, Esq., John Kelly, Kilpecan aforesaid, man-servant to said Richard Villiers.

Memorial witnessed by: Thomas Croker, Dublin, Esq., Edmd. Doyle, Dublin, gent.

176, 70, 117110 Richd. Villiers (seal)

167 MOONY, OWEN, Doone, King's Co., Esq.

4 Sept. 1753. Narrate 2½ pp. 6 May 1755.

His wife Mary Moony. John Moony his eldest son. Edward Moony second son of testator. His brother William Moony. Owen Moony, nephew of testator. Francis Enraght grandson of testator. Owen Enraght grandson of testator. Simon Bradstreet, Kilmainham, Co. Dublin, Esq., and John O'Connor, Mount Pleasant, King's Co., Esq., trustees. Dr. Lewis Pritchet, Lither [? Letter], King's Co., Esq., and Francis McAulay, Frankford, King's Co., Esq., joint exors.

Esker Castle, Cap[p]an[a]los[s]et, Ballycap, Carrowcolm, Coolderrogh, Doone, Killtawragh, Aghafin, Lawaghbegg, in Barony Garrycastle, King's Co.

Witnesses: Stephen Reynolds, Dublin, apothecary, Samuel Kathrens, Dublin, gent., Henry Stevens Reily, Dublin, public notary.

Memorial witnessed by: Samuel Kathrens, Henry Stevens Reily.

174, 472, 117111 O. Moony (seal)
Owen Moony the younger, nephew of testator

168 PITT, ANNE, Dublin.

15 July 1747. Full ¼ p. 17 May 1755.

To my dear mother my real and personal estate. My uncle Skerrett her brother. My aunt Susanna Flack. Mr. William Powell apothecary.

My whole and sole interest in house and ground in Wine Tavern Street that the Common Pleas Office is now kept in. My estate on Cock Hill.

Witnesses: Randall Slack, Dublin, gent., Christopher Rice, Dublin, cutler, Wm. Cosgrave, Dublin, merchant.

Memorial witnessed by: Christopher Rice, Thomas Biggs, Dublin, gent.

172, 431, 117255 Jane Pitt (seal)
mother of testatrix.

169 KINGSBOROUGH, RT. HON. ROBERT LORD

13 Jan. 1752. Full 1¾ p. 13 June 1755.

My brother Henry King (under age). My brother Edward. My late father Sir Henry King. Mark Whyte, Dublin, Esq., trustee.

My real and personal estate. The demesne of Rockingham [Co. Roscommon].

Witnesses: Sarah Chamberlaine, Dublin, spinster, Charles Gardiner, Boyle, Co. Roscommon, gent. [? agent] to the testator, Hugh Maguire, Dublin, servantman, since deceased.

Memorial witnessed by: Charles Gardiner, Edward Mathews, Dublin, gent., clerk to Mark Whyte, Dublin, Esq.

176, 83, 117512 Hen. King (seal)

170 PALMER, ELIZABETH otherwise COTTON, wife of Wm.

Palmer of Dublin, Esq. 17 May 1750. Full 1¾ p. 18 June 1755.

To my husband Wm. Palmer all my fortune in England and £10 out of my fortune in and about Dublin. My sister Hannah Davison otherwise Cotton; her husband. Edward Fole, Dublin, gent.; his wife. £100 due by Mr. Throp. Money due from Doctor Mosse. John Goodwin of the Royal Hospital near Dublin, Esq., exor.; his wife. Mrs. Jane Delgarno. Eliz. Hansard.

My ground in Kildare Street, Dublin, and my house thereon erected to Christopher Robinson (exor.) Dublin, Esq., one of H.M. Counsell at law, upon trust, remainder to Robt. Robinson, Dublin, Doctor of Physick. " I desire to be buryed near dear Mrs. Robinson." My house in Finglass wherein Mr. Connolly now lives.

Witnesses: Michael Clarke, Dublin, Esq., Anthony Coane, Strabane, Co. Tyrone, Esq., Edward Croker, Dublin, apothecary.

Memorial witnessed by: Edward Croker, Daniel Huleatt, Dublin, gent.

177, 81, 117561 Robt. Robinson (seal)

171 HOVENDEN, NICHOLAS, Toulaghten [Towlerton], Queen's Co., gent. 19 March 1755. Narrate ½ p. 26 June 1755.

His son Arthur Hovenden exor. His son Richard Hovenden. A legacy bequeathed to testator by Will of Thos. Hovenden then late of Gurteen, Queen's Co., deceased, dated 13 April 1744.

Witnesses: David Price, Castletown, clerk, William Supple, Toulerton, butcher, Laughlin Dowling, Toulerton, all Queen's Co.

Memorial witnessed by: Richard Hovenden, Dublin, gent., Wm. Magin, Dublin, gent.

177, 98, 117603 Arthur Hovenden (seal)

172 DALTON, RICHARD, Snugborough, Co. Westmeath, gent. 1 April 1755. Full 1½ p. 27 June 1755.

To be buried in churchyard of Ballymore. James Nugent only son of my nephew Edmond Nugent. My nephew Dalton Smyth, son of Mr. James Smyth of Moyvore and who has lived with me. My servant Mary Dun. Money due to me by Anthony Malone, Esq. My servant Bryan McCormick, his son Andrew McCormick. Said nephew Dalton Smyth and George Meares of Ballymore, Esq., exors.

House and garden whereon Mr. James Dalton, tailor, now lives to my said servant maid at rent of £2 per annum.

Witnesses: Richd. Meares, Killinboy, Co. Westmeath, gent., James Dalton, Ballymore, Co. Westmeath.

Memorial witnessed by: John Brady, Dublin, merchant, Patk. Corbet, Dublin, clerk to Geo. Meares, Esq.

177, 103, 117650 Dalton Smyth (seal)

173 TURNER, ANN, Dublin, widow. 18 June 1747. Précis ½ p. 12 July 1755.

Her sister Palmer. Her sister Bernard, her husband. Her nephew George Dunbarr, Esq.

Lands of Killelongford, part of lordship of Clonmore, Co. Carlow.

Witnesses: Thomas Groves, Dublin, servant to said testator, Edward Cullen, clerk to George More, Dublin, public notary, and said George More.

Memorial witnessed by: Edwd. Cullen, George More.

177, 150, 117848 George Dunbar (Dunbarr) (seal)

174 HUNTER, DAVID, Orangefield, Co. Down, Esq.

20 Feb. 1747. Précis 1 p. 15 July 1755.

Lands etc. of Orangefield, Co. Down, to be sold by Ralph Knox and Samuel Craghead, London, merchants, trustees; money arising from such sale to become part of residue of said testator's personal estate.

Witnesses: Saml. Parmenter, then of Basinghall Street, now of Inner Temple, London, gent., Benjamin Chandler then of Basinghall Street aforesaid, gent., since deceased, John Clarke then of Inner Temple and now of Basinghall Street aforesaid, gent.

Memorial witnessed by: William Lucas, Middle Temple, London, Esq., John Clarke.

176, 455, 117862 Ralph Knox (seal)

175 RANELAGH, ARTHUR LORD

7 Jan. 1748. Narrate 2½ pp. 19 July 1755.

His wife Selina Lady Ranelagh. His nephew John Cole of Florence Court, Co. Fermanagh. William Cole son of said John Cole. His nephew Henry Brooke, Esq., son of his sister Catherine Brooke and his worthy friend Albert Nesbitt, Coleman Street, London, Esq., trustees.

His manors, castles, towns, lands, tenements and hereditaments etc. in counties of Waterford, Tipperary and Dublin, and in cities of Dublin and Waterford, and in counties of said cities. Real estate etc. in Co. Clare which was the estate of Captain Michael Cole his late brother deceased.

Witnesses: Nathaniel Cole, Basinghall Street, London, gent,, Samuel Parmenter, then of same now of Inner Temple Lane, London. gent., Godfrey Kettle, Basinghall Street, gent.

Memorial witnessed by: Nathaniel Cole, Basinghall Street, London, gent., John Clarke, clerk to said Nathaniel Cole.

172, 540, 117906 Henry Brooke (seal)

176 RULLAND, JOHN, Templebar, Dublin, gent.

29 Oct. 1751. Narrate ½ p. 8 Oct. 1755.

His wife Jane Rulland extx. His good friend Joseph New, Temple Bar, hatter, trustee. His daughter Sarah Leazonby then wife of Edwd. Leazonby.

His house and premises known by the sign of The Cock in Dame Street, Dublin, wherein Mr. Cottingham Mercer then dwelt.

Witnesses: John Mathews, Temple Bar aforesaid, carver, Richd. Rowland, Temple Bar, yeoman, Henry Stearne, Dublin, gent.

Memorial witnessed by: Saml. Morgan, Dublin, gent., Henry Stearne.

178, 200, 118566 Jane Rulland (seal)

177 WILDE, WILLIAM, Dublin, gent.

18 Jan. 1755. Narrate ¾ p. 8 Oct. 1755.

William Wilde, Dublin, ironmonger, the natural son of testator, exor. His [testator's] brother John Wilde, exor. Edwd. Bolton, Brazeel, Co. Dublin, Esq., and Boleyn Whitney, Dublin, Esq., trustees. His nephew Henry Nixon; his eldest son William Nixon.

Real and personal estate etc. in city of Dublin or Kingdom of Ireland. Holdings on east side Frederick Street, Dublin.

Witnesses: Rev. Jones Burches, parish of St. Mark, Dublin, clerk, John Sault, Sir John's [Rogerson's] Key, in [said] parish and city, victualler, Thos. Clarke, Lazers Hill in said parish and city, gent.

Memorial witnessed by: Chris. Deey, public notary, Dublin, Thos. Aungir, Co. Dublin, farmer.

178, 201, 118567 William Wilde (seal)

178 LYSTER, JOHN, late of Athleague then of Dublin, Esq.

7 Jan. 1753. Narrate ¾ p. 16 Oct. 1755.

All his real estate to his mother the Rt. Hon. Margaret Lady Viscountess Mayo. Said real estate is described on re-publication of said Will 13 June 1753 as consisting of the Mannor of Athleague otherwise Athleig with mills, fairs and markets, Carrownekelly otherwise Quillagh, Kynogh other Keanagh, Lissereger, Clonekelly, Cloneen otherwise Cloyne, Carrowreagh, Cloneowris otherwise Clonejowris, Toberkeogh otherwise Blindwell, Araght otherwise Araghty, Lissenoud, Lisskemane, Gortree, Corralea otherwise Corraleagh, Lisscorr, Ballylyon, Cartron otherwise Tryne, all in Barony Athlone, Co. Roscommon. House in parish of St. Audeon, county of city of Dublin.

Witnesses: Rev. Wm. Darby, Dublin, clerk, George Gunning, Hollywell, Co. Roscommon, gent., John Hopkins, Dublin.

Witnesses to re-publication: Wm. Darby, George Gunning, Dennis Kelly, Dublin, gent.

Memorial witnessed by: Wm. Darby, Paul Ryan, Dublin.

178, 216, 118612 M. Mayo (seal)

179 LYSTER, JOHN, late of Athleague, Co. Roscommon, then of Dublin, Esq. Codicil 1 Nov. 1753. Précis ¼ p. 16 Oct. 1755.

Whereby he devised all his estates as therein mentioned [no further information].

Witnesses: Wm. Darby, Dublin, clerk, James Dillon, Dublin, Esq., George Gunning, then of Dublin but now of Holywell, Co. Roscommon, gent.

Memorial witnessed by: Wm. Darby, Paul Ryan, Dublin.

178, 216, 118614 M. Mayo (seal)

180 LARGE, THOMAS, Carriglea, Co. Waterford, gent.

1 Oct. 1755. Narrate 1¼ p. 11 Nov. 1755.

Ann Large otherwise Keily his wife. John Large, city of Cork, his eldest son. Richard Large, George Large, Jno. Allin and David

Coughlan to divide residue of an estate to be sold. John Keily, Knockalahin, Co. Waterford, Esq., and Geo. Coughlan, Cappoquin, Co. Waterford, Esq., trustees. Money due to testator from King Willington, late of College Hill, Co. Tipperary, Esq., by bond to testator and Jno. Keily, Esq., deceased, bequeathed to said John Large, his [testator's] said wife, Richard Large, George Large, Nancy Large, John Allin and David Coughlan. Said Richard Large, John Allin and David Coughlan exors.

Lands of Ballystannelly [Ballystanly], Glassclone and part of Ballybrack, upwards of 300 acres and 107 acres part of lands of Ballystannelly aforesaid purchased by testator from Mary Large otherwise Doolin late of Ballycapple, Co. Tipperary, widow and from Wm. Large of Nenagh, Co. Tipperary, apothecary, son to said Mary, in Barony Clonlisk, King's Co.

Witnesses: John Floyd, Ballyduff, Co. Waterford, schoolmaster, Bryan O'Bryan, Knockane, Co. Waterford, yeoman, Wm. Fowlow, Coolcormuck, Co. Waterford, farmer.

Memorial witnessed by: Wm. Fowlow, Michl. Fowlow, Carriglea, yeoman.

178, 255, 118807 Dav. Coughlan (seal)

181 HOFFSHLEGER, JOHN BERNARD, Dublin, merchant.

21 Jan. 1747. Précis ½ p. 24 Dec. 1755.

Residue of his personal estate and all his real estate to Daniel Falkiner, Dublin, alderman, exor.

Witnesses: William Lennox, Dublin, Esq., John Wallace, Dublin, book keeper to said William Lennox, John Julien, Dublin, book keeper to testator.

Memorial witnessed by: John Julien, Benjamin Geale, Dublin, merchant.

176, 443, 119483 Dan. Falkiner (seal)

182 DOBSON, ANNA MARIA otherwise TOMKINS, wife of Captain Robt. Dobson the Earl of Home's Regiment of Foot. 2 Dec. 1751. Narrate ½ p. 3 Jan. 1756.

Articles made previous to her intermarriage with her husband dated 13 June then last, Andrew Knox and Roger Morris, trustees. Devises to her said husband lands of Colonedy, parish Maghera, Gershedon, parish Cumber, Knockbrack, Ardkill, Lower Tullyally, Upper Tullyally, parish Clondermot, all in Co. Londonderry.

Witnesses: Richd. Thwaites and Robert Jones, clerks to Benj. Johnston, public notary, Dublin, and by said Benj. Johnston.

Memorial witnessed by: John Rooke, Benj. Johnston.

176, 457, 119523 Robt. Dobson (seal)

183 LENNOX, BOYLE, Dublin, Esq.

24 Nov. 1755. Full ¼ p. 20 Jan. 1756.

Real and personal estate to wife Elizabeth Lennox, extx.

Witnesses: Henry Benson and John Preston, clerks to Robert Wallis, Dublin, public notary, and by said Robt. Wallis.

Memorial witnessed by: Henry Benson, John Preston.

178, 463, 119622 Elizth. Lennox (seal)

184 ARTHUR, THOMAS(1), Ballyquin, Co. Clare, gent.

12 Dec. 1752. Codicil 16 Aug. 1755. Narrate 1 p. 29 Jan. 1756.

His wife Elizabeth Arthur otherwise Butler, extx., and guardian of his only daughter Ann Arthur (under 25 years, unmarried) and his only son Thos. Arthur (under 25 years). His real, freehold and personal estate.

Witnesses: Thomas Arthur Thomas, Cloneconry, Co. Clare, gent., Luke Wall, Dublin, gent., John Linehan, Ballymullowny, Co. Clare, farmer.

Codicil witnessed by: Luke Wall, John Linehan, Edmd. Vaughan, Killeagy, Co. Clare, farmer.

Memorial witnessed by: Luke Wall, William McNeboe, Dublin, chaiseman.

180, 99, 119714 Elizabeth Arthur (seal)

(1) Thomas Arthur Piers. Betham's Will Pedigrees, Vol. 24, p. 178, Genealogical Office, shows the testator as Thomas Arthur son of Piers Arthur.

185 McCAUSLAND, OLIVER, Strabane, Co. Tyrone.

19 Dec. 1753. Narrate 1¼ p. 5 Feb. 1756.

Reciting deed of settlement of part of his real estate in 1744, provision made thereby for his wife Jane McCausland. His younger children Margaret, Oliver, Allice and Ann Jane. His eldest son John McCausland. Rev. Robert Spence, Donaghmore, Co. Donegal, clerk, and Alderman James Dunn, Dublin, trustees. His dwelling house in Strabane.

Witnesses: Saml. Moore, Londonderry, Doctor of Physick, Rev. Victor Ferguson and Simeon Rouse, both of Strabane, aforesaid.

Memorial witnessed by: Simeon Rouse, Rev. Chas. Rea, Donaghmore, clerk.

181, 62, 119823 Robt. Spence (seal)

186 McQUILIN, ALEXANDER, Dublin, cloth worker.

25 Jan. 1756. Narrate ½ p. 4 March 1756.

His grandchildren by his daughter Mary Walsh, that is to say Elizabeth Walsh, Elinor Walsh, Patrick Walsh and Alexander Walsh. Her husband Patrick Walsh. Said daughter Mary Walsh extx.

His house in Pill Lane, Dublin and his warehouse in Mass Lane otherwise Lucy's Lane, Dublin, and a house in Pimlico in parish of St. Catherine.

Witnesses: Chas. Connelly, Dublin, tailor, Isaac Wilson, Dublin, gent.

Memorial witnessed by: William Magin and John Hutton, Dublin, gents.

181, 122, 120156 Mary Walsh (seal)

187 CATHCART, CARLETON, Ghent, Northern Netherlands, Life guardsman. 10 Dec. 1742. Précis ½ p. 17 March 1756.

Personal and real estate to Alexander Cathcart "my beloved kinsman." Judy in London, testator's washer-woman.

Witnesses: Jonathan Robinson, Paul Bradshaw, William Kennedy, gent.

Memorial witnessed by: Jonathan Robinson, William Magin, Dublin, gent.

181, 167, 120295 Alexr. Cathcart (seal)

188 RAYNER, JOHN, Tubberlynan, Co. Meath, gent.

3 March 1756. Narrate 1½ p. 22 March 1756.

His wife Mary Rayner otherwise Nugent and his cousin Robert Bonham, Esq., trustees and exors. and guardians of his children until respectively aged 21 years. His daughter Martha. His daughter Mary. His daughter Mehittabell. His brother Captain Robert Rayner.

Real estate in city of Dublin and county of Meath.

Witnesses: George Nugent, Castlerickard, Co. Meath, Esq., George Lewis, Stoneford, Co. Meath, yeoman, Saml. Totherinton, Tobertynan, Co. Meath and Rev. John Payne, Castlerickard, Co. Meath, clerk.

Memorial witnessed by: Thos. Tudor, Dublin, gent., Percival Irwin, clerk to Wm. Crowe, Dublin, gent.

177, 579, 120338 Mary Rayner (seal)
one of the devisees and exors.

189 THOMPSON, JAMES, Leitrim, Co. Londonderry.

20 May 1734. Précis 1 p. 26 March 1756.

His wife Katherine. His two sons Joshua and James. His son Robert. His youngest son John. His daughter Jane Typpin and husband. His son Wm., his [testator's] wife, and his neighbour William Man exors.

Witnesses: Rev. Hugh Wallace, Magherafelt, Co. Londonderry, Thomas Man and Wm. Man both of Leitrim, farmers.

Memorial witnessed by: Hugh Wallace, James Crawford, Magherafelt, innkeeper.

180, 247, 120382 Joshua Thompson (seal)
John Thompson (seal)

190 SHEWELL, GEORGE, Liverpool, County of Lancaster.

18 Aug. 1755. Narrate 1 p. 7 April 1756.

His wife Elizabeth Shewell. His daughter Mary Frazier, wife of Joseph Frazier, mariner. His daughter Anne Shewell. His son Michael Shewell. His son Rev. John Shewell, clerk.

His real estate in Dundalk, Co. Louth, to be recovered from John Pepper of Ballyhow, Co. Meath, Esq., and sold by exors. His wife, Wallop Brabazon, Rath, Co. Louth, Esq., and Benjamin Stockley, Liverpool, cooper, exors.

Witnesses: Robert Blackburn, Liverpool, schoolmaster, Elizabeth Tueson otherwise Watkinson, wife of Herman Tueson, Liverpool, mariner, Rachel Billinge otherwise Watkinson, wife of James Billinge, Liverpool, mariner.

Memorial witnessed by: Elizabeth Tueson, Joseph Rathborn, Liverpool, mariner.

177, 589, 120493 Elis. Shewell (seal)

191 BLAKE, SIR THOMAS, Somervill, Co. Galway, Bart.

31 July 1748. Full 3 pp. 21 April 1756.

To be interred in tomb of my ancestors at Galway. My wife Dame Elizabeth Blake extx. and guardian of my only daughter Anna Blake (under 21 years). Real estate in remainder to " my only son and heir apparent Ulick Blake, Esq." (his present wife), failing whose heirs to Valentine Blake, Esq., my brother, then to Thomas Blake of Brendrum, Co. Mayo, gent., and in remainder to Walter Blake of Brendrum, Isidore Blake of Galway, gent., and to his son Maurice Blake of Galway, Isidore Blake eldest son of said Isidore, Walter Blake second son of said Maurice Blake, Patrick Blake second son of said Isidore. His brother John Blake. Thomas Burke, Dublin, counsellor at law, Thady McNamara, Oyle, Co. Clare, Esq., and Thomas Blakeney the elder, Cullagh, Co. Galway, gent., attorney at law, trustees. A bond passed by me to Jonack Bodkin, merchant.

Witnesses: Julia Martin, then of town of Galway, spinster, but now married to Walter Blake of the Co. Galway, Esq., Robert Martin then of Dangen but now of Dublin, Esq., George Cusacke, Dublin, surgeon, Patrick Larkin, then servant to testator.

Memorial witnessed by: John Hutton, Dublin, John Savage, Dublin, upholder.

178, 572, 120582 Eliza Blake (seal)

192 WARD, JOHN, Dublin, baker.

31 March 1749. Narrate ½ p. 6 July 1756.

His wife Elizabeth Ward. His son Thos. Ward (under 21 years). His dwelling house in King Street, his bake house, baking utensils and all his back concerns.

Witnesses: Henry Holdbrook, Dublin, slater, John Cassidy, Dublin, baker, Valentine Kaven, Dublin, gent.

Memorial witnessed by: Christopher Dalton, Dublin, public notary, William Williams his clerk.

183, 56, 121542 Thos. Ward (seal)

193 HIPPISLEY, WILLIAM, heretofore of Staunton, Wiltshire, Esq., and parish of St. Andrew, Holborn, Middlesex.

4 Feb. 1754. Précis 1 p. 7 July 1756.

Lands etc. in parishes of Staunton, North Bradley, Durneford and Highworth, Co. of Wilts. Lands in parish of Bourton on the Water, county of Gloucester or elsewhere in Gt. Britain and his lands etc. in Ireland to be sold by trustees John Hippisley Cox, Stone Easton, Co. Somerset, William Calley, Burdropp, Wilts, and John Hippisley, Lambourne, Berks., Esqrs.

Witnesses: Samuel Dukinfield, Fenchurch Street, London, gent., Charles Du Buc of Ship Yard, Bartholomew Lane, London, gent., Hugues Hebrand, Hog Lane, Soho, gent.

Memorial witnessed by: Thos. Ludbeg, clerk to Thos. Brigstock of Bartletts Buildings, Holborn, London, gent., George McLean.

180, 502, 121546 J. Hippisley (seal)

194 DALY, MORGAN, Kilcleagh, Co. Westmeath, Esq.

24 May 1756. Narrate 1½ p. 31 July 1756.

His uncle Arthur Morgan and his kinsman Henry Boyle Carter, Esq., trustees. His brother Peter Daly (under 26 years). His cousin Joseph Daly, Moysaghly, gent. Dennis Daly eldest son of said Joseph. John Daly, second son of said Joseph. His sister Elizabeth Daly.

Real estate in Counties of Westmeath and Roscommon and elsewhere in Ireland.

Witnesses: John Curry, Dublin, Doctor in Physick, Thomas Mulock, Dublin, public notary.

Memorial witnessed by: Alexr. Stuart, Hugh Reynolds, Dublin, gents.

179, 450, 121802 Jos. Daly (seal)

195 ASHBROOKE, HENRY VISCOUNT.

25 June 1752. Full 11 pp. 10 Nov. 1756.

John Folliott of the Royal Hospital near Dublin, Esq., and Rev. Hugh Dawson, Banford, Co. Kilkenny, trustees. My wife Elizabeth Viscountess Ashbrooke and Henry Lord Viscount Palmerston exors. and guardians. My son William Flower (a minor). My daughters Elizabeth Flower and Mary Flower (under 21 years and unmarried). Alexr. King and Crofton Warren, gents., trustees. My sister Rebecca Agar.

Lands of Cappenelanwood, Parkwood commonly called Bishopswood, the Course wood, Knockatrina Wood and the Derry wood by the side of the mountain. All other my real estate. To said wife use of house and demesne etc. during her natural life and residence at Castledurrow [Queen's Co.].

Witnesses: Jane Ponsonby, Dublin, widow, Charles Magauran, Dublin, gent., Miles Henshaw, servant to testator.

Memorial witnessed by: Anthony Dempsy, William Magin, Dublin, gent.

186, 40, 122602 Crofton Warren (seal)

196 COLHOUN, WILLIAM, Strabane, Co. Tyrone, Esq.

26 Aug. 1756. Narrate 1 p. 17 Nov. 1756.

His wife Patience Colhoun. James Colhoun second son of Rev. Alexr. Colhoun of Ballyhallachan, Co. Tyrone, clerk. Alexr. Colhoun, third son of Alexr. Colhoun the elder. Chas. Ussher, Dublin, Esq., and Wm. Stewart, Newtownstewart, Co. Tyrone, gent., trustees.

Lands of Garvachullen [Garvaghhullion], Laught Upper and Lower, Scraghey Upper and Lower, Cross, Ballinree and Tullymuck and Duntague [Dunteige], Classmullagh and Lisnacreagh[t] mill, all in Co. Tyrone. The house wherein Wm. Maxwell, Esq., now dwells, and part of his own dwelling house which he purchased from John Gordon, deceased, both in Strabane. Lands of Drumra[g]h, Co. Tyrone. Aghamore, Meencaragh [Meencarriga], Meencloghore, Killmore Upper and Lower, and part of Coolnacrumiagh, Co. Tyrone, Knockigarran, Co. Donegal.

Witnesses: John Sproull, apothecary and Thos. Parkison, merchant, both of Strabane, Richard Cowan, Lifford, Co. Donegal, gent.

Memorial witnessed by: Richard Cowan, James McMunn, Dublin, yeoman.

185, 190, 122690 Cha. Ussher (seal)

197 JOHNSTON, JAMES, Cordoolough, Co. Monaghan, gent.

26 June 1756. Narrate 1 p. 18 Nov. 1756.

His wife Hanna Johnston. His son James Johnston. His daughter Sarah Johnston. His brother Francis Johnston. His brother David Johnston. Richard Grahams, Esq., and Francis Lucas, Greenmount, Esq., exors. and John Ker, Dublin, to be joint exor. and guardian to his said children during their minority. His real estate.

Witnesses: John Moore, gent., Letitia Ker, wife of John Ker, both of Dublin, gent., Alice Templeton, Dublin, spinster.

Memorial witnessed by: John Moore, John Hutton, Dublin, gent.

186, 59, 122714 John Ker (seal)

198 GREEN, MICHAEL, Rocksborough, Co. Tipperary, Esq.

19 Aug. 1756. Narrate 1 p. 6 Dec. 1756.

His wife, extx. His son Michael, his present wife. His son Francis Green. His son Wm.

Town and lands of Kilnemack and other lands mentioned in deed of release 15 April 1755. Curraghcloney, Co. Tipperary. To his son Wm. part of the town and lands of KilmcCumo([1]) which he held by a fee farm grant made by his father Rodolphus Green unto his brother Thos. which afterwards became vested in testator. Lands in Co. Tipperary held by lease from the Bishop of Waterford [situation not mentioned]. Lands of Crin[n]aghtane, Co. Cork.

Witnesses: Eccles Disney, Churchtown, Co. Waterford, Esq., Rev. Wm. Downes, Clonmell, Co. Tipperary, clerk, Robt. Shaw, Clonmell, apothecary, Wm. Connor, Dublin, gent.

Memorial witnessed by: Wm. Connor, Thos. Hodgson, Dublin, gent.

182, 565, 122926 Mi. Green (seal)

199 SLICER, SAMUEL, Rathfarnham, Co. Dublin, Esq.

4 April 1753. Codicil 27 July 1753. Narrate ½ p. 21 Jan. 1757.

His wife Jane Slicer, extx. His sister-in-law Deborah Isaac.

Town and lands of Micknanstown and Culfore, and part of East Booli[e]s then in possession of Samuel Slicer and his undertenants, in Co. Meath.

Witnesses to Will and codicil: Rev. Jeremy Walsh and George Thomas, Rathfarnham, Co. Dublin, clerks, John Pilkington, Dublin, gent.

Memorial witnessed by: John Pilkington, Mathew Henderson, Isaiah Parivisol, Dublin, gent.

185, 309, 123268 Jane Slicer (seal)

([1]) Possibly the townland of Kilmaculla, Co. Cork is intended.

200 HUNT, CHRISTIAN otherwise HIGGINS otherwise HEWETTSON wife of Alderman Percival Hunt of Dublin.

6 March 1749. Full 3¾ pp. 22 Jan. 1757.

My husband Alderman Percival Hunt. Alderman Percival Hunt of Dublin, the younger, and John Hunt, Dublin, merchant, sons of my said husband. Richard Higgins my son. James Browne my grandson. My daughter Christian Paine, her husband. My grandson Laurence Paine.

Robt. Robinson, Dublin, Esq., Doctor of Physick. Christopher Robinson, Dublin, Esq., one of H.M. council at law and Robert French, Monivea, Co. Galway, Esq., trustees. My estate in Castledermot, Co. Kildare and in Co. Kilkenny.

Witnesses: Wm. Marshall, Richd. Thwaites, Ben. Johnston, notary public.

Memorial witnessed by: Richd. Thwaites, Mark Whyte, Dublin, Esq.

187, 39, 123270 Chr. Robinson (seal)

201 TAFFE, GEORGE, Dolphin's Barn Lane, Co. Dublin, weaver.

16 April 1756. Narrate ½ p. 6 April 1757.

His wife Ann Taffe extx. His several sons and daughters.

House and tenement in Dolphins Barn Lane wherein he then dwelt.

Witnesses: John Towson, Dolphins Barn Lane, Co. Dublin, tanner, William Whitehead, Brown Street, Co. Dublin, threadmaker, Mathew Daniel, Dublin, scrivener.

Memorial witnessed by: William Magin, Dublin, gent., Wm. Whitehead.

184, 505, 124070 Ann Taffe her mark (seal)

202 DEHAYS, JAMES, Youghal, Co. Cork, Esq.

18 Sept. 1756. Narrate 1¾ p. 17 May 1757.

His cousin Elizth. Langdon then wife of Lieut. Henry Davison. To Mary Ducros £100 per annum for life, plate and household furniture. His cousin John Godart, watchmaker. His cousin Margaret Langdon otherwise Godart, wife of Nathaniel Langdon. His cousin Solomon Godart, Dublin, gent. His cousin James Mitchell, London, watchmaker. His god-daughter Susanna Rouvier, wife of Thomas Day of Youghal. To his godson James Bassett son of Henry Bassett £50 when 21 years. His god-daughter Elizabeth Kelynge, widow of John Kelynge, city of Westminster, deceased. Peter Ducros, Dublin, gent. Augustus Fryard, perukemaker. Col. Wm. Strode, 3rd Regt. of Foot Guards, £20 on condition he accepts the executorship. Said Wm. Strode and said Mary Ducros executors.

Reciting that lands etc., part of the estate of Robert Cooke, Esq, deceased, were conveyed by deeds to him or in trust for him subject to redemption on payment of certain sums of money. Stock secured to testator by the Governors and Company of Merchants trading to the East Indies. Testator was executor of Will of Major Richard Bassett.

His houses and land in Youghal, the rent if let or produce if sold to the French Protestant Hospital called the Peste House, near Moorfields, London. £100 to Protestant poor of parish of Youghal. To Incorporate Society in Dublin for Promoting English Protestant working Schools any overplus when all legacies and annuities paid.

Witnesses: Colonel William Hore, Dublin, —— Gorges, Dublin, staymaker, John Ducros, Dublin, apothecary.

Memorial witnessed by: John Ducros, William Magin, Dublin, gent.

183, 593, 124494 Mary Ducros (seal)

203 LODGE, GEORGE, the elder, Gragueavoice, Queen's Co., gent. 12 Jan. 1748. Narrate ¾ p. 26 May 1757.

His wife. His daughter Elinor Lodge. His son George (who is to take care and manage for his mother). His son Christopher Lodge. His son Francis. His daughter Caroline. His farm of Gragueavoice.

Witnesses: Jeremy Lodge, Derreen, Queen's Co., gent., George Lodge, Freshford, Co. Kilkenny, gent., Christopher Lodge, Cullenabegg, Queen's Co., gent.

Memorial witnessed by: James Scott, Kilkenny, gent., Richard Washington, Kilkenny, malster.

183, 597, 124586 Chr. Lodge (seal)
(eldest son and heir of George Lodge the elder and witness to his Will).

204 EMPEY, ANTHONY, Ballyleehan, Queen's Co., farmer.

20 March 1757. Narrate ½ p. 18 June 1757.

His wife Edy Empey otherwise Hovenden. His sons Anthy. and Robert. His son Thos. His son George Empey. His son Francis Empey.

The farm and lands he then lived on in Ballyleehane, part held by his son John Empey (executor).

Witnesses: Simon Sucksmith, Doonane, shopkeeper, Thos. Dixon, Ballyleehane, schoolmaster, both in Queen's Co.

Memorial witnessed by: Michael Argent, William Hall, both of Dublin, gent.

189, 126, 124878 John Empey (seal)

205 CROOKE, KATHERINE, Dublin.

8 June 1757. Narrate 1 p. 7 July 1757.

By virtue of Will of Mark Nowlan, Dublin, gent., the testatrix was seized and possessed of a share of houses etc. in tenancy of Thomas Throp or his representatives in Patrick Street, and Plunket Street, Dublin, and ground and holding at Naas, Co. Kildare, and a large house situate at corner of High Street and Christ Church Lane, Dublin. This she left to trustee Rev. Chas. Jones (executor), Vicar of Stradbally, Queen's Co., for use of Miss Elizabeth Palmer then lodging in same house with the testatrix (at Mr. James's then bookseller and stationer in Dame Street, Dublin). Testatrix's mother Mrs. Elizabeth Parry residuary legatee and to have benefit of a lease near Chappleizod and the estate in Wales.

Witnesses: Joshua Sheppard, Dublin, bookbinder, Benjamin Doyle, Dublin, clerk, James Lyons, Dublin, bookseller.

Memorial witnessed by: Benj. Doyle, Henry White, Dublin, gent.

190, 21, 125102 Cha. Jones (seal)

206 ALEXANDER, JOSEPH, New Market, Combe, Co. Dublin, tallow chandler. 26 Jan. 1747. Précis ½ p. 25 Aug. 1757.

His wife Mary Alexander. His grandchild Margaret Burriss. His dwelling house in Newmarket on the Combe aforesaid.

Witnesses: John Hutton, clothier, Edward Williams, carpenter, Michael Connor, slater, all of Dublin.

Memorial witnessed by: Michael Connor, William Magin, Dublin, gent.

186, 476, 125512 Mary Alexander (seal)

207 NOWLAN, DARBY, Tingaran, Co. Kilkenny, gent.

1 Sept. 1742. Narrate 1 p. 9 Nov. 1757.

His nephew Timothy Nowlan and his wife Mary Nowlan, their son Darby Nowlan the younger (under 21 years). Mary Nowlan the younger. James Poe, Rossneharly, Co. Tipperary and Thomas Scott, Modishill, said county, executors, His leases and holdings in Crookeswood [situation not mentioned].

Witnesses: Rev. Leonard Funnadine, late of Callan, Co. Kilkenny, clerk, deceased, John Russell, Graige, said county, farmer, Timothy Nowlan, Killalowe, said county, schoolmaster.

Memorial witnessed by: John Russell, Jas. Scott.

188, 386, 126085 Darby Nowlan (seal)

208 COANE, ANTHONY, Esq., Collector of Strabane, Co. Tyrone. 3 April 1756. Précis ½ p. 12 Nov. 1757.

His wife Ann Coane. His nephew Robt. Coane.

His freehold of Ballymountriggen or Higginstown in the manor of Ballyshannon, and lands of Cordiver [? Co. Leitrim].

Witnesses: George Buchanan, apothecary, John Dunlap, sadler, John Holliday, tailor, all of Strabane.

Memorial witnessed by: George Buchanan, James Nesbitt, Strabane, Esq.

187, 486, 126137 Robt. Coane (seal)

209 DOBBS, ANNE, Rathcoole, Co. Dublin.

25 Oct. 1757. Narrate 1 p. 19 Nov. 1757.

Her daughter Mary Walsh. Her son-in-law Edwd. Stevens, executor. Her two younger children Eliz. and Jane. Her grand-daughter Ann Egan. Her daughter Jane Stevens and her children. John Clinch, Rathcoole, exor. [No lands mentioned].

Witness: John Donohoe, Rathcoole, farmer.

Memorial witnessed by: John Donohoe, Jas. Croke, Dublin, merchant.

191, 1, 126309 Mary Walsh her mark

210 USSHER, BEVERLY, Kilmeadan, Co. Waterford, Esq.

30 Sept. 1755. Full 7½ pp. 26 Nov. 1757.

My eldest daughter by my first marriage Mary Ussher, exor. My second and third daughters of my first marriage Elizabeth Ussher and Ann Ussher. A sum of £3,000 my marriage portion with my late wife Elizabeth Ussher otherwise Schuldam, to my only daughter of my second marriage Elizabeth Catherine, my brother-in-law Edmond Schuldam, Esq., and Jno. Lysaght, Esq., guardians of said daughter Elizabeth Catherine during her minority. My good friends John Lysaght, Mount North, Co. Cork, Esq., and Shapland Carew, Woodstown, Co. Waterford, Esq., trustees and exors. My uncle Arthur Ussher, Cappagh, Esq. My brother-in-law John Lysaght, Esq., and Shapland Carew guardians of my three daughters of my first marriage during their minority.

By default of issue male of both my marriages I now stand seized in fee simple of the several towns, lands, tenements and hereditaments following: Glen[n]anore, Shanakill, Boley, Thomastown, Ballnacurr

[? Ballynacurra], Ballygarrett, Knocknacrohy, Ballydiscart, Ballynabb, Scart, Glenavadora, Killeshalls (part set to John Keane, Esq., late of Cappoquin), Garranfadda, Knockacullen, East Ballylemon and West Ballylemon, all in Co. Waterford. My lands of Kilmeadan. £20 to poor of parish of Kilmeadan.

Witnesses: Rev. Daniel Sandoz, Waterford, clerk, Jno. Lyon, Saml. Taylor, Waterford, gents.

Memorial witnessed by: Saml. Taylor, Agnes Taylor wife of said Samuel Taylor.

190, 200, 126422 Mary Ussher (seal)

211 GOUGH, GEORGE, Ballyclogh, Liberties of city of Limerick. gent. 20 June 1753. Narrate ¾ p. 1 Dec. 1757.

His brother Thomas Gough. His father Wm. Gough. His brother James Gough. His sister Jane Franklin [? otherwise Gough]. His sister Mary.

Lands of Ballyclogh, Towgreen and Carrigaparson, all in S. Liberties of city of Limierck.

Witnesses: Hickman Rose, Limerick, gent., Richd. Studdert, Claunderalaw, Wm. Franklin, Aylerowe, both Co. Clare, gents.

Memorial witnessed by Hickman Rose, Richd. Rose, Dublin, gent.

191, 19, 126474 Thos. Gough (seal)
city of Limerick, gent.

212 DAWSON, JOHN, Dromore, Co. Monaghan.
7 Oct. and 19 Dec. 1754. Narrate ½ p. 2 Dec. 1757.

His son John Dawson, a minor. His daughter Elizabeth. His son Wm. Dawson. His nephew Francis Dawson his sister's son. Chas. Mayne, Maynefield, Richard Mayne, Carson, and John Rogers, all in Co. Monaghan, exors. His freehold known by the name of Donore, Co. Monaghan.

Witnesses: Richd. Roe, Dyan, Hugh O'Neil, Killcrow, both Co. Monaghan, Thos. Maunsel, Corlinan, Co. Cavan.

Codicil witnessed by: Edwd. Lee and Edwd. Mayne of Cootehill, Wm. Roe, Rakam, all in Co. Cavan.

Memorial witnessed by: Thos. Noble, Potea, Co. Fermanagh, Cornelius Wynne, Dublin, gent.

189, 531, 126483 Chas. Mayne (seal)

213 GIBSON, WILLIAM, Dublin, cabinet maker.
8 Jan. 1758. Full ¾ p. 18 Jan. 1758.

My wife Jane (enceinte) and my father-in-law John Curry exors. My sister-in-law Elizth. Curry. My nephew William Mooney. My nephew Anthony Mooney.

The house in Pool Street, in the Earl of Meath's Liberty, in possession of Mr. McCormuck. Houses and premises in Bridgefoot Street, Dublin.

Witnesses: James McFann, carrier, Thomas Green, silversmith, William Dixon, public notary, all of Dublin.

Memorial witnessed by: William Dixon, Wm. Wilkinson, Dublin, joyner.

190, 308, 126912 John Curry (seal)

214 WATSON, JOHN, Clonmackshoneen, Barony Forth, Co. Carlow, farmer. 7 May 1756. Full 2 pp. 21 Jan. 1758.

Susanna my wife. My son Thomas Watson, exor. My daughter Patience Thornton, her husband Thomas Thornton. My eldest daughter Susanna, her husband Thos. Brennan. My son-in-law John Swanton. My daughter Mary, Patrick Bermingham her husband. My son John. My grandson John Moffitt (under 14 years). My friends Samuel Watson the younger and Robert Lecky to assist my son Thos. to see this my Will put in force.

Lands of Clonmackshoneen and other lands which I have settled on my son Thomas.

Witnesses: John Perkins, Ballintraine, Co. Catherlough, gent., Daniel Mackasay and George Ellis, both of Ballybromell, Co. Catherlough, blacksmiths.

Memorial witnessed by: said John Perkins, and John Perkins, Dublin, gent.

192, 161, 126988 Thos. Watson (seal)

215 ARMSTRONG, MARTIN, Drumlivan, Co. Leitrim, gent.
4 July 1747. Précis ½ p. 3 Feb. 1758.

To his only son Edmund Armstrong all his real and personal estate.

Witnesses: Francis Johnston, Sheafield, Co. Leitrim, gent., John Johnston, Tubberline, Co. Cavan, gent., Hugh McPharlane, Killduff, Co. Cavan, Doctor of Physick.

Memorial witnessed by: Francis Johnston, James Irwin, Drumsillah, Co. Leitrim.

191, 97, 127169 Ann Armstrong (seal)

216 MASSY, HUGH, Duntrileage, Co. Limerick, Esq.
5 Oct. 1757. Codicil 10 Oct. 1757. Full 1¾ p. but not a complete copy. 7 Feb. 1758.

My eldest son Hugh Massy of Newforest, Co. Tipperary, Esq. My second son Rev. George Massy of Elin, Co. Limerick. My fifth son Major Eyre Massy, now in America. My youngest son Charles Massy of Duntrileage, Esq.

A mortgage made by Mr. Bridgeman to my brother the Rev. Dean Massy in trust for me. My unsettled estates of inheritance Killcully and Killcronan in North Liberties of County of city of Cork, and Bally(n)anema, Killenane, Ballylisdonagh, Aghnagurra and Ballylacken in Co. Limerick. Ballybrownmore and Ballybrownbegg, Broskeymore and Broskeybegg, " Kealioganna otherwise lands in Controversy," Garrane, Wenlome, Ballekoeny, Elm otherwise Keelnekeely(1), Doon, Clariney, Knockreney and part of Realine had been conveyed to testator's second son George Massy. My estate of Duntrileage.

(1) The location of these townlands is not stated. The modern Index of Townlands shows Elm Park Demesne in parish of Kilkeedy, Co. Limerick.

Witnesses: Daniel Crone, Dublin, gent., Brooke Brasier, Rivers, Liberties of city of Limerick, Esq., George Benson, Dublin, gent.

Codicil witnessed by: Elizabeth Briggs, Limerick, George Benson, Dublin, gent., George Black, Duntrileage, Co. Limerick.

Memorial witnessed by: Francis P. Turton, Dublin, gent., Edmond English, Dublin, gent.

187, 517, 127227 Hugh Massy (seal)

217 HALL, EDWARD, Strangford, Co. Down, Esq.

13 March 1713/14. Full 3 pp. 13 Feb. 1758.

If I die in Co. Down to be buried in churchyard chancell of the parish church of Clonallen with my dear father and mother. Rowland Savage, Portaferry, Esq., Roger Hall of Mounthall and my wife Ann Hall and Elizabeth Rowley sister to my wife exors. John Moore (my nephew), Drumbaneagher and Toby Hall son of my said brother Hall to succeed as exors. if said Rowland Savage my nephew and my brother Roger Hall should die. My eldest son Francis Hall. My second son Rowley Hall (under 21 years). My eldest daughter Catharine. My second daughter Lettice Hall. My two daughters Ann Hall and Elizth. Hall. My sister Christian Hall.

Money due by Patrick Savage of Portaferry, Esq., and by Thos. Meredith, soap boiler in Strangford, Wm. Wallace, Newry, merchant, Wm. Smith, St. John's Point, Mr. Patk. Savage of Ballygalgate and Rev. Mr. Smith, Dissenting Minister; money due by Andrew Patterson, weaver "which my brother Patk. Savage promised by note to see paid me," and Thos. Fortescue, Esq., Dromniskin, Hector McNeill of Portaferry and Francis Wootton of Down. My brother and sister Rowley. £300 in cash now in the Castle of Portaferry under the care of my sister Ann Savage. My nephew Thos. Fortescue, Dromiskin, Esq. Hercules Rowley, Dublin, Esq.

My estate of freehold in Barony Fews, Co. Armagh. A lease from Mr. Lawrence in Lower Evagh [? Barony Lower Iveagh], Co. Down. A lease from Bishop of Dromore [situation not mentioned]. £5 yearly charged on the Ferry of Narrow Water bequeathed to me by my father. My lease of The Point with all houses and land therein. My lease of Rosglass [? Co. Down] purchased from Patk. Byrne. The two Tollum Granges [Tollumgrange Lower and Upper] and Ballybegg, Barony Lecale, Co. Down. Lease of Ballyhornan [Co. Down], lately taken from Earl of Kildare. Lands of Ballynahy [? Ballynanny, Co. Down].

Witnesses: Hugh McMasters, Strangford, Robert Echlin, Portaferry, Charles Maxwell, all of Co. Down, gents.

Memorial witnessed by: Patk. Savage, Saintfield, Co. Down, one of the Attornies of the Exchequer, Robert Hamilton Smith, clerk to said Patk. Savage.

193, 144, 127280 Rowley Hall (seal)
(Rev. Rowley Hall, Killileagh, Co. Down, clerk).

218 TYNTE, Rt. Hon. JAMES, Oldbawn, Co. Dublin, Esq.

20 Feb. 1755. Full ½ p. 11 April 1758.

To Robert Tynte, Esq., Counsellor at law, exor. all my real estate and freehold in Ireland and Wales.

Witnesses: Sir Robert Deane, Dromore, Co. Cork, Bart., John Stratford, Belan, Co. Kildare, Esq., Wm. Austen, Cork, Esq.

Memorial witnessed by: John Smith and James Maddock, Dublin, gents.

187, 534, 127781 Robert Tynte (seal)

219 CLIBBORN, JOHN, Moatgranogue, Co. Westmeath, gent.

30 June 1754. Full 3 pp. 18 April 1758.

My wife Sarah, exor. My eldest son Joshua Clibborn. My daughter Sarah Pim alias Clibborn. My daughter Jane Clibborn. My son Robert Clibborn. My daughter Ann Pim alias Clibborn. My daughter Abigail Clibborn. My son George Clibborn (under 21 years). My son Abraham Clibborn (ditto). My brothers Abraham and James Clibborn. My brother Robert Clibborn, Dublin, merchant, exor.

My estate in the lands of Newtown and Lurgan, King's Co. Town and lands of Turphelim granted in fee farm to me by Earl of Cavan [situation not mentioned]. My estate in Moatgranogue, Killenboylegan, Tolskenrow and Killenahinch were settled on son Joshua Clibborn upon his marriage. The part with three houses etc. which I hold from my brother George Clibborn deceased. Houses, towns and lands of Turphelim held by lease from Thos. Tipping, Esq. Loughanameena(gh), King's Co., joining to Newtown and Lurgan aforesaid leased from Henry Marsh Esq., deceased. Aughenarget, Co. Westmeath. I now am possessed of half of the lands of Lissesisse [Lissanisky, King's Co.], Kilbride and Killcollin [King's Co.] the estate of Capt. Joseph Maddock who has been several years abroad; by letter of attorney to Dr. Robert Roberts and Councillor James Maddock said lands were leased to my brother Robert Clibborn and me in partnership.

Witnesses: Samuel Whinrey, Ballyboughlan, Co. Westmeath, gent., Benj. Parvin, Moat, Co. Westmeath, Wm. Jones, Moat.

Memorial witnessed by: Theophilus Perkins, Dublin, gent., John Perkins, Dublin, clerk to said Theophilus Perkins.

193, 293, 127893 Geo. Clibborn (seal)

220 [CLAYTON], ROBERT, BISHOP OF CLOGHER,

2 Aug. 1748. Narrate ½ p. 18 April 1758.

Remainder of his real and personal estate in England and Ireland to his wife Catherine Clayton, extx. After her death to his nephew Robt. Bayly his estate of Cloghrane, Co. Limerick, and to his nephew Samuel Bayly his estate of Danistown [? Co. Meath]. To his sister Ryves his estate of Collcashin [? Co. Kilkenny] purchased from Mr. Ryves. To his sister Brown his estate near Chaplizod by Dublin. All his nephews and nieces.

Witnesses: Rev. John Burgh of the Diocese of Clogher, clerk, Wm. Dougherty, servant to testator, Richard Sampson, Clogher, notary public.

Memorial witnessed by: Denis George, Dublin, gent., Rev. Thos. Bernard, Diocese of Derry, clerk.

191, 258, 127909 K. Clayton (seal)

221 [CLAYTON], ROBERT, BISHOP OF CLOGHER.

Codicil 23 Feb. 1758. Narrate ½ p. 18 April 1758.

His wife. His niece Ann Bernard. To his niece Ann Croker the house and lands of Backstown [? Co. Dublin] then in lease to her husband Thomas Croker. The estate of St. Wolstanes and all his estate in Co. Kildare.

Witnesses: Rev. John Burgh, Diocese of Clogher, clerk, Denis George, Dublin, gent., and Ann Daly, Dublin, maid servant to testator.

Memorial witnessed by: Denis George, William Gold servant to said Mrs. Clayton.

191, 259, 127910 K. Clayton (seal)

222 HARMAN, WESLEY, Moyle, Co. Carlow, Esq.

21 April 1758. Précis ½ p. 20 April 1758.

To his wife Mary Harman real and personal estate etc. James Agar, Gowran, Co. Kilkenny, Esq., trustee.

Witnesses: John Curtis, Dublin, Esq., James Byrne, Dublin, merchant, Samuel Jenkins, Dublin, gent., John Kelly, Dublin, gent., one of the Attornies of the Court of Exchequer in Ireland.

Memorial witnessed by: James Byrne, John Kelly.

193, 320, 127940 Mary Harman (seal)
widow of testator

223 JONES, EDWARD, Stridagh, Co. Sligo, gent.

21 Nov. 1757. Narrate ½ p. 27 April 1758.

His uncle Jas. Jones. Thos. Jones, third son of said Jas. Jones. His freehold lease of Ballyscanill [Co. Sligo].

Witnesses: Thomas Soden, Kilkat, Morgan Sweeny, Carney, Alexander Campbell, Carney, all in Co. Sligo, farmers.

Memorial witnessed by: Alexander Campbell, Wm. Chambers, Dublin, gent.

190, 533, 128091 James Jones (seal)

224 THOMPSON, ELIZABETH, Derryree, Co. Fermanagh, widow. 19 March 1754. Narrate ¾ p. 2 June 1758.

Her son Wm. Thompson. Her daughter Catherine Thompson.

Moiety of Lettercullum, Co. Armagh (as set forth in a deed from her husband Edward Thompson deceased and testator to said son Wm. Thompson), Culla McKee tenant; another part perfected to her said daughter, John Hall and Alexr. Hall tenants.

Witnesses: Rev. John Dundass, Aughalon, clerk, Andrew Leonard, Drumbrocas, gent., and Edwd. Little, Maguiresbridge, merchant, all in Co. Fermanagh.

Memorial witnessed by: Andrew Leonard, Hugh Cunningham, Beltaran, Co. Armagh.

194, 59, 128620 Wm. Thompson (seal)

225 KER, ANDREW, Portatrave, Co. Monaghan, Esq. 28 Feb. 1753. Narrate 1½ p. 8 June 1758.

His son John Ker. His eldest son Robert Ker. His daughter Margt. Pettygrew. His daughter Alice Ellis. His sisters children.. His niece Susanna Little. Nichs. Coyne and William Ker trustees. £5 to poor of parish of Aughnamullen [Aghnamullen].

Lands of Mt. Kermell otherwise Carrickanallen, Lissnegallorigh [Lisnagalliagh] and Fermoyle purchased from Capt. Richard Pockridge, in Barony Cremorne, Co. Monaghan. Lands of Corfinlough, Carbofin [Corrabofin], Drumlangfield and Corenure purchased from Ralph and John Wilman in parish of Tullycorbill [Tullycorbet], Co. Monaghan, and lands of Anaghabane and Bellinegarry, Co. Monaghan, and his lands of Carrowcarrow [Corracharra] purchased from Rice Moore, in Co. Monaghan. Aughnamullen, Mullenanalt and Latton. Skeagh, Dromnickin, Carrowbarrow, Anieldrin(1) and Cahir. Cornewall, Aniabane [Annaghybane] in Barony Dartry, Co. Monaghan.

Witnesses: John Wallace and Edw. Dawson, both of Newtown Corry, Co. Monaghan, Andrew Brekey, Lismagonaway, Co. Monaghan.

Memorial witnessed by: John Wallace now of Dublin, Wm. Hall, Dublin, gent.

191, 402, 128685 John Ker (seal)

(1) I cannot trace this townland but suggest it may be the townland of Anny in Aghamullen parish.

226 MATHEWS, EDWARD, Dublin, Esq.

10 Jan. 1756. Narrate $1\frac{1}{4}$ p. 19 June 1758.

His wife Sarah Mathews and his sons Daniel, Hill and Edward Mathews trustees and exors. His sons Andrew Mathews and John Mathews. His eight daughters Elizabeth, Grace, Sarah, Jane, Ann, Charlotte, Leslie and Mary Mathews. His said son Daniel when he gets any preferment in the church is to pay back value of books in his hands.

His real estate. His lease in or near Newry. Testator's law books and manuscripts to his son Edward.

Witnesses: Pierce Byrne, Dublin, gent., Valentine Ramsay, Dublin, merchant, William Owen, Dublin, gent.

Memorial witnessed by: Valentine Ramsay, Thomas Gardiner.

191, 435, 128819 Sarah Mathews (seal)

227 PARRY, THOMAS, Dunleary, Co. Dublin.

10 Feb. 1733/34. Full $\frac{3}{4}$ p. 19 June 1758.

My wife Jane Parry, extx. My son Richard Parry. My daughter Rachel Parry. My daughter Mary Parry (all under age). My sisters Rachel Parry and Mary Connor.

My house in Dunleary wherein John Lewis now dwelleth, another in Dunleary wherein Thomas Collis now dwells, my house in Dunleary wherein Mr. Maguire now dwells, my house in Dunleary wherein I now dwell and the shops etc.

Witnesses: Thos. Collis, Dunleary, gent., deceased, John Clements, Ringsend, Co. Dublin, gent., deceased, Richard Evans, Mountain, Co. Dublin, schoolmaster.

Memorial witnessed by: John Hutton, Dublin, Wm. Magin, Dublin, gent.

195, 25, 128824 Rachel Dun (seal)
Rachel Parry otherwise Dun widow
of Patrick Dun deceased.

228 MAUNSELL, JOSEPH, the elder, Carah [? Carragh], Co. Galway, gent. 19 Jan. 1758. Narrate 1 p. 28 June 1758.

His wife Elenore Maunsell, her brother. His daughter Ann Burke, her husband Anthony Burke. His grandson Maunsell Burke. His grandson Joseph Maunsell. "£5 to his eldest son Thomas Maunsell during his natural life so long as he remained unmarried." His son Standish Maunsell. His natural daughter Mary Maunsell. All his estates real and personal to his second son Joseph Maunsell, exor.

Witnesses: Anthony Burke, Springfield, Co. Galway, gent., Charles O'Connor, Knockalegane, Co. Roscommon, gent., Patrick Clancy, Loughrea, Co. Galway, gent.

Memorial witnessed by: Anthony Burke, Peter Carry, Dublin, gent.

187, 588, 128924 Joseph Maunsell (seal)

229 SEWRIGHT, ANDREW, Ballymacombs, parish Ballyscullion, Co. Londonderry. 11 Oct. 1748. Narrate ¾ p. 5 Oct. 1758.

His wife Mary. His son Martin.

Lands in Ballymacombs, parish of Ballyscullion, proportion of Vintners, Co. Londonderry.

Witnesses: Bryan Mulhollan, Ballyneece, proportion of Vintners, Co. Londonderry, schoolmaster, John Steel, Joseph Jonkin, John Dickson all of Ballymacombs, farmers.

Memorial witnessed by: Bryan Mulhollan, John Walsh, Magherafelt, Co. Londonderry, tailor.

197, 93, 129708 Mary Sewright (seal)
her mark

230 BEWLEY, DANIEL, Dublin, merchant.

24 June, codicil 28 June 1758. Narrate 2¼ pp. 11 Oct. 1758.

His wife Hannah Bewley. His daughter Miriam Lapham, his son-in-law William Lapham. His son George exor. His son-in-law John Clibborn. His daughter Hannah Bewley (under 21 years and unmarried). His stepsons Joseph and Ambrose Barcroft. His niece Jane Barcroft, her daughters Jane Byrne and Sarah Smith. His brother-in-law Francis Russell exor. Garrett Hassen.

His lands, tenements, fee farm rents, ground rents etc. His dwelling house on Lazars Hill, Dublin. Lease from Richard Maguire of a holding in Dawson Street. His lease in Bridgefoot Street, Dublin, from Thomas Pearson, Esq., then set to James Duff. Concerns held under Richard Witherall in Crow Street, Dublin. Legacy to poor of people called Quakers in Dublin.

Witnesses: Philip Smyth and James Smith, clerks to Richard Thwaites, public notary, Dublin, and said Richard Thwaites.

Codicil witnessed by: William Palmer also clerk to said Richard Thwaites, James Smith and said Richard Thwaites.

Memorial witnessed by: Richard Thwaites, Robert Jones his clerk.

194, 350, 129749 Geo. Bewley (seal)

231 WARING, HUGH, Kilkenny, Esq.

27 Sept. 1758. Narrate ¾ p. 9 Nov. 1758.

His wife Mary Waring. His daughter Elizabeth. His own son John. His son Hugh Waring. His son Edmond.

Lands of Archerstown otherwise Warington, Ballogh, Cloneen and the Glebe land adjoining, Briskalagh and Moun[?t]more. The house in city of Kilkenny wherein Mr. Laffan dwells. Lands of Oldtown etc. and a house and garden going to Gallows Green; piece of ground in Patrick Street, Kilkenny purchased from Mr. Cook.

Witnesses: Thomas Goddard, Kilkenny, Esq., Joseph Evans, Bellevan, Co. Kilkenny, Esq., Michael Hairey, Warrington within the liberties of city of Kilkenny, gardener.

Memorial witnessed by: Thos. Goddard, Henry Hoban, of same, yeoman.

196, 255, 129930 Edmd. Waring (seal)

232 FERGUSON, ANDREW, Mullaghagarry, Co. Donegal. 29 June 1758. Précis ½ p. 13 Nov. 1758.

His brother John Ferguson exor. His freehold of Lifford, his freehold of Mullaghagarry. His lease of Stranorlar.

Witnesses: Rev. John Mackie, Stranorlar, clerk, Joseph Barclay, Ballybofey, gent., James Ferguson, Magrycorran, farmer.

Memorial witnessed by: John Mackie, James Ferguson.

195, 225, 130031 John Ferguson (seal)

233 WIGGANS, JOHN, Cloncaran, parish of Drummully, Co. Fermanagh. 24 March 1735/6. Précis ½ p. 29 Nov. 1758.

My son Thomas Wiggans. My son-in-law John Rosbrough.

Lease of Drumesky, parish of Drummully, Co. Fermanagh.

Witnesses: Patk. Connally, Newtownbutler, Co. Fermanagh, James Thompson, late of Fargreen, Co. Fermanagh.

Memorial witnessed by: Patk. Connally, John Johnston, Dublin, gent.

196, 336, 130262 John Rosbrough (seal)

234 McNEILL, ANN, alias MONTGOMERY, widow of Hector McNeill, Dunseverick, Co. Antrim, Esq. 17 July 1756. Narrate ¾ p. 7 Dec. 1758.

Reciting indenture 14 May 1756 between testator, the Hon. Michael Ward one of H.M.'s Justices of the Court of King's Bench, and Archibald McNeill, second son of testator. Her said son Archibald McNeill exor.

The manor of lordship of Drumbracklin, that is to say the town and lands of Duneah, Clogher, Lisno, Ballyacklis, Ballycarne, Ballylessan, Milagh otherwise Melough, Knockbracklin otherwise Knock-brackan, the mill and mills thereon etc.

Witnesses: Adam Humble, Dublin, doctor of physick, Arthur Thomas, Dublin, gent., Henry Crawford, then of Dublin now of Rapho, Co. Londonderry, surveyor of excise.

Memorial witnessed by: Patrick Savage, Dublin, gent., Robert Hamilton Smyth, clerk to said Patrick Savage.

195, 302, 130360 A. McNeill Mt. Gomery (seal)
Archibald McNeill the devisee, now called Archibald McNeill Montgomery.

235 MEARES, JAMES, Aghaga, Co. Monaghan, gent.

1 Jan. 1748. Narrate ½ p. 23 Oct. 1758.

His five daughters. His son James. His sons John and Samuel Meares. Humphrey Evatt, Esq., Wm. Pettigrew, Crolly, and Wm. Meares, gent., exors.

Lands of Aghaga, Elegish and Seeagh, Co. Monaghan. Holding in Drumgarnan, Drumaveal and his part of Annasragh belonging to the mill in Co. Armagh.

Witnesses: Wm. Blakely, John Blakely, both of Granshagh, Co. Monaghan, gents., and James Meares, Drumgarran aforesaid, gent.

Memorial witnessed by: James Meares, and Abraham Meares Sandhills, said county, gent.

196, 415, 130579 Wm. Meares (seal)

236 ASHE, JOHN, Glanworth, Barony Fermoy, Co. Cork.

29 March 1741. Narrate ½ p. 14 Sept. 1758.

To his wife Catherine Ashe otherwise Croker, extx., lands of Knockancorbally, Barony Fermoy, Co. Cork, leased to him by Michael Roberts of Glanworth, and all other real and personal estate.

Witnesses: Rev. Randall Roberts, Glanworth, Co. Cork, clerk, Elizabeth Widenham, Glanworth aforesaid, widow, Thomas Lucan, Richfordstown, Co. Cork, gent.

Memorial witnessed by: Thos. Lucas, James Bennett, Cork, victualler.

195, 430, 130943 Cathre. Bennett otherwise Ashe otherwise Croker (seal)

237 HOEY, PAUL PERCY, Dublin, Esq.

27 Jan. 1748. Précis ½ p. 14 Feb. 1759.

To his mother Hannah Hoey, widow, extx. all his lands, tenements and hereditaments in this Kingdom, and personal estate.

Witnesses: William Ryves, Dublin, Esq., John Eustace, Dublin, apothecary, John Griffith, Dublin, aledraper.

Memorial witnessed by: William Ryves, Theodore Cooke, Waterford, gent.

194, 606, 131105 Han. Hoey (seal)

238 HETHERINGTON, SIDNEY, Ballinriddery, Queen's Co.

1 April 1755. Narrate ½ p. 3 March 1759.

His wife M. Hetherington, her daughters. His eldest son Wm. Hetherington. His son Richard Hetherington. His daughter Sebella. Easter Hetherington [? another daughter].

His freehold lands in Ballinriddery, Laraugh and part of Danganstown, in parish Coolebanagher, Queen's Co. His freehold in Mountmellick set to Jno. Jordan and Wm. Slate.

Memorial witnessed by: Jno. Porter, Doolaght, George Mitchell, Clonmyland, Denis Hyllem, Laraugh, all in Queen's Co., farmers.

196, 595, 131279 Will. Hetherington (seal)

239 MACARTNEY, GEORGE, Dublin, Esq.

7 Aug. 1755. Narrate ¾ p. 14 May 1759.

His son Clarles Macartney. His grandson George Macartney. Daniel Mussenden and George Portis, of town of Belfast, Esqrs., trustees.

All his real estate in counties of Down and Antrim and the county of the town of Carrickfergus. Lands partly lying in Co. Antrim and partly in the county of the town of Carrickfergus to which he became entitled in right of his late wife Elizabeth Macartney otherwise South. Lands in city and county of the city of Dublin and in city and county of the city of Kilkenny and in King's Co. His house in Earl or Henry Street, Dublin.

Witnesses: Rev. George Philips, Dublin, clerk, Henry Benson, then clerk to Robt. Wallis, Dublin, public notary, and by said Robt. Wallis.

Memorial witnessed by: James Maddock, James Mildmay, Dublin, gent.

201, 131, 132075 George Macartney (seal)
grandson of testator

240 MACARTNEY, CHARLES, Dublin, Esq.

10 July 1758. Narrate 1 p. 14 May 1759.

His brother and nephews. His nephew George Macartney of Lincoln's Inn. Elizabeth Hadsor and Sarah Wittewrong. His friend, John Sheen, Dublin, Esq., and Robert Wallis, Dublin, public notary trustees.

Testator was seized of estates in city and county of the city of Dublin, and in the city and county of the city of Kilkenny and in King's Co. in his own right and under his late father George Macartney, Esq. Estates in counties of Down and Antrim and county of town of Carrickfergus.

Witnesses: John Lodge, Michael White, chirurgeon, and James Maddock, gent., all of Dublin.

Memorial witnessed by: James Maddock, James Mildmay, Dublin, gent.

201, 132, 132076 George Macartney (seal)
nephew of testator

241 SPENCE, ROBERT, Strabane, Co. Tyrone, Esq.

15 Feb. 1759. Narrate 1½ p. 6 June 1759.

His wife Hannah Spence. His issue then living by his said wife only one son John Spence. Connolly McCausland, Fruithill, Co. Londonderry, Esq., and testator's brother-in-law Robert McClintock trustees. William McClintock brother of said wife. Her brother John McClintock. His nephew Nixon Stevenson. Robt. Griffith son of Anthy. Griffith of Strabane, merchant. All his real and personal estate.

Witnesses: John Sproull, apothecary, Robert Porter, merchant, Simeon Rouse, merchant, all of Strabane.

Memorial witnessed by: John Sproull, Robert Porter.

201, 184, 132380 Hanna Spence (seal)

242 LELAND, MARGARET, Dublin, widow.

7 Feb. 1759. Narrate 1 p. 12 June 1759.

Her son-in-law Thos. Bond, Dublin, merchant, trustee and exor. Her son-in-law Edwd. Mockler, exor. Her daughter Mary Mockler his wife. Her child[ren] Jane Bond, Robt. Leland and Deborah Leland. Her daughter Jane Bond. Her son Robt. Leland. Her daughter Deborah Leland. Her daughter-in-law Margt. Leland. Her grandchildren Saml. and Ann Leland. Her late servant maid Catherine Hendrick.

The house on Ormond Quay. Devised residue of real and personal estate to her children Mary Mockler, Jane Bond, Robt. Leland and Deborah Leland.

Witnesses: Henry Hawkskaw, surgeon, Margt. Gilmore, widow, James Saunders, gent., all of Dublin.

Memorial witnessed by: Wm. Hall, Michael Argent, both of Dublin, gent.

201, 200, 132457 Thos. Bond (seal)

243 JOHN LAW, Ballydown, parish of Seapatrick, Co. Down died lately intestate but before his death directed that notes be taken as to the distribution of his real and personal estate. [Deed, Law to Law to Law, dated 8 Nov. 1758].

My wife Sarah. My son John. My son James. My son Samuel. My sons William and Joseph. My sons James, Aughtry and George. My three daughters Sarah, Mary and Elinor.

Rents of Gargory and Glenmaghry. The tenement late Mrs. Rowans. The farm in Ballymony, the farm in Corbitt. My farm in

Ballydown with all houses, bleach green and mill. The green now held by Archibald Knight. The bleach green on the north side of the River Bann commonly called the New green.

Said Notes not being taken before witnesses to carry the same into a nuncupative Will, said Sarah the widow and James the eldest son and heir of said John Law, the other children being minors, registered an agreement in order to carry into execution the intentions of said John Law.

Deed witnessed by: Rev. Henry Jackson and Robert Cumine, both of Ballymony, parish of Magherally, Co. Down.

Memorial witnessed by: said Henry Jackson and Robert Cumine.

196, 580, 132525 Sarah Law (seal)

244 HOSACK, THOMAS, Dennyhora, parish Mullaghbrack, Co. Armagh, farmer. 4 Nov. 1756. Narrate ½ p. 6 Jan. 1759.

His son Michael Hosack. His son George Hosack. John Hosack, son to said Michael Hosack.

His dwelling house, farm, etc. in Dennyhora, parish of Mullabrack, Barony of Onie [Mullaghabrack, Barony of Oneilland West], Co. Armagh.

Witnesses: Arthur Brown, Market Hill, William Magill, Cornamuch, Hugh Hosack, Shaniraken, William Daly, Drumleck, all in Co. Armagh, yeoman.

Memorial witnessed by: Arthur Brown, John Scott, Armagh, gent.

195, 599, 132545 Michael Hosack (seal)

245 BUTLER, EDMOND, Newtown, Queen's Co., Esq.

2 Dec. 1751. Narrate 1 p. 20 June 1759.

His brother William and [testator's] wife Ann exors. and guardians of his younger children. His second son Francis. His second daughter Catherine. His fourth son Edmond. His daughter Bridget and her husband Theobald Butler, Esq.

Lands of Newtown and all other real and personal estate. Residue of fortune to be distributed amongst his younger children exclusive of his eldest son and his said daughter Bridget. The £100 testator gave as apprentice fee with his son Edward he deemed a part of his distributive share of the residue.

Witnesses: Mark Gerard, Dublin, gent., William Williams, Dublin, gent., Christopher Dalton, Dublin, public notary, deceased.

Memorial witnessed by: William Williams, Samuel Corbet, Castledurrow, Co. Kilkenny, gent.

200, 171, 132571 Edward Butler (seal)

246 BUTLER, EDMOND, Edmondsbury, Queen's Co.

Codicil 5 Feb. 1759. Narrate ½ p. 20 June, 1759.

His son Edward. His farm of Newtown, Barony Ossory, Queen's Co. to his [testator's] wife Anne Butler " that thereby she may keep his children together and maintain and educate his son Edmond." His niece Ester Butler. His son Francis Butler. Excludes his son Piers Butler from any right to his farms or personal estate. The farm of Burrismore, Co. Kilkenny.

Witnesses: Bryan Mulhall, Castlemarket, Co. Kilkenny, Esq., doctor of physick, Hugh Bathorn, Durrow, Co. Kilkenny, gent., Thomas Richardson, Durrow, gent.

Memorial witnessed by: Hugh Bathorn, Samuel Corbet, Durrow, gent.

201, 225, 132575 Anna Butler (seal)
widow of testator

247 GASON, JOHN, Killoshalloe, Co. Tipperary, gent.

5 July 1757. Précis ½ p. 21 June 1759.

Ratifies settlement made on his intended marriage with Araminta Williams by deeds of lease and release dated 1 and 2 of said month of July. To Theobald Wolfe and Richd. Maunsell, trustees in said settlement, the lands etc. therein mentioned.

Witnesses: Mathew Lyster, Joseph Green, Christopher Comyn Gardiner, all of Dublin, Esqrs.

Memorial witnessed by: Joseph Green, Alexr. Castell, gent., one of the attornies of the Court of Exchequer in Ireland.

199, 389, 132613 Theod. Wolfe (seal)

248 KIRK, JANE, widow of Jno. Kirk, deceased.

19 Sept. 1744. Full ½ p. 28 June 1759.

My son John Kirk. Robt. Cole and Joseph Copland husbands to my daughters Jane and Mary. My daughter Jane Cole. My daughter Mary Copland. My grand-daughters Jane Cole and Mary Cole. My worldly substance.

Wintesses: Jno. Cantwill, Benjamin Walker and Alexr. Clark, all of the Coombe, Co. Dublin, weavers.

Memorial witnessed by: Benjamin Walker, Thos. Butler.

199, 417, 132714 Joseph Copland (seal)

249 KIRK, JOHN, Elbow Lane, Co. of Dublin, weaver.

3 Feb. 1743. Narrate, part in full ¾ p. 28 June 1759.

My wife Jane, extx. My son John Kirk. My daughter Mary Copeling [Copland] otherwise Kirk. My daughter Jane Cole otherwise Kirk. My two grandchildren Jane and Mary Cole.

My house in Elbow Lane. " The adventured lands when recovered."

Witnesses: Thomas Purcel, Alexr. Clerk, Wm. Beeden.

Memorial witnessed by: Wm. Beeden, Thos. Butler.

199, 418, 132715 Mary Copland (seal)
John Copland (seal)
her husband

250 WILSON, CHRISTIAN, Scar, Co. Wexford, gent.

16 May 1755. Narrate 1 p. 5 July 1759.

His wife Elizabeth Wilson. His eldest son John Wilson. To his second son Benjamin Wilson, exor., estate he purchased from his brother-in-law William Radford deceased, that is Killmenan, mill and pond of Kilmenan, town and lands of Clonbologue, Ragans, the town and lands known by the name of the Cottier's holding and three corner Park. His son-in-law John Bowers. His son-in-law Nathaniel Davis. His son-in-law Wm. St. John.

His estate in Co. Wexford and Co. Kilkenny. Arpinstown joining Kilmenan [Kilmannan]; tythes great and small of the parish of Rathmacknee. Sle[e]dagh, Sleackestown, Cherrytown, Synottstown otherwise Cardiff's holding, Foxeshole, the mill of Sle[e]dagh and Rochestown Little, all in Barony Bargy, Co. Wexford.

Witnesses: Rev. Francis Shudall, late of Duncormuck, Co. Wexford, clerk, deceased, Henry Boyd, Charles Shudall, both of Duncormuck, gents.

Memorial witnessed by: Alan Kelly, David Jonathan Clarke, both Dublin, gents.

197, 599, 132803 Ben. Wilson (seal)

251 WILSON, ARTHUR, Leminaroy, in the proportion of Vintners, parish of Termaney [Termoneeny], Co. Londonderry, farmer. 11 June 1759. Narrate ¾ p. 23 July 1759.

To his wife Jane and his daughters Margery and Jane all his farm or holding in Leminaroy [Lemnaroy] in three equal parts. His son Thomas Wilson. His son-in-law Thomas Faucet. His son-in-law Charles McKaghey. His brother Morgan Wilson, Francis Dickson and Thomas Kane, exors.

Witnesses: Adam Downing, Leminaroy, farmer, Davis Steel, Drumlamph, said county, James Downing, Leminaroy, gent.

Memorial witnessed by: Adam Downing, David Steel.

200, 238, 133004 Margery Wilson (seal)

252 McDANIEL, DANIEL, Forechester, Co. Wexford.

15 Sept. 1759. Narrate ½ p. 1 Oct. 1759.

His son and exor. Edward McDonald(1) and to his wife Elizabeth McDonald £24 then in hands of Joseph Payn of Collgreny. His grandson Edwd. McDonald. His grandson Daniel McDonald. His granddaughter Catherine McDonald. His son the said Edward's three youngest children. Testator's daughter Mary Murphy. His daughter Elenor Earl. His daughter Susana Murphy.

Lands of Forechester, held by lease from Mathew Ford.

Witnesses: Charles Doran, Monalee, Co. Wexford, farmer, Mathew Murphy, Mullane, Co. Wexford, servant man and Mary Murphy, Fennock, said county, mother to said Mathew Murphy.

Memorial witnessed by: Charles Doran, William Magin, Dublin, gent.

200, 361, 133488 Edward McDaniel (seal)

253 PILKINGTON, ELIZABETH, Dublin, widow.

16 Aug. 1759. Précis ½ p. 13 Nov. 1759.

Real estate which came to her by Will of her late husband Richd. Pilkington and by death of her brother Joseph Wilson, late of Ballymore, Co. Galway, as one of his co-heiresses. Mathew Carter, Dublin, Licentiate in Midwifry and Jno. Carroll, Dublin, gent., trustees and exors. Rev. Oliver Carter, exor. and Mary Carter his wife.

Witnesses: Joshua Carter, Dublin, gent., an attorney of the Common Pleas, James Bradley, New Row near Thomas Street, Dublin, thread and tape maker, Neal McMullan, Caple Street, Dublin, apothecary.

Memorial witnessed by: James Connor and Timothy Ryan, both of Dublin, writing clerks to Mr. John Carroll, attorney.

202, 232, 133841 Oliver Carter (seal)

(1) In both original and transcript of this memorial the surname of the son Edward and his family is written as McDonald. This is incorrect as he signs as " Edward McDaniel " when registering the memorial.

254 SINGLETON, HENRY, Dublin, Esq., Master of the Rolls.
9 Sept. 1754. Codicils 22 Feb. 1757, 1 Aug. 1758, 30 Nov. 1758, 18 July 1759. Full 15½ pp. 15 Nov. 1759.

My nephew Wm. Foster, Esq., trustee. My niece Charity Yorke, her husband Wm. Yorke, Chief Justice of the Court of Common Pleas. My niece Mary Tisdall (sister of Charity Yorke), her husband Philip Tisdall, H.M.'s Solicitor General. Elizabeth Tisdall, eldest daughter of said Philip and Mary Tisdall. Mary Tisdall second daughter of said Philip and Mary Tisdall. My niece Ann Corbett, her son Robt. Corbett, her sister Sarah Leigh (my niece), her husband Dr. Edwd. Leigh. My sister Mary Leigh, her grandson John Leigh, her grandson Edwd. Leigh. My nephew Francis Leigh. My sister Patience Fowke, her husband John Fowke. Sydenham Fowke eldest son of my sister Patience. John Fowke younger son of my sister Patience, exor. Said Robt. Corbett, Sydenham Fowke and John Fowke the son and respective issue male as they shall come into possession of lands shall take surname of Singleton only. Pictures of Genl. Fowke, my brother Rowland Singleton deceased and my own picture which properly belong to my said sister Patience or her husband. My niece Sarah Rochfort, her husband Arthur Rochfort. My nephew Edward Meade, exor. My niece Elizabeth Meade. My nephew Alderman Edward Hardman. My niece Sarah Hardman. My niece Ann Gartside, money I owe her as exor. of my brother Rowland Singleton deceased. My niece Alth. Barlow, wife of James Barlow, Esq. My niece Patience Ford. My nephew Alderman Henry Ogle. My niece Patience Ogle. My nephew Capt. John Morris (money which I have advanced for his promotion in the Army), his brother Thomas, his brother Henry and sister — Morris. My nephew John Morris his father. My nephew Robert Madder. Mrs. Ferguson, daughter of my said niece Patience Ford, her husband. The daughters of my niece Sarah Rochfort. My niece Patience Colpois, wife of John Colpois. My nephew Wm. Howard. My nephew Ralph Howard. My niece Patience Howard. My sister-in-law Mary Singleton.

Sir Thomas Taylor, Bart. John Bradshaw, Dublin, merchant. The two daughters of Alderman Edmund Schoals of Drogheda. To Lord Newport, Lord Chancellor of Ireland, my three vols. of the Monasticon Anglicanum. Thomas Marlay late Chief Justice of King's Bench. Robt. French now a Justice of the Common Pleas. Wm.

Bristow, Esq. Anthony Foster, Esq. Arthur Hill, Esq. My servant Charles Adams.

The manor or reputed manor of Drumcon[d]ra, lands of Balrath, Upper and Lower Dromconra [Drumcondra], Aclare, Rathrasney, Clonpartin, Corstown, Keirnstown, Moonistown [Mooneystown], Piercetown, Bellsedrick, Upper and Lower Drumsawry, all in Barony Slane, Co. Meath. Ardagh, Carrick, Tueran, Street, Rathnally, Bawn, Begsrew [Begsreeve] and Lisboy, Bellpatrick, Stonehouse, Brownstown, Carrickshenagh [Carricknashanagh, Co. Louth], Mell, Deanrath, all in Co. Meath, Louth and Co. of town of Drogheda. The manor or reputed manor of Kilsallaghan and all my lands in parish of Kilsallaghan, Co. Dublin, which I purchased from Mr. Ellis. The manor or reputed manor of Kenagh, and Cashell alias Piercecourt and all my lands in Co. Cavan which I have purchased from Mr. Fitzherbert. Lands of Moonygall, Drumsillagh, Millecroghery and Grenan [Co. Meath]. My dwelling house etc. in Jervais Street, Dublin. My dwelling house in Lawrence Street, town of Drogheda. My dwelling house etc. commonly called Belvidere, and all lands which I hold from Dr. Marmaduke Coghill deceased, or from Charles Moore, Baron of Tullamore in Drishoge or elsewhere in Co. Dublin. To be buried in vault lately made for me in St. Peter's Church, Drogheda.

Second codicil 1 Aug. 1758: My nephew Alderman Henry Ogle's legacy by his death is become lapsed. The five children of the said Henry Ogle. Patience Colpoys is since dead. Ann Colpoys daughter of said Patience Colpoys. Third codicil 30 Nov. 1758: My sister Mary Leigh is lately deceased. Her daughter-in-law Sarah Leigh, widow of John Leigh, deceased. Fourth codicil 18 July 1759: My sister Patience Fowke is now in a declining sate of health. My nephews Francis Leigh, Edward Hardman, alderman, and Wm. Ogle, alderman, the elder, and my nieces Ann Corbett and Sarah Leigh her sister. My nephew Wm. Ogle, second son of Henry Ogle deceased to be exor. in case Edward Meade should die in my lifetime. My nephew John Leigh to be a trustee and exor. if John Fowke should die in my lifetime.

Witnesses: Richard Dawson, Dublin, Esq., Jno. Thompson and Wm. Robinson, Dublin, gents. To codicil (1): Richd. Dawson. Jno. Thompson, Br. Noble, Dublin, gent. To codicil (2): John Lodge, Dublin, gent., Edwd. Blackburne, Dublin, grocer, Corns. Wynne,

Dublin, bookseller. To codicil (3): John Lodge, Thos. Hunt, Dublin, sadler, Edwd. Blackburne. To codicil (4): John Lodge, Corns. Wynne, Edwd. Blackburne.

Memorial witnessed by: Richard Dawson, John Lodge.

202, 12, 133868 Sydm. Singleton (seal)
(Sydenham Fowke now called Sydenham Singleton, Esq.)
Jno. Fowke (seal)

255 CHAMBERLAIN, JOSEPH, Knockfinn, Queen's Co. farmer.

21 Sept. 1757. Narrate 1¾ p. 19 Dec. 1759.

His three sons. His son Joseph and his two other sons (under 21 years). His brothers John Chamberlain and Theophilus Chamberlain and his friend Robert Palmer, trustees and exors. Second son William. His third son John. His house and farm in Knockfinn.

Witnesses: Joseph Smith, Knockfin, comber, Roger Vanston, Burress in Ossory, comber, Thomas Ringwood, Craigadrisley, gent., all in Queen's Co.

Memorial witnessed by: Joseph Smith, Roger Vanston.

204, 53, 134265 Theop. Chamberlain (seal)

256 BOLTON, JOHN, Lis[s]odeige, Co. Kerry, Esq.

25 May 1759. Narrate ½ p. 22 Dec. 1759.

His wife extx. His son James Bolton and his daughter Ann Boucher, his children by his former wife. His son Lucius Bolton. His children [? by] Margaret Bolton. His other children. His son-in-law Arthur Saunders, Esq., exor. His freehold lease and farm of Lis[s]odeige.

Witnesses: Michael McMahon, Patrick Riordan, Maurice Rourke, all of Lis[s]odeige.

Memorial witnessed by: Michael McMahon, Thomas McDonagh.

203, 105, 134286 Arthur Saunders (seal)

257 JONES, RICHARD, Booterstown, Co. Dublin, Esq.

11 Dec. 1759. Narrate 2½ pp. 8 Jan. 1760.

His wife Mary Jones, exor. His daughter Deborah, under 21 years and unmarried. His sister Mary Blakely. His sister-in-law Susanna Medlicott. His daughters Martha and Mary under 21 years. His sister Ann Harrison. His nephews John Harrison and Robert Harrison. His former servant Mary Flannigan, Thomas and Grace the children of said Mary Flannigan. Theobald Wolfe and Theobald Medlicott exors.; they are to be guardians of said daughter Deborah until she shall attain 21 years. His wife and Theobald Wolfe to be guardians of his daughters Martha and Mary.

His estate in Co. Wexford. His dwelling house lately built in the lands of Feas and the demesne lands about 11 acres [situation not mentioned]. His dwelling house at Booterstown and interests near the town of Booterstown.

Witnesses: Mar. Izod, Chapple, Co. Kilkenny, spinster, Ann Waring, spinster, sister of the testator's wife, Christopher Comyn Gardiner, Dublin, Esq., barrister at law.

Memorial witnessed by: Christopher Comyn Gardiner, Francis Johnson, Dublin, servant to said Theobald Wolfe.

204, 69, 134398 Theod. Wolfe (seal)

258 BOSWELL, ROBERT, Ballycurry, Co. Wicklow, Esq.

24 Jan. 1760. Full 8½ pp. 6 March 1760.

To be interred in burial place of my family in the church of Wicklow. My wife Mary Boswell, a settlement made upon my marriage with said Mary by deed 16 March 1731. Charles Coote, Cootehill, Co. Cavan and Mark Whyte, Dublin, Esq., trustees and exors. My daughter Frances Boswell " my only younger child." My half-brother William Boswell. The children of my half-brother Alexander Boswell. John Boswell, eldest son of my half-brother Alexander Boswell deceased, Whitley Boswell, second son and Alexander Boswell the third son of my half-brother Alexander Boswell deceased. My sister Arabella Magrath.

Legacy to Protestant poor of parish of Wicklow. My estate and mansion house of Ballycurry. Lands of Tomcoyle and other lands in Co. Wicklow held from Benjamin Wolley and Mary his wife. Cullahill in manor or lordship of Mount Kennedy held by lease unto Henry Boswell, the son of my half-brother Henry Boswell deceased. Lands in counties of Sligo, Roscommon and Wicklow mentioned in settlement dated 26 Aug. 1755 made on marriage of my son John Boswell deceased with Frances Coote. My brother-in-law John Craddock. My grand-daughter Mary Boswell. My grand-daughter Frances Boswell. If daughters of my daughter Frances Boswell or my said grand-daughters shall become entitled to my estate such person's husband and their issue shall use surname and bear arms of Boswell.

Witnesses: Sir George Ribton, Stillorgan, Co. Dublin, Knight, Alderman Overstreet Grogan, Dublin, mercer, Edwd. Grogan, Dublin, gent.

Memorial witnessed by: Overstreet Grogan, Thos. Tudor.

203, 244, 135000 Frances Boswell (seal)
daughter of testator
Mark Whyte (seal)

259 LAWE, GEORGE, Dublin, gent.

31 July 1756. Narrate ½ p. 12 May 1760.

His wife Margaret Lawe otherwise Wrightson, extx. His brother Robt. Lawe.

Rents of lands of Anahagh, Co. Monaghan, lease thereof granted by Brigadier Robt. Echlin to Rev. John Lawe, clerk, his father, deceased.

Witnesses: Richd. Battersby, Geo. Johnston and Jno. Dunlap, all of Monaghan, merchants.

Memorial witnessed by: Geo. Wrightson, Forbes White, both Dublin, merchants.

202, 517, 135064 Margt. Lawe (seal)

260 COBBE, JOHN, Deer Park, Queen's Co., farmer.

9 Feb. 1760. Narrate $\frac{3}{4}$ p. 24 March 1760.

Richard Cobbe his eldest brother, of Deer Park, Queen's Co., farmer, exor. Roger Hanlon, Deer Park, exor.

His freehold lease which he bought from Susanna Cobbe otherwise Guiot otherwise Terris about 12 acres, in Deer Park, Barony Portnahinch, Queen's Co.

Witnesses: Edward Fotherell, Kilbride, farmer, Patrick Neal, William Lawler and Roger Hanlon, of Deer Park, farmers.

Memorial witnessed by: Roger Hanlon, James Dunn, Portarlington, Queen's Co., town clerk.

203, 266, 135167 Richard Cobbe (seal)

261 PRECIOUS, MATTHEW.

8 June 1756. Full $\frac{1}{4}$ p. 19 June 1760.

" To my daughter West the holding she is now in possession of " [situation not mentioned]. Precious West and John West her two sons.

Witnesses: James Dignan, then of Castlewarden, Co. Kildare, servant to Rev. Mr. Ward, Wm. Coulter, Coosscollharbour [Crosscoolharbour], Co. Wicklow, farmer.

Memorial witnessed by: Wm. Coulter, Henry Stearne, Dublin, gent.

205, 282, 136091 John West (seal)

262 REFORD, LEWIS, Antrim, linendraper.

3 April 1760. Narrate $3\frac{1}{2}$ pp. 20 June 1860.

His wife Frances. His eldest son Lewis Reford. His younger son Joseph Reford, exor., Susana his wife. His grandson Lewis Reford (his mother Susana), son of said Joseph Reford. His son-in-law Thomas Hoope (exor.), his wife Sarah daughter of testator, their second son Lewis Hoope. His daughter Hanna Reford.

His fulling mill six acres of lands and houses thereon in which testator then dwelt. Testator's grandmother's tenement on east side of the mill dam; rents etc. payable to Lord Massareene. His lands called Tanabrack [? Tamybuck] adjoining Kells Water, Co. Antrim, occupied by Robert Owens. His son Joseph Reford to deliver barley and oats to testator's wife yearly out of Moyliny [? Moylinny, Co. Antrim] farm. Farm held under Lord Massereene known by the name of Spring or Killcrests farm, Co. Antrim. Lands near Muckamore Bridge, parish of Antrim, held under Lord Massereene formerly called Wilson's or Wilkinson's farm and lately known as Moyliny farm. His tenement possessed by his son-in-law Thomas Hoope opposite the church in town of Antrim. Tenements in Antrim town; the Quaker meeting house and burying place of said people called Quakers adjoining the road leading from Antrim to Muckamore Bridge.

Witnesses: Saml. McCormick, Esq., doctor of physick, James Dobbin, Postmaster and Senischall, both of town of Antrim, Francis Joy, Feehoge, Co. Antrim, papermaker.

Memorial witnessed by: James Dobbin, Francis Joy.

207, 96, 136098 Joseph Reford (seal)
Tho. Hoope (seal)

263 FLEMING, ELINOR, Kells, innkeeper.

28 June 1760. Narrate ½ p. 28 July 1760.

Her son-in-law Thos. Clinton, exor. Her son Rev. Christopher Fleming. Her son Joseph Gaghegan. Her son John Fleming. Michael Smyth, Modlin, Co. Meath, exor.

Her dwelling house, shop, brewing utensils etc. in Market Street, Corporation of Kells.

Witnesses: Thomas Weldon, skinner, Patrick Macken, distiller, Denis McAuley, schoolmaster, all of Kells.

Memorial witnessed by: Patrick Macken, James Byrne, Kells, merchant.

209, 8, 136458 Michl. Smyth (seal)

264 CASSEDY, WILLIAM, Francis Street, Dublin, merchant.

14 May 1754. Narrate ½ p. 30 July 1760.

His wife Margaret Cassedy, extx. His son Jno. Cassedy, under 24 years. His son William. His daughter Mary. His son Thomas, a legacy if alive. His daughter Ann.

His lease held under Jno. Taylor, Esq., in Francis Street.

Witnesses: Jno. Hussey, Dublin, gent., Michl. Gaul, Dublin, gent.

Memorial witnessed by: Michl. Gaul, Wm. Magin, Dublin, gent.

206, 370, 136484 Margt. Cassedy (seal)
her mark

265 HOLLISTER, PHILIP, Dublin, gent.

3 June 1758. Narrate ½ p. 31 July 1760.

His wife Deborah Hollister. His daughter Elizth. Hollister. His daughter Charlot(1), her fortune if she married with the consent of her mother Deborah Hollister and his son-in-law Alexr. Casstels and his wife Charlot Castle(1). His wife Deborah Hollister, his son-in-law Alexr. Casstle, Wm. Cooper, trustees, guardians and exors.

His holding in Little Forrest: his holding in York Street and Love Lane [Dublin].

Witnesses: Charles Armstrong, Dublin, gent., Thomas Peacocke, Dublin, gent. and Elinor Peacocke his wife.

Memorial witnessed by: Thomas Peacocke and Elinor his wife.

205, 358, 136490 Deborah Hollister (seal)

266 KIRKWOOD, GEORGE.

13 April 1759. Narrate ½ p. 25 Aug. 1760.

My wife; her house at Ballyduff where she now dwells. My sister Sophia Kirkwood. My brother Loder Kirkwood. Margt. and Mary Kirkwood. Jane Brinn. Ann McPartlon.

---

(1) The Christian name of one of these daughters must be incorrect unless Alexr. Castle had married a second time.

The farm of One Galles in the County Kaven and parish of Templeport leased from Lord Tyrone.

Witnesses to Will and memorial: Richard Story, Bray, Co. Wicklow, gaiger, Thos Phillips, Windgate, said county, innkeeper and Ursula Phillips his wife.

205, 388, 136649 Elizabeth Kirkwood (seal)

267 STEWART, REV. ARCHIBALD, Ballintoy, Co. Antrim, D.D. 23 Nov. 1751. Narrate 1 p. 4 Nov. 1760.

His sister Jane Stewart. Arthur Dobbs, Castle Dobbs, Esq., James Stewart, Billy, Esq., Counsellor at law, James Smyth, clerk, Vicar of Armoy, all Co. Antrim, exors. and trustees.

Ballyloghmore, parish of Billy, Co. Antrim. Mill etc. at Dunsevrick, parish of Ballintoy.

Witnesses: William Hutcheson, Ballycastle, Co. Antrim, landwaiter, Rev. Alexander Cuppage, curate of Ballywilling, Co. Londonderry, Rev. James Young, curate of Ballintoy.

Memorial witnessed by: Alexr. Cuppage, John McAllester, Ballycastle, Co. Antrim, gent.

208, 67, 137115 Jane Stewart (seal)
of Ballylogh, Co. Antrim.

268 GODWIN, EDWARD, Brabston Street otherwise Truck Street, Liberty of Thomas Court and Donore, Co. Dublin, chandler. 8 July 1757. Précis ½ p. 27 Nov. 1760.

His wife Jane Godwin. His town and lands of Irishtown, Co. Dublin, and concerns in Co. Dublin on the Upper Coomb. His dwelling house in Truck Street.

Witnesses: John Clapham, Truck Street, Co. Dublin, shoemaker, George Mathews, Truck Street, butcher, Thomas Clapham, son of said John Clapham, since deceased.

Memorial witnessed by: Daniel Bourne, Patrick's Close, Co. Dublin, gent., John Martineau, of same place, clerk to said Daniel Bourne.

212, 26, 137472 Jane Godwin (seal)

269 OWEN, NICHOLAS, Raconnell, Co. Monaghan, gent.
1 May 1759. Narrate 2½ pp. 27 Jan. 1761.

His wife Mable Owen. His daughter Prudence White wife of Robert White of Dagon, Co. Cavan. His eldest son Thomas Owen. His second son Jno. Owen already provided for. His third son Nicholas Owen. His fourth son Blayny Owen. Rev. Dr. Obins, and Samuel Blacker, Esq., trustees. His friends and relations Edwd. Lucas, Castleshane, Esq., and Rev. Dr. Joseph Grace now of Trinity College, Dublin, clerk. Robert Montgomery, Brandrum, Co. Monaghan, and James Hamilton, Monaghan, Esqrs., exors.

His freehold estate. Newgrove otherwise Monaghandought, Raconnell East and Raconnell West. The two Tullycrumons [? Tullycroman] and Aughaboy and all his other real estate in Co. Monaghan,

Witnesses: Geo. Scott, Aughnamullagh, Co. Monaghan, gent., Ralph Semple and Edwd. Campbell both of Monaghan, gents.

Memorial witnessed by: Edwd. Campbell, Alexr. Campbell, Raconnell, Co. Monaghan, gent.

211, 103, 137961 T. Owen (seal)

270 STEWART, WILLIAM, Newtownstewart, Co. Tyrone, Esq.
14 Dec. 1750. Narrate 1½ p. 3 Feb. 1761.

His wife Mary Stewart. His eldest son John Stewart. His second son Nicholas Stewart. His youngest son Charles Stewart, under 21 years. William Edie, Killydart, Co. Tyrone, gent., trustee.

Ballykelly, Manor of Newtownstewart, Co. Tyrone. Mulholland's field and Carrigan's in said manor. The house wherein testator dwelt in Newtownstewart and Bog Park and Deer Park part of his freehold. Tan house, park, field and Printy's field in said manor. Legland in said manor.

Witnesses: Jane Lane, spinster and Rev. Pelissier both of Newtown Stewart(1) and Richd. Cowan, Lifford, Co. Donegal.

Memorial witnessed by: Jane Lane, Peter Pelissier, Richd. Cowan.

207, 487, 138073 Mary Stewart (seal)

(1) Probably Rev. John Pelissier, rector of Ardstraw 1753-81. Betham shows him as brother of Rev. Peter Pelissier.

271 DONNELLAN, SARAH otherwise ORMSBY, Dublin, widow.

19 Jan. 1761. Full 2 pp. 27 Feb. 1761.

My eldest son Gilbert Donnellan, Esq. My only daughter Frances Donnellan extx. My youngest son John Ormsby Donnellan, his father Edmond Donnellan, Esq., deceased, his grandmother Sarah Ormsby. Rev. William Donnellan. Capt. James Donnellan. Myles Reilly.

My dwelling house in Sackville Street, Dublin. Lands of Ballinamona and all my lands in Co. Limerick. Streamstown, Kingstown otherwise Ballinrink, Knockanroe and Ranahinch and other lands in Co. Westmeath.

Witnesses: John Whiteway, Wm. Bury, Mark Synnot.

Memorial witnessed by: Mark Whyte, Dublin, Esq., John Whiteway.

212, 66, 138366 Frances Donnellan (seal)

272 BOWLES, WILLIAM PHINEAS, Dublin, Esq.

25 June 1760. Full 1¼ p. 16 March 1761.

My son Phineas Bowles, a minor, to be under care of Hannah Crofton, Dublin, spinster, extx. My brother Richard Bowles. My sister Anna Maria Haywood otherwise Bowles.

My estate and leasehold interests in Co. Tipperary, city of Dublin, and elsewhere.

Witnesses: Joseph Hall, Dolphin's Barn, Co. Dublin, gent., Luke How, Royal Hospital, Esq., John Pilkington, Dublin, gent.

Memorial witnessed by: John Pilkington, John Robinson, Dublin, gent.

208, 303, 138519 Hannah Crofton (seal)

273 WYLY, ROBERT, Thomastown, Co. Kildare.

28 Jan. 1761. Précis ½ p. 3 April 1761.

Joseph Barcroft and William Greenhow, Dublin, merchants, trustees. Lands of Thomastown and Tullylost, held from Earl of

Kildare. Coolcaragon held from Lord Courtown, Timahoe held from Arthur Dobbs, Esq., Stickins held from Thomas Carr, clerk, all in Co. Kildare. His leasehold estate of Aghnamelick, King's Co. held from Anthony Henderson.

Witnesses: John Lawler, Thomastown, weaver, John Flood, of same, farmer, John Bencraft, servant to testator.

Memorial witnessed by: William Wyly, brother and one of the exors. of testator, William Bolger, Dublin, gent.

212, 117, 138622 Wm. Greenhow (seal)

274 SPROULE, THOMAS, Strabane, Co. Tyrone.

2 April 1759. Précis ½ p. 14 April 1761.

His wife Mary Sproule. His three sons James Sproule, Samuel Sproule and John Sproule.

His freehold lands of Altamullan, Minacheeran and Pollygerrybane, Co. Tyrone.

Witnesses: Thos. Short, merchant, Patrick Wilson, gent., and John McCollagh, merchant, all of Strabane.

Memorial witnessed by: Thos. Short, John McCollagh.

210, 262, 138802 Jas. Sproule (seal)
Sam. Sproule (seal)
John Sproule (seal)

275 CROKER, WALTER, Ballygrillahane, Co. Cork, gent.

20 May 1741. Narrate 2 pp. 26 May 1761.

His brother Thos. Poole and Mary his wife. His nephew Walter Poole, eldest son of said Thos. and Mary. His nephew Wm. second son of said Thos. and Mary. His nephew Jonathan Bowles. Anthy. Stawel, Ballydoole, Co. Cork, gent., guardian to said nephew Jonathan Bowles during his minority. To his god-daughter Mary Green, daughter of Wm. Green, £40 as an help and provision for said Mary in marriage. Cathleen Roch otherwise Sheehy. £100 to poor Protestants of parish of Castletownroch.

Ballyanker, Co. Waterford. Ballygrillahane, Barony Fermoy, Co. Cork.

Witnesses: Richd. Verling, Glananore, Henry and Thos. Browne, Ballinvoher, all Co. Cork, gents.

Memorial witnessed by: Henry Browne, Wm. Anderson, Aghacross, Co. Cork, gent.

209, 477, 139184 Jonathan Bowles (seal)

276 NEWSOM, SOLOMON, Cashell, Co. Tipperary.
28 March 1742. Narrate 1 p. 9 June 1761.

Confirms release dated 8 Aug. 1738 made on his marriage with his wife Sara Newsom then Sara Chandlee. His wife Sara Newsom extx.

Lands of Dually, [Co. Tipperary] purchased from Richard Sparrow. Lands mentioned in said deed of settlement.

Witnesses: John Eustace and Alexander Ryves both of Dublin, merchants, John Burrows, Dublin, gent.

Memorial witnessed by: Alexander Ryves, John Nicholson, Dublin, gent.

213, 60, 139363 Sara Newsom (seal)

277 PARKINSON, ROBERT, Atherdee, Co. Louth, Esq.
29 July 1754. Précis 1 p. 15 June 1761.

His good friends Theobald Wolfe, Counsellor at law and John Barlow, one of the attorneys of the Common Pleas, trustees and exors. with testator's wife Diana Parkinson. Testator had in Trinity term last suffered a recovery of the lands comprehended in his marriage settlement [situation not mentioned].

Witnesses: William Harward, Dublin, Counsellor at law, John Hamilton, Strabane, Co. Tyrone, Esq., Counsellor at law, Wm. McCausland, Dublin, Esq., one of the attorneys of the Court of Exchequer in Ireland.

Memorial witnessed by: William McCausland, Fairfax Mercer, Dublin, gent.

211, 208, 138445 Jn. Barlow (seal)

278 RINGWOOD, GRACE, Closeland, Queen's Co., widow of Thomas Ringwood late of Tinnoran, Co. Wicklow, farmer, deceased.

17 Jan. 1759. Narrate ½ p. 20 June 1761.

Her sister Jane Barry, wife of Stephen Barry, Monastereven, Co. Kildare, innholder. Testatrix's mother Jane Landey and Thos. Gaugain Landey then of Closeland exors.

Witnesses: Thomas Gaugain Landey, Dublin, Elias Landey then of Closeland but now a volunteer in Gen. Dejeans Regt. of Horse, Patrick Byrne, Closeland, gardener.

Memorial witnessed by: Thomas Gaugain Landey, Robt. Parke, Moone, Co. Kildare, gent.

212, 351, 139513 Jane Landey (seal)

279 BRUCE, WILLIAM, Drumlamph, parish of Maghera, Co. Londonderry. 24 Aug. 1745. Précis ½ p. 25 June 1761.

His wife Mary. His son Samuel. His son Robert. His son Hugh. His house and lands.

Witnesses: John Dickey, Bellaghy, Co. Londonderry, shoemaker, Darby Kinan, farmer, Isabel Kinan, then spinster, daughter of said Darby, both of Drumlamph.

Memorial witnessed by: John Dickey, Fergus Kennedy, Bellaghy, malster.

208, 501, 139574 Samuel Bruce (seal)
his mark
Hugh Bruce (seal)

280 RANSON, WILLIAM, Dublin, gent.

2 July 1761. Full 1½ p. 22 Sept. 1761.

My wife extx. My son William Ranson now living with me. My daughter Mary Cooper otherwise Ranson. My sons John and Benjamin Ranson who have been in foreign countries for some years past. My present dwelling house in Drogheda Street, Dublin.

Witnesses: William Dixon, public notary, Thomas Clark his apprentice.

Memorial witnessed by: William Dixon, Thomas Clark.

212, 529, 140263 Benj. Ranson (seal)

281 McWHINEY, ADAM, Killyberry, parish of Ballyscullion, Co. Londonderry. 27 March 1761. Narrate ¾ p. 3 Oct. 1761.

To Thomas McWhiney of Killyberry aforesaid all his houses and gardens etc. in Killyberry. David Lockard and Thomas Lockard, the sons of Adam Lockard deceased. Robert Simeral.

Witnesses: Thomas Roney, Castle Dawson, John McWhiney, Leitrim, John Cooper, Killyberry, all in Co. Londonderry, farmers.

Memorial witnessed by: John McWhiney, John Cooper.

212, 558, 140364 Thos. McWhiney (seal)

282 PILSWORTH, RALPH, Milltown, Co. Kildare, farmer. 14 Jan. 1745. Précis ½ p. 9 Oct. 1761.

To his sister Elizabeth Pilsworth, extx., all his leasehold farms, etc. and all his worldly substance.

Witnesses: Thos. Burrowes, Milltown, gent., since deceased, Thos. Pilsworth, Milltown, gent., Dennis Gorman then of Milltown and now of Fox Grace, Co. Dublin, schoolmaster.

Memorial witnessed by: Dennis Gorman, John Gelling, Dublin, gent.

208, 597, 140392 Eliz. Pilsworth (seal)

283 WRIGHT, JOSEPH, Gola, [Co. Monaghan]. 19 March 1761. Narrate 1¼ p. 22 Oct. 1761.

His wife Elinor Wright. Failing any issue by her his lands etc. to Joseph Wright son of his cousin Henry Wright of Monaghan. His brother William Wright exor. James Wright of Karrach. Jas.

Whittsitt of Knocknagratt. Jno. Wright of Drummond's bond to the testator to be given up to his son Thomas. Money due to his uncle Henry Owen.

His real estate. His lands in Barony of Dartry, and part of the townland of Forevas [? Foremass, Co. Monaghan] which he purchased from the Bradys. Lands of Knocknagratt [Co. Monaghan] leased from Jno. Mitchell.

Witnesses: Rev. Jno. Cranston, Tysloughlan, Co. Monaghan, clerk, Arthur Robinson, Ballynametagh, Co. Armagh, Esq., doctor of physick, Jno. Mitchell, Cornock, Co. Monaghan, gent.

Memorial witnessed by: Jno. Cranston, Patk. Frener, Monaghan.

213, 160, 140464 William Wright (seal)

284 GIFFARD, SIR THOMAS, Castle Jordan, Co. Meath.

4 Nov. 1755. Précis 1 p. 10 Nov. 1761.

Lands of Castle Jordan, Ballymullagh otherwise Moyunsfurry, Ballickbrack, Drunane otherwise Dryne, Carrickgarr [? Co. Meath] and Corlettstowne(1) charged for portions of his several daughters.

Witnesses: Owen Butler, Dublin, gent., Robert Edgeworth, Kilshrewly, Esq., Luke Magivney, then servant to Edward Edgeworth of Park, King's Co., Luke Magiveney, then servant to Edward Edgeworth of Kilshrewly, Esq.

Memorial witnessed by: Robt. Edgeworth, Andrew Nesbitt, Dublin, Esq.

214, 161, 140627 Francis Nesbitt (seal) who is married to one of testator's daughters.

285 MAGUIRE, LAWRENCE, Mallow, Co. Cork, farmer.

25 March 1749. Précis ½ p. 11 Nov. 1761.

His wife. His son John Maguire. His daughter Catherine. His son Lawrence. Holdings in Mallow leased from William Jephson. Rev. James Kingston, Kilpadder and Arthur Norcott, Waterhouse, exors.

---

(1) Possibly Corbetstown, parish Castlejordan is intended.

Witnesses: Robt. Philpot, Patk, Tarrant, John White, all of Mallow, Co. Cork, gents.

Memorial witnessed by: Patk. Tarrant, Mathew Braddock, Mallow, gent.

214, 163, 140643 John Maguire (seal)

286 POWER, DAVID, Boulibane, Co. Galway.
12 April 1761. Précis ½ p. 17 Dec. 1761.

To Joseph Power, Loughrea, Co. Galway, gent., all my real estate in Co. Galway, that is to say the lands of Boulibane and Ballyboggan and lands of Keeloges. Rev. Archdeacon William Pigot and Hyacinth Daly, Esq., both of Loughrea, exors.

Witnesses: James Burke, Robert Hardiman, Anthony Tracy, all of Loughrea, gents.

Memorial witnessed by: Robert Hardiman, Peter Kilkenny, Dublin, gent.

213, 300, 141193 Joseph Power (sea)

287 LAWRENCE, THOMAS WORSOPP, Waringstown, Co. Down, Esq. 31 Aug. 1741. Full 1 p. 19 Dec. 1761.

My wife Joanna Frances Lawrence. My son Henry Lawrence (under 21 years). My nephew Thomas Dawson. My nephew Richard Frost. My nephew John Lawrence Dawson. My nephew Gustavus Dawson. Samuel Waring, Waringstown, Co. Down, Esq., and Holt Waring, Henry Street, Dublin, Esq., trustees and exors. My real estate.

Witnesses: Rev. Archdeacon George House, Harrymount, Co. Down, John Stothard, Maralin, Co. Down, Esq., John Huey, servant to said Saml. Waring.

Memorial witnessed by. Henry Steevens Reily, Dublin, notary public, Frances Ussher, Dublin, widow.

218, 35, 141221 Joanna Frances Lawrence (seal)

288 PARKER, NATHANIEL, Dublin, gent.

9 Dec. 1761. Full 3 pp. 15 Jan. 1762.

My wife Rebecca Parker and my son John Parker exors. My son Daniel Parker. My daughter Rachel Wickham, her husband. My daughter Rebecca White, her husband. My daughter Ann May, her husband. My grandchildren John Gibson and Nathaniel Gibson.

My estate and freehold interests in New Roe on the Poddle in the Earl of Meath's Liberty, four houses therein, Mr. Connor and Mr. Cantwell, Mr. Grundy and Mr. Pidgeon my undertenants. To said daughter Rachel from my wife's decease my chattle interest and concern in Crooked Staff wherein she now lives. Houses etc. in Mutton Lane, Black Pills [? Pitts], Meetinghouse Yard [Dublin]. Concern which I purchased from Mr. Hagrie [situation not mentioned]. Blackrock, Co. Dublin. New Markett in Earl of Meath's Liberty. King Street near St. Stephen's Green, Foredom's Ally near the Combe, Dublin.

Witnesses: Peter Tomey, Dolphin's Barn Lane, carpenter, Thomas Barrow, Dolphin's Barn Lane, skinner, William Dixon, Dublin, notary public.

Memorial witnessed by: William Dixon and George Hughes his apprentice.

214, 327, 141384 Jno. Parker (seal)

289 ANGLESEY, RICHARD EARL OF, of Newport Pagnell, Viscount Valentia and Baron of Mountnorris and also of Altham. 7 April 1759. Full 8 pp. 23 Jan. 1762.

To be buried in church Rossmanoge or any other church. My wife Juliana Countess of Anglesey; I have had several children by her of which three daughters and one son are now only living, that is to say Richearda Annesley otherwise called Lady Richearda, my eldest daughter, Juliana Annesley otherwise called Lady Juliana my second daughter, Catherine Annesley otherwise called Lady Catherine my third daughter and Arthur Annesley otherwise called Lord Annesley my only son by my wife Juliana (under 21 years). My wife Juliana Countess of Anglesey, Chas. Tottenham, Ross, Co. Wexford, Esq., and Rev. Chas. Huson of Wexford, clerk, and Edward Donovan,

Dublin, Esq., Counsellor at law, trustees. Mr. Cornelius Donovan, brother of my said wife. Richard Donovan, Rickard Donovan and Deane Donovan my said wife's brothers.

" Before my intermarriage with my said dear wife Juliana Countess of Anglesey I have had sevll. natl. children by different women during the time of my living separate from my first wife Mrs. Ann Phrust afterwards Countess of Anglesey, that is to say by Mrs. Ann Simpson Dorothea Annesley my eldest daughter, Carolina Annesley my second daughter and Elizth. Annesley my third daughter, and by Mrs. Ann Saulkeld of London deceased I had one natl. son Richd. Annesley, and by Mrs. Mary Glover late of Newport Pagnell in the Kingdom of Great Britain I had one natl. daughter named Ann Annesley otherwise Glover." " My aforesaid natl. daughter Dorothea now wife or reputed wife of one Duboies a fidler."(1). Said natural daughter Carolina now wife of Wm. White, Esq.

All my real and personal estate in Great Britain and Ireland. Woods in the park of Camolin, Co. Wexford.

Witnesses: Nicholas Viscount Loftus of Ely, Robt. Boyd, Glensansaw, Co. Kilkenny, Esq., Darius Drake, Camlin, Co. Wexford, Esq., Rev. Jno. Nixon, Mount Julia, Co. Wexford, clerk.

Memorial witnessed by: Nicholas Viscount Loftus of Ely, Mark Whyte, Dublin, Esq.

211, 550, 141447 Edw. Donovan (seal)

290 KIRKWOOD, ELIZABETH, widow of Geo. Kirkwood, Arklow, gent. 22 Nov. 1761. Précis ½ p. 8 Feb. 1762.

To Andrew Nesbitt, Dublin, Esq., half of the town and lands of Owengallis, Co. Cavan, the other half to his brother Edward Kinch.

Witnesses: Thomas Kavanagh the elder, Thomas Kavanagh the younger both of Cabinteely, Co. Dublin, gents., Thomas Crawford, Dublin, gent., one of the attorneys of H.M. Court of Exchequer in Ireland.

Memorial witnessed by: Thomas Crawford, Saml. Corry, gent., clerk to said Andrew Nesbitt.

215, 233, 141653 And. Nesbitt (seal)

(1) The will of Dorothea Dubois, proved 1774, mentions her two sons by Peter Dubois, John Herbert Valentia Dubois and Frederick Peter Dubois. (*Betham Wills*, Vol. 10, p. 46, Genealogical Office).

291 BOLTON, Rev. RICHARD, Lagore, Co. Meath, clerk, Vicar of Ratoath. 14 March 1761. Précis ½ p. 24 April 1762.

To his nephew Rev. Thos. Norman, Iniskeen, Co. Monaghan, clerk, (exor.), all his freeholds and estate of inheritance in Ireland.

Witnesses: Wm. Gamble, merchant, Geo. Gamble, merchant, Thos. Craige, clerk and book keeper to said Wm. and Geo. Gamble, all of Dublin.

Memorial witnessed by: Thos. Craige, Andrew Makilwaine, Dublin, gent.

216, 173, 142286 Thos. Norman (seal)

292 BOLTON, THOMAS, Lagore, Co. Meath, Doctor in Physick. 24 Feb. 1762. Narrate ¾ p. 24 April 1762.

Rev. Bigoe Henzell, Minister of the parish church of Dunshaughlin and Connolly Norman, Dublin, Esq., trustees. His nephew Thomas Norman, exor. Robert Norman, son of said Thomas Norman. His nephew Joshua Warren of Galtrim, Co. Meath, gent.

Lands of Loughbracken, Co. Meath. Lands called Street's farm and lands near Ratoath, Co. Meath. Houses etc. in Cook Street, Dublin. Lands near Dunboyne, Co. Meath held under the choir of Christ Church, Dublin and then in possession of James Hamilton, Esq.

Witnesses: Patk. Supple, Dunshoghlin, innkeeper, John Smith, Kilbrew, gent., Robt. Londy, Lagore, testator's butler.

Memorial witnessed by: Robt. Londy, Andrew Makilwaine, Dublin, gent.

214, 558, 142287 Thos. Norman (seal)

293 BRADSTREET, SIR SIMON, Kilmainham, Co. Dublin, Bart., Counsellor at law. 2 Nov. 1760. Full 5 pp. 3 May 1762.

My wife Ellinor. My son Samuel. My son Simon Bradstreet, a settlement made previous to the marriage of my son Simon with

Ann daughter of Sir Henry Cavendish[1]. My grandson Simon Bradstreet. My grandson Samuel Bradstreet. My grand-daughter Ellinor Catherine Bradstreet. My daughter Charlotta Viscountess Mountgarrett wife of Edmond Viscount Mountgarrett. My grandson Edmond Butler. My grandson Richard Butler. My grandson Simon Butler. My grand-daughters Ellinor Butler and Ann Butler. My daughter Emilia wife of Samuel Zobell, Esq., Captain in Whitmore's regiment. My nephew Lieut. Colonel John Bradstreet, Governor of St. Johns in Newfoundland. My sisters Susanna and Mary [Bradstreet]. My father Simon Bradstreet of Portland, Co. Tipperary, Esq., deceased. My grandfather John Bradstreet of Blanchvilles Park, Co. Kilkenny, Esq. Said Sir Henry Cavendish, Dublin, Bart., and my cousin James Agar, Ringwood, Co. Kilkenny, Esq., trustees.

My mansion house etc. in Kilmainham. My lands of inheritance in Kilmainham, Dubber, Mitchers Mount, Merryfalls and Killmacree. Ballymount otherwise Little Ballymount, Esker, Monagher, Arsdillagh, Colewinter otherwise Coldwinter otherwise Johnstown otherwise Great Johnstown in Co. Dublin. Tenements etc. in Plunkett Street, Francis Street, Skinner Row, Castle Street, Cork Hill, James Street; tenements, garden, orchard etc. "near and adjoining the Bason situate in the County of the city of Dublin." Ballynattin, Co. Catherlogh. Ballynockmore and Keatingstown, Co. Kilkenny.

Witnesses: Thomas Pasley, clerk to Henry Steevens Reily, Dublin, public notary, Richard Thwaites, Dublin, public notary and said Henry Steevens Reily.

Memorial witnessed by: Henry Steevens Reily, Thomas Pasley.

213, 490, 142385 Ellenor Bradstreet (seal)

294 BRAY, RICHARD, Youghall, Co. Cork, cabinet maker.

9 Jan. 1762. Précis ¼ p. 22 June 1762.

To his wife Mary Bray, extx., his goods and chattles. His brothers Jno. Bray and Wm. Bray and his sister Mary Knight otherwise Bray.

---

(1) Betham's abstract of this will at the Genealogical Office states that Ann was the sister of Sir Henry Cavendish.

Witnesses to Will and memorial: Mathw. Walsh, Youghall, clockmaker, Hugh Pollock, Youghall, potter.

218, 215, 143088 Mary Bray (seal)

295 FOLLIOTT, JOHN, Lickhill, Worcestershire, Colonel in H.M. Royal Regiment of Foot in Ireland. 9 March 1750. Narrate 2½ pp. 25 June 1762.

To Francis Folliott eldest son of Capt. Jno. Folliott of the Royal Hospital £10 and his niece Anna Ormsby £100. To nephew Owen Wynne rents of Garryduffe. To nephew Jno. Wynne £500. His cousin Gilbert Folliott's widow. Capt. Jno. Folliott of the Royal Hospital near Dublin, Jno. Folliott second son to said Jno. Folliott, Henry Folliott and Peter Folliott third and fourth sons of Capt. Jno. Folliott. His sister Catherine Wynne. Owen Wynne, senr., and Jno. Arabine, Esq., trustees. Owen Wynne of Hazelwood, Esq., Col. Jno. Arabine and Capt. Jno. Folliott exors.

To Mary Harlow £5 per annum during widowhood. To Francs. Gillespie (a servant) an annuity for life out of lands of Uragh, Muckrum and Monicomrit, Co. Leitrim and to his wife Dorothy all the wearing apparel of the late Mrs. Luggs.

Colgaugh or Culagh, Co. Sligo. His estate etc. in Wishaw in Warwickshire. A messuage called Four Oaks and several pieces of land in neighbourhood of Sutton Colefield, Warwickshire and farm of Lickhill, and Lordship etc. of Lower Mitton; lease of the Burlagh and a lease of Woodgreen, parish of Kidderminster. Possessed of several estates in fee left to him by his late cousin Robt. Folliott of Holybrook, Co. Sligo, deceased, and of a small estate near Sligo which he purchased from Mr. Ross and a small estate in Co. Leitrim called Uragh, Muckrum, Park and Monicomrit which he purchased from William Barret. Mullagh, Farna, Aghanagh, Donna Vera [Doonaveeragh], Drumdony and Carrowkeel in the union of Townagh, Co. Sligo and other leasehold interests in and about the town of Sligo. Farm of Ballymacward held by lease from Trinity College; farm of Cloonin and a tenement for building on near to the church of Ballyshannon, farm of Drumcrin and farms of Fennor and Dunmuckrum in the Moygh near Ballyshannon [Co. Donegal] all leased from Wm. Conolly, Esq.

Witnesses: Jno. Bayly, late of Dublin, Esq., deceased, Jno. Clark, Dublin, Esq., Nathaniel Weld, then clerk to said Jno. Bayly.

Memorial witnessed by: Wm. Ross, Bartholomew Delandre, clerks to Edwd. Scriven, Dublin, gent.

218, 219, 143123 (Capt.) J. Folliott (seal)

296 MURDOCK, JOHN, Liverpool, Lancaster.

15 Feb. 1762. Narrate ¾ p. 10 Aug. 1762.

His late father John Murdock late of Liverpool, mariner, deceased, bequeathed eighteen hundred pounds to his [? testator's] daughter Elizabeth, out of lands of Heathstown and Macgraham, Co. Westmeath. His wife.

Witnesses: Robt. Wainwright, Foxteth Park, Co. Lancaster, husbandman, John Brownell and George Proctor both of Liverpool, gents.

Memorial witnessed by: Robert Parker, Liverpool, merchant, George Proctor.

213, 601, 143553 Hannah Murdock (seal)
(widow of John Murdock the son)

297 JESSOP, THOMAS, Fairbane [Ferbane], King's Co.

2 Feb. 1753. Full 1¾ p. 21 Dec. 1762.

My wife, exor. My eldest son William Jessop, exor. My two sons John, exor., and George. My daughter Rodia. Hanna Downs and Susanna Downs. My youngest daughter Elizabeth Jessop.

Lands of Killmore, Corrageen and Coshbeka, Kincorr [King's Co.]. Thos. Nugent, Darby Mulpether and Philip Hinsey, Mathew Dillon, Murtogh Murrin tenants of houses and gardens. The house and garden James Gorman now holds from me by lease in the name of Robert Whitton. John Forster and Patrick Coghlan tenants in town of Ferbane. The house where John Carr and Jeremiah Lilly now dwell.

Witnesses: Robert Sherwood, Athlone, Co. Roscommon, gent., Luke Daly, Nogusduff, King's Co., farmer, Robert Whitton, Kincorr King's Co., farmer.

Memorial witnessed by: Luke Daly, John Weekes, Dublin, gent.

213, 606, 143637 George Jessop (seal)

298 PLUNKETT, PATRICK, Lowart, parish of Donagh, Co. Monaghan. [Date not recorded]. Narrate 1½ p. 27 Aug. 1762.

His wife Isabella Plunkett. His son Robt. Plunkett. His (testator's) three sons and daughter: his son Thomas, his son Wm. Plunkett, his daughter Margaret Baxter, his son James Plunkett. Exors. his sons Robt. and Thos. Plunkett and Charles Baxter. Debts due to him by heirs of Baptist Johnston, Esq., deceased. His lease of Lowart.

Witnesses: Andrew Moore, Armagh, Co. Armagh, wheelwright, Samuel McMullen, Lowart, James Baxter, New Mills, Co. Monaghan, gent.

Memorial witnessed by: Samuel McMullan, Thomas Noble, Summerhill, Co. Fermanagh, gent.

219, 283, 143471 Chas. Baxter (seal)

299 NEDHAM, ROBERT, Newry, Co. Down, now at Beckenham, Co. Kent, Esq. 22 Jan. 1760. Codicil 8 Aug 1762. Précis 1 p. 9 Nov. 1762.

Concerning a rent charge out of his freehold lands etc. within the lordship and town of Newry.

Witnesses: John Shuckburgh, parish of St. Dunstan in the West, London, bookseller (since deceased), Richard Cocks, Inner Temple, London, Esq., Jacob Collinvaulx, parish of St. Dunstan, gent.

Codicil witnessed by: Elizabeth Proctor, parish of St. James, Westminster, Co. Middlesex, spinster, Richard Ansell, Greatford, County of Lincoln, yeoman, William Mathews, Wolingford, Co. Berks, gent.

Memorial witnessed by: Jacob Collinvaulx, Robt. Stockdale.

216, 522, 144193 Catherine Nedham (seal)
a devisee in said Will mentioned

300 GRAHAM, JOHN, Strabane, Co. Tyrone.

25 Feb. 1745/6. Narrate ½ p. 11 Nov. 1762.

His son John Graham, exor. His son Francis Graham. His son Thos. Graham. To his daughter Jean £10 to be disposed to her family. John Colhoune, Strabane, exor. His real and personal estate.

Witnesses: James Knox, Walter Parry and Allan Campbell all of Strabane, Co. Tyrone.

Memorial witnessed by: said Allan Campbell, John Thompson, Strabane, public notary.

218, 447, 144285 John Graham (seal)

301 GREEN, MICHAEL, Roxborough, Co. Tipperary, Esq.

19 Aug. 1756. Précis ½ p. 12 Nov. 1762.

To his wife Ellinor Green real and freehold estate.

Witnesses: Eccles Disney, Churchtown, Co. Waterford, Rev. Wm. Downs, clerk, Robt. Shaw and Wm. Connor, gents., all of Clonmell, Co. Tipperary.

Memorial witnessed by: Wm. Chadwick, Dublin, gent., Martin McGwire, Clonmell, servant to said Elinor Green.

218, 454, 144309 Ellinor Green (seal)

302 SUMMERS, SAMUEL, Dublin, merchant.

26 Dec. 1762. Narrate 1 p. 4 Jan. 1763.

His cousin Richd. Summers, Bristol. His brother-in-law William Tuckett, Philipstown, Co. Carlow. His brother-in-law Amos Strettell. His brother-in-law John Dawson, Dublin, merchant, exor.

His piece of land called the Strive Close in Pembrokeshire, S. Wales. His fee simple estate in George's Lane and Fade Street, Dublin, which he lately purchased from the assignees of the Bank lately kept by Willcocks and Dawson. Three houses in Bolton Street (Sackville Gardiner, Esq., lessor). Confirms sale of lands of Philipstown to said William Tuckett. To his brother-in-law Amos Strettell his concerns in Meath Street and Earl Street which he held by lease from the representatives of Jonathan Strettell. To his clerk Walter White his houses in Newmarket, Co. Dublin. To John Rook, Dublin, calender, his houses in Clothworkers Square, Co. Dublin. To his servant Edward Middleton house etc. in Fordams Alley, Co. Dublin, held by lease from Col. Joshua Paul.

Witnesses: Walter White, Dublin, merchant, Edward Middleton, of the same, one of the Battleaxe Guards, Christian Roeder, clerk to Thos. Mulock, Dublin, public notary.

Memorial witnessed by: William Noble, Dublin, gent., Richard Cudmore, clerk to William Crowe, Dublin, gent.

221, 136, 144961 John Dawson (seal)

303 BROWNE, JOHN, Neal, Co. Mayo, afterwards called Sir John Browne, Bart. 14 Sept. 1747. Narrate 1 p. 19 Jan. 1762.

Testator devised his castles, towns, lands and hereditaments mentioned in articles dated 1 March 1744 made between testator, Geo. Browne of the Neal aforesaid, Esq., his eldest son and heir apparent, to Sir Jno. Bingham, Castlebar, Co. Mayo, Bart., and Poole Cosby, Stradbally, Queen's Co., Esq., as trustees for use of his said eldest son Geo. Browne in tail male. Jno. Browne second son, Dodwell Browne third son, Henry Browne fourth son, and Palmer Browne fifth son of testator.

Witnesses: Geo. Fitzgerald, Rockfield, Co. Mayo, Esq., Patk. Fitzgerald, Castlebarr, Co. Mayo, Esq., William Fergus, Raheens, Co. Mayo, gent.

Memorial witnessed by: Wm. Magin, Jno. Hutton, both of Dublin, gents.

220, 345, 145042 Jno. Browne (seal)

304 LAWTON, TRAYER, Cork, merchant.

25 May 1758. Précis ¾ p. 28 Jan. 1763.

His wife Ann Lawton. His son Hugh Lawton exor. His daughter Sarah Lawton. Lucia Lawton one other daughter of said testator. Ann Leslie and Lawton Leslie grand-children of testator.

Wintesses: James Aickin, Daniel MacCarthy and Michael MacCarthy all of Cork.

Memorial witnessed by: Sampson Towgood French, Dublin, Esq., James Flaherty, Cork, writing clerk.

221, 144, 145147 Hugh Lawton junior (seal)

305 BIRNIE, JOHN, Templepatrick, Co. Antrim.

6 Nov. 1745. Narrate 1 p. 7 March 1763.

His son William Birnie. His son John Birnie. His son Alexr. Birnie and his son Saml. Birnie exors.

His freehold house and tenements he was then possessed of and the eight acres of land [situation not mentioned]. Lease of farm he possessed in Kilmakee adjacent to Dunathry Bridge. His bleach green and mills.

Witnesses: William Livingston, Cloghanduff, Co. Antrim, linen draper, David Bell, linen draper and William Bell, weaver, both of Templepatrick.

Memorial witnessed by: William Livingston, William Bell.

217, 451, 145662 Will. Birnie (seal)
eldest son of testator

306 MARTIN, GEORGE, Curren, parish of Maghera, Co. Londonderry, smith. 10 Feb. 1752. Narrate 1½ p. 29 April 1763.

His wife Margaret Martin. His son Edward Martin. George Martin fourth son of his son Henry Martin. His son Henry Martin.

His farm in Curren by lease under Rt. Hon. William Connolly, Esq. Two tenements, houses and gardens called Thomas Pear's and Peter Scullin's.

Witnesses: Bernard Mulhallen, the elder, Moyagoll, in the proportion of Vintners, Co. Londonderry, farmer, Adam Downing, Lemnaroy in the proportion aforesaid, farmer, Roger Tochill, Moyagoll, farmer.

Memorial witnessed by: Adam Downing, John Kirkpatrick, Magherafelt, said county, glazier.

227, 129, 146248 Edward Martin (seal)

307 TYRONE, MARCUS EARL OF

18 May 1762. Narrate 2½ pp. 2 May 1763.

His wife Catherine Countess of Tyrone, extx. His eldest son Geo. De La Poer Beresford. His second son Jno. Beresford. His third son William Beresford (youngest son, under 21 years). His six daughters. Hamilton Gorges, Catherine's Grove, Co. Dublin, Esq., and Rt. Hon. the Earl of Arran trustees.

His advowson or right of presentation to the living of Termonmaguirk, Co. Tyrone. His fee farm and other estates in and about the town of Carrick, Co. Tipperary. Town and lands of Knocknecrew, Co. Waterford and all other lands etc. in said counties of Tipperary and Waterford. His dwelling house in Dublin and house in possession of Richard Gorges, Esq. [situation not mentioned]. His leasehold lands of Aghalow and all other lands held under the See of Derry. His leasehold interests in Coleraine. His real estate of Young's Castle and all other his real estate in the city of Dublin. Reciting that the Hon. Lieut. Genl. Frederick Hamilton deceased, before testator's marriage assigned the manor of Walworth, Co. Londonderry in trust for testator after his said Frederick Hamilton's death, and by deed of settlement 2 April 1726 the said manor of Walworth was assigned to trustees for use of testator's younger children. Said Frederick Hamilton died in 1748 and the testator obtained from the Corporation of Fishmongers, London, a new lease, expending £7,215, and £200 yearly rent more than the former rent. Reciting that the manor of Freemore, Co. Londonderry and Manor of Beresford, Co. Cavan were also vested in trustees for his younger children and testator has paid the portions of his four eldest daughters and charged said lands with £9,998 10s. 0d. for his two youngest daughters.

Witnesses: Hans Bailie, Edward Sterling, Dublin, Esq., Benjamin Higgins, Dublin, gent.

Memorial witnessed by: Edward Sterling, Benj. Higgins.

226, 80, 146279 C. Tyrone (seal)

308 BELL, Dr. GEORGE, Bellsgrove, Co. Tyrone, Doctor of Physick. 29 June 1739. Full 2¼ pp. 11 May 1763.

My eldest son John Bell. A deed of settlement made on my intermarriage with Martha Ewing deceased his mother. My other younger children Samuel Bell, Barbara Bell, Anna Bell, Eliza Bell and Martha Bell (all unmarried and under 21 years). George Bell, Armagh, merchant and William Delap, Dublin, merchant, exors. My real estate in Co. Tyrone.

Witnesses: Clotworthy O'Neill late of Shains Castle, Co. Antrim, deceased, John Gordon, Belfast, Co. Antrim, merchant, Alexr. Young, late of Belfast, merchant, deceased.

Memorial witnessed by: Michael Duffey, James Dobbin, both Dublin, gents.

225, 334, 146434 Samuel Bell (seal)

309 RATH, JAMES, Irishtown.

26 Feb. 1757. Narrate 1 p. 30 June 1763.

His wife Jane. His son Patrick Rath. His son Law Rath. His daughter Mary Wall. Mary Russell, Ann McGloughlin, Ann Faulkner. James Carrolan's children. William Filgate, Lisreny, Pat. Johnston, Dromcashell, exors.

His leases of Irishtown [situation not mentioned] adjoining northerly Lilburn's holding, westerly Terence Byrne's holding, Neal McCan's holding easterly, Thomas Hoyes [or Hayes] holding westerly.

Wintesses: Patt. McDavitt, Atherdee, John McLoughlin, Downstown, smith, Patrick Gurish, Drumcashell, farmer, all in Co. Louth.

Memorial witnessed by: Patk. Gurish, John Hutton, Dublin, gent.

226, 201, 147045 Patrick Rath (seal)
his mark

310 SLATOR, HENRY, Summerhill, Co. Dublin, gardener.

31 Oct. 1762. Narrate ¾ p. 18 July 1763.

His wife Mary Slator, exor. His brother John Slator. Patrick Cahill, exor. His holding wherein he then dwelt, with the garden ground thereunto belonging, Col. Joshua Paul lessor. A house and garden leased to James Reilly [situation not mentioned].

Witnesses: John Neal, Dublin, ale draper, Patrick Farrell, Dublin, gardener, John Tyldesley, Dublin, instrument maker.

Memorial witnessed by: Patk. Farrell, Owen Brady, Dublin, gent.

222, 114, 147251 Mary Slator (seal)
her mark

311 RAINSFORD, MICHAEL, Dublin, gunsmith.

11 Dec. 1756. Précis ½ p. 19 July 1763.

To his daughter Mary Rainsford £800 when 21 years or on marriage. Her brother James Rainsford. His daughter Frances Hutchinson, her son Michael Hutchinson. His real and personal estate.

Witnesses: Jno. Govers, gunsmith, Wm. Hughes, grocer, Robt. Wallis, notary public, all of Dublin.

Memorial witnessed by: Edward Glass, Dublin, gent., Hannah Barker, wife of Thomas Barker, Ratoll, Co. Kildare, gent.

226, 265, 147255 Wm. Barker (seal)
the now husband of said Mary Rainsford

Mary Barker (seal)
otherwise Rainsford wife of said William Barker

312 IRWIN, CHRISTOPHER, Ratoath, Co. Meath, gent.

21 Nov. 1758. Narrate ¾ p. 17 Aug. 1763.

Testator was eldest son and heir at law of Christopher Irwin late of Ratoath aforesaid, and formerly of Rockfield, Co. Roscommon, Esq. deceased.

His real and personal estate to his brother Percival Irwin, provided he lived to attain the age of 21 years: in case his said brother should die before attaining said age all to his mother Elizabeth Irwin, extx.

Witnesses: James Currin, John Dalton, grocers, Wm. Crowe, gent., all of Dublin.

Memorial witnessed by: Wm. Crowe, Richd. Cudmore, clerk to said Wm. Crowe.

220, 598, 147463 Eliza Irwin (seal)

313 BUCKLEY, JOHN, Bray, Co. Wicklow, farmer.

7 April 1758. Narrate ½ p. 20 Aug. 1763.

To his brother Leonard and Anthony Buckley one shilling each. To Rev. Dr. John Lyons (exor.) of Bray parish benefit of a lease then held under Lord Fitzwilliam known by the name of Kilbride, also another lease under same Earl called Proctor's holding, and a lease under the Earl of Meath all said lands being in the parish of Bray, half Barony of Rathdrum, Co. Wicklow.

Witnesses: James Bowden, Bray, clerk and schoolmaster, Christopher Harland, Bray, wigmaker, Martin Dugin, Bray, smith.

Memorial witnessed by: James Bowden, William Magin, Dublin, gent.

223, 122, 147495 John Lyon (seal)

314 SODEN, JAMES, Sligo, Co. Sligo, Esq.

24 April 1763. Narrate 1½ p. 19 Nov. 1763.

His wife Jane Soden. Five shillings to each of his brothers and sisters.

His estate of Grange, Runroe and Castlecorn, Barony Carbury, Co. Sligo. Houses etc. in Holburn(e) Street, Sligo, Benjamin Burton, lessor. Farm of Mo(n)ynean, parish of Dromclive [Drumcliff] held from Owen Wynne, Esq. Farms held under Lord Palmerston that is to say the Island of Dernish, Contemplish([1]), the west part of Drumfads and the Black Park in said Barony of Carbury.

([1]) Farm described as Clonteprocklish in memorial No. 148428 Thos. Tibboe to Jane Soden and others dated 3 Oct. 1763.

Witnesses: Abraham Martin, Barrett Knott, Christopher Jones, all of town of Sligo.

Memorial witnessed by: Barrett Knott, Thos. Tibboz, Sligo, gent.

223, 320, 148427 Jane Soden (seal)

315 VAUGHAN, GEORGE, Buncranagh, Co. Donegal.

23 June 1753. Précis 1½ p. 23 Nov. 1763.

Nephew Basil Brooke, Esq., Gustavus Brooke, nephew of testator, brother of said Basil Brooke.

George, Lord Archbishop of Armagh, Primate of all Ireland, William, Bishop of Derry, the Bishop of Clogher, the Bishop of Raphoe, Edward, Bishop of Elphin, Joseph, Bishop of Kilmore, Henry, Bishop of Meath, St. George Caulfield, Esq., Lord Chief Justice of H.M. Court of King's Bench, Henry Singleton, Lord Chief Justice of H.M. Court of Common Pleas, Rev. Thos. Barnard, clerk, rector of Magheral, Rev. Edward Golding, clerk, Archdeacon of Diocese of Derry, Rev. Richard Leake of Londonderry, Anthony Foster, Dublin, Esq., and Andrew Knox, Prehen, Co. Londonderry, Esq., trustees. His estates in Co. Fermanagh and all other lands.

Witnesses: Henry Bartly and Thomas Bartly both of Buncranagh, smiths, George Gillasphy, Buncranagh, wheelwright, Rev. Richard Leslie, Londonderry, Edward Gillasphy the younger, Buncranagh, yeoman.

Memorial witnessed by: Thos. Bartly, Richd. Cowen, Lifford, Co. Donegal, gent.

221, 432, 148461 Gustavus Brooke (seal)

316 JOHNSTON, JAMES, Park Street, Co. Dublin, clothier.

13 Sept. 1749. Narrate 2 pp. 10 Dec. 1763.

His wife Mary Johnston. Her mother Martha Leigh. Francis and Robert Leigh her brothers. Isaiah Johnston his brother's son. Testator's sister's daughter Mary Feairbrother wife of Abraham Feairbrother. Her brother Benjamin Robinson, testator's nephew. Abraham Johnston his brother Phineas Johnston's son. His brother

Phineas Johnston. His brother's son James Johnston. His cousin Abraham Fairbrother and Samuel Gale, weavers, trustees. Money to be equally divided between testator's wife and the children of his brothers George and Phineas Johnston and the children of his sister Elizabeth Robinson.

His lease from the Earl of Meath on the Comb. Lease from Andrews and wife now under Thomas Litton [situation not mentioned]. Lease from Elizth. Willcocks, Joseph and Hannah Barcroft; lease from Martha Verscoyle [situations not mentioned]. A lease under Richard Witherall in Coles Alley. Lease from Richd. Wilemott in Dunchans Ally. A lease from Wm. Craigale in Parks Street and now the testator's dwelling house.

Witnesses: John Woodman, Spittlefields, Dublin, weaver, John Whitlock, Park Street, Dublin, silk weaver.

Memorial witnessed by: John Whitelock, Thomas Callaghan, Dublin, gent.

227, 469, 148712(1) Mary Feairbrother (seal)

317 BATTERSBY, WILLIAM, Cloonybreny, Co. Meath, gent.

14 April 1759. Narrate 2 pp. 20 Dec. 1763.

His wife Mary Battersby. His son Robert Battersby, exor. His son Thomas Battersby, exor. His son John Battersby. His grandson William Battersby. His three daughters Martha Kellet, Mary Sherrock and Caroline Hawkins. His brother-in-law Ambrose Sharman, Killcarty, Co. Meath, exor.

His farms of Pickettstown (Puckettstown, Buckettstown) and his part of Diamor, Co. Meath. His lease and farm of part of Cloonybreny and the Parks whereon he then dwelt Hilleherry (Hillebarry, Hillabarry). His lease and farm of Little Park next adjoining the Gray Bog in Smithstown and Dogstown, Co. Meath. Lease of Corlough, part of Thomastown and lease and farm of Philipstown both in Co. Meath.

(1) The pagination of this book of transcripts is incorrect; it runs pages 1 to 523, then 424 to 635. Memorial number 148712 will be found in the second sequence following page 523.

Witnesses: Luke Toole, Cloonybreeny, gardener, Worship Bocker, Cloonbreeny, gardener, Myles Reilly, Loghcrew, schoolmaster, all in Co. Meath.

Memorial witnessed by: Francis Lowndes, gent., attorney, Terence Coghlan, writing clerk, both of Dublin.

229, 19, 148831 Robert Battersby (seal)

318 READING, ROBERT, Dublin, Esq.

Died Sunday 8 Jan. 1764. 25 Dec. 1763. Full 1½ p. 11 Jan. 1764.

My friends Michael Chamberlain and Barry Colles both of Dublin, Esqrs., trustees. My brother Benjamin Reading. My sister Elenor Reading otherwise Coughlan.

My estate and lands of Derrycooly and other lands in King's Co. now in lease to Vance Wetherall, Esq. My part of Tullymorehan and Derrooly in said county, part of Derrooly in lease to John Holmes, Wm. Higgins, and Terence Cassidy tenants of part of Tullymorehan lands.

Witnesses: Richd. Jackson, Dublin, Doctor of Laws, Franklin Drury, Dublin, gent., Constantine Cullen, Dublin, Esq., Deputy Registrar of the High Court of Chancery.

Memorial witnessed by: William Costello, Dublin, gent., Joshua Meredith, Clonegown, King's Co., Esq.

223, 455, 148982 Barry Colles (seal)

319 DAVIES, BENTON, Galway, apothecary.

27 Nov. 1763. Narrate 1 p. 31 Jan. 1764.

Anne Mathews otherwise Davies, exor., wife of Arthur Mathews of said town of Galway and sister to testator. Her eldest daughter Mary Mathews, Deborah Mathews second daughter, Isabella Mathews third daughter and Bridget Mathews fourth daughter of said Arthur and Anne Mathews, all unmarried. His cousin Thos. Davies, Newcastle, Co. Galway, gent., exor. His real and personal estate.

Witnesses: Rev. Michael Gilway, Galway, clerk, John Hamlin, Galway, alderman, Charles Westlake, Galway, gent.

Memorial witnessed by: Charles Westlake, John Hamlin.

229, 51, 149208 Anne Mathews (seal)

320 DOMVILLE, WILLIAM, Queen Street, London, formerly of Jermyn Street, parish of St. James within the Liberty of Westminster, Middlesex, Esq. 7 July 1759. Full 3½ pp. 3 Feb. 1764.

My cousin the Rt. Hon. Sir Compton Domville of Templeoge Co. Dublin, Bart., one of the Privy Council in Ireland, exor. Theodore Clements, Dublin, Esq., Edward Knatchbull, Templeoge, Esq., late one of the Masters of the High Court of Chancery in Ireland, trustees. My nephew Rev. Benjamin Barrington, Dublin, son of my sister Barrington; said Benjamin Barrington or any male issue to take name of Domville when in possession of testator's estates. To Hon. Admiral John Forbes, second son of Earl of Granard all my books in England and also all my French manuscripts relating to the Revenues of France in England, and all my books and manuscripts in Ireland. Capt. Thomas Forbes of the parish of St. Marylebone, Middlesex. Miss Jane Hooke, daughter of my friend Nathaniel Hooke, Esq. Capt. George FitzGerald of St. James Street. Felix MacDonnagh, surgeon. Edward Dickinson, parish of St. Clement Danes, Middlesex, gent., exor. Legacies to servants Judith Berry, John Dennis, Elizabeth Ford, Thomas Steel, and the Incorporated Society of Dublin for promoting English Protestant working schools in Ireland.

All my manors, messuages, farms, lands, tenements and hereditaments in city of Dublin, in counties of Dublin and Meath and elsewhere in Ireland. My houses in Jermyn Street and at Brompton, Middlesex.

Witnesses: William Heineken, Frederick Kandler, John Garden, London.

Memorial witnessed by: Michael Nowlan, Dublin, Daniel Hogan, Dublin, gent.

222, 372, 149267 C. Domvile (seal)

321 BRAUGHALL, RICHARD, Kildare, Co. Kildare, victualler. 14 Jan. 1759. Narrate 1 p. 20 March 1764.

His wife Mary Braughall exor. His eldest son Jno. Braughall. His youngest son Michl. Braughall. His daughters Mary Ann Braughall and Elizabeth Braughall. Rev. Robt. Caulfield, clerk, exor.

His farm and lands of Knocknagally, Co. Kildare leased from Mr. White of Pitchfordstown. His lands of Youghall leased from Earl of Drogheda. Lands called the Half Acres near Kildare and the farm and lands called Broadhooks near Kildare leased from Earl of Kildare and lands, premises etc. in town of Kildare. Farm and lands of Clondown. Farm and lands of Ballynague(1) leased from the widow Stephens.

Witnesses: Henry White, Dublin, gent., Patk. Nowland, Kildare, victualler, Chas. Geoghegan, Naas, Co. Kildare, merchant, James Moore, Ballyneage, Co. Kildare, woodmonger.

230, 147, 149894 Richd. Braughall (seal)

322 NEALE, HANNAH otherwise PAUL, widow of Archdeacon Benj. Neale. 16 Jan. 1764. Précis ¾ p. 20 March 1764.

One fifth part of her towns and lands to her grandson the Hon. Edward Stratford.

Town and lands of Ballyhackett otherwise called Ballynackett, Coole, Barnhill otherwise called Barnekill, Knocklissonemore otherwise called Knocklessinemore, Knocklissenebegg otherwise called Knocklessinebegg, Rathvilly and Knockavagh, Co. Carlow. Ballycolane, Ballyvass and Hubberstown, Co. Kildare.

Witnesses: Thomas Eyre, Dublin, Esq., Morley Saunders, Saundersgrove, Co. Wicklow, Esq., William Crowe, Dublin, gent.

Memorial witnessed by: William Crowe, Richard Cudmore clerk to said William Crowe.

229, 174, 149900 Edward Stratford (seal)

---

(1) Possibly the townland of Ballyneage or Hybla, Co. Kildare.

323 SAMPSON, ROBERT, Killbrook, parish of Castleknock, Co. Dublin. 16 Sept. 1760. Précis ½ p. 26 March 1764.

His wife Elinor Sampson, exor. James Glascock, Dublin, Esq., exor.

The house and lands of Killbrook, Co. Dublin, leased by testator from the Rt. Hon. William Connolly, Esq., deceased by the name or description of part of the lands of Dunsink, Co. Dublin.

Witnesses: Henry Glascock, Daniel Magusty, William Finlay, all of Dublin, gents.

Memorial witnessed by: Daniel Magusty, Henry Kempston, Dublin, gent.

231, 251, 149963 Elinor Sampson (seal)

324 GASCOIGN, ELIZABETH, Dublin, widow of Rev. Thomas Gascoign. 4 Oct. 1763. Précis ½ p. 20 April 1764.

To Luke Annelly, Dublin, cabinetmaker, exor., all the residue of her effects, goods and chattels.

Witnesses: James Rothery, Dublin, stone cutter, William Sharman, Dublin, shoemaker.

Memorial witnessed by: James Rothery, Thomas Judge, Dublin, writing clerk.

229, 246, 150272 Luke Annelly (seal)

325 COPE, ANTHONY, Dean of Armagh.

7 June 1760. Codicil 26 March 1764. Full 8 pp. 5 May 1764.

My wife Sarah. My brother Arthur Cope exor. My brother Barclay Cope. My brother John Cope. My brother Robert Cope. Wm. Viscount Grimston, Harbottle Luckyn, Esq., brother to said Lord Grimston, and Samuel Wegg, Lincoln's Inn Fields, Middlesex, Esq.

My estates in Co. Armagh, in city of Dublin and elsewhere in Ireland. My manor of Mount Norris, Co. Armagh being the town and lands of Killcarraneightra, Killcarranoughtra, Macknavarry, Moytoone, Cornure, Cullentra, Dromer, Dromero, Kiddebegg, Tullallin, Tullyharrin, Kiddimore, Ballygorman, Derryclincan, Derrychucan and mill, Mount Norris, Two Shesraghs, the moiety of Kiercon, Kinkon, Dunclaire and Drumclarre, 4,300 acres. Also the town and lands of Granges of O'Neillan [? Grange Lower and Grange Upper, Barony Oneilland West] otherwise the Grange of O'Neiland otherwise the Grange of Oneland, Barony O'Neland, Co. Armagh, 586 acres. My house at Hoghill in Dublin in which I now live(mentioned in codicil).

Witnesses: Frances Austen, Thomas Gregory, John Mockcallah, London, gents.

Codicil witnessed by: Rev. William Tisdall, Rev. Henry Blacker, clerks, Denis Doran, gent., all of Dublin.

Memorial witnessed by: David Buttle, Dublin, gent., Talbot Forde, Dublin, gent.

223, 610, 150365 Artr. Cope (seal)

326 ARMSTRONG, ANDREW, Ballencard, King's Co., gent.

19 March 1764. Narrate 1 p., 26 June 1764.

His wife Elizabeth Armstrong. His nephew Harry Wilson. Alexr. Piersy, Garradice, Co. Leitrim, Esq., George Tares, Mackin, Co. Cavan, Esq., trustees. Lands of Nedd and Cornagie, Co. Cavan.

Witnesses: John Judge, Moyally, King's Co., gent., William Whitfield, County Glass, King's Co., and Arthur Higgs of same.

Memorial witnessed by: John Judge, Thos. Bole, Mackin, Co. Cavan, farmer.

237, 2, 151324 Eliza Armstrong (seal)

327 OWENS, JAMES, Killbreedy, Co. Limerick, gent.

9 April 1764. Narrate 1½ p. 26 June 1764.

Reciting that Jeoffery Owens late of Killbreedy, gent., being seized in fee farm and possessed of the lands of Killbreedy died lately intestate without issue leaving the said James Owens his only brother and heir-at-law, and that the said James Owens (the testator) demised the said lands to his nephew John Hiffernan of Killbreedy. Testator confirms said lease of said lands in Barony Cushma, Co. Limerick to said nephew subject to a jointure payable to said Jeffery Owen's widow.

Witnesses: John Rourke, Killmalock, Co. Limerick, merchant, Luke Speerin, Rahamarkig, Co. Limerick, gent., Dominick Sheahan, Rostkenys, Co. Kerry, gent.

Memorial witnessed by: Dominick Sheahan, Dennis Hiffernan, Killbreedy, said County, gent.

233, 47, 151326 John Hiffernan (seal)

328 QUIN, LAWRENCE, Henry Street, Dublin, bricklayer.

29 Nov. 1763. Précis ½ p. 10 July 1764.

His wife Mary Quin. His three children. Effects "to be divided between his . . . . ."(1). His house in Henry Street.

Witnesses: Edwd. FitzSimons, Moffeet, Dublin, bricklayer, Wm. FitzSimons, Phrapper Lane, Dublin, bricklayer, John Long, Dolphins Barn Lane, Dublin, tanner.

Memorial witnessed by: Terence Coghlan and John Hutton, both Dublin, gents.

232, 187, 151632 Mary Quin (seal)
her mark

329 BROWN, JOHN, Dublin, merchant.

18 Feb. 1762. Narrate ¾ p. 27 July 1764.

His wife Margaret, extx. His three sisters Mary Baker, Alice Moore, and Margaret Brown. His three nieces Jane, Mary and Elizabeth Baker. His brother Robert Brown died at Kingston, Island of Jamaica and left his father John Brown, since deceased, sole heir and exor. The father John Brown renounced in favour of testator.

Witnesses: Robert Leigh, Killner Swettenham, merchant, Murray Kathrens, gent., all of Dublin.

Memorial witnessed by: Killner Swettenham, William Hall, Dublin, gent.

226, 629, 151853 Mary (recte Margt.) Brown (seal)

(1) There is a blank in both original and transcript but the words "wife and children" might be inferred here.

330 CAMPBELL, CATHERINE, wife of Colin Campbell, Esq., then a lieut. of 42nd Regiment of Foot or Royal Highlanders, formerly of Athlone now of Dublin. [Date not recorded]. Narrate ¾ p. 28 July 1764.

Her husband Colin Campbell exor. Her sister Frances Glass. Lands of Clonowen, Ballymullee, Cox Castle and Bonegard with her lands of Sliebane, Co. Roscommon.

Witnesses: Allen Campbell, Capt. in said 42nd Regiment of Foot, Alexr. Drummond, Ensign in said regiment, and John Grant a private soldier in said regiment.

Memorial witnessed by: John Campbell, Dublin, Esq., William Magin, Dublin, gent.

229, 591, 151871 C. Campbell (seal)
(Colin Campbell, testator's husband)

331 CALDWELL, SARAH, Dublin, spinster.

26 June 1761. Précis ½ p. 15 Aug. 1764.

All real and personal estate to her mother Bridget Caldwell, Dublin, widow.

Witnesses: Saml. Evans, Dublin, gent., James Plunkett, Dublin, gent., Alexr. Carroll, Dublin, Esq.

Memorial witnessed by: James Plunkett, Henry White, Dublin, gent.

230, 436, 152092 Bridget Caldwell (seal)

332 ONGE, JOHN, Hayestown, Co. Dublin.

" Lately deceased " [Date of Will not recorded]. Narrate 1 p. 25 Aug. 1764.

Lieut. Abel Onge, eldest son of his cousin Samuel Onge of Luke Street, Dublin, merchant. Lieut. Walter Onge, second son of said Samuel Onge. Francis Onge third son of said Samuel Onge. Samuel Onge fourth son of said Samuel Onge. Joshua Davis, Dublin, counsel at law and Charles Alder, Dublin, attorney, trustees and exors.

Town and lands of Hayestown, Co. Dublin. A house in Cuckoo Lane, Dublin, held by testator by virtue of a lease for lives from -Stepney, Esq., to Hannah Doddridge.

Witnesses: Arthur Maguire, Francis Harvey and Joseph Bayly, all of Dublin, Esqrs.

Memorial witnessed by: Joseph Bayly and Wm. Bayly, Dublin, gent.

233, 76, 152201 Abel Onge (seal)

333 KENNEDY, DAVID, Ballymaglack, parish Comber, Co. Down. 30 Sept. 1763. Full 1¼ p. 27 Aug. 1764.

My wife Mary Kennedy. My father-in-law Thos. Jackson, exor. To my son David Kennedy 11/4½d. If said Mary Kennedy remarries Thomas Jackson, Ballyregan, Hugh Kennedy, Ballyneglack and James McNawel of Ballybean, all Co. Down, to dispose of part of [my] lands for support of my children " till my son James arrives at age, first my daughter Mary Kennedy, James Kennedy, Susanna Kennedy and Martha Kennedy if she comes home and John Kennedy." Remainder of goods to be divided equally between " my wife and younger children viz. my wife Mary Kennedy, my son Thos. Kennedy, my daughter Mary Kennedy, my son James Kennedy, my daughters Martha, Susanna Kennedy and my son John Kennedy."

My farm in townland of Ballyalley(1).

Witnesses: James McNall, Ballybean, farmer, deceased, James Neill, Dunlady, and John McHaffey, Ballymaglack, farmers.

Memorial witnessed by: James Neill, Henry Joy, Belfast, Co. Antrim, printer.

236, 118, 152207 Thomas Jackson (seal)

334 KEON, AMBROSE, Dublin.
2 Sept. 1748. Précis ½ p. 11 Sept. 1764.

All real and personal estate to his daughter Ann Keon.

Witnesses: James Nixon, then Dublin, gent., one of the attorneys of H.M. Court of Exchequer in Ireland, Edwd. Warren, then Dublin,

(1) Situation not mentioned. Possibly Ballyalloly in Cumber parish is intended.

gent., one of the attorneys and an officer of the said Court of Exchequer, Geo. Sparks, Dublin, gent., one of the attorneys of said Court of Exchequer.

Memorial witnessed by: Geo. Sparks, Thos. Tyrrell, Dublin, now serving man to the said Ann Keon.

230, 470, 152316 Ann Keon (seal)

335 PARKS, SAMUEL, North Street, Newry[1].

11 April 1747. Narrate ¾ p. 1 Oct. 1764.

His brother John Parks, Dublin. His sisters Anne and Bell[a] Parks. His servant man Bryan O'Hear. His sister Elizabeth Parks, extx., [of Ruskie, Co. Down]. His real and personal estate.

Witnesses: Edmond McGoirk, gent., Thomas Seaton, weaver, both of Ruskie, John Young, Donaghy, Co. Tyrone, Thomas McNaughton, Ruskie, gent.

Memorial witnessed by: John Hutton and Terence Coghlan, Dublin, gents.

232, 314, 152471 Elizabeth McNaughton otherwise Parks (seal)

336 BALL, JOHN, Frederick Street, Dublin, Esq.

6 March 1763. Full 4 pp. 20 Dec. 1764.

My wife Margaret Ball, Thomas Ball, Seapark, Co. Wicklow, Esq., Richard Jackson, Colraine, Esq., and Richard Jackson, Forkhill, Co. Armagh, Esq., trustees and exors. My dear step-daughter Martha Ransford. My stepson Robert Ransford. My sister Araminta Caulfield. A ring and plate to my daughter Dorothea Margt. Shinton and her children quite out of power of her husband Richard Shinton. My cousin Captain Saml. Ball now in Germany. My old servant Bryan Murphy. My old friend Mrs. Eliz. Adams alias Kyle. My friend Mar. Paterson, Serjeant at Law, Esq. My friend Doctor Chas. Lucas.

---

(1) This will is not listed in "*Index of the Prerogative Wills of Ireland*" (Vicars), but is included by Betham in his abstracts of Prerogative Wills where it is shown as proved 5 May 1747 (Genealogical Office MS. 242, p. 362).

Lands of Loughross, The Island of Loughross, Creenkill, Tullyard, Clarbane, Ratreelan, Creeockeeran and the moiety of the customs of the Fair of Cross and the commonage thereunto belonging, Ballyonan otherwise Ballsmoore Upper and Lower, Scarve McKea, Anahecussy Darsy, Mullag[hg]lass, Stripe of Camolly Darsy, Lisdromgrany, Carcacullen, Cargarovaddy and Tullynamaloge [Co. Armagh]. Three Castles and other lands in Co. Kilkenny. A lease of the house, gardens and 70 acres of land [situation not mentioned] to Folliott Warren, Esq., dating from March 1763.

Witnesses: John Shee, Charles Butler, Robert Murphy.

Memorial witnessed by: Mark White, Dublin, Esq., John Hill, clerk to said Mark White.

238, 147, 153561 Richd. Jackson (seal)

337 POWER, JOSEPH, Loughrea, Co. Galway.

25 Dec. 1764. Narrate 1¼ p. 29 Jan. 1765.

His wife Julian Power. His only son David Brandon Power. James Daly, Carrownakilly, Co. Galway, Esq., trustee. His kinsman James Burke of Iserclearan, Co. Galway, gent.

Rathruddy, Cahernamuck, Gortnamanagh and Liscub, Co. Galway. Real estate devised to him by David Power late of Boulybane, Co. Galway, Esq., deceased, that is to say Boulybane, Ballyboggin and all the rest of the real estate in Co. Galway devised by him to testator. Breafaninlare, Barony Tyrawly, Co. Mayo. His leases of Caher, and several houses etc. he held in town of Loughrea from Earl of Clanrickard.

Witnesses: Thomas Burnet, John French, Philip Mayne and Redmond Stapleton, all of Loughrea, Co. Galway.

Memorial witnessed by: Philip Mayne, Thomas Burnet.

238, 190, 153953 Julian Power (seal)
widow of testator

338 GRAHAM, RICHARD, Ballymascad, Co. Down, farmer.

31 Jan. 1761. Full 1 p. 5 Feb. 1765.

To my wife Elizth. Graham, extx., and my daughters Ann

Graham, Elizth. Graham and Mary Graham half of my farm in Ballymascad leased from James Ross of Portavoe, Esq. The other half to my three daughters Sarah Graham, Jane Graham and Margt. Graham. My two sons Francis Graham and John Graham and my grandson John Graham a British shilling each. My daughter Letitia Graham otherwise Frizell, wife of John Frizell of Ballyloughans, Co. Down.

Witnesses: Thomas Jackson, Ballyregan, Co. Down, farmer, John Houston, Church quarter, parish of Dundonald, Co. Down, farmer, James Savage, Ballyregan, farmer.

Memorial witnessed by: Thomas Jackson, Henry Joy, Belfast, Co. Antrim, printer.

238, 214, 154098 Elizth. Graham (seal)
her mark

339 DARCY, DANIEL Dublin, cordwainer.

23 Dec. 1757. Précis ½ p. 12 Feb. 1765.

His wife Sarah Darcy, extx. His son George and daughter Mary Darcy. All his worldly substance and effects.

Witnesses: William Stewart, Dublin, gent., Gregory Maguire, Dublin, weaver.

Memorial witnessed by: Wm. Stewart, John Bath, Dublin, breechesmaker.

238, 226, 154210 Sarah Darcy (seal)

340 DOOLAN, THOMAS, Portumna, Co. Galway.

20 April 1764. Narrate 1 p. 24 March 1765.

His wife. His son William. Testator's brother William. His brothers Nicholas and John. His sisters. His brother-in-law Mr. Williams. His father, his wife and brother William exors.

His Portumna concerns, Cappahubbuk, cowpasture and two tenements, cabbins and gardens. To his eldest son his leasehold interests and lands subject to payment of £400 to his younger children equally between them. Reversions he is entitled to on the death of his father and mother-in-law should go for use of his wife and children equally during their lives and afterwards to young Mr. Richard Tidd to whom he leaves Mr. White's note.

Witnesses: Walter Hardiman, James Frith, Edward Burke.

Memorial witnessed by: Edward Burke, Nathl. Coates, Eyrecourt, Co. Galway, farmer.

238, 281, 154478 Wm. Doolan jr. (seal)
Wm. Doolan the younger.

341 CURTIS, HENRY, Ham[m]on[ds]town, parish of Clonalvy, Co Meath. 24 Sept. 1764. Narrate ½ p. 21 March 1765.

His wife Agnes Curtis exor. His second son Collumb Curtis exor. His eldest son John Curtis. His youngest son Peter Curtis. His daughter Mary, unmarried. His leases. The house of Haminstown [Hammondstown] in which he dwelt.

Witnesses: Michl. McCanna, of the Naul, Co. Dublin, land surveyor, Andrew Dougherty, Hannontown, servant to testator, Zacherias Ralp [? Ralph], servant to testator.

Memorial witnessed by: Wm. Magin, Wm. Fitzgerald, Dublin, gents.

233, 387, 154643 Collumb Curtis (seal)

342 GRAMES(1), RICHARD, Ballymesca, parish Dundonald, Co. Down, farmer. 20 Feb. 1760. Full 1¼ p. 29 March 1765.

My wife and my daughter Ann Grames exors. My sons John Grames and Francis Grames. My daughter Letitia Grames. John Grames son to my son Richard Grames deceased 1/1d. Richard Grames son to my son James Grames deceased 1/1d. My farm or land, one side next to John Glenholme's [situation not mentioned].

Witnesses: Robert Orr, Portgribb, parish of Castlereagh, Co. Down, farmer, James Grames, Ballylisbredan, parish of Dundonald,

(1) Surname probably Graham. Compare with No. 338.

farmer, Thomas Nightengeal late of Carryreagh parish of Dundonald, farmer, deceased.

Memorial witnessed by: Robert Orr, David Henderson clerk to Henry and Robert Joy of Belfast, Co. Antrim, printers.

238, 322, 154706 Elizabeth Grames
her mark
widow of testator (seal)

343 CUPPAIDGE, RICHARD, Moate, Co. Westmeath.
1 May 1764. Narrate 2½ pp. 4 April 1765.

His nephew John Loftus Cuppaidge. His nephew George Cuppaidge. Mary Cuppaidge eldest daughter of his brother John Cuppaidge. Jane Cuppaidge second daughter of his brother John Cupppaidge. Elizabeth Stothard eldest daughter of his sister Jane Stothard. Rachel Stothard second daughter of his said sister Jane Stothard. George Cuppaidge, Dublin, paper frame maker, son of John Cuppaidge, deceased, late of Drumcondra Lane, gardener. Samuel Waring, Warringstown, Co. Down, Esq., and Holt Waring his brother, trustees.

Lands of Ballybroder, Capalaghy Low [? Lower], Derrygoland, Derryreaghand, Ralurton, Co. Westmeath. His two leases in Clara, King's Co.

Witnesses: Richard Homan, Moat Grenogue, Co. Westmeath, gent., Rev. John Mulock, Bellair, King's Co., clerk, John Potts, Moat Grenogue, distiller.

Memorial witnessed by: John Potts, Thomas Dease, Dublin, gent.

235, 393, 154757 John Loftus Cuppaidge (seal)

344 NICHOLSON, THOMAS, Upper Ballykineen, Queen's Co., gent. 17 March 1723/4. Full 2 pp. 26 April 1765.

My wife Jane Nicholson. My son Richard Nicholson exor. My grandson Thomas Nicholson, under 21 years. My son-in-law Darby Kennedy. To my grand-daughter Jane Peirce one heifer that grazes with Morrish Grumly. My two sons-in-law John Peirce, exor., and William Mossop. Lands of Upper Ballykineen, John Edgill and his wife lessees.

Witnesses: Thomas Cantrell, late of Gortnaclay, Queen's Co., gent., Loughlin Finlay, Fordras, said Co., farmer. Dennis Delany, Killurin, King's Co., schoolmaster.

Memorial witnessed by: John Corbitt, Castlegoff, Queen's Co., shoemaker, John Edgill, Ballykineen, farmer.

235, 416, 154963 Richd. Nicholson (seal)

345 PENROSE, SAMUEL, Waterford city, gent.

19 Jan. 1764. Précis ½ p. 18 May 1765.

To George Randle and Cooper Penrose of Cork, merchants, trustees, his real and personal estate.

Witnesses: Thomas Boyse, Waterford, Esq., Saml. Sprigg, Waterford, gent., Theodore Cooke, Waterford, notary public.

Memorial witnessed by: Thos. Boyse, John Lymbery, Waterford, gent.

238, 423, 155399 Anne Penrose (seal)
widow of said Samuel and guardian of his children named in said Will.

346 FRENCH, MARY otherwise TOWGOOD, wife of Savage French, parish of St. Nicholas, Cork. 1 Nov. 1764. Full 2¼ pp. 20 June 1765.

My husband Savage French exor. My eldest son Sampson Towgood French. My three younger sons Savage French, Richard Temple French and Mathew Deane Towgood French. My five daughters. My daughter Elizabeth Savage French, my daughter Catherine French, my daughter Melian Towgood French, my daughter Sarah French, my daughter Dorcas French.

My estate in [Baronies of] East and West Carbery [Co. Cork] which devolved to me from my father and my deceased uncle Sampson Towgood.

Witnesses: John McDonald, Cork, linen weaver, William O'Brien, of South surburbs of said city, nailor, Thos. Costello, Glasseen, surburbs of said city, linen weaver and bleacher.

Memorial witnessed by: Thomas Costello, James Wherland the younger, Cork, gent.

238, 482, 155887 Savage French (seal)

347 MITCHELL, ANNE, Bellagalda, Co. Roscommon, widow. 11 April 1761. Narrate 1¼ p. 5 July 1765.

Her son Thomas Mitchell of Bellagalda. Her cousin Thomas Davis son to her cousin Geffry Davis of Cloonfinouge. Her daughter Catherine Knight. Her grandson John Knight. Her said son Thos. Mitchell and Rev. James Blear, clerk, exors. £10 to buy a piece of plate with the Ormsby's arms to her cousin Thomas Davis in token of his father's friendship to her in her troubles. Annuity arising out of lands of Derrynall (Derrynale) to William Lennon of Greyford, Esq., as trustee.

Witnesses: Susy Mathews, Cloonfinouge, widow, Theobald Burk, Tumard, farmer, James Dunnagher, Cloonfinouge, servant, all in Co. Galway.

Memorial witnessed by: James Dunnagher, Geffry Davis, Cloonfinouge, gent.

242, 156, 156129 Will. Lennon (seal)

348 WEIR, ELIZABETH alias BENNETT alias WALKER, Dublin. 24 Oct 1737. Narrate, part in full, 1½ p. 3 Aug. 1765.

Reciting indenture 28 Dec. 1705 made between John Sproule, Dublin, clothier, of the one part, and Samuel Bennett, Dublin, tallow chandler and William Colles, Dublin, brewer, of the other part, whereby said John Sproule conveyed to them a house or tenement in Thomas Court alias Thomas Court Bawn within the liberties of Thomas Court to the use of William Walker for life and after his death to use of Elizabeth Bennett otherwise Walker otherwise Weir late wife of said Wm. Walker. Said William Walker and said Elizabeth Bennett intermarried soon after executing said deed.

My son Samuel Walker, exor. 1/- to my son John Walker. To be buried in parish churchyard of St. James.

Witnesses: Phil Portal, Hugh Carmichael, John Speer, junior, Will. Sumner, notary public.

Memorial witnessed by: Jonathan Morgan, Dublin, goldsmith, Henry Stearne, Dublin, gent.

242, 240, 156492 Saml. Walker (seal)

349 SHEERER (SHURER), HUGH, Cessnagh, Co. Londonderry, farmer. — Jan. — Narrate 1 p. 10 Aug. 1765.

His wife Mary Morrison. His daughter Margaret. Her sister Ann and Mary. His brother John Morrison of Clagan and William Morrison of Dromore and his brother Jonathan Shurer of Cessnagh, Londonderry, exors.

Witnesses: Hugh Morrison, Dromore, John Sheerer, Ballymore, Joseph Morrison, Dromore, all Co. Londonderry.

Memorial witnessed by: John Sheerer, Dominick McCausland, Dublin, gent.

244, 110, 156564 William Morrison (seal)

350 KEATING, JOHN, Dorset Street, Dublin. [Date not recorded]. Précis ¼ p. 27 Aug. 1765.

His daughter Catherine Keating.

Witnesses: Paul Smith, Dorset Street, gent., John Laurent, Mountrath Street, Dublin, merchant, Elizth. Darassue, Blank Street, Dublin, spinster.

Memorial witnessed by: John Laurent, Robt. Ormsby, Dublin, gent.

233, 580, 156716 Catherine Keathing (seal)

351 BALDWIN, SIR BRIDGES, Wallington, Co. Surrey. By name of Bridges Baldwin, Esq., of Dublin, 13 Feb. 1745. Narrate part in full 2 pp. 27 Sept. 1765.

Settlement made 25 May 1738 previous to his marriage with his wife by name of Frances Ne[y]noe, spinster, daughter of Joseph

Ne[y]noe, Dublin, merchant of the lands of Ballysumaghan, Barony Tyrrell, Co. Sligo, held from See of Elphin. Leasehold interest and houses in Winetavern Street formerly called The Pied Horse Inn but then known by the name of Baldwin's Court, were assigned to Rev. Charles Baldwin and Urmston Pepys, Esq., trustees in said indenture named. Testator confirms said settlement to his wife Frances Baldwin otherwise Ne[y]noe, extx.

Dwelling house on South side of Molesworth Street near Stevens Green which he purchased from Charles Bucknall, Esq. His real and personal estate in Great Britain and Ireland which he was possessed of by virtue of the last Will of his uncle John Bridges then late of Wallington, Surrey, deceased. His house wherein he then dwelt with the coach house, stables, vaults and cellars etc. situated on Abby Street in the lordship of St. Mary's Abbey, surburbs of city of Dublin, which testator purchased from Anna Maria Pollard, widow of Dillon Pollard, deceased. Goods, chattles and personal estate to which he was then entitled by the last Will of his aunt Elizabeth Bridges then late of Wallington, Surrey, spinster, deceased.

Witnesses: Joseph Malone, Dublin, hosier, Richard Campsie, late of same, cabinetmaker, deceased, Michael Carter, Dublin, sadler.

Memorial witnessed by: Joseph Malone, William Williams, Dublin, notary public.

238, 568, 156924 Fra. Baldwin (seal)

352 BROWNE, JOHN, commonly called SIR JOHN BROWNE, the Neal, Co. Mayo. A further codicil 12 Sept. 1762. Narrate, 1 p. 8 Nov. 1765.

Reciting that by his first codicil to his Will testator had left the house and farm of Raheens [? Co. Mayo] to his third son Dodwell Browne in tail male. He now empowers said Dodwell Browne to make leases of said house and farm.

Witnesses: James French and Francis French, both of the Neal aforesaid, Bartholomew Nowlan, servant to said John Browne.

Memorial witnessed by: Bartholomew Nowlan, Jackson Walsh Delacour, Dublin, gent.

242, 414, 157311 Dodwell Browne (seal)

353 SHAW, ALICE, Galway town, widow of Robert Shaw late of Galway, Esq. 8 Dec. 1748. Narrate 1 p. 9 Nov. 1765.

Her son Robert Shaw. " Legacies to the children of the said Alice Shaw therein named" [not recorded](1). Her brother-in-law James Molony and her nephew Croasdaile Miller, Esqrs., exors.

Farm and lease of Clostokin, Co. Galway, a deed concerning said lands was executed between testator and the rest of the heirs at law of her father Thomas Croasdaile, Esq., deceased.

Witnesses: John Johnson then of Galway, burgess, but now of Ballinasloe, Co. Galway, watch and clock maker, Edward Shields and John Hamlin, both then of town of Galway, burgesses, but now of said town, aldermen.

Memorial witnessed by: John Johnson, Edward Shields, John Hamlin.

245, 59, 157341 — Robt. Shaw (seal) son of testator, Capt. in H.M.'s 43rd Regt. of Foot.

354 McDONNELL, ALEXANDER, Gort, Co. Galway. 29 May 1760. Narrate ¾ p. 14 Nov. 1765.

" To his well-beloved son-in-law Richard Allen the house which he then possessed and enjoyed in the town of Gort." His son Charles McDonnell. His daughters Mary and Cecilia. A lease which he held in town of Gort. Rev. Dean Nethercotes, trustee. His friend Thomas Allen and James Gardner, exor.

Witnesses: Thomas Allen, Monivae, Richard Allen, Kilbegg, both Co. Galway, linen weavers, Martin Mannin, Galway, shoemaker.

Memorial witnessed by: Richard Allen, John French.

244, 223, 157562 — John McDonnell (seal) (" John Donnell, Woodford, Co. Galway, wheelwright, one of the exors. and residuary legatees of said Alex. McDonel.")

(1) The Will of her husband Robert Shaw, dated 20 Oct. and proved 23 Dec. 1737, mentions his wife Alice Croasdaile, sons Robert, William, George Croasdaile, John, Richard and Thomas Shaw, daughters Mary, Mercy and Elizabeth Shaw. (Genealogical Office MS. 246, p. 144).

355 JOHNSTON, THOMAS, Dublin, Major of 56th Regt. of Foot.
4 Oct. 1765. Narrate 2 pp. 5 Dec. 1765.

His wife Angel Johnston. His son Jno. Johnston. His son Henry Johnston. His brother-in-law Adam Noble, Longfield, Co. Monaghan, Esq., his brother-in-law Jackson Wray, Ballycastle, Co. Antrim, and his brother John Johnston, Urchar, Co. Armagh, Esq., trustees. His niece Elizabeth Johnston, daughter of his brother Graham Johnston. The children of his sister Charity Shekleton. The children of his brother John Johnston.

His estate of town and lands of Camilly, Co. Armagh, and Coolfoord, Co. Meath. His dwelling house in Suffolk Street, Dublin.

Witnesses: Thos. Benson, Dublin, clerk, Stephen Reynolds, Dublin, apothecary, John Wolverston, Dublin, gent.

Memorial witnessed by: John Wolverston, Jno. Hunter, clerk to said John Wolverston.

241, 183, 157946 Jackson Wray (seal)

356 CUTLER, GEORGE, Banagher, King's Co., shopkeeper.
12 Jan. 1763. Narrate 1 p. 10 Dec. 1765.

To his wife Bridget Cutler farm and lands of Kilnemeelcum and his house, shophold and tenements in Banagher and all other his real and personal estate. His brother Richard Cutler.

Witnesses: Bryan Flyn, Cloonbegny, Co. Roscommon, yeoman, Thomas Coy, Loughrea, Co. Galway, carpenter.

Memorial witnessed by: Thomas Coy, Andrew Tierney, Kellygrove, Co. Galway, gent.

246, 314, 158016 Richard Cutler (seal)

357 TYLER, JOSHUA, M[o]ygara, Co. Sligo, gent.
4 Dec. 1764. Narrate ¾ p. 17 Dec. 1765.

My brother John Tyler. To Bridget Tyler otherwise Ford £5 per annum for life. All good and chattles to my two daughters Susanah

Tyler and Elinor Tyler and their mother Bridget Tyler. My nephews Wm. Tyler and Arthur Tyler. Jas. Tyler son of Jas. Tyler, Claragh, Co. Sligo. Mr. Jas. Tyler, Claragh, Co. Sligo, gent., and Mr. Andrew Baker, Colstlaghlane, said Co., gent., exors. My farms of Cabragh, Collmullen (Collmullin) and Cloghane, Co. Sligo.

Witnesses: Mathew Baker, Ragwood, Thos. Powell, Cloghane, Bartly Flanagan, Moygara, all Co. Sligo, gents.

Memorial witnessed by: Thos. Powell, John Doe of said county.

241, 205, 158112 Jas. Tyler (seal)

358 READING, JOHN (BORR), Readingstown, Queen's Co., Esq.

20 Aug. 1739. Full 2½ pp. 7 Jan. 1765.

My eldest sister Margaret Reading. My brother Robert Reading. My sister Ellinor Coghlan, a jointure on the estate of Kilcolgan, King's Co., to which she will be entitled upon the death of her husband Anthony Coghlan. My sister Begnet Reading. My father John Reading, Esq. My brother Benjamin Reading, merchant, exor. Debts due to Terence Geoghegan, Dublin, lately deceased, Ralph Briscoe, Ballycowen, King's Co., gent., Francis Geoghegan, Channell Row, brewer, lately deceased, James Bradshaw, Dublin, mercer, Maurice O'Connor, Cappagarron, King's Co., Esq., William Graham, Platten, Esq., Daniel Conyngham, Dublin, merchant, John Barker, Dublin, linen draper, and Thos Tailford, Ballyna, King's Co., gent., and by me and brothers and sisters to said Briscoe.

My estate in the manor, towns and lands of Reddingstown, a mortgage thereon due to John Damer, Esq., and portions already charged thereon for " my brothers and sisters by my father's marriage settlement."

Witnesses: Thomas Tailford, King's Co., James Keays, Killena, King's Co., Charles Stewart, Old Conagh, Co. Dublin.

Memorial witnessed by: Charles Stewart, Michael Heagerty, Dublin, writing clerk.

249, 7, 158320 Benj. Reading (seal)

359 FALKINER, SARAH, Dublin, widow.

27 Sept. 1765. Full 1 p. 9 Jan. 1766.

To be buried in churchyard of St. Patrick's church in the same grave with my father. All residue of my estate to my only son Frederick Falkiner, exor. To Miss Sarah Spence the daughter of Mr. Abraham Spence now of London, merchant, £150 when 21 years or married. To Rebecca, Mary and Melinda Mathews £20 each. My servants Peter Barnwell and Sarah Gibbons. To my kinsman Capt. Robert Spence and to Dr. John Spence £400 each. The widow of my late kinsman Abraham Spence. Malinda Gavan. My great grand-daughters Elizabeth and Anne Gale. The two daughters of Mr. John Betagh. The three sons of Alderman Benjamin Gale now Lord Mayor of Dublin. Rev. Mr. Hopkins.

Witnesses: Robert Hamilton, Esq., James Maddock, gent., both of Dublin.

Memorial witnessed by: Robert Jones, public notary, Dublin, John Robinson his clerk.

242, 570, 158350 Fredk. Falkiner (seal)

360 JOHNSTON, JOHN, Castle Dawson, Co. Londonderry, clothier. [Date not recorded]. Sworn 2 Dec. 1765. Narrate 1 p. 14 Jan. 1766.

His wife Mary Johnston. His two sons Duncan Johnston (elder) and John Johnston. His daughter Jane Johnston, unmarried. His daughters Sarah Hamersly and Margaret McNeil. His grand-daughter Mary McNeil. Said Duncan Johnston and Samuel Laird, Magherafelt, Co. Londonderry, apothecary, exors.

The mill tenement in the town of Castle Dawson with the land thereunto belonging.

Witnesses: Mathew Webb, mason and Robert Johnston, clothier, both of Castle Dawson, Ezekiel Richardson, Magherafelt, yeoman.

Memorial witnessed by: Ezekiel Richardson, Robert Dawson, Magherafelt, yeoman.

248, 55, 158400 John Johnston (seal)
son of testator

361 TAYLOR, RICHARD, Askeaton, Co. Limerick, Esq.

3 Dec. 1763. Narrate 1 p. 27 Jan. 1766.

His son Richard Taylor. His daughter Sarah Crowe. His grandson Francis Crowe.

His farm held by Patrick and Martin Fitzgerald called Moye in said county and Barony Sheiny [? Shanid]. The house and garden held by testator from Robt. Hewson [situation not mentioned].

Witnesses: William Devenport, John Busteed, Wm. Aherrin, Mathw. Connor, all of Askeaton, farmeis.

Memorial witnessed by: John Busteed, Robt. Hickson, Ballykeale, Co. Limerick, gent.

244, 404, 158540 Sarah Crowe (seal)

362 LEISTER, THOMAS, Dublin, farrier.

17 Sept., 1753. Précis ¼ p. 28 Jan. 1766.

To his wife Elinor Leister otherwise Mehard (exor.) all his estate.
Witnesses: Mich. Mitchell, John Dawson, William Keating, all of Dublin.

Memorial witnessed by: William Magin, William Fitzgerald, Dublin, gents.

246, 444, 158608 Elinor Leister (seal)

363 STAINES, ROBERT, Great Newtown, Co. Dublin, farmer.

5 Sept. 1751. Narrate 1½ p. 20 Jan. 1766.

His wife Martha Staines. His son Robert. His daughter Jane Staines. His daughter Margt. His daughters Martha, Mary, Ruth and Susanna. His friend Thomas Taylor, Clarkstown, Co. Dublin, gent., and his son-in-law Peter Newman, Chambers Street, tailor, exors.

Lands called Bracknehill, 10 acres [situation not mentioned]. His leasehold, 20 acres, being part of Great Newtown.

Witnesses: James Midgley, Chambers Street, weaver, Mat. Daniell, of same, scrivener, William Luke, of same, clothier.

Memorial witnessed by: William Magin, William FitzGerald, Dublin, gent.

246, 445, 158609

John Anderson (seal)
Martha Staines (seal)

Martha Staines, wife of testator.
" John Anderson wife [husband] of the within named —Staines one of the daughters of the said Robert Staines."

364 FOORD, NICHOLAS, Limerick, Esq.

7 Dec. 1763. Narrate, part in full, 1¾ p. 8 Feb. 1766.

His wife Elizabeth Foord. His second son Abraham Foord exor. His daughter Martha Foord otherwise Royce now the wife of Thos. Henry Royce. If her heirs become entitled to testator's estates they are to take the surname of Foord. My eldest and undutiful son Nicholas Foord.

The town and lands of Clounkeen, Caherilly West and Ballyblake, Co. Limerick, and of Cloonclenan, Ballyneclogh and Carnarry in county of the city of Limerick, and of Ballyrichard Morris in Co. Tipperary. Town and lands of Carron, Shanbally, Mahung and Adrigain, Co. Tipperary and Drumsillagh, Co. Clare. " All my houses, tenements and hereditaments in the cities of Cork, Waterford and Limerick."

Witnesses: Henry Hunt, Fishamble Street, Dublin, apothecary, William Gibbons, Wine Tavern Street, livery lace weaver, James Canter, Wine Tavern Street, gent.

Memorial witnessed by: James Canter, Wm. Magin, Dublin, gent.

241, 273, 158834 Abraham Foord (seal)

365 WARREN, MARY, wife of Folliott Warren, Lodge, Co. Kilkenny, Esq. 8 March 1764. Full 1¼ p. 27 Feb. 1766.

My husband. Money deposited in my hands by my late dear sister Morres to be paid to Haydock Evans Morres her only son. My nieces Isabella and Mary Morres. My sister Sarah Warren. My brother Lieut. Eben. Warren. My sisters Anna Maria and Eliza Warren.

Lands bequeathed to husband. "Any lands I have right in Counties of Tyrone, Derry or any other county after my dearest husband's life which I became intitled as heir to my grandfather Sir Robt. Staples to my dearest cousin Sir Robert Staples, Bart. for life" . . failing his issue said lands to eldest son of my uncle the late Rev. Thomas Staples. The three daughters of my late uncle. To Sir Robert Staples my father's picture. Anty Coddy £20. Alderman Hans Bailey and Rev. Nicholas Martin, exors.

Witnesses: Nichs. Mackey, Burnchurch, Co. Kilkenny, gardener, John Kennedy, late of Three Castles, Co. Kilkenny, late butler to said Folliott Warren, Jane Russell, late of Three Castles aforesaid, waiting maid to said Mary Warren and now of Kilkenny and married to said John Kennedy.

Memorial witnessed by: Nichs. Mackey, Thomas Armstrong, Dublin, writing clerk.

24, 299, 159091 Robt. Staples (seal)
Ebenezer Warren (seal)

366 CROWE, ROBERT, St. Francis Abbey, near Limerick, skinner. 29 April 1763. Full ½ p. 27 Feb. 1766.

My wife Hannah Crowe exor. Wm. Holland, only son of Philip Holland Sword Bearer of Limerick, exor. All my worldly substance houses leases and tenements.

Witnesses: Joseph Holland, junr., Richd. Speve, John Bently, all of Limerick.

Memorial witnessed by: Joseph Holland, Wm. Fitzgerald, Dublin, gent.

239, 394, 159092 Wm. Holland (seal)

367 FULLER, JOSEPH, the younger, Thomas Court, Liberty of Thomas Court and Donore, Dublin, gent. 12 July 1762. Full 1 p. 8 March 1766.

My brother Abraham Fuller. Joseph Thomas Fuller, son of my said brother Abraham Fuller. My brother John now unmarried.

Said two brothers exors. I am intitled to an estate in the lands of Crossintown, Barony of Farbill, Co. Westmeath, expectant on the death of my father Joseph Fuller.

Witnesses: Luke Reilly, St. Thomas Court, Dublin, hatter, Thomas Bewley, junr., Clare Street, grocer, Thos. Reilly, Dublin, serving man to testator.

Memorial witnessed by: Thos. Reilly, Samuel Hatch, gent., clerk to Adam Williams, Dublin, Esq.

243, 206, 159251 Abm. Fuller (seal)

368 PERKINS, JOHN, Dublin, gent.

13 May 1763. Précis ½ p. 14 March 1766.

Francis Harvey, Dublin, Esq., and John Fenn, Johnstown, Co. Carlow, gent., trustees.

Lands of Ballintrane and Ballymogue, Co. Carlow purchased by testator from Marinus James Kennedy, Esq. Part of lands of Oldtown, Co. Carlow, held by lease from Beauchamp Bagnall, Esq., for lives of testator, his brother Theophilus Perkins and his cousin Theophilus Perkins.

Witnesses: William Harvey, Thornton Francis Ryan, James Hornidge, all of Dublin, gents.

Memorial witnessed by: William Cotton, linen draper, Joseph Waddy, gent., both of Dublin.

243, 221, 159309 John Fenn (seal)

369 BELL, GEORGE, Creighton's Grove, Co. Tipperary.

20 April 1747. Narrate ½ p. 17 March 1766.

His wife Mary then enceinte. His eldest son Saml. Bell. To his daughter Jane Bell (under 10 years) £500 when 21 years or on marriage. Jno. Scott, Limerick, Geo. Tutehill, Flaha, Co. Limerick, and testator's said wife Margaret Bell, exors. His real and personal estate.

Witnesses: John Barrett, James Jordan, John Carden.

Memorial witnessed by: James Jordan, Modereny, Co. Tipperary, farmer, Talbot Carroll, Emill, King's Co., gent.

241, 337, 159335 Jane Labatt (seal)
Jane Labatt otherwise Bell,
daughter of testator

370 JOHNSTON, LETITIA, wife of George Johnston, Dublin, Esq.
8 Feb. 1764. Full 1½ p. 29 April 1766.

Reciting indenture of 29 June 1757 between said George Johnston of the first part and the said Letitia Johnston otherwise Molesworth of the second part, and John Moland, Dublin, Esq., and Richd. Holmes, Dublin, gent. of the third part. George Johnston my present husband. My brother Capt. Robt. Molesworth. My brother Richard Molesworth. My sister Juliana Herbert. My niece Letitia Herbert. Said John Moland and Richard Holmes trustees. My cousin Lieut. Oliver Richard Lambert. John Lambe, Esq., Counsellor at law. My uncle John Moland, Esq. My sister Elizabeth Holmes, wife of Richard Holmes, Dublin, gent. My sister Jane Clootwyk. My sister Amelia Molesworth. My sister Isabella Molesworth. Thos. Coghlan, Dublin, merchant, son to the late John Coghlan, Esq., and grandson to the late Dr. Henry Maule Bishop of Meath, exor.

Witnesses: John Lambert, Lawrence Pearson, both Dublin, gents., and Henry Maguire, clerk to said Thos. Coghlan.

Memorial witnessed by: Bryan Meheux, gent., John Lambert.

241, 385, 159932 Juliana Herbert (seal)

371 CURTIS, ROBERT, Inane, Roscrea, Co. Tipperary, clerk.
19 Oct. 1764. Codicil 14 Feb. 1765. Narrate ½ p. 30 April 1766.

His second son Chas. Curtis, Inane, Esq. Lands of Mucklow, Ballynagh, Clonagh and Clare all in Barony Ballycowen, King's Co. Part of Killananay set to Gilbert Tarlton and part set to Robt. Drought Esq., Killaghy set to Michael Duigan, all in Barony Ballyboy, King's Co.

Witnesses: Chas. Colombine, Cliveden, Co. Clare, clerk, John Samrose, Inane, servant to said testator.

Codicil witnessed by: Robt. Carew Armstrong, Mount Heaton, King's Co., John Minchin, Busherstown, King's Co., Esq., Mathias Walker, Roscrea, Co. Tipperary, clerk, and said John Samrose.

Memorial witnessed by: John Samrose, Wm. Dale, Dublin, clerk to John Evans, Dublin, gent.

241, 396, 159982 Chas. Curtis (seal)

372 TROTTER, STEPHEN, Duleek, Co. Meath, Esq.

22 March 1764. Full 1 p. 7 May 1766.

My son Thos. Trotter. My sister Ram. My sister Jane Stuart. My friend Jas. Grattan, Esq., Recorder of Dublin and Richd. Levinge, Dublin, Esq., trustees and exors. Stephen Ram, son of Humfries Ram of London, Esq. My nephew Chas. Stuart, his sister Rebecca. Mr. Edward King. Wm. Knowles my apprentice to be paid £50 when 25 years. My real and personal estate.

Witnesses: Abel Ram, Ramsfort, Co. Wexford, Esq., Edwd. Curtis, Dublin, apothecary, Richd. Cooke, Dublin, butler to testator.

Memorial witnessed by: Edwd. Curtis, Edwd. King, Dublin, gent.

241, 415, 160123 Thos. Trotter (seal)

373 VESEY, MARY, alias DIXON alias ORMSBY, Dublin, widow of Wm. Vesey late of Dublin, Esq. 2 Feb. 1761. Full 3¾ pp. 22 May 1766.

To be buried in vault in St. Mary's Church, Dublin, near late husband Wm. Vesey, Esq. My sister Mrs. Frances Vandaleur, Dublin, widow. My nephew John Ormsby Vandaleur, second son of said sister Vandaleur; my nieces Frances Vandaleur and Mary Vandaleur. My nephew Francis Vandaleur, Esq. My nephew Richd. Vandaleur. Mrs. Mary French my aunt's daughter. My sister Mrs. Sarah Donnellan. My niece Frances Donnellan the only daughter of my said sister Sarah Donnellan. My nephew Gilbert Donnellan, Esq., his brother John Ormsby Donnellan.

Mrs. Mary Wilcock my old servant. My own maid Catherine Hawks. My old servant Wm. Gratty. Mary Brookes the widow of my old servant Henry Brookes. Major Thomas Marlay second son of the late Lord Chief Justice Marlay. My friend and companion Ann Maxwell. £20 to poor of St. Mary's parish. My sisters Frances Vandaleur and Sarah Donnellan exors.

Town and lands of Ballinamona and all my lands etc. in Co. Limerick. Lands which I hold under the See of Ossory. Reciting indenture of 19 July 1735 made by testator by name of Mary Dixon, Dublin, widow, and others charging £500 for use of my sisters Frances Vandaleur then wife of John Vandaleur, Esq., and Sarah Donnellan then the wife of Edmd. Donnellan, Esq., on the lands of Innis Jordan otherwise Enis Jordan, Gortdorabogher alias Gortderaghboher alias Gorterabogher, Gortsheely alias Gortshely, Upper Verdins alias Verdons, Lower Verdins alias Verdons, John Lynch FitzGeffry and Jeffry Lynch FitzDominick's gardens, Gortenore alias Gortenone, Gortalake alias Gortnelecky, Gortnecappa alias Gortnecappagh, Seaghnamawooly alias Seaghnamawwooley, the two Lenaboys alias Leneaboys, Gortelangin alias Gortalangan, Lowsichill alias Lowsyhill, Gortnatebbar alias Gortatubber, Stonegartaboge alias Clonegurtebogue, part of Gortnadronagh alias Gortedronagh, Cappalagin alias Cappalagan, Gortnecaskey alias Gortcaskin alias Gorteaskin, Gortnecanna alias Gortacumna, Gortneflemings alias Gortnafleming, Cappadroniagh alias Cappadronagh alias Cappadronogh alias Capparonagh, Cappoghloghmore alias Cappacloghmore, Cappatellaghan(e), Killuricky alias Killcorky, Cappaboncarnea alias Cappaghboncanera, Cappabanngure alias Cappaleamger, Cappaneplay alias Cappaghneplay, Dunagh, Tempane alias Tempine, Carrow Jordan, Cappareandony alias Cappaghriandonagh alias Cappaghriondara, Cappanecorky, Gortunna alias Gortunagh alias Gortuna, Cappaseda alias Cappaghsadda, Omeryfaddy and several parcels of land late the property of Ann Blake, Geoffry Lynch, Geoffry Font and Mathew Martin FitzNicholas and Richard Blake in the county of the town of Galway. My dwelling houses and offices and houses in Henry Street, Dublin.

Witnesses: Richard Dawson, Wm. Bury and Mark Whyte, all of Dublin, Esqrs.

Memorial witnessed by: Mark Whyte, Dublin, Esq., Joseph Chalmondeley, Dublin, butler to Frances Donnellan, Dublin, widow.

241, 464, 160379

Frances Donnellan (seal)
the surviving exor.

374 WEST, ANDREW, Drumcondra Lane, dairyman.

27 March 1735. Full 1½ p. 30 May 1766.

My wife (extx.) to have £20 " to be divided among my nearest relations at the direction of the parish priest." My niece Mary West alias O'Hara. John Mathews. Mary Mathews. Joan Hurtwood. Christopher West. Lawrence West. Lawrence Mathews. Jude Kelly's daughter. Michael McAway, Easter McAway. My house and gardens and field [situation not mentioned].

Witnesses: James Carbery, Edward FitzGerald, Edward Heley, all of Drumcondra Lane, Co. Dublin, gardeners.

Memorial witnessed by: William Keeling, bricklayer, William Grantham, shoemaker.

248, 418, 160474 Mary O'Hara
her mark

375 LOVETT, JOHN, Rathlyon, King's Co., Esq.

13 Nov. 1765. Précis ½ p. 2 June 1766.

His wife Mary Wheeler alias Lovett. His son John Lovett. Sir Wm. Parsons of Birr, Bart., and his cousin John Loyde of Gloster, King's Co., exors. His real estate. His lease of Glascarig.

Witnesses: John Hamilton, Whitehaven, Great Britain, surgeon, Geo. Twentyman, Breyton near Cockermouth, Great Britain, steward, John Younghusband, Cockermouth, ale draper.

Memorial witnessed by: Wm. Crowe, Dublin, Bury Blakeney, Dublin, clerk to said Wm. Crowe.

241, 488, 160519 Mary Ann Lovett (seal)

376 AKIE, WILLIAM, Lisalong, Co. Monaghan.

[Date not recorded](1). Narrate ¾ p. 26 June 1766.

To his brother Andrew Akie and his sister Margaret Akie one half each of his lease of Lisnalong.

(1) An abstract of this, a Clogher Diocesan Will, in the Swanzy Collection of Wills at the Genealogical Office, gives its date as 30 April 1765.

Witnesses: Michael Connolly, Raw, Margaiet Akie, testator's sister who since intermarried with James Nixon of Rock Corry, Co. Monaghan, Martha McCorry, Lisnalong, Co. Monaghan.

Memorial witnessed by: Michael Connolly, Richard Dawson, Loughony, Co. Monaghan, attorney at law.

245, 198, 160967 James Nixon (seal)
guardian to above Andrew
Akie who is a minor

377 BARRY, MARY, Ballindreat, Co. Donegal, gentlewoman.
31 Aug. 1758. Narrate 1 p. 4 July 1766.

Half of Sheercloon near Ballindreat, Co. Donegal to her brother John Fitzgerald of Ballyshannon, Co. Donegal the half of remaining half to Robert Armstrong, Ballindreat, the remaining quarter to Isaac Fitzgerald and John Fitzgerald her nephews. Alice Keys wife to Roger Keys of Lifford. Her nephews Isaac Armstrong and Christopher Aimstrong. Mary McKim her grandniece. Mr. David Armstrong of Murlagh, Co. Donegal and Robert Armstrong exors.

Witnesses: David Jenkins, John Keys and John Thompson all of Strabane, Co. Donegal, gents.

Memorial witnessed by: John Thompson, John Keys.

245, 215, 161103 Dav. Armstrong (seal)

378 MOUNTCASHELL, STEPHEN VISCOUNT, Moore Park, Co. Cork. (" Stephen Moore the elder of Moore Park, Co. Cork, Esq., and late the Rt. Hon. Stephen Lord Viscount Mountcashell "(1). 29 May 1763. Full 9 pp. 2 Aug. 1766.

Mentions a suit concerning the validity of a Will set up and pretended to be the Will of Robert Colvill, Esq., deceased, and verdict found against said pretended Will. My late wife Alice Moore otherwise Colville was the only sister and heiress at law of the said Robert Colvill(2). Reciting indenture dated 25 June 1762 made by

(1) Stephen Moore of Kilworth, Co. Cork was created Baron Kilworth of Moore Park in 1764 and Viscount Mountcashell 22 Jan. 1766.

(2) *The Complete Peerage* by G.E.C. states that he married 21 Nov. 1719 Alicia sister and heir of Robert Colvill and daughter of Hugh Colvill who was son and heir of Rt. Hon. Sir Robert Colvill.

testator and said Alice his wife whereby Charles Caldwell, Dublin, Esq., became trustee for them of said Robert Colvill's estate in counties of Antrim, Dublin and Kildare. Having already provided for my daughter the Rt. Hon. Mary Countess of Inchiquin now make provision for my younger sons and other daughters by the said Alice. My second son Colvill Moore. My third son William Moore. My fourth son Robert Moore. My daughter Elizabeth Moore (unmarried). My daughter Catherine Moore (unmarried). My eldest son Stephen Moore, exor. Rt. Hon. John Ponsonby, Esq., now one of the Lords Justices of Ireland and Speaker of the House of Commons of Ireland and Rt. Hon. Charles Earl of Drogheda trustees. My daughter Sarah San(d)ford and her husband.

Lands etc. in Co. Antrim: The late Dissolved Abbey or Monastry of Kells otherwise Dysert, Galgorm, Ballykyle, Ballynecloss, Tyson otherwise Thyson, Tannebrannan, Fenagh, Carmacky, Killelea otherwise Killelees, Carondonby otherwise Carrondonny, Broghlimont otherwise Broghnemolt, Maghiylosk, Carumeny otherwise Carnumnick, Ballycloys, Tullybacky otherwise Collnabacky, Derrygarreen, Broghdone otherwise Broghdohane, Tullygrilly otherwise Tavaghgreely, Tullypatrick, Crankill otherwise Cramkilly, Cabra, Cornelea, Drumfine, Tirrereagh otherwise Tirreagh, Killdony, Ballywatermoy, Moylarg otherwise Moighlargy, Fenaghy, Tullaghgarly, Glenwry otherwise Glenwhirry, Knockboy, Broghshane otherwise Little Broghshane, Buckna, Ballynecard [Ballynacaird] otherwise Ballymucknecard, Carustroan otherwise Ballycarustroany, Douglass, Crossneladdy otherwise Ballycarustroany, Douglass, Crossneladdy otherwise Crosslady, Menishmore, Cashell, Tecloy otherwise Ballytickleagh, Milldreen, Tonoghbreck otherwise Tanenaghbreck, Altiho otherwise Antenenam otherwise Altnehana, Clegan otherwise Clegny, Glanravell, Tulloge, Ballygally, Cloghnenermy, Rukeel otherwise Ballyruckall, Lissneheld otherwise Lissnekilge, Rufftine otherwise Rukan otherwise Ballyrukan, Donnemulcan, Ballynermy, Lisbreen otherwise Ballylisbrine, Lisselistry otherwise Lisnesilistrie, Ballycloghan, Eglish otherwise Ballyeglish, Kenbelly, Rossharry, Erghmagh, Aghafatan, Lisnechroghery, Coreen, Shillnavoggy, Slemish, Ballysallagh, Dunduffe, Ballygonespick, Ballynulto, Kells otherwise Templemurry, Ballylisnagumgall, Cornaugh otherwise Ballycarnake, Tullymoyland otherwise Ballytullaghmoyland (Ballytulloghmoland), BallyMcVey, Farnisky otherwise Cornaugh otherwise Ballyfagisky, Freballyvilly, Applety otherwise Avelty,

Killdrum, Ballycromkelly, Ballyneslate, Ballyardilioframay, Ballyhagere, otherwise BallyMcCowan, Ballytanaghbreck, Ballygilgad, Frenagh otherwise Tullogharly(1), Glancurry otherwise Glanwhirry, Killconriola, Ballymena, Corminick, Ballyloghan, Loghnegarly, Drunveagh, Cabra, Carnelea, Ballyarvey, Donsoan, Killelug, Antecomitus, Clonteconnell, Clogher, Killflugh and Lennore and advowsons etc. of Killconriola, Ballymonagh and Kells, Co. Antrim. Lands of Ballycutland otherwise Ballycottland otherwise Cottlanstown, Donade, Fryanstown, Sillagh, Great Morganstown and Rahesker, Co. Kildare. Ballymore otherwise Ballymore Eustace, Ardenode otherwise Adenwood otherwise Adrdenought otherwise Ardnaright, Silverhill, Morganstown, Bryancann, Lugaclay, the two Ballydalys [? Ballydallagh], Tenihinch, Glasshamon, Season(s), Glassknock, Burrowsland, Beckfords Lands and Austins Land being five acres near the place commonly called the Horses Pass, Co. Dublin [recte Co. Kildare].

Witnesses: Dominick Sarsfield, Esq., Counsellor at Law, Richard Chartres, Dublin, surveyor and Inspector of the Custom House Quay, John Boland, Dublin, one of the attornies of H.M. Exchequer in Ireland.

Memorial witnessed by: Richard Chartres, Anthony Dempsy, Dublin, notary public.

245, 270, 161474 Colvill Moore (seal)

379 NESBITT, HUGH, Tullydonnell, Co. Donegal, Esq.

12 Dec. 1764. Précis ½ p. 5 Aug. 1766.

To his brother George Nesbitt, Esq., exor., his freehold of "Couladason in Cavan estate" [? Cooladawson], Co. Donegal.

Witnesses: James Smylie, Killtoole, John Stinson, Ardvarnock, Alexr. Finlay, Tullydonnell, all said county, farmers.

Memorial witnessed by: James Smylie, John Stinson, Alexr. Finlay, John Thompson, Strabane, writing clerk.

252, 14, 161500 Geo. Nesbitt (seal)

(1) It will be noted that some townlands are listed more than once. The order and variants of spelling found in the transcript have been adhered to.

380 PETERSON, WILLIAM, Ballynafoy, parish Anaghlone, Co. Down. 7 July 1766. Narrate ¾ p. 12 Aug. 1766.

His only son James Peterson. His farm of land then in his actual possession held under Bernard Ward, Esq., in Ballynafoy, Barony Upper Iveagh, Co. Down.

Witnesses: Saml. McMahen, James Sprot, both of Ballynafoy, farmers, Robert Thompson, Lissnasligan, Co. Down, farmer.

Memorial witnessed by: Saml. McMahen (McMahon), John Colvill, Dromore, Co. Down, gent.

247, 266, 161577 James Patterson (seal)

381 TRACY, JOHN, Dublin, carpenter.
27 June 1766. Narrate 1 p. 22 Aug. 1766.

My five grandchildren viz. Susanna Langin (now inter-married to John Nailor, Sergt. in 39th Regiment of Foot), Hannah Langin, Mary Langin, Elizabeth Langin, Rachel Langin. My six houses on north side of Tighe Street in parish of St. Paul, Dublin, Robert Barrett, the widow Wall, Thomas Kelly, John Coates, John Stewart and Owen Tommins tenants thereof. Robert Barnett, Dublin, cordwainer, John Stewart, Dublin, victualler, exors.

Witnesses: Zacharia Toulton, Dublin, cordwainer, John Fotteral, Dublin, gent.

Memorial witnessed by: John Fotteral, James Malloy, Dublin, writing master.

247, 290, 161707 John Stewart (seal)

382 EDKINS, GEORGE, Millstreet, Co. Dublin, gent.
10 April 1762. Narrate 1¾ p. 3 Sept. 1766.

His eldest son Rev. James Edkins. His second son Peter. His son George Edkins. His other children John Edkins and Rebecca Turner. His grandchildren George, Elizabeth and James Edkins (under 21 years) children of said son Peter. His four grandchildren.

His holding in Mill Street, Blackpitts, Wardshill and Newmarkett, Co. Dublin, held under Earl of Meath. His holding in Blackpitts leased from Merriott Dalway, Esq.

Witnesses: Ann Coulson, widow, Hugh Jefferies, grocer, Gilbert Allason, all of Dublin.

Memorial witnessed by: Christopher Lynham, Mill Street, Co. Dublin, brewer, Gilbert Allason.

247, 305, 161820 Peter Edkins (seal)

383 YARNER, CATHERINE, Dublin, widow.
9 May 1765. Full 1½ p. 7 Oct. 1766.

To be interred near my dear son in the family vault of the Yarners in St. Michan's, Dublin. All residue of real and personal estate to my brother Richard Bouchier, exor. My eldest sister Mary Bouchier. My brother Rev. Edward Bouchier of Hertford. My nephew the Hon. John Warde, Esq. My niece Mary Torkington. My nephew Rev. Edward Bouchier, son to my brother Edward Bouchier of Hertford. My nephew Henry Prittie. My niece Elizabeth Bouchier. My nephew John Bouchier. My nephew Chs. Bouchier, son to my brother Rev. Edward Bouchier. My niece Sarah Bouchier. My niece Emilia Bouchier. My friend Mrs. Mary Westby. My friend William Crookshanks, attorney at law, exor.

Witnesses: Samuel Cooke, Dublin, painter, Henry Stearne, Dublin, gent., Gilbert Allason, Dublin, public notary.

Memorial witnessed by: Geo. Crookshank, Dublin, gent., Gilbert Allason.

252, 150, 162161 Wm. Crookshank (seal)

384 BASTIFILL, JOHN, Russburrough, parish of Blessington, Co. Wicklow, victualler. 7 June 1760. Narrate ½ p. 16 Oct. 1766.

His wife Mary Bastifill. His son William Bastifill. His house built on part of his freehold [situation not mentioned].

Witnesses: Joseph Eager, Blessington, parish clerk, James Rily, Glasshina, Co. Wicklow, farmer, Robert Hoyle, Burgage, Co. Wicklow, farmer.

Memorial witnessed by: Joseph Eager, Terence Coghlan, Dublin, gent.

245, 381, 162252 William Bastifill (seal)

385 DAWSON, RICHARD, Drumintine, Co. Monaghan.
11 Oct. 1746. Narrate 3 pp. 14 Nov. 1766.

His wife Alice Dawson. To his two sons William Dawson, clerk, and Jeremiah Dawson lands of Maghernokelly, Barony Dartry, Co. Monaghan, John Lipton, Neal Smith, Bryan Finly tenants and half in possession of testator's son Jeremiah Dawson. His son [William's] Richard Dawson. His [William's] second son William Dawson, his third son John Dawson. Testator had provided for his other children upon their respective marriages. His eldest son James Dawson. His daughters Ann Drumgoole, Susanna Hall, Prudence Mitchell, Rebecca McClure otherwise Phillips and Sarah Harper. £1 2s. 9d. to poor of parish of Ematris.

Witnesses: William Whitesitt, Joseph Jackson, Ralph Semple, Monaghan, gent.

Memorial witnessed by: Ralph Semple, Edward Campbell, Dublin, gent.

254, 106, 162724 Jeremiah Dawson (seal)

386 MURGITROD, JANE, widow of Jonathan Murgritrod, merchant.
2 May 1761. Précis ½ p. 31 Jan. 1767.

To Mary Needham, Dublin, spinster, extx., rents etc. of her personal estate, being an interest in houses on the Upper Comb and in Fordom's Ally in trust for use of testator's daughter Mary Lindsay otherwise Murgritrod.

Names of witnesses not recorded.

Memorial witnessed by: Robert Acheson, Dublin, Saml. Adams, clerk to said Robert Acheson.

252, 416, 163892 Mary Lindsay (seal)

387 CUFFE, MAURICE, St. Albans, Co. Kilkenny, Esq.

7 May 1752. Codicil Feb. 1764. Narrate 3¼ pp. 5 Feb. 1767.

His wife Hannah Cuffe alias Bligh extx. His eldest daughter Mary Cuffe extx. His second daughter Ann FitzGerald alias Cuffe extx. Samuel Mathews, Bonnetstown, Co. Kilkenny, Esq., Joseph Evans, Belevan, Co. Kilkenny, Esq., trustees. Barnaby Demeve, stonecutter at Kilkenny. Codicil revokes bequest to testator's wife and confirms to his daughter Ann then married to Denny Baker Cuffe all the bequests in said Will made to her by description of Ann Cuffe alias FitzGerald.

Town and lands of St. Albans alias Killagh, Co. Kilkenny. His house of St. Albans. Trenchardstown, Co. Kilkenny, Fairfax Wallis, Dublin, Esq., lessor. Lands of Grange, Queen's Co., with rectorial and vicarial tythes and mills thereof (George Hartpole of Shrewle, Queen's Co., Esq., lessor), Killaree, Banenough alias Three Castles, Co. Kilkenny (Redmond Morris, Esq., lessor).

Witnesses: William Williams, notary public, Mark Gerrard, gent., Christopher Dalton, notary public, all of Dublin.

Witnesses to codicil: Elizth. Hartpole, Carlow, spinster, Richard Williams, St. Albans, steward, Francis Creery, St. Albans, gardener.

Memorial witnessed by: Joseph Evans, Esq., and Joseph Evans, junr., Esq., both of Belevan, Oliver Lodge, Shildrinagh, gent.

239, 597, 163984

Mary Cuffe (seal)
Denny B. Cuffe (seal)
Anne Cuffe (seal)
widow of Denny Baker Cuffe

388 DRAYCOTT, DOROTHY other LENTHALL, Dublin, widow.

25 Nov. 1765. Narrate ¾ p. 5 Feb. 1767.

Testator as only child and heir at law of her late father Wm. Lenthall the younger, Dublin, Esq., deceased, was entitled to lands in Co. Tipperary: Gortrowan, Killcormick otherwise Collecormick, Barnacallnilegan and part of Killward in parish of Templemore, Barony Eliogarty and Ikerrin. Having no issue she devised said lands etc. to her cousin Mrs. Susanna Curtis wife of Mr. Robert Curtis of Summerhill. Said Robt. Curtis exor.

Witnesses: George Hadsor, Dublin, merchant, Theophilus Perkins, Dublin, gent., Henry Fitzakly formerly servant to said Robt. Curtis.

Memorial witnessed by: George Hadsor, William Brown, shop-keeper to the said George Hadsor.

254, 251, 163988 Robt. Curtis (seal)

389 WILLINGTON, JOHN, Killoskehane, Co. Tipperary, Esq.

12 March 1756. Narrate 3 pp. 14 Feb. 1767.

His wife Mary Willington. His eldest son John Willington (under 21 years). His second son Jonathan Willington (do.). His nephew, John Willington, eldest son of his brother James Willington (do.). His nephew James Willington eldest son of his brother Jonathan Willington (do.). His nephew Jonathan second son of his brother Jonathan Willington. Testator's wife and said brother Jonathan Willington exors. and guardians of his said children. Lands of Killoskehane and Lisnegatt, Stephen Moore lessor.

Witnesses: Joseph Hall, Dolphins Barn, Co. Dublin, gent., John Humphreys and John Hayes, Dublin, gents.

Memorial witnessed by: John Humphrys, Edward King, Dublin, gent.

252, 465, 164138 John Willington (seal)
son of testator

390 SHARP, ANTHONY, Roundwood, Queen's Co., Esq.

30 May 1763. Narrate 2 pp. 14 Feb. 1767.

His wife Catherine Sharp. Rents of estates to his grandson Robt. Anthony Flood provided he takes surname of Sharp. His daughter Frances Flood. His brother Isaac Sharp. His brother Joseph Sharp. His sister Rachel Delany. His friends John Parnell and Martin Delany trustees.

His real estate of Cloneheen, Clarahill, Ballentine, Coolesane and Boyle with Upper Coolmoy in Queen's Co.; his freehold estate and houses in the county of the city of Dublin and in the Earl of Meath's Liberty and all other his real and freehold estates in Ireland. His estate and houses in Bristol in England (deeds in the hands of Mr. Henderson in Bristol).

Witnesses: Joseph Calcutt, Thomas Morton, both of Mountrath, Queen's Co., gent., Thomas Conway, Queen's Co., gent.

Memorial witnessed by: Joseph Calcutt, John Humphrys, Dublin, gent.

255, 176, 164143 Anthony Sharp (seal)

391 McCRAITH, ROBERT, Loughlogher, Co. Tipperary, gent.

18 Oct. 1766. Précis ½ p. 18 Feb. 1767.

To Thomas Grady, Killballyowen, Co. Limerick and William Lane, Dublin, Esq., his freehold lands and estates [situation not mentioned] upon trusts.

Witnesses: Hugh Callanan, Cashell, Doctor in Physick, John Hayman, Clonmell, gent., William Meagher, Carrigata, gent., all in Co. Tipperary.

Memorial witnessed by: James Tothall, James Gollock, both Dublin, gent.

252, 484, 164199 Thos. Grady (seal)
Wm. Lane (seal)

392 KING, THOMAS, Dublin.

14 Feb. 1767. Précis ½ p. 3 March 1767.

To his sister Ann King, extx., his house in Dublin being a lease under the Earl of Meath [situation not mentioned] "and a lease which he held from the Corporation of the town of Wicklow in the possession of William Hodgins." Sarah Nevin, Thomas Street. George Bennett, son of Carden.

Witnesses: Rev. John Croasdaile, curate of parish of Kennyty, King's Co.

Memorial witnessed by: John Humphrys, senr., John Humphrys, junr., Dublin, gents.

252, 526, 164398 George Bennett (seal)

393 ROACH, THOMAS, Balleese, Co. Wicklow, farmer.

23 June 1766. Full ½ p. 23 March 1767.

My mother Mary Roach. My brother John Roach. My child March (Mary) Roach. Richard Ask, Balleese, my friend. My freehold lease of part of lands of Balleese.

Witnesses: James Jones, sadler, Elizabeth Jones wife of said James Jones, Ann Ask, wife of said Richard Ask, all of Balleese.

Memorial witnessed by: Ann Ask, James Jones.

252, 631, 164689 Richard Ask (seal)

394 BAKER, MARY, Littlegrange, Co. Wicklow, widow.

14 Feb. 1765. Précis ½ p. 2 May 1767.

Her daughter Mary Baker, John Hays and John Warren exors. Patrick Bryan, Ballynapark, Co. Wicklow, gent., trustee.

Her estate in town and lands of Cranerobin, Barony Gorey, Co. Wexford held from Sir Laurence Esmond, Bart., deceased. Her interest in lands of Farrenslate, Co. Wicklow, being a lease for life of Henry Pigeon which she purchased from Capt. John Archer.

Witnesses: Edwd. Archer, Mountjohn, Co. Wicklow, Henry Pigeon and Peter Pigeon, both of Blackditch, Co. Wicklow, gents.

Memorial witnessed by: Wm. Hamilton, Dublin, brasier, John Chamley, Dublin, gent.

257, 5, 165052 Mary Baker (seal)

395 SETTLE, JOHN, Finglasbridge, Co. Dublin, Esq.

22 Jan. 1759. Précis ¼ p. 4 May 1767.

To his cousin John Bayly, Dublin, Esq., exor, all his lands etc. both freehold and leasehold in Ireland or elsewhere.

Witnesses: Rev. Henry Bate, Worcester, Great Britain, clerk, I. Thornloe and Wm. Skillicome, both of Worcester aforesaid, gents.

Memorial witnessed by: Christopher Abbott, Dublin, gent., John Chamley his clerk.

254, 363, 165073 Jno. Bayly (seal)

396 BINDON, SAMUEL, Templemargaret, Co. Limerick, Esq.

17 Sept. 1764. Précis ½ p. 12 May 1767.

His son Burton Bindon. His daughter Anne Bindon. His nephew John Carleton Whitelock, Esq., and Rev. Geo. Massy exors.

Witnesses: Rev. Cornelius Crowley, Pallas, Co. Limerick, clerk, Francis McMahon, Margarett, liberties of Limerick, writing clerk, John Gonan, Limerick, yeoman.

Memorial witnessed by: John Gonan, John Towhy, Ballycahane, Co. Limerick.

247, 602, 165266 Geo. Massy (seal)

397 MURDOCK, JOHN, Liverpool, mariner.

6 Oct. 1757. Narrate 3 pp. 26 June 1767.

His son John Murdock exor. His daughter Sarah Williamson, her husband. His sisters Mary Thompson, Jennett Murdock and Isabell Murdock. Sarah daughter of his late brother William Murdock. His nephew John Murdock son of his brother Robt. His nephew John Murdock son to his late brother William Murdock. Arthur Heywood and Joshua Biggs (exor.) both of Liverpool, George Maquay, Wm. Toone and James Campbell, all of Dublin, merchants, trustees.

His lands of Heathstown and Ma(c)grahan, Co. Westmeath.

Witnesses: Thos. Aspinwall, Robt. Eaton and Fletcher Orred, all of Liverpool, gents.

Memorial witnessed by: Fletcher Orred, Gerard Potter, Liverpool, gent.

263, 36, 166100 Joshua Briggs (seal)
of Liverpool, tabocconist, an exor.

398 PIGEON, THOMAS, Geashill, King's Co. gent.

5 March 1765. Précis ½ p. 30 June 1767.

A lease of the lands of Ballynacarrige, King's Co. devised to his brother Henry Pigeon, exor.

Witnesses: Thomas Page, late of Woodbrook, Queen's Co., farmer, James Vicars, Geashill, King's Co., gent., Denis Costoly, Geashill, yeoman.

Memorial witnessed by: James Vicars, John Chamley, Dublin, gent.

256, 301, 166175 H. Pigeon (seal)

399 SAYERS, ARTHUR, Saffronheart, Co. Cork, clerk.

27 July 1759. Narrate ½ p. 3 Sept. 1767.

His wife Martha Sayers. His brother Mathew Ottiwell of Mallow, trustee and an exor. His son Edward Sayers, exor. His daughter Martha. His farm of Cro[a]ghnacree otherwise Saffronheart.

Witnesses: Robert Houston, late of Mallow, Esq., deceased, George Sayers, Mallow, gent., Maurice Welsh, Cro[a]ghancree, farmer, all in Co. Cork.

Memorial witnessed by: George Sayers, William Bowen Webb, Mallow, gent.

255, 548, 167017 Matt. Ottiwell (seal)

400 COPE, CATHERINE, widow of late John Cope, Esq.(1).

16 July 1767. Précis ¾ p. 19 Sept. 1767.

Her mother Mary Russell. Her father Henry Russell. Her brother-in-law Arundell Madden exor. Her sister Rachel Madden otherwise Russell.

Witnesses: James Russell, John Barker, Jane Barker.

Memorial witnessed by: Thomas Dalton, Murray Kathrens, Dublin, gent., John Barker.

264, 3, 167173 Arundell Madden (seal)

(1) John Cope's Will dated 11 June 1766 mentions his wife Catherine Russell. They married July 1760 and he died Oct. 1766. (*Betham MSS.* Ist Series, Vol. IX, p. 79 Genealogical Office).

401 PIGEON, HENRY, Geashill, King's Co., gent.

[Date not recorded]. Précis ½ p. 26 Oct. 1767.

His brother Peter Pigeon exor. His sister Margaret Pigeon. His lease of Ballinacarrig.

Witnesses: John Hannan, Geashill, merchant, John Oxlay, Geashill, gent., James Vicars, Geashill, parish clerk.

Memorial witnessed by: James Vicars, John Chamley, Dublin, gent.

263, 274, 167648 Peter Pigeon (seal)

402 WATTS, HENRY, New Street, Co. Dublin, nailer.

18 April 1766. Précis ½ p. 29 Oct. 1767.

His wife Mary Watts extx. His son Wm. Watts and his daughter Mary Watts both minors. His house in New Street, Dublin.

Witnesses: Felix Corrin, Cavan Street, Dublin, nailer, Richard Prowse, Duke Street, Dublin, gent.

Memorial witnessed by: Felix Corrin, Wm. FitzGerald, Dublin, gent.

264, 182, 167663 Mary Watts (seal)
her mark

403 BULL, WILLIAM, William Street, Dublin.

8 July 1767. Précis ¼ p. 30 Oct. 1767.

His estate in town and lands of Dalkey, Co. Dublin to Attiwell Wood and William Lane, both of Dublin, Esqrs., as trustees.

Witnesses: J. Watson, Bullock, Co. Dublin, gent., Edwd. Chetham and Toby Purcell, both of Dublin, gents.

Memorial witnessed by: Richd. Supple, Aghadoe, Co. Cork, Esq., Richd. Waller, Dublin, gent.

259, 334, 167669 Wm. Lane (seal)

404 HUSSEY, JAMES, Dublin, Esq.

6 Jan. 1763. Full 1½ p. 2 Dec. 1767.

My wife. My father Stafford Hussey. My brother-in-law Sir Edwd. Montague, Knight of the Bath (exor.) and my cousin Thos. Fitzgerald, Esq., Counsellor at law, trustees. My cousin Jane Barry widow of Capt. Edwd. Barry. Lieut. James Hussey my brother-in-law.

Lands etc. in Co. Meath whereof Stafford Hussey, Esq., my father, is in possession of, and all other my real estate.

Witnesses: Robt. Clements, Dublin, Esq., Fred Gore, late of Dublin, since deceased, Robt. Tighe, Dublin, Esq.

Memorial witnessed by: Robert Clements, William FitzGerald, Dublin, gent.

267, 17, 168326 Thomas Fitzgerald (seal)

405 TIGHE, ROBERT, Mitchelstown, Co. Westmeath, Esq.

2 July 1766. Narrate 4½ pp. 12 Dec. 1767.

His wife Mary Tighe. His daughter Ann Chapman. His son-in-law Benjamin Chapman, Esq. His son Robert Tighe, exor. His brother-in-law Rt. Hon. Nat. Clements, Esq., and Henry Sandford, Castlerea, Co. Roscommon, Esq., guardians of his grandchildren during minority. His grandson Robert Stearne Tighe, a minor. His eldest son Richard Stearne Tighe had lately died possessed of lands of Sheepstown, Stonestown and Scurlogstown [Co. Westmeath] " which he formerly conveyed to him " and left issue Robert Stearne Tighe his eldest and then his only son and one daughter Mary Ann Tighe and by his wife Arabella Tighe a second son since born called William Fitzgerald Tighe.

Rathgeerin and Ballyknockvicar and other lands in parish of St. Mullins, Co. Catherlogh which he purchased from Simon and Geo. Cavanagh. Lands of Ballykildivean, Co. Westmeath. Part of Mitchelstown, Muckeltown (Muckleton) [? Mucklin] and Castletown and Ellintown [Co. Westmeath] held under a lease and three plots of ground in Castledelvin which he purchased. His estate of Kilpatrick, Co. Westmeath.

Witnesses: Rev. Manly Gore, clerk, Joseph Hopson and Andrew Keary both of Mitchelstown, Co. Westmeath, farmers.

Memorial witnessed by: Andrew Keary, Robert Reynell, Dublin, gent.

267, 58, 168484 Robert Tighe (seal)

406 BURKE, RICHARD, Corr, Co. Galway.

17 Nov. 1766. Narrate 1 p. 27 Jan. 1768.

His sister Honora Shepheard otherwise Burke. His son Richd. Burke then or lately living at the sign of the Hope [? Harp] and Anchor on Aston's Quay, Dublin. His brother John Burke. His sister Mary Burke. Exors., trustees and guardians of his son Richd. Burke: Redmond Dolphin, Corr, Esq., (his friend), Thomas Dowling, Dublin, gent., one of the attorneys of the Exchequer (his friend), Bryan Stapleton, Usher's Quay, Dublin, one of the clerks of Richard Nelson, Esq., Mrs. Elinor Boyle, Aston's Quay, Ulick Burke. "One Mr. Maddin a poor reduced gent. who sometimes came for relief to Corr." His nurse Elinor Griffin otherwise Roach.

Lands of Gortymaddin, Co. Galway and all rest of his personal fortune.

Witnesses: Robt. Hamilton, Patk. Hamilton, both of Fairfield, Co. Galway, gent., Silvester Devenish, Cappasale, said County, Esq.

Memorial witnessed by: Wm. Fitzgerald and John McCabe, both of Dublin, gent.

260, 284, 168954 Bryan Stapleton (seal)

407 ARMSTRONG, HENRY, Dublin, gent.

11 April 1767. Full 1¼ p. 10 Feb. 1768.

My wife Catherine Armstrong. My daughter Jane Browne wife of Thos. Browne. My daughter Sarah Armstrong wife of Alexander Armstrong. My daughter Mary Daniel widow. George McMullen, merchant and John Salt, both of Dublin, trustees and exors.

My real and freehold estates. My house and concerns in Blackmore Yard, Dublin.

Witnesses: Robt. Jones, Dublin, public notary, John Ashenhurst, John Robinson his clerks.

Memorial witnessed by: John Ashenhurst, Robt. Jones.

268, 134, 169216 George McMullen (seal)
John Salt (seal)

408 BODKIN, EDMOND, Kilcloony, Co. Galway.

7 Dec. 1767. Full 3 pp. 23 Feb. 1768.

My son and heir James Bodkin. My brother Anthony Bodkin of Tuam, Co. Galway, gent., and his eldest son, my nephew, James Bodkin FitzAnthony. My nephew Thomas Bodkin, second son to my said brother Anthony. My brother Andrew Bodkin of " Sanctacruz in America." My brother James Bodkin of Santacruz aforesaid. My youngest brother Valentine Bodkin. John Bodkin, Kiltroge, Co. Galway, Esq. My uncle Andrew Bodkin. My two natural sons Nicholas and Hyacinth Bodkin, under 21 years. My niece Mabella Lynch daughter of my sister Elinor Lynch. My brother Anthony Bodkin and my brother-in-law Andrew French of Galway, merchant, exors. The Rt. Hon. Earl of Louth and James Daly of Dunsadine [? Dunsandle], Co. Galway, Esqrs., guardians to my son James Bodkin. My faithful friend and servant Anthony Daly. My servant Patrick Connolly. Sums owed by John Holliday, Knock, Co. Galway, gent., by bond and mortgage of Clonfadda, Co. Roscommon.

My real and personal estate. My household furniture etc. now in the custody of Messrs. John and Andrew French in Galway.

Witnesses: Derin O'Connor, John Cheevers, Roger McClancy.

Memorial witnessed by: John Kirwan, Dublin, Esq., John Bodkin, Ballydavid, Co. Galway, Esq.

264, 298, 169429 Anthy. Bodkin (seal)

409 ABBOTT, MORDECAI, Wexford, Esq.

1 Dec. 1760. Full $2\frac{1}{4}$ pp. 23 Feb. 1768.

My wife Charlotte Abbott, extx. and guardian of children during their minority. My eldest son Thomas Abbott. Benjamin Daniel,

Dublin, merchant, trustee. My friend Michael Swift, Caple Street, Dublin, gent., trustee. My lands etc. in Co. Wexford.

Witnesses: Francis Perry, Hoy's [? Hoey] Court, Dublin, gent., William Watson of same, court staymaker, John Perry, Dublin, tailor.

Memorial witnessed by: William Watson, Benjamin Watson, Dublin, gent., one of the attorneys of H.M. Court of Exchequer in Ireland.

266, 156, 169441 Michl. Swift (seal)

410 HENDERSON, MATHEW, Dublin, merchant.
27 July 1765. Full 2 pp. 29 Feb. 1768.

My wife Susanna. My son John, his present wife Olivia. My niece Elizabeth Henderson daughter of my brother James. My nephew Mathew Henderson now in America, son of my brother William Henderson. My friends Thomas Reed (Read) and Robert Montgomery, Esqrs., and James Long, merchant, all of Dublin, trustees and guardians of grandchildren during minority. My real and personal estate.

Witnesses: Christopher Deey, Dublin, public notary, Thomas Collins and Edwd. Bourke, clerks to said Christopher Deey.

Memorial witnessed by: David Buttle, Dublin, gent., Cornelius O'Brien, clerk to said David Buttle.

266, 171, 169493 John Henderson (seal)
of Dorsett [? Street], city of Dublin, Esq.

411 DOMVILLE, SIR COMPTON, Templeogue, Co. Dublin, Bart.
27 July 1761. Full 2 pp. 23 March 1768.

Real and personal estate to my kinsman William Domvile now of London, Esq., failing whose issue same to my nephew Charles Pocklington (exor.); said Charles Pocklington is to take name of Domvile and bear the arms of my family. Rt. Hon. Nathaniel Clements, Esq., and Edward Knachbull, Esq., trustees. The widow of my nephew the late Lord Santry. My two old servants Charles Plessey and Richard Stevenson.

All my lands, houses, hereditaments etc. in Ireland. The mansion house etc. in Templeogue which came to me at the death of my father Thos. Domvile of Templeogue as his only son and heir. Lands etc. in Ireland which I am entitled unto under Will of my nephew the late Lord Santry (to said Charles Pocklington). My leasehold interest, plate, household furniture and pictures which shall be in the house in Santry at the time of my death.

Witnesses: William Kingston, Timothy Cox, clerk to Mr. Ferguson in Bath, George McCartney, Michael Carr.

Memorial witnessed by: David Broghill, Thomas Armstrong, Dublin, writing clerks.

266, 207, 169779 Charles Domvile (seal)
late Charles Pocklington

412 PARKE, FRANCIS, Farnagh, Co. Leitrim.

5 Nov. 1761. Narrate 1¼ p. 21 April 1768.

His eldest son Wm. Parke. His second son Edwd. Parke. His third son Francis Parke. His fourth son Chr. His daughter Rebecca Street. His daughter Jane Parke. His daughter Letitia Carter. His son-in-law Henry Street, of Sligo, and John Algoe, exors. A sum due to widow "Craffd."(1) of Lurganboy. His estates, leases and effects.

Witnesses: Wm. Crawford, Lurganboy, Co. Leitrim, tanner, Geo. Spence, Drumidillier, said county, farmer, David Weir, Sligo, gent.

Memorial witnessed by: David Weir, Thomas Deane, Sligo, gent.

263, 416, 170089 William Parke (seal)

413 LEE, RICHARD, Prussia Street, Co. Dublin, gardener.

8 Dec. 1767. Narrate 2½ pp. 18 May 1768.

His wife Elizth. Lee. John Maddock the younger, Dublin, hatter, Geo. Brooks, Summerhill, Co. Dublin, gent., trustees and exors. His niece Jane Maddock, wife of said John Maddock. His nephews John Lee and Richard Lee, his niece Mary Lee. His cousin Hanover Lee.

(1) Probably Anne Crawford alias Nixon of Lurganboy whose Will, proved in the Prerogative Court 1766, mentions a son William. (*Betham MSS.* Genealogical Office).

His nephew Mathew Lee. His servants Thomas Curry, Nicholas McAnnally, Ann Palmer. His old servant Eliz. Grantham otherwise Ball, her husband.

His holdings in Cabrah Lane, Co. Dublin, held by lease from late Mr. Thomas Walsh, deceased, and in Blackhorse Lane, Co. Dublin, held by leases from late Mrs. Yarner deceased and Chas. Gordon, Esq. £5 for shoes and stockings for poor children of Finglas School, Co. Dublin.

Witnesses: Wm. Oates, Stoneybatter, Co. Dublin, grocer, Wm. Swan, clerk to Thos. Dalrymple, Dublin, gent., and said Thos. Dalrymple.

Memorial witnessed by: William Fitzgerald, Michael Smith, both Dublin, gents.

268, 349, 170734 John Maddock (seal)

414 BALDWIN, RICHARD, Angier Street, Dublin, Esq.
17 Oct. 1764. Full 2 pp. 22 June 1768.

To be buried in St. Peter's Churchyard in the same grave as my late wife and children. To my wife Mary Baldwin otherwise Usher £400 per annum etc. Her deceased mother Mrs. Barbara Usher, her father Henry Usher, Esq., deceased. To my son Richard Baldwin (exor.) all residue of real and personal estate. My three daughters Barbara Baldwin, Elizabeth Baldwin and Mary Baldwin, my wife to be guardian of my daughter Mary until she is 21 years. My relation Mrs. Sarah Phillips. Lieut. William Leaver who married my relation Miss Elizabeth Phillips. My niece Mrs. Elizabeth Swift. William Swift, Esq., trustee and overseer of my Will. My nephew Sir Bridges Baldwin and his lady. Mrs. Arabella Broadway. Miss Editha Phillips. My servant William Heyden, his wife Alice Heyden. James Martin my coachman, his wife Susanna Martin.

Witnesses: Samuel Kathrens, Dublin, public notary, Samuel Boursiquot, writing clerk and Richard Thwaites, notary public both of Crampton Court, Dublin.

Memorial witnessed by: Samuel Bourisquot, Michael Swift, Caple Street, Dublin, gent.

263, 470, 171320 Richd. Baldwin (seal)
only son and sole exor. of testator

415 CAULFIELD, Rev. and Hon. CHARLES, Dublin, clerk, late of Castlestewart, Co. Tyrone. 9 Jan. 1765. Full 3¾ pp. 9 July 1768.

To be buried in church of Armagh, Co. Armagh. My eldest son James Caulfield, exor. My daughter Ann Moore, her mother Mary Moore. My second son Thos. Caulfield. My fourth son John Caulfield. My daughter Grace Caulfield (unmarried and under 21 years), her sister Ann Moore. My third son Charles Caulfield, exor.

Stephen Booker my servant. Mrs. Underwood. Debt of £100 due by Major John Morris to be given to poor of parish of Donaghenry, and £30 to poor of parishes of Ardboe [Arboe] and Donaghenry. Accounts etc. in hands of Geo. Campbell attorney and his father John Campbell. Duplicate copy of my Will lodged in hands of Annesly Stewart, Dublin, Esq. £20 to Incorporated Society for promoting Protestant charter schools in this kingdom.

Real estate purchased by my brother Staples and me from Alexr. Earl of Antrim in Barony Kilconway, Co. Antrim; all other my real estate in counties of Antrim and Tyrone and elsewhere. The estate of Castle Stewart which I am seized of under the Will of John Houston, Esq., deceased, a settlement made between the Rev. Thomas Staples clerk, and Grace Staples(1) otherwise Houston his wife, me the testator and Alice my late deceased wife [date not mentioned](2).

Witnesses: Andrew Carmichael, H. Carmichael, John Rose.

Memorial witnessed by: David Broghill and Thomas Armstrong, both of Dublin, writing clerks.

265, 94, 171632 Jas. Caulfield (seal)

416 MOONEY, RICHARD, Blackrath, Co. Kildare, farmer. 13 April 1764. Précis ½ p. 29 July 1768.

All goods, estate, etc. to his son Walter Mooney of Blackrath, exor.

Witnesses: Henry Claxton and Arthur Claxton both of Killcullen-bridge, Co. Kildare.

(1) The name of Grace Staples is left out of the transcript.

(2) The testator married in 1728 Alice daughter of John Houston of Craigs. *Clogher Parishes and Clergy* (Leslie).

Memorial witnessed by: John McCabe, John Hutton both of Dublin, gents.

267, 309, 171821 Walter Mooney (seal)

417 PLESSY, CHARLES, Templeoge, Co. Dublin.

29 July 1766. Full ½ p. 13 Aug. 1768.

To be buried in Crumlin. Mrs. Mary Plessy, extx., of Chancery Lane and her children. My two leases [situation not mentioned].

Witnesses: Thomas Hunt, Dublin, goldsmith, James Cleland, Dublin, gent.

Memorial witnessed by: Thomas Hunt, Neal Cassidy, Dublin, apothecary.

261, 396, 171953 Mary Plessy (seal)

418 HOWARD, ADAM, Cortcloon, Co. Westmeath, gent.

20 Sept. 1768. Narrate ¾ p. 1 Oct. 1768.

To his sisters Hannah and Mary Ann Howard his interest in lands of Milltown and Ballinagreny [Ballynagrenia], Co. Westmeath. Cortcloon with the bleach yard etc. to his brother Michael Howard with his interest in the lands of Milltown, Co. Dublin.

Witnesses: Nicholas William Brady, Joseph Tempest, both Dublin, merchants, David Davis, Dublin, apothecary.

Memorial witnessed by: Joseph Tempest, and William Dale and Joseph Cahill both of Dublin, gents.

261, 498, 172423 Michael Howard (seal)

419 MARTIN, JASPER, Birchall, Co. Galway, Esq.

15 Feb. 1749/50. Précis ½ p. 4 Oct. 1768.

To his cousin Richard Martin then of Dang [? Dangin] in the liberties of the town of Galway, Esq., but since deceased, his estate in Ireconnaught, Co. Galway.

Witnesses: John Concannon, Samuel Fletcher and Laurence Browne, all of Dublin, gents., since deceased, and Patrick Martin, Galway, gent.

Memorial witnessed by: Patk. Martin, John Lynch, Galway, gent.

261, 502, 172440

Robert Martin (seal)
of Dangin, Esq., heir at law of said Richard Martin.

420 CANE, JAMES, Dublin, Esq.

15 April 1755. Full 2 pp. 14 Oct. 1768.

My wife extx. My daughters Jane and Alice Cane (under 21 years and unmarried). My son James Cane (under 21 years). My eldest son Wm. Cane. To my mother £20 per year for life. My brothers and sisters. Martha Beates, her husband. My friend John Carroll, gent. My brothers John Cane and Hugh Cane. My real and personal estate.

Witnesses: Nichs. Nettervill, R. Moore, Luke Gaven.

Memorial witnessed by: Tottenham Howlin, clerk to John Carroll, Dublin, gent., Maurice Daly, Dublin, writing clerk.

259, 443, 172507

Jane Cane (seal)
widow of testator

421 BUSBY, JOHN, Dublin, victualler.

23 Dec. 1742. Narrate ½ p. 31 Oct. 1768.

To his niece Mary Flood, spinster, (extx.) for the care she had taken of him since his wife's death the interest of a lease of his holding in Drumcondra Lane demised by him to Charles Campbell then deceased, his household goods and furniture in the house [in which] he then dwelt and all real and personal estate.

Witnesses: Charles Reilly, ale draper, Robert Granger, shop keeper, Mathew Dunnigan, baker and James Donnelly, gent., all of Dublin.

Memorial witnessed by: John McCabe, Richard Jenkinson, both Dublin, gents.

261, 541, 172660 Dunn Flood (seal)
her mark
Mary Flood otherwise Dunn, extx.

422 YOUNGE, ELIZABETH, King's Street, Oxmantown, parish of St. Paul, widow. 20 Sept. 1766. Full 1½ p. 24 Nov. 1768.

To be buried in St. Paul's Churchyard with my late husband. My daughter Elizabeth Houlsten wife of Owen Houlsten of Gracely Hall in Cheshire, farmer. My eldest grandchild Mary Houlsten (unmarried and under age), my second grandchild Hanna Houlsten (ditto), my third and youngest grandchild John Houlsten (under age). Rev. Theobald Disney, Dublin, clerk, and James Goddard, Dublin, gent., trustees and exors. Mrs. Alice Kelly wife of Bryan Kelly of King Street, Stephen's Green, grocer. James and Thomas Kelly, sons of Alice and Bryan Kelly.

My house on north side of King Street, Oxmantown. Money in hands of Stephen Wybrants secured to testator by his and Mathew Staunton's joint bond.

Witnesses: Rebecca Howard, Dublin, widow, Alfred Howard, Dublin, gent.

Memorial witnessed by: Rebecca and Alfred Howard.

266, 467, 173163 Theo. Disney (seal)
James Goddard (seal)

423 PALLISER, WILLIAM, Rathfarnham, Co. Dublin, Esq. 2 Feb. 1765. Narrate 2 pp. 7 March 1769.

His late wife. To his cousin Rev. John Palliser (exor.) of Rathfarnham, D.D., town and lands of Stephenstown, Co. Kildare, Councillor Rowan lessor, and also Oldtown, Co. Kildare, Michael Hogan lessee. Archerstown, Tinvire, Grennan and the Glebe in Queen's Co. Sums due to him by Wm. Pole, Ballyfinn, Co. Kildare and by James Hutchinson, Knockballymeagher, Co. Kildare, gent., by mortgages on their estates. His lease under the See of Cashel [situation not mentioned]. His houses, lands etc. in and about the town of Rathfarnham.

To Rev. Walter Thomas, eldest son of his cousin the Rev. Geo. Thomas the town and lands of Cornagoure, Co. Wicklow. His cousin Ann Thomas, Rathfarnham, spinster. His cousin John Barrington, Ballynakill, Queen's Co., Esq. Mrs. Mary Thomas to receive rents of lands of Killnasure, Carrick, Clonkeenahanbegg and the Islands thereon, Queen's Co., Mrs. Frances Leeds to have an annuity out of said lands. To his cousin Rev. Oliver Wheeler lands of Fryar's Inch and Glandine near the city of Kilkenny. To Jane Taylor, daughter of Alderman Thomas Taylor, deceased, his house in Molesworth Street, Dublin. To the eldest son of his cousin Wm. Groome late of Strongfield, Co. Galway, deceased, his interest in a lease held under Welbore Ellis in the city of Dublin [situation not mentioned].

Witnesses: Richard Wilson and Richard Fenner, both Dublin, Esqrs., John Pilkington, Dublin, gent.

Memorial witnessed by: John Pilkington, John Perry both of Dublin.

270, 503, 174667 John Palliser (seal)

424 ROWE, RICHARD, Ballyharty, Co. Wexford, Esq.

13 Jan. 1769. Full 7½ pp. 10 April 1769.

My nephew Ebenezer Radford (exor.), son of William Radford and Dorothy Radford otherwise Rowe, to take surname of Rowe. My nephew Richard Boyse, Craige, Co. Wexford, Esq., (ditto, if said Ebenezer has no issue male). My nephew Rev. Nathaniel Boyse (ditto). My nephew William Hobbs, Waterford (ditto). My nephew George Hobbs (ditto). My sister Elizabeth Boyse. My sister Dorothy Radford wife of said William Radford. My sister Ann Hobbs, wife of Michael Hobbs of Waterford, alderman. My nephew Richard Hobbs " who is visited with blindness " son of said Ann. To my niece Elizabeth Hobbs £300 on marriage. Cornelius Grogan, Johnstown, Co. Wexford, Esq., and Dr. Ebenezer Jacob, Mount Edwards or Bettystock, near Wexford, trustees. Joseph Nunn, Killcastle, Co. Wexford, Esq., exor.

Lands in Baronies Forth and Bargy, Co. Wexford. £40 to poor of parish and Union of Mulrankin.

Witnesses: Mathew Cardiffe, Thomas Robinson, John Bury, public notary.

Memorial witnessed by: Mathew Cardiffe, Rogerson's Quay, Dublin, ship carpenter, Edward Butler, Dublin, gent.

272, 315, 175007 Ebenzr. Radford Rowe (seal)
Ebenezar Radford now Ebenezer Radford Rowe

425 STEWART, JANE, Ballylogh, Co. Antrim, spinster.

1 Aug. 1760. Narrate 3 pp. 22 April 1769.

Rev. Archibald Stewart late of Ballylogh, Co. Antrim, D.D., deceased, brother to said Jane the testator. Alexander Stewart of Ballintoy, Co. Antrim, nephew to testator. Jane and Sophia Stewart daughters of said Alexander Stewart her nephew. Richard Dobbs, second son of Conway Richard Dobbs and Randal Dobbs, third son of Conway Richard Dobbs, Alexander first and eldest son of said Conway Richard Dobbs and Ann Dobbs niece of testator. Sons of said Conway Richard Dobbs to take surname and bear arms of Stewart as they become entitled to testator's real estate. Her grand-nephew Edwd. son of her late niece Rose Brice otherwise Stewart. Rev. Richard Dobbs, Lisburn, Co. Antrim, D.D. James Stewart, Coleraine, Co. Londonderry. James Leslie, Stranocum, Co. Antrim, Esq., and Rev. James Smyth, Vicar of Armoy, Co. Antrim, trustees.

All her real and personal estate. Lands of Ballyloghmore, parish of Billy, Barony Dunluce, Co. Antrim and the mill of Dunseverick in the parish of Ballintoy, Barony Carey, Co. Antrim which had been devised by her said brother Archibald Stewart to testator.

Witnesses: Alexander Boyd, Esq., and Jno. McAllester, merchant, both of Ballycastle, Co. Antrim, Andrew Stewart, late of the Park in the parish of Ballintoy, Co. Antrim, gent., deceased.

Memorial witnessed by: Alexander Boyd, John Stewart, Ballintoy, Co. Antrim, gent.

273, 138, 175316 Jas. Leslie (seal)

426 BALDWIN, DAME FRANCES, Dublin, widow of Sir Bridges Baldwin late of Dublin. 5 Jan. 1769. Narrate 9 pp. 10 May 1769.

Her brother William Neynoe, Dublin, Esq. Her nephew Joseph Neynoe eldest son of said brother. Her niece Sarah Lynam otherwise Neynoe, her nephew William Lynham her husband. Her niece Frances Ball otherwise Neynoe. Her nephew John Neynoe. Her nephew John Lynham. Her nieces Sarah and Ann Lynam spinsters. Frederick Bridges Schaw, Isabella Schaw his wife. John Bridges Schaw. Elizabeth and Charlotte Schaw daughters to Charlotte Schaw otherwise Baldwin and nieces to her said husband. Her niece Ormsby otherwise Pepys. The children of Elizabeth Hudson otherwise Neynoe. Elizabeth Swift otherwise Longfield and her daughter Elizabeth. Mrs. Jane Lynam wife of Joseph Lynam. Mary Dalton otherwise Smith and her children. John Stokes and George Phillips exors. Rt. Rev. Charles [Jackson] Lord Bishop of Kildare and Rev. Isaac Mann, D.D., Archdeacon of Dublin, trustees of her real estate. Rev. John Stokes, D.D., Senior Fellow of Trinity College, Dublin, and Rev. Geo. Phillips, Dublin, clerk, trustees of her personal estate.

A rent of £100 arising out of ground on east side of Kildare Street, Dublin, on which a large stone house, coach house and stables etc. were built, purchased from Edward Nicholson, Esq., by her husband. Two houses on east side of Merrion Street, in the manor of Bagotrath, Dublin, Lord Fitzwilliam lessor, purchased by her late husband from John Connell, merchant. Ground and dwelling house etc. on west side of Frederick Street, parish of St. Ann, Dublin, Wm. Wilde lessor, purchased by her late husband from Catherine Hamilton widow of Arthur Hamilton Maxwell, Esq., or from Edward Nicholson; ground, dwelling house etc. in Granby Row, parish of St. Thomas, Dublin, purchased by her late husband from Andrew Reid. Dwelling house etc. on south side of Molesworth Street purchased by her late husband from Charles Bucknall, Esq. Dwelling house on north side of Great Britain Street, Dublin held under a lease made by Richard Ball to Joseph Ball which her husband purchased from said Reid. Wine vaults on north side of Strand Street, Lordship of St. Mary's Abbey, Dublin. Lands of Ballysummaghan, Co. Sligo, the Bishop of Elphin lessor.

Witnesses: James Sparrow, rector of Walcot near Bath, Rev.

John Waller, Fellow of Trinity College, Dublin, Lewis Clutterbuck, town clerk of Bath.

Memorial witnessed by: John Waller, Will. Williams, Dublin, notary public.

272, 435, 175664 J. Stokes (seal)
Geo. Phillips (seal)

427 KEATING, THOMAS, Dublin, coachmaker.

6 Oct. 1764. Codicil 25 Jan. 1769. Narrate 1¾ p. 18 May 1769.

His wife Arabella Keating. His daughter Susanna Keating. His son Thomas Keating. His uncle Wm. Keating. His brother-in-law Jno. Chaigneau. Fras. Booker, Dublin, Esq., late one of the Sheriffs of Dublin, and Oliver Nelson, Dublin, printer, trustees.

Leasehold interests in part of lands of Booterstown, Co. Dublin, and in city and surburbs of city of Dublin. Dwelling house in Booterstown with garden etc. demised to testator by Viscount Fitzwilliam. Three houses built by testator in Merrion Square (ground demised by said Lord Fitzwilliam), Col. Montgomery lessee. The house wherein testator lately lived situate in Merrion Street.

[Name of witnesses not recorded].

Memorial witnessed by: Susana Keating, Samuel Adams, Dublin, gent.

275, 121, 175755 Ara. Keating (seal)

428 KAVANAGH, GARRETT, Barnhill, Co. Kildare.

18 March 1765. Narrate ½ p. 22 May 1769.

To his wife and his youngest son Robert half the furniture of his house, half of his stock and half of his book debts. To son Darby £20 and a bed if he should marry with the consent of his mother and brothers. To son James one shilling. To his son Laurence Kavanagh (exor.), his house and land and other half of stock and book debts. One guinea each to Rev. Father Byrne and Rev. Father Commins.

Witnesses: Thomas Browne, Barnhill, farmer, John Corcoran, Derryfarm, said county, farmer.

Memorial witnessed by: Wm. Fitzgerald, John McCabe, both Dublin, gent.

275, 135, 175831 Laur. Kavanagh (seal)

429 McGRAYNOR, THOMAS, Mullinestillen, Co. Dublin, farmer. 22 Nov. 1762. Codicil 19 March 1763. Narrate 1 p. 23 May 1769.

His wife Margaret. His son Thomas McGraynor. Son Owen McGraynor. Son Terance McGraynor. His grand-daughter Elizabeth McGraynor daughter to his son Terance. Rev. Mr. John Byrne and Robert Towson, exors.

Witnesses to Will and codicil: John Sandford, "Caventeely," Co. Dublin, gent., Edward Kennedy, Mullenestillen, farmer.

Memorial witnessed by: John Hutton, John McCabe, Dublin, gents.

276, 11, 175844 Thos. McGraynor (seal)

430 NEWELL, JOHN, Kinkell, Co. Down, gent.

3 July 1769. Narrate 1½ p. 4 July 1769.

Town and lands of Kinkell, and corn mill and kiln thereon and residence etc. to his daughter Elizabeth Cowan otherwise Newell. Her eldest son John Cowan. His grand-daughter Mary Cowan. His grand-daughter Margaret Cowan. To his son George Newell six shillings and no more. Person inheriting his estate to take surname of Newell. His two sons-in-law Joseph Cowan and David Cuming exors.

Witnesses: Robt. Wallace, Newry, gent., David Richardson, Newry, gent., William Rankin, Newry, shoemaker.

Memorial witnessed by: Robt. Wallace, David Richardson.

272, 579, 176552 John Newell (seal) the testator
Eliz. Cowan (seal)

431 IEVERS, AUGUSTINE, Great Connell, Co. Kildare.

6 Jan. 1768. Narrate, part in full, ¾ p. 13 July 1769.

My wife Susanna Ievers otherwise O'Brien. Thos. Clutterbuck and Ellen Clutterbuck otherwise Prendergast his wife my niece. James Rice son of Cornet James Rice who lately died and recommended his said son to me on his death bed. My freehold of the house and demesne of Great Connell.

Witnesses: John Mangan, Piercetown, farmer, Thos. Ward, Great Connell, schoolmaster, Redmond Bourke late manservant to testator, all Co. Kildare.

Memorial witnessed by: Thos. Ward, Benj. Johnston, Dublin, gent.

275, 256, 176704 Sus. Ievers (seal)

432 DAVYS, CHARLES, Hampstead, Co. Dublin, Esq.

30 March 1769. Codicils 30 March 1769, 5 April 1769. Full 7 pp. 19 August 1769.

To be interred with my father and mother at the church of St. Michan's, Dublin, Mary Davys otherwise Hely my wife. Provision made " in case I shall happen to die without issue " by which rents etc. to be held by the trustees for use of Rt. Hon. Cadwallader Lord Blayney for life and then to his heirs male, failing male issue to John Caulfield, Esq., and his heirs for ever. Said John Caulfield, my cousin, Captain in 56th Regiment. Faithfull Fortescue, Corderry, Co. Louth and Adam Noble of Longfield, Co. Monaghan, exors. John Barlow, Park, Co. Meath and Elinor his wife. Lieutenant Thomas Barlow and Edward Barlow, surgeon, sons of said John Barlow. Miss Elizabeth Purdon of Curristown, Co. Westmeath, her brothers and sisters. £1,000 to be laid out at interest upon securities to be approved of by Henry Hunt, Dublin, apothecary or after his death by Elizabeth Hunt his now wife, the yearly interest to be paid to said Elizabeth Hunt and after death of said Henry and Elizabeth Hunt £400 to be paid to their eldest daughter Susanna Hunt, the remaining £600 for the other children of the said Henry Hunt which shall then be living.

£100 to minister and churchwardens of Finglas parish Co. Dublin, for the use of the Charity School. My holdings or concerns at

Hampstead, Co. Dublin to be sold; all my other lands etc. in counties of Antrim, Kildare and Dublin, and in town of Carrickfergus or elsewhere to be held by exors. for payments of annuities. A pair of large silver candlesticks belonging to me now at Castle Blayney. Lands in Dublin and Kildare, except holdings at Hampstead, to use of Hon. Francis Caulfield. Residue to Incorporated Society for Promoting Protestant Schools in Ireland. To wife Mary Davys otherwise Hely my house on east side William Street, Dublin, purchased from Samuel Broadstreet, Esq., Recorder of city of Dublin [second codicil].

Witnesses to Will and first codicil: Michael Aigoirs [Aigoin] and David Aigoirs [Aigoin], Dublin, merchants, John Rawlins, Dublin, Esq.

Second codicil witnessed by: Arthur Guiness, Dublin, brewer, Benjamin Ball, Dublin, ironmonger, John Rawlins.

Memorial witnessed by: John Rawlins, John Purdon, Dublin, gent.

277, 185, 177151 Faith. Fortescue (seal)
Adm. Noble (seal)

433 FERGUSON, ANDREW, Strabane, Co. Tyrone, gent.
6 Aug. 1769. Narrate 1 p. 30 Aug. 1769.

To his friend George Buchanan, apothecary in Strabane lands etc. in and near city of Londonderry formerly occupied and possessed by the testator's late father from the London Society. A suit then depended between John Hamilton, Esq., Counsellor at law and the testator relative to the last Will of testator's late aunt Mrs. Dorcas Ferguson.

Witnesses: William Orr, merchant, William Campbell, innholder, John McCollagh, merchant, all of Strabane.

Memorial witnessed by: William Orr, John McCollagh.

276, 277, 177260 Geo. Buchanan (seal)

434 LANESBOROUGH, HUMPHREY EARL OF
24 Dec. 1761. Full 3½ pp. 16 Sept. 1769.

If I die in Dublin to be buried in church street of St. Ann's in Dawson Street. My late wife. My son the Hon. Brinsley Lord Newtown exor. My daughter [in-law] Rt. Hon. Jane Lady Newtown. My brothers Hon. Robt. Butler and John Butler, Esqrs., trustees. My grandson Wm. Butler. My grand-daughter Elizabeth Butler. My grand-daughter Mary Butler. Miss Anna Jones. Miss Rebecca Jones who lives with my aunt Butler. Sums owed to my said son Brinsley Lord Newtown by Mrs. Margery Nesbitt. Mr. John Ross who was formerly tutor to my son Brinsley Lord Newton. My servants Wm. Cormick, Darby Kennedy.

My house and lands in Booterstown, Co. Dublin. My house and offices in Stephen's Green. My dwelling house etc. in the town of Belturbet, Co. Cavan. £30 to the Widows Almshouse in Belturbet subject to the same conditions as money left to said Almshouse by Mrs. Mary Mansell deceased. My several estate in counties of Cavan and Fermanagh.

Witnesses: David Freeman, Mary Clegg, Patk. Brady.

Memorial witnessed by: Michael Black, Dublin, gent., John Carroll, Dublin, gent.

269, 365, 177419 Lanesborough (seal)
(Brinsley Earl of Lanesborough)

435 EDWARDS, EATON, Doctor of Physick.

3 July 1769. Narrate 2 pp. 18 Sept. 1769.

His wife. His son William Edwards. His daughter Mary Jameson. His son Eaton Edwards. Hans Wallace, Waterford, merchant, trustee. All his real estate in Co. Wexford. His lands of Newtown, Co. Kilkenny. His house in Meath Street, Dublin.

Witnesses: Rev. Daniel Sandize, Waterford, clerk, John Lyon, Waterford, alderman, John Lymbery, Waterford, gent.

Memorial witnessed by: John Lymbery, John Allen, Waterford, merchant.

276, 328, 177436 Hans Wallace (seal)

436 BLESINTON, WILLIAM EARL OF(1)

17 Sept. 1760. Précis ½ p. 7 Oct. 1769.

His wife Elenor Countess of Blesinton and Charles Ussher, Dublin, Esq., exors. and trustees.

(1) *The Complete Peerage* by G.E.C. states that apparently the testator and his wife adopted the spelling " Blesinton."

His manors of Newtown Stewart and Rash, Baronies of Strabane and Omagh, Co. Tyrone. His manor of Aghentoan [Aghintain] otherwise Rash, Mount Stewart, Barony Clogher, Co. Tyrone, and his freehold manors, lands, etc. in counties of Donegal and Tyrone. His manor of Mount Joy, which he held by lease from the crown, in Barony Dungannon, Co. Tyrone.

Witnesses: Hugh Hamersly, Esq., Giles Hitchcock, gent., Richd. Gilbert, gent., all of London.

Memorial witnessed by: John Dowdall, clerk to Richard Nelson, Dublin, Esq., Michael Coghlan, man servant to said Charles Ussher.

261, 625, 177640 Chas. Ussher (seal)

437 KELLETT, CHARLES, Cornas[h]esk, parish of Lurgan, Co. Cavan. 28 April 1768. Narrate 1½ p. 16 Nov. 1769.

My wife Susanna Kellett. To my mother Elizabeth Kellett a bond due by Francis Young. My brother David Kellett. My brother-in-law John Kellett of Fordstown, Co. Meath. John Betty, eldest son to Rev. Christopher Betty, Cherrymount, Co. Meath. As there is no probability of my having lawful issue I bequeath to my nephew Charles Kellett eldest son of my brother-in-law John Kellett of Fordstown, my farm in Enagh, parish of Mullagh, Co. Cavan. My nephew Charles Kellett youngest son of my brother David Kellett of Mullagh, Co. Cavan. Rent of lands of Enagh parish of Mullagh. Lease of lands of Enagh parish of Castle Raghan. Rev. Christopher Betty, Cherrymount and my mother Elizabeth Kellett exors.

Witnesses: Christopher Betty, Cherrymount, clerk, Richard Young, Bellwood, Co. Meath, gent., Owen McCann servant to said Christopher Betty.

Memorial witnessed by: Owen McCann, John Young, Dublin, gent.

275, 426, 178303 Charles Kellett (seal)
son to John Kellett of Fordstown

438 MANWARING, WILLIAM, George's Lane, Dublin, toyman. [Date not recorded]. Narrate 1 p. 29 Nov. 1769.

His wife Virtue Manwaring guardian of children and exor. His only son James Manwaring, under 14 years. His four daughters

Catherine, Virtue, Mary and Sarah Manwaring (under 18 years and unmarried). A lease in Pudding Rowe next adjoining Castlemarkett.

Witnesses: John Kiernan, Edmond Dunn, both Dublin, gents.

Memorial witnessed by: William Fitzgerald, Dublin, gent., Henrietta Fitzgerald his wife.

273, 376, 178532 Virtue Manwaring (seal)

439 ROCHE, MARY otherwise HOWARD, widow of Richd. Roche of Dublin, Esq. 12 Oct. 1756. Narrate ¾ p. 1 Dec. 1769.

Her son Thos. Roche. No children of her said son Thomas Roche's present wife daughter of the late Captain John Waller to inherit any of her real or personal estate. Her friend James Goddard, Dublin, gent., trustee and exor. Her nephew Alfred Howard. Lands of Scribblestown, Co. Dublin, leased from the family of Luttrell of Luttrellstown. Her Bowbridge rents[1].

Witnesses: Edwd. Mathews, Dublin, Esq., Richd. Moore, Val. Ramsay, Dublin, gent.

Memorial witnessed by: Val. Ramsay, Patk. FitzGerald, Dublin, vinter.

277, 392, 178565 Jam. Goddard (seal)

440 BROWNE, SIR JOHN, Neale, Co. Mayo, Bart.

Codicil 3 Aug. 1761. Narrate 2 pp. 2 Dec. 1769.

Codicil making provision in case testator's eldest son George Browne should die without issue male. Testator's second son John Browne (" his son Jack."). His son Henry. His third son Dodwell who bore his late dear wife's family name[2]. Reciting that testator's wife Dame Catherine Browne otherwise Daly had conformed to the Church of Ireland and that several suits were then carrying on for recovering her fortune and mentioning debts formerly paid off by her father Sir Walter Blake, Bart., then late of Dublin, he in reality

(1) Possibly Bow Bridge Street in parish of St. James, Dublin, is intended.

(2) The testator had five sons and a daughter by his first wife Margaret Dodwell. His second wife Catherine, daughter of Sir Walter Blake of Menlo, and widow of Denis Daly of Carrownakelly, died without issue 1775.

at the time of his death being no ways indebted but his son Quin [? Blake] to Mr. Damer and Mr. Vincent. His daughter Bourke(1). Bequeathed to his son Palmer Browne by his wife's particular order and direction £2,000 as by articles perfected between him and his wife 23 Nov. 1754.

A debt due by testator to the late John Mills, alderman, once of Galway. His faithful friend James McDonagh of the Neale, a sum due to said James McDonagh by order of Alexander Bodkin. To "his poor kinswoman Margaret Maly of Eden fifty pounds to industure upon untill she should receive her fortune from her brother." Fany Shiels. His servants Bartholomew Nolan and his wife Elizabeth. Five lodgings to be built for poor tenants of his estate at the Neale. The farm and house of Raheens [? Co. Mayo]. His Bishop's lease near the Neale reserved with the Archbishop of Tuam.

Witnesses: Rev. Cecil Crampton, Headford, Co. Galway, clerk, Edmond Burke, Ballyhean, Co. Mayo, Doctor of Physick, George Jenning, Dublin, gent.

Memorial witnessed by: Terence Coghlan, William FitzGerald, Dublin, gent.

274, 307, 178584 Dodwell Browne (seal)

441 GRANARD, GEORGE EARL OF

26 June 1764. Narrate 2 pp. 9 Dec. 1769.

His son George Lord Forbes, exor. His grandson George Forbes, only son of said George Forbes. His youngest son John Forbes. The Attorney General and Solicitor General, and their successors in those offices for the time being, trustees. All his manors, messuages, lands, tenements and hereditaments in counties of Longford, Leitrim and Westmeath.

Witnesses: Richard Steele, then of Dublin, Esq., but now Sir Richard Steele of Dublin, Bart., Thomas Kennedy, Dublin, gent., since deceased, Daniel Grogan, Dublin, then servant to said Earl and since deceased.

Memorial witnessed by: Patrick Palmer, Dublin, Esq., Barrister-at law, Thomas Lee, Dublin, attorney.

267, 603, 178681 Granard (seal)
(George, Earl of Granard, grandson of testator)

(1) Julia wife of Edmund Bourke.

442 TAAFFE, JOHN, Stephenstown, Co. Louth, Esq.

15 May 1769. Narrate 2 pp. 14 Dec. 1769.

Half of residue etc. to his grand-nephew John Maginnis, only son of his nephew Doctor Arthur Maginnis, to take surname of Taaffe. The other half to his nephew Thomas Dillon, only son of Robert Dillon, to take surname of Taaffe. His nephew Hugh Maginnis to take surname of Taaffe if he inherits. Gifford Nesbitt and Simons Isaac, Esqrs., Barristers at Law, and Hugh Reilly, Cruicetown, Co. Meath, Esq., trustees. Said nephew Arthur Maginnis and his brother-in-law Robt. Dillon, gent., exors. His real estate and freehold leases in Co. Louth.

Witnesses: John Taaffe, Raneety, Henry Byrne, Allardtown, both Co. Louth, gents., Philip Reilly, Boynagh, Co. Meath, gent.

Memorial witnessed by: Philip Reilly, James Connelly, Dublin, merchant.

277, 431, 178754 Robt. Dillon (seal)

443 ROWAN, REV. ROBERT, Mullans, Co. Antrim, clerk.

16 May 1742. Full 2¾ pp. 20 Dec. 1769.

My wife Letitia Rowan. My daughter Margaret Rowan. My brother William Rowan of Sea Patrick, Co. Down, clerk, and Mr. Archibald McNealle of Belfast, chirurgeon, trustees and exors. My younger children Archibald, Stewart, William and Margaret Rowan, under 21 years. My eldest son John Rowan. My second son Archibald Rowan. My third son Stewart Rowan. My fourth son William Rowan. My estate of freeholds [situation not mentioned].

Witnesses: Rev. Skeffington Bristow, Halebrook, Co. Antrim, clerk, Rev. John Brett, Ballywillan, Co. Antrim, clerk, Jas. Blair, Ballymena, Co. Antrim, Doctor of Physick.

Memorial witnessed by: Skeffington Bristow, Henry Dunkin, Dublin, William Rowan, Ballymoney, Co. Antrim, gent.

277, 478, 178891 Stewart Rowan (seal)

444 STEWART, JAMES, Coleraine, Co. Londonderry, Esq.

23 Dec. 1769. Précis 1 p. 21 Feb. 1770.

His wife Helena Stewart. His son Robert. His son James. John Stewart, Ballantoy, Co. Antrim, Esq., and Richard Lloyd, Coleraine, gent., trustees and exors. Mark Kerr O'Neill, Flowerfield, Co. Londonderry, Esq., and testator's wife Helena to be guardians of his children.

Lands of Moghratendry and Camanreigh, [? Co. Londonderry], held under Earl of Antrim by deed of 1739. Rest of real and leasehold estate. Testator had entered into an agreement with Mr. George Martin of Artimecormicke to convey to said George Martin the lands of Eagery [situation not mentioned]. Leases to be granted to John Etcheson, Alexander Stewart and Gaen Allen [? Aken].

Witnesses: William Shaw, Antrim, Co. Antrim, Richard Lloyd and John Tittle, junior, both of Coleraine.

Memorial witnessed by: Baxter Spencer Sanders, Coleraine, labourer, John McKim, Coleraine, sadler.

277, 553, 179784 Helena Stewart (seal)
John Stewart (seal)

445 FLOYD, JOHN, parish of Conwell, Co. Donegal, farmer.

4 Dec. 1758. Narrate $\frac{3}{4}$ p. 26 Feb. 1770.

To Isabella, then the wife of his son Richard Floyd, his dwelling house etc., and all lands in town of Bogg in Ards(1), for her children. To his grand-daughter Sarah Floyd, from age of 16 years to age of 26 years, "twenty shillings out of Ezekiel Wilson's rent and the benefit of the meadow that his sons William and Richard then held." Said Richard his son to deliver to testator's grand-daughter when 16 years the said meadow being part of the farm wherein said Ezekiel Wilson lives [situation not mentioned]. His grandson John Floyd.

Witnesses: Francis Sam. Wilson and Richard Jamison, both Raphoe, Co. Donegal, gents.

Memorial witnessed by: Francis Jammison, Edwd. Morris, Strabane, Co. Tyrone.

269, 420, 179839 Richard Floyd (seal)
the father and guardian of the several orphans
in said memorial mentioned.

(1) Probably the townland of Ards Big in Conwal parish, Co. Donegal.

446 PALMER, ROGER, Palmerstown, Co. Mayo.

31 Aug. 1769. Narrate 4½ pp. 28 March 1770.

Articles of agreement entered into on the intermarriage of his son Francis Palmer with Elizabeth Echlin daughter of Sir Robert Echlin, Bart. Reciting that said Francis was since dead leaving issue two sons, Roger his eldest and Francis his younger, and two daughters, Frances and Elizabeth.

The Rt. Hon. the Lord Strange, Preston, Lancaster, John Knox, Cottlestown, Co. Sligo, and Oliver Burke, Palmerstown, Co. Mayo, Esq., trustees and exors., Francis Evans, Dublin, Esq., trustee.

Lands etc. in counties of Mayo, Sligo and Dublin and in Northumberland and Lancaster and town and lands of Ross and Killibrone, Clon[o]anass, Kilroe, Glanedagh, Cloonaghbegg, Ballyduffy, Ballymayoge, Knocks, Aghaleage, Carrowmore, Attycarragh, Trustimore, Rathlackan, Creganbegg, Carrickbarrett and one part of manor town and lands of Bellehahan[1], Clonlee, Mullaghclery, Lissgown [? Lisgowel], Clooncurry, Tawnabegg, Knockshanvally, Knockmore, Garanard, Gral[l]aghbegg, Carnanease, Knocklegan alias Knockgarrane, Ardcloon, Carrowgonois alias Carrowgow[a]n, Oughtragh alias Uctnass, Fartagh, Shimaghmuiny alias Shimaghmuny, Gortnegar alias Gorteens, Annaghagh, Killtimagh, Carrowentyane, Tawnycraft, Faghny alias Fahiny, Killean alias Cullane, Carrowkean alias Carrowbane, one part of Balltigarruff and one part of Lissdorane, and lands of Killmullogh, Ballineety, Moyn, Killroe and Glanedagheighter, all in Co. Mayo. House and lands of Rush, Dromanagh, Kinwel, Cornhill, Kinure and a part of Kinure in the possession of James Farren and John Farren, Tool's garden, Teeling's meadow (part of Kinure lands), part of Drumlattery and Ballykea and all the towns and lands of Rush with the green, rabbit warren and windmill thereon etc. Lands of Raharton, Ballytrea otherwise Ballykea with the part called Chapman's holding, Kinure with the lands of Cospell's and Chapman's holding, Drumlattery and Dearcetown otherwise Piercetown with the lands of Leamount with a sub-denomination of Thomastown and Ballykea, Thomastown and Ballustrees being part of a sub-denomination of Thomastown, lands of Bullrudder, Darcystown, Castleland and Cliffordspark, Folkstown otherwise Fookstown otherwise Foulkstown, Tubberstekin otherwise Tubbertekin otherwise Stabledeskin and Doolagh, Millstown with the mill race, part

(1) Belladooan, Barony Tirawley, parish Kilfian may be intended.

of Milestown cut across by the river adjoining Christopher Darcy's holding, Knock, the castle lands and Plunkets parks, Turkinstown and Stephenstown with the mill thereof, in Co. Dublin.

Witnesses: Rev. Moses Magill, Dublin, clerk, Sankey Denis, William Palmer, Dublin, gents.

Memorial witnessed by: Sankey Denis, Chris Bowen, Hollymount, Co. Mayo, gent.

281, 51, 180358 John Knox (seal)

447 HILL, PETER, Gillynahirk, Co. Down, farmer.

29 Dec. 1769. Full 1½ p. 5 May 1770.

My wife and five sons. My son Hugh Hill. My son Jno. Hill. To Alexr. Hill and Hugh Hill exors., my two sons, the leasehold of Gillinahirk (Gillynahirk). My daughter Margaret Hill. The Brenyall [Braniel] lease, Samuel Smith [lessor or lessee]. To Alex. Hill the farm he now possesseth [situation not mentioned].

Witnesses: Peter Hill, Hugh McDowell, Robert McQuoid.

Memorial witnessed by: Robert McQuoid, Gillynahirk, Co. Down, carpenter, Jno. Mackay, Lisburn, Co. Antrim, writing clerk.

271, 423, 180817 Alexr. Hill (seal)
Hugh Hill (seal)

448 CHAYTOR, JOHN, Kilmacurragh, Co. Wicklow, farmer.

6 Aug. 1768. Narrate ½ p. 3 May 1770.

To his three daughters Ann Chaytor, Susanna Chaytor and Hannah Chaytor his leasehold interests in lands of Ballybeg, Killmacurrow and Knocknattin, Co. Wicklow, held from Wm. Acton, Esq., and of Ballydonnell, Co. Wicklow, held from Arthur Baldwin, Esq.

Witnesses: Joseph Pim, Ballymurrew, Co. Wicklow, farmer, John Ashton, yeoman and Grace Ashton, spinster, both of Ballymurrew.

Memorial witnessed by: Wm. Acton, Dublin, Esq., Thos, Acton, Dublin, gent.

269, 500, 180829 Ann Chaytor (seal)

449 MACARTNEY, JAMES, Hanover Square, Middlesex, and Granard, Co. Longford. 17 Oct. 1769. Précis ¾ p. 7 May 1770.

To Rt. Hon. the Earl of Hillsborough and Rt. Hon. Viscount Barrington his manor of Granard, Co. Longford and other lands etc. in counties of Longford and Westmeath as trustees. His daughter Catherine Macartney and said trustees exors.

Witnesses: Thomas Goostrey, parish of St. James, Westminster, gent., Cornelius Vanderstop, Cunies Street near Hanover Square aforesaid, gent., Christopher Killett,clerk to said Thomas Goostrey.

Memorial witnessed by: Thomas Goostrey, Dyonisia Day, housekeeper to said Catherine Macartney.

280, 142, 180904 Catherine Macartney (seal)

450 KIRWAN, FRANCIS, Blindwell, Co. Galway, gent. 16 Oct. 1768. Full 1½ p. 7 May 1770.

Dominick Blake, Fertygare, Co. Galway, Esq., trustee and exor. Michael Kirwan and Richard Kirwan (under 21 years), both of Blindwell and both my natural sons by Unity Linsky of Blindwell. My brother Martin Kirwan late of Blindwell, gent. My estate in houses and otherwise in town of Galway. Part of lands of Blindwell to which I am entitled by virtue of the Gavel Act(1). Mrs. Mary Lynch wife of Edmund Lynch of Ashgrove, Go. Calway, gent. Martin Lynch, Drimcong, Co. Galway.

Witnesses: Sibby Blake, Castlegrove, Co. Galway, widow, Walter Blake, Moneygannon, said Co., gent., John Lyons, Castlegrove, farmer.

Memorial witnessed by: James Maely, servant to said Dominick Blake, Alexr. Spawn, Dublin, attorney at law, notary public and one of the Proctors of H.M. Prerogative Court in Ireland.

273, 619, 180851 Dominick Blake (seal)

451 MORRIS, RICHARD, Prussia Street, Co. Dublin. 1 Feb. 1770. Précis ½ p. 9 June 1770.

To his wife Ann Morris, his dwelling house and garden in Prussia Street and all other real and personal estate.

(1) Where this form of tenure exists, real estate, in cases of intestacy, passes to the sons in equal shares instead of to the eldest.

Witnesses: Edmond M'Can and Jno. Alexander, both Dublin, gents., Wm. Jones, Dublin, shoemaker.

Memorial witnessed by: Jno. Alexander, Wm. Jones.
280, 282, 181603 Ann Morris (seal)

452 MAYNE, JOHN, Goland, Co. Fermanagh, Esq.

6 July 1762. Narrate $\frac{3}{4}$ p. 21 June 1770.

His wife Rebecca Mayne. His eldest son Samuel Mayne. His son Francis. His kinsman Charles Mayne, of Coothill, Co. Cavan. A provision made by testator for his younger children, save his son Francis. James Noble, Clentever, Co. Fermanagh, and James Betty, Clownish, Co. Monaghan, exors. His estate of Goland, Co. Fermanagh. Lands of Lammy which he held from Robert and Charles Eccles.

Witnesses: James Noble, Mahonstown, Co. Meath, Esq., James Browne, rough rider to testator, since deceased, Wm. Irwin, Corbally, Co Fermanagh, farmer, also since deceased.

Memorial witnessed by: Saml. Kathrens, Dublin, gent., John McCabe, Dublin, gent.

276, 600, 181825 S. Mayne (seal)
(Samuel Mayne eldest son of testator)

453 LOVETT, JONATHAN, Kingswell, Co. Tipperary.

8 Aug. 1770. Précis $\frac{1}{2}$ p. 14 Sept. 1770.

To his second son Verney Lovett (exor.) lands of Kingswell and Marshallswrath. Farm and lands of Carrons Reddy. Two houses in town of Tipperary sett to John Bluett and two small fields sett to Patrick Mangan which were left to testator by the Will of Mrs. Jane King, interest in lands of Montgasty, commonly called the Hills of Tipperary which testator purchased from Mr. Solomon Delane, all in Barony Clanwilliam, Co. Tipperary.

Witnesses: William Russell, Tipperary, Esq., Hugh Massy, Pegsborough, Esq., James Russell, Tipperary, Esq., all Co. Tipperary.

Memorial witnessed by: Bryan Meheux, Dublin, gent., William Russell.

274, 624, 182901 Verney Lovett (seal)

454 McGACHIN, Rev. STEPHEN, Ardillas, King's Co.

10 April 1769. Narrate ¾ p. 15 Sept. 1770.

His wife Susanna McGachin otherwise Lewis extx. Mrs. Hannah Palmer wife to Mr. Joseph Palmer of Glanncorra and sister to his said wife Susanna. Testator's sister Elizabeth Rutherford. Lands of Ardillas, in half Barony of Phillipstown, King's Co.

Witnesses: Rev. Adam Blair, Liss, King's Co., Michael Carroll, Glancroe, King's Co., schoolmaster, William Cowen, Glanacorra, servant to said testator.

Memorial witnessed by: William Cowen, James Ferrall, Dromoyle, King's Co., farmer.

282, 234, 182919 Susanna McGachin (seal)
Hannah Palmer (seal)

455 WILDE, JOHN, Kileeke, Co. Dublin, farmer.

24 April 1770. Narrate ¾ p. 4 Oct. 1770.

His eldest son Michael Wilde (already provided for). His daughter Jane who was then a lunatic. His daughter Mary Doyle wife of Christopher Doyle. His youngest son, John Wilde (exor.). His son James Wilde also then a lunatic. His daughter Bridget Wilde, spinster, under 21 years. His friend Thomas Savage, Finglas Wood, tanner, exor.

Witnesses: Thomas Butler, Richd. Dunn, both of Dublin, gents.

Memorial witnessed by: Jno. Hutton, Jno. McCabe, Dublin, gent.

283, 135, 183095 Thos. Savage (seal)
Michl. Wilde (seal)

456 DRUITT, JOSEPH, Dublin, merchant.

21 Oct. 1770. Narrate 2¼ pp. 28 Nov. 1770.

His wife Elinor Druitt. His son Edwd. Druitt, exor. His son Thos. Druitt. His daughter Jane Emerson otherwise Druitt wife of Henry Emerson deceased. His brother John Druitt, then surveyor of Excise in " Lisborn."

Houses etc. in Grafton Street, Dublin, a yard warehouse, etc. at rere of Mr. Wm. Hill's which he held by lease from late Anthony Barrodall. Shares in five ships or vessells, *The Love, The Law, The Marlborough, The Saltham* and *The Lovely Nelly of Whitehaven.* His sloop called *The Morning Star.* Three houses he built in Henry Street and corner Marlborough Street, ground leased from Mr. John Penrose, and then inhabited by Rev. Stewart Plunkett, Henry Talbot, Esq., and James Hussey, Esq. House he then lived in on the Bachelor's Walk, purchased from the children of late Jacob Jones. Two houses in Grafton Street, Mrs. Mary Butler lessor of ground, then inhabited by Luke Dempsey, upholder, and the representatives of Samuel White. Two houses in Stoneybatter purchased from Chas. Meares. Two houses on North side College Green, purchased from widow Manfield, then inhabited by Mr. John French and Thos. Smith. Houses in Cook Street purchased from widow Smith. Ground in Liffey Street. Houses on South side of College Green and a house in Trinity Lane held by lease from City of Dublin. Two houses in Back Lane held by lease from Corporation of Taylors. A house in Grafton Street, which he took from Eusebius Low.

Witnesses: James Mathews, gent., Michael Rourke, saltmaker, Jno. Wilmott, Esq., all of Dublin.

Memorial witnessed by: James Mathews, Jno. McCabe, Dublin, gent.

284, 261, 183947 Edward Druitt (seal)

457 RUSSELL, JOHN, Edenderry, Co. Down, linendraper.

1 Nov. 1770. Full 1 p. 28 Jan. 1771.

My wife Jane Russell. I confirm grant by deeds of lease and release to my son John Russell of my farm in Edenderry, and two other farms in counties of Down and Antrim. Said son John exor. My daughter Elizabeth Scott, otherwise Russell, her husband Patrick Scott. Agnes Lyons, otherwise Russell, my daughter and wife of Wm. Lyons of Belfast, merchant. My daughter Jane McCormick widow, Elinor McCormick, a minor, daughter of said Jane by Cornelius her late husband. Jno. McCormick, a minor, son of said Jane by said Cornelius. Mary McCormick, a minor, daughter of said

Jane by said Cornelius. My daughter Mary Russell, spinster. My stepson James Scott, Elizabeth Swandell, the sister of the said James Scott. My sister Grizell Davidson. My sister Ann Coates. My sister Sarah Davidson. My brother Hugh Russell.

Witnesses: Samuel Heron, Lisburn, Co. Antrim, and Jane his wife, Alexr. Arthur, Lisburn, gent.

Memorial witnessed by: Samuel Heron, John Mackay, Lisburn, writing clerk.

284, 314, 184566 John Russell (seal)

458 SMYTH, ALICE, otherwise MERCER, wife of Rev. Thos. Smyth, Treasurer of St. Patrick's, Dublin. 31 Dec. 1770. Narrate 1 p. 31 Jan. 1771.

After decease of her late father Fairfax Mercer, Esq., she was entitled to a moiety of the land of Clea, Co. Down. An agreement dated 9 Jan. 1770 entered into upon her intermarriage with said Thos. Smyth. Her sister Mary Fitzgerald. Her said husband Thos. Smyth exor.

Witnesses: John Morrison, John Barlow, both Dublin, Esqrs., John Barlow junior, second son of said John Barlow.

Memorial witnessed by: John Barlow junior, John Barlow.

284, 322, 184614 Thos. Smyth (seal)

459 GILBERT, ROBERT, Humphreystown, Co. Wicklow. 3 June 1769. Codicil [not dated]. Narrate 1 p. 7 Feb. 1771.

To his brother Richard Gilbert, his lands of Humphreystown and Lognagrove [Lugnagroagh], Co. Wicklow, for life only and then to his children save by Martha Barker daughter of Wm. Barker of Baltiboys, Co. Wicklow. His sister Frances wife of John Wills, extx.

Will and codicil witnessed by: Howard Humphrey, Esq., Richard Talbot, Matthias Dowse, gents., all of parish of Donard, Co. Wicklow.

Memorial witnessed by: Matthias Dowse, John Waddy, Dublin, gent.

284, 341, 184754 Frances Wills (seal)

460 DONELAN, NEHEMIAH, Caheroin, Co. Galway, Esq.
7 Oct. 1770. Codicil 12 Dec. 1770. Narrate 2½ pp. 5 March 1771.

His wife Mercy Donelan otherwise Shaw. His eldest son Nichs. Donelan. His second son Robt. Donelan. His third son Thos. Donelan. His youngest son John Donelan. His daughter Alice Burke otherwise Donelan, her intermarriage with Patk. Burke. His younger children Rebecca Donelan, Robt., Thos. and John. Robt. French, Moniva, Esq., and said wife Mercy, trustees. Exors. his said wife Mercy, Rev. Jeremiah Marsh and said Robt. French. Codicil mentions a settlement on his daughter Rebecca Kirwan otherwise Donelan and Mr. Thos. Kirwan her husband.

Lands of Toberpader, Licknebegg, Gortmaskehy, Cartron, Co. Galway. Lands of Cahirateige, Co. Galway. Lands and farms of Parke, Caherain (Cahiroen), Ballydavid, Garranamrahir and Island Rorey, Co. Galway.

Witnesses: Revd. Robt. Lewis, Athenry, Co. Galway, clerk, John Kirwan, Dublin, gent., Dominick Burke, Athenry, gent.

Codicil witnessed by: Stephen Donelan, Kelagh, Co. Galway, Chs. Donelan, Blackgarden, Co. Galway, Esq., David White, Athenry, shoemaker.

Memorial witnessed by: Dominick Burke, David Whyte.

288, 32, 185159 Mercy Donelan (seal)

461 SMITH, JOSEPH, Tigh Street, Dublin, ale draper.
9 March 1771. Narrate ¾ p. 28 March 1771.

His daughter Jane Jackson. His son John Smith exor. His sister Jane Jackson. The house with the lease thereof he then possessed in Tigh Street. His daughters Jane Jackson and Mary Cowley. His son-in-law Jno. Cowley exor. Simon Shiptrap's two daughters Ann and Mary.

Witnesses: Robt. Badcock, Tighe Street, clothier, Wm. Wills, Stoneybatter, Oxmantown, schoolmaster.

Memorial witnessed by: Robt. Badcock, Richd. Kean, Dublin, gent.

289, 10, 185388 John Cowley (seal)

462 LORD, CASSANDRA otherwise ARNOLDI, wife of Edward Lord, Dublin, gent. and youngest daughter and one of the co-heiresses of Samuel Arnoldi late of said city, Doctor of Physick, deceased.

24 Aug. 1766. Narrate 1¼ p. 3 April 1771.

Her husband Edward Lord exor. Testator at the time of her marriage to said Edward Lord with her sisters Catherine Arnoldi, Mary Arnoldi and Ann Jane Arnoldi, three other of the daughters and co-heiresses of the said Samuel Arnoldi, shared in a house in Carrow Lane, city of Limerick, formerly held by Jno. Furnell, a house near the Citadell in the Irish town of city of Limerick formerly held by Francis Williams, a house formerly held by Wm. Franklin, several houses formerly held by Robt. Wilkinson in the Irish town of said city, a piece of waste ground on east side of Carrowlane formerly held by said Robt. Wilkinson and Wm. Davis, another piece in the Irish town formerly held by Francis Sargent, a rent charge out of a house, tanyard etc. in Carrowlane, aforesaid, now or formerly belonging to Major Maguire, another rent charge out of a house and ground in city of Limerick now or formerly belonging to Jno. Jephson Esq., a rent charge out of lands of Killbarron, Co. Tipperary, and Townlewith, Co. Meath, then held by representatives of Robt. Vincent deceased, and also lands of Robertstown, and parts of Killeagh in the Island of Allen, Co. Kildare, expectant on the death of her mother, Ann Arnoldi. Testator also held an undivided fourth part of Little Bellingstown and Loughmartin, Co. Dublin, leased by said Samuel from the Archbishop of Dublin. Reciting that her said mother is since dead.

Witnesses: Stephen Radcliff, Dublin, Esq., Samuel Clossy, then of Dublin, Doctor of Physick. Thomas Campbell, Dublin, yeoman.

Memorial witnessed by: Stephen Radcliff, Jno. Bromwell, Dublin, yeoman.

284, 472, 185436 Edward Lord (seal)

463 KEAN, WILLIAM, Clontarf, Co. Dublin.

20 March 1770. Full 2¾ pp. 6 April 1771.

To be buried in churchyard of Clontarf near my father and mother. My friends Thos. Harrison, principal surveyor on the Customs House

Quay in Dublin, Michael Swift, Caple Street, Dublin, gent., trustees. My dear namesake Wm. Kean now residing with me, the son of my late brother John Kean. Richard Hingley, Orisdall, Isle of Man. Mrs. Jane Boles, any debt which my late brother Edward did or might owe to said Jane Boles. Miss Mary Boles, niece of said Jane Boles. All my lands etc. in Co. Wicklow, Co. Dublin, the County of the city of Dublin, and Co. Meath and elsewhere.

Witnesses: Rev. John Usher, rector of parish of Clontarf, Jonathan Swift, Stephen's Green, Dublin, gent., Deane Swift, Little Brittain Street, Dublin, surgeon.

Memorial witnessed by: John Usher, Jonathan Swift, Deane Swift.

282, 487, 185464 Will Kean (seal)

464 FINLAY, MARGARET otherwise THOMPSON, Ballygunnichan, Co. Down, widow. 29 July 1768. Narrate $\frac{3}{4}$ p. 13 April 1771.

Her two sons Isaac Finlay and James Finlay. Her farm of Ballygunnichan and profits arising to which she was entitled by Will of her late husband.

Witnesses: Alexr. Colville, Dromore, Co. Down, John Carlisle, Anaghmacowan, Co. Down, gent.

Memorial witnessed by: John Carlisle, Joseph Dickson, Dromore, Co. Down, gent.

283, 452, 185539 Isaac Finlay (seal)

465 GRAYDON, GEORGE, Killishe, Co. Kildare.
4 March 1762. Codicils: 1 July 1762. 23 July 1762. 10 Jan. 1770. Full $7\frac{1}{2}$ pp. 17 April 1771.

To be buried in the church of Gilltown next my late wife Jane Graydon. A settlement made in 1739 previous to my intermarriage with her, Thomas Graydon, Greenhills, Co. Kildare, gent., and John Hamilton, Dublin, goldsmith, were trustees. My eldest son Alexr. Graydon, exor. My sons Robt. Graydon (third son, exor.), and George Graydon (fourth son) and my daughter Avis Mary Graydon.

Said Alexander to be guardian of my children Hamilton Graydon, Robert Graydon, George Graydon and Avis Mary Graydon until they severally arrive at age of 21 years, (but in codicil Sir K. D. Burrowes appointed guardian in his place). My second son Hamilton Graydon, sums laid out equipping him for the Army, I have procured my son a Cornet's commission. My brother Thomas Graydon. A bond perfected to me by Arthur Hemphill. My nephew George Graydon son of my brother Erasmus Graydon. My friend Sir Kildare Dixon Burrowes, Dublin, Bart., and Charles Neal, Shean Castle, Co. Antrim, Esq., trustees. Mr. Robert Bray.

Lands, premises etc. in Naas, Co. Kildare, and part of the commons of Naas known by the name of Monacaka. Lands of Killishee and Sword Wallstown, Co. Kildare held by lease from Hon. Richard Fitzpatrick, Esq.

Witnesses: Geo. Perkins, Dublin, attorney, deceased, Richd. Cudmore, Dublin, attorney, Bartholomew Cliffe, Carlow, gent.

Codicil witnessed by: Richard Tracy, Naas, Co. Kildare, slater, deceased, Jno. Cosker, Killishee, farmer, Anthony Munilly, servant to testator.

Second codicil: Following death of eldest son Alexander Graydon in England 10 July, testator's son Robert inherits instead.

Codicil witnessed by: Rev. Wm. Donnellan, Naas, clerk. Christopher Hawkins, Giltown, farmer, John Mitchell, late of Co. Kildare, writing master, deceased.

Third codicil: Charles O'Neill, trustee, is dead. Thos. Ryves Rassalagh, Co. Wicklow, appointed in his place. I have purchased part of Sir Henry Echlin's estate, the wood of Killishee. Son Robt. Graydon to be sole exor. of Will and Codicils.

Codicil witnessed by: Rev. Wm. Digby, Geashill, King's Co. clerk, Rev. Wm. Taverner, Kildare, clerk, James Fagan, Killishee, farmer.

Memorial witnessed by: Richd. Cudmore, Rev. Wm. Donnellan, Jno. Cosker, James Fagan.

282, 495, 185581 Robt. Graydon (seal)

466 SINCLAIR, JOHN, Holyhill, parish of Leckpatrick, Co. Tyrone. 6 Feb. 1770. Full 1 p. 20 April 1771.

My wife Elizabeth Sinclair. To my son William Sinclair the quarter land of Argry, parish of Lifford, Co. Donegal as settled upon him at his marriage by deed between his elder brother James Sinclair, since deceased and me. My son George Sinclair (under 21 years). John James Perry second son of George Perry of Mullaghmore. Exors. my wife Elizabeth, John Hamilton of Strabane, Esq., Samuel Perry, Mullaghmore Esq., and Mr. George Buchanan, Strabane, apothecary. Andrew Knox to " inspect into the conduct of my son George." Lands of Holyhill and Kenachan (Kinachan), Legfordrummon [? Ligfordrum or Douglas], Beaghs and Knockaniller. My house and Demesne of Holyhill.

Witnesses: James Stevenson, Esq., Robt. Porter, merchant, both of Strabane, Robt. Orr, Gallony, farmer, both Co. Tyrone.

Memorial witnessed by: Robt. Orr, Gallony, Thomas Buchanan, Strabane, gent.

286, 151, 185663 Elizabeth Sinclair (seal)

467 COOKE, GEORGE, Drom, Co. Tipperary, gent. 15 July 1768. Précis ½ p. 24 April 1771.

To his second son George Cooke his interest in lands of Gurtnaduff, Ardkeen, Ardkeenbegg, Gurteenvillen, and the two Raths, part of the lands of Drom, situate in Barony Eliogarty, Co. Tipperary, held by lease from James Butler of Drom to the testator's father Randal Cooke, deceased, and testator's part of the Commons of Monemore.

Witnesses: John Willington, Killoskehan, Minchin Carden, Fishmoyne, Geo. Bennett, Lorane, Co. Tipperary, Esq.

Memorial witnessed by: John Willington, James Hodgson, Dublin.

279, 676, 185810 Geo. Cooke (seal)

468 READING, BENJAMIN, Pelletstown, Co. Dublin, Esq. 17 and 25 April 1771. Narrate 1 p. 13 May 1771.

His friend Barry Colles, Dublin, Esq., trustee and legatee. Rebecca Tomly then married to Wm. Read of Aston's Quay, master porter.

Mrs. Mary Gumly who lodged in his house at Pelletstown.

Lands of Pelletstown, Co. Dublin. His houses etc. in Borr's Court, Michael's Lane and Schoolhouse Lane, Dublin, Derrycooly, Derrooly and Basteele otherwise Tullymorahan, King's Co. Ballynunry and Kilcoole, then in tenancy of Owen Coghlan and . . . Butler in Co. Carlow, and all other lands which testator was in possession of or entitled to "as heir to Gerard Borr the younger, and as heir to Christian Borr his grandfather and to Margaret Borr, the mother of the said Christopher." A house opposite the mansion house of Pelletstown then set to Edward Buckley, Esq.

Witnesses: Wm. Smart, Borr Court, Dublin, writing clerk, Pat. Conlan of same, writing clerk, Pat. Butler, Michael's Lane, Dublin, grocer.

Codicil witnessed by: Pat. Conlan, Wm. Fleming, Christ Church Lane, peruke maker, Peter Dillon, The Combe, weaver.

Memorial witnessed by: Wm. Costello, Dublin, clerk to Barry Colles, Edwd. George, Dublin, gent.

281, 265, 186195 Barry Colles (seal)

469 REED, ROBERT, Annagh, parish of Clonfeckle, Co. Tyrone.

23 Oct. 1764. Codicil 8 July 1769. Narrate ¾ p. 5 June 1771.

His wife. James Reed and Isaac Reed sons of testator. William Fluker, his son-in-law and his wife Mary Fluker. His sons John Reed, Thomas Reed, Archibald Reed. Exors. William Stewart and Wm. McDoell both of Annagh and William Hodgens, Benburb, all in parish and Co. aforesaid. His ten acres of land and houses.

Witnesses to Will and Codicil: Bry. Carbery, Joseph Stewart, Abraham Plunket, all of or near Annagh.

Memorial witnessed by: Abraham Plunket, Joseph Stewart of Annagh, Co. Tyrone, gent.

287, 202, 186500 William Stewart (seal)
William McDoell (seal)

470 SMYTH, Rev. HENRY, Limerick, clerk.

4 Nov. 1752. Précis ½ p. 19 July 1771.

His wife Diana, extx. His brother Geo. Smyth. Lands of Kileegy, Shan[n]aknock and Carhumeer, Barony Tulla, Co. Clare.

Witnesses: Rev. Wm. Maunsell, Limerick, clerk, Andrew Shepherd, late of Limerick, Esq., deceased, Wm. Byrenn, Limerick, carpenter.

Memorial witnessed by: William Furlong, Dublin, gent., John Smith, Newcastle, Co. Limerick, gent.

283, 552, 187183 G. Smyth (seal)

471 BEARD, RICHARD, Athy, Co. Kildare.

18 July 1771. Narrate part in full, ¾ p. 9 Aug. 1771.

My son William. Son Richard. My son Joseph. My son Charles My daughter Margt. Harrison. My daughter Anne. My daughter Hannah. George Daker and Geo. King, both of Athy, exors.

His dwelling house, shop, cattle, etc. Lands of Ardura [? Andrew, Co. Kildare]. His interest in Wm. Orr's holding, and the holding he had from Rachel Roche, and the meadow that Mr. Chambre held [situation not mentioned ? all in Athy]. Lands of Dunbrin, Garro[o]nagh and Whitebog, Queen's Co. except part of Garro[o]nagh that his son Richard then grazed.

Witnesses: Hunt Calcott Chambre, Athy, gent., Daniel Mansergh, brewer, George Daker, junr., tanner., William Roche, Athy., merchant.

Memorial witnessed by: Wm. Roche, Timothy Delany, Dublin, gent.

287, 334, 187453 Wm. Beard (seal)

472 BURKITT, ROBERT, Cookstown, Co. Wexford, farmer.

28 Jan. 1767. Narrate ¾ p. 26 Aug. 1771.

Wife Sarah Burkitt and daughter Ann exors. His daughters Phiana [? Diana] Burkitt and Ann Burkitt. His daughter Sarah Fearon. His son Robert Burkitt. Rents to children of his said son

Robert Burkitt, Allen Loyd, Ballyfarrel and Wm. Fearon of Colecannon, both Co. Wexford, farmers by their present wives. Lands of Cookstown, part set to Silvester McGrah, George Wafer, and Marks Wafer.

Witnesses: Thomas Daith, Glasscarrigg, Co. Wexford, farmer, Jno. Johnson, of same, farmer, Wm. Johnson, Coolotrindle, said Co., linen weaver.

Memorial witnessed by: Jno. Johnson, Castell, gent., and attorney of H.M. Court of King's Bench.

287, 368, 187586 Robt. Burkitt (seal)

473 KIRWAN, MARTIN FITZTHOMAS, Knock, Co. Galway.

26 April 1771. Narrate 1 p. 12 Sept. 1771.

His nephew Joseph Kirwan, Cornanty, Co. Galway Esq., eldest son of John Kirwan deceased the brother of testator. Martin Kirwan, second son of said John. Richard Kirwan, Cregg, Co. Galway, Esq., Capt. Andrew Kirwan the brother of said Richard. Capt. Hyacinth Kirwan, third brother of the said Richard Kirwan of Cregg. Richard Kirwan of Woodfield, Co. Galway, Martin Kirwan, the eldest son of said Richard. Nicholas the second son of said Richard. Andrew the brother of said Richard Kirwan. Patrick the eldest son of said Andrew. Denis Kelly, Castlekelly, Co. Galway, trustee and with Jno. Blake, Windfield, Co. Galway, Esq., exor. To his brother Ambrose Kirwan £50 per annum. To Edward Kirwan of Turin, Co. Mayo, Esq., £24 per annum. Quarter land of Knockdronnadough otherwise Knockadrong, Barony Clare, Co. Galway.

Witnesses: Marcus Brown, Moyne, Thomas Nolan, Caple Street, Dublin, attorney, John Burke, York Street, Dublin, attorney.

Memorial witnessed by: John Burke, Laurence Keating, Dublin, attorney.

286, 339, 187801 Joseph Kirwan (seal)

474 TUTHILL, GEORGE, Faha, Co. Limerick, Esq.

27 May 1768. Narrate 1 p. 12 Nov. 1771.

Rev. Wm. Maunsell, Limerick, Jno. Westropp, Atyflin, Co. Limerick, Esq., trustees. His wife Dorothy Tuthill. His son John

Tuthill. His son Christopher Tuthill (under 21 years). His daughter Ann Tuthill (unmarried). His daughters Frances and Ann.

Lands of Faha and the two Ballyanra[h]ans [Ballyanrahan East and West, Co. Limerick]. His estate of Ballinleeny, Kilmore and both Doorlesses, Ballyteige, Ballinstona, [Co. Limerick], part set to his tenants Beanell and Maxwell, Killenure otherwise Knockeen, [Co. Limerick]. His farms of Garrankea and Lisnemucky, [? Co. Limerick]. His farm of Newtown.

Witnesses: John Harrison, Limerick, gent., Robt. Harrison, Garrureagh, Co. Clare, Esq., Seps. Hewson, Brushy, Co. Limerick, gent.

Memorial witnessed by: Robt. Harrison, Percival Harte.

285, 359, 188485 Christr. Tuthill (seal)

475 STRINGER, JOHN, Ballykean, Co. Wicklow.

5 Jan. 1771. Narrate ¾ p. 25 Nov. 1771.

His wife Grace Stringer. His son Joseph Stringer (under 21 years). His daughter Elizabeth Stringer and his daughter Ann Stringer (both under 21 years and unmarried). To his brother Joseph Stringer that part of the lands of Ballykean now in his possession. His lease of lands of Ballykean.

Witnesses: Henry Revell, Redcross, yeoman, Wm. Radford, Ballykean, yeoman, Talbot Ashenhurst, Wicklow, gent., all in Co. Wicklow.

Memorial witnessed by: Henry Revell, Thomas Acton, Dublin, gent.

290, 17, 188798 Joseph Stringer (seal)

476 TOOLE, LAURENCE, Clondalkin, Co. Dublin.

21 Nov. 1771. Précis ½ p. 25 Nov. 1771.

His daughter Jane Toole (exor.) widow and relict of Michael Toole deceased. Two acres of ground in scrubby pasture in lands of Clondalkin then in possession of Pierce Aspell, farmer, as tenant to testator.

Witnesses: James White, Dublin, writing clerk, Walter Lacy, Clondalkin, smith, Thomas Duggan, Kilmainham, publican.

Memorial witnessed by: James White, John Fitzpatrick, writing clerk.

287, 684, 188810 Jane Toole (her mark) (seal)

477 POE, JOHN, Solsborough, Co. Tipperary, Esq.

13 Oct. 1771. Narrate 1¼ p. 3 Dec. 1771.

His brother James Poe of Solsborough exor. Edward Poe eldest son of testator's brother Emanuel Poe of Moyroe, said county, gent., Richard Gason the younger, Killashalloe, and Joshua Minnet of Annabeg, both Co. Tipperary, Esqrs., trustees. Town and lands of Solsborough otherwise Clonmuck and one moiety of lands of Belleen, all in Barony Lr. Ormond, Co. Tipperary.

Witnesses: Richard Gason, the elder, Killashalloe, Esq., George Franklin, Nenagh, said Co., land surveyor, Patk. Leary, Killashalloe, servant of said Richard Gason the elder.

Memorial witnessed by: George Franklin, George Smith, Nenagh merchant.

289, 18, 188941 Jam[es] Poe (seal)

478 SHAW, SAMUEL, Melough, Co. Down, gent.

31 May 1748. Codicil 13 April 1749. Full 2 pp. 19 Dec. 1771.

My son John Shaw. My son Andrew Shaw. My son Samuel Shaw. That part of my freehold estate in the town and lands of Ballynegarrick, Co. Down, known by the name or names of Jno. Maharg's and John Macoghfry's farms. Part of my said freehold estate in Ballynegarrick now held by Jno. Young, the remaining part of my said estate in said townland of Ballynegarrick commonly called Andrew Pattersons, Joseph Pattersons and Widow Gardeners and Arthur Rayney Maxwell's farms and holdings. Codicil concerns the cutting of turf at Marland Moss.

Witnesses: Wm. Beers, Edenderry, Jno. Murdogh, Ballylesson, Hugh Hana, Ballylesson, Co. Down, gent.

Witnesses to Codicil: John Barckly, Drumatigg, James Camlin, Toddstown, Rachel Todd, Toddstown, spinster, all in Co. Down.

Memorial witnessed by: Jno. Murdoch, Jas. Camlin, Toddstown, said Co., gent.

290, 102, 189222 Andrew Shaw (seal)

479 STEPHENS, GEORGE, Knockanree, Co. Wicklow.
5 July 1760. Précis ½ p. 7 Jan. 1772.

To three executors [not named] as trustees, lands of Blindwood and Oughill, Co. Wicklow, and lands of Monegrena [Monagreany], Co. Wexford. The Will registered at the desire of one of the executors Frances Butler otherwise Stephens, now wife of Henry Butler of Ballinvallon, Co. Wicklow, gent. [No witnesses to Will].

Memorial witnessed by: Edward Bury, Dublin, gent., Richd. Bury, Knockanree, Co. Wicklow.

285, 452, 189360 Fras. Butler (seal)

480 HOWARD, BRIDGET, Dirty Lane, Dublin, widow.
23 March 1771. Full, partly narrate ½ p. 7 Jan 1772.

" To be interred by my husband Patrick Howard at the expense of my brother." Sisters Margt. Kelly and Mary Hardford's children. Her brother Patrick Wolton, exor. Gives nothing to his [her exor.'s] daughters Mary Langan and Jane Wolton. Her nephew Patrick Wolton.

Witnesses: James Mitchell, weaver, Patk. Rooney, merchant, Dublin.

Memorial witnessed by: Patk. Rooney, James Mitchell.

290, 128, 189365 Pat. Wolton (seal)

481 BURTON, JOSEPH, Shinrone, King's Co.
7 May 1771. Narrate ¾ p. 21 Feb. 1772.

His wife Mary Burton. His sons Thomas, William and Joseph. To his daughter Martha, his daughter Elizabeth, his daughter Ann, legacies when 21 years. His son Richard. His daughter Folomsby.

Farms of Skehanagh and Lackagh, [? King's Co.] held by lease from John Lloyd, Esq. The house he then lived in. The lands of Dromonduff. Lands of Shinrone. His holding in Shinrone, known as Richard Hurst's holding. His holding in Shinrone that Robert Grace lives in with the lands of Gurtgreen and the Pollough thereunto belonging.

Witnessed by " three credible subscribing witnesses."

Memorial witnessed by: John Doolan, Shinrone, King's Co. one of the three witnesses above mentioned, Thomas Collins, Dublin, gent.

285, 518, 189985 Jos. Burton (seal)

482 AUSTEN, WILLIAM, Dublin, Esq., one of the Masters of H.M. High Court of Chancery in Ireland. 23 Aug. 1763. Narrate ¾ p. 2 April 1772.

His wife Elizabeth Austen exor. His son Wm. Tynte Austen. His brother-in-law John Lawton, Cork, merchant, Wm. Perry, Woodroffe and Wm. Lane, Dublin, Esq., trustees and exors. His son Thomas Bowes Austen.

Lands of Ballybredoe and Old Rouskagh, Co. Tipperary, leased to Joshua Fennell and rest of real and personal fortune. Lands of Kilgrogy and Carrigateary, otherwise Rocksborough and the Spittle Lands of Ardfinin [Co. Tipperary], purchased from Sir Thomas Prendergast and leased to Thos. Clutterbuck, Stephen Moore and John Prendergast.

Witnesses: John Smith, Dublin, gent., James Maddock, Dublin, gent., Robt. Wallis, Dublin, public notary.

Memorial witnessed by: Henry Walter French, Dublin, gent., Robt. Wallis.

288, 271, 190521 Eliz. Austen (seal)

483 NEALE, EVAN, Dublin, measurer.

12 Nov. 1750. Narrate ½ p. 8 April 1772.

To his friends Hugh Wilson and Patrick Wall (exors.) the house in which he then dwelt with the smith's forge adjoining in trust [situation not mentioned]. His wife Catherine Neale exor. His two daughters Anne Neale and Mary Neale (under 21 years and unmarried).

Witnesses: Joseph Willcocks, Dublin, gent., Jno. Kathrens, Dublin, public notary.

Memorial witnessed by: Joseph Willcocks, Wm. Williams, Dublin, public notary.

289, 236, 190581 Cathern Neale (seal)

484 RAWLINS, JAMES, Dublin, weaver.

28 Jan. 1772. Narrate ½ p. 2 May 1772.

His wife Ann Rawlins. His son Thomas Rawlins. Lease of his house on Lazor's Hill and lease of a piece of ground in Harvey's yard on said hill, both held from Mrs. Lucy Sterling, Dublin, widow. Debts due to Wm. Percivall, New Ross, Dublin, rope maker. Exors. said Wm. Percivall and James Classon, Rathmines, gents. Thomas Doyle, Lazor's Hill, gardener.

Witnesses: Jno. Moss, Jno. Devereaux, Edwd. English, all of Dublin.

Memorial witnessed by: Jno. Devereux, Jno. Macabe, Dublin, gent.

289, 273, 190786 William Percival (seal)

485 WELDON, ROBERT, Birr, King's Co.

7 Feb. 1769. Narrate ¾ p. 26 May 1772.

His wife Mary Weldon otherwise Parsons exor. Elizabeth Weldon testator's mother. His only daughter Mary Weldon, (under 18 years, unmarried). His sisters Elinor, Celia, Mary, Jane and Hester [Weldon]. James Frazer, Dublin, Esq., Wm. Parsons, junr., exors. His real and personal estate.

Witnesses: James Jackson, Birr, King's Co., gent., Richd. Hansard, an officer in the — Regt. of Foot, Edwd. Lowry, Birr, merchant.

Memorial witnessed by: James Jackson, James Hastler, Dublin, gent.

288, 359, 191315 M. Weldon (seal)
(Mary Weldon otherwise Parsons)

486 HAMILTON, ANDREW, Ballymacdonnell, Co. Donegal.

10 May 1771. Narrate 1 p. 18 June 1772.

His wife Euphemia (exor.) guardian of his children during minorities. His eldest son Andrew Hamilton. His three daughters. His second son William Peter Hamilton. Rev. James Montgomery, Cloverhill, Alexr. Montgomery of the Hall, and Thos. Nesbitt of Killmacredon, Co. Donegal, Esqrs., trustees. Cuthbert Smith Esq., Captain in the 5th Regt. of Dragoons, exor. Town and lands of Ballymacdonnell, Dunkanelly and Ballymagowan and other his real estate.

Witnesses: Francs. Fawcett, Killybeggs, gauger, John Law and Hugh Langan, both of town of Dunkaneley, gents., all in Co. Donegal.

Memorial witnessed by: Francs. Fawcett, Thos. Arnold, Killybeggs, gent.

291, 323, 191658 Euphemia Hamilton (seal)

487 BARNEWALL, MATHIAS, son of Lord Trimlestown.

28 June 1764. Précis ½ p. 14 July 1772.

His brother the Hon. Thomas Barnewall. Lands in counties of Dublin, Meath and Galway and in the King's Co. to which he was entitled to the reversion in fee expectant on the death of his father Robt. Barnewall, Esq., commonly called Lord Trimlestown.

Witnesses: Thomas Earl of Westmeath, Thomas Earl of Louth, Jno. Egan, Dublin, gent.

Memorial witnessed by: Thos. Earl of Westmeath, Jas. Crowe Dublin, gent.

290, 319, 192142 Thos. Barnewall (seal)

488 WILLIAMS, RICHARD, Charleville, Co. Cork, gent.

4 Nov. 1771. Narrate 1 p. 16 July 1772.

His wife Ann Williams otherwise Gibbings. His brother-in-law Bartholomew Gibbings, Gibbings Grove, Co. Cork, Esq. His nephew Richard Williams and his present wife Elizabeth Williams otherwise Smith. Lands of Dromarig, Barony Duhallow, Co. Cork. Mullahard otherwise Highmount and Clashnespirlogh.

Witnesses: Lawrence Donegan, Esq., James Donegan, apothecary, Joseph Rains, gent., all of Charleville.

Memorial witnessed by: Joseph Rains, Andrew Batwell, Fortland, Co. Cork, gent.

274, 646, 192175 Ann Williams (seal)

489 MAGILL, JOHN, Dublin, perukemaker.

21 July 1772. Narrate ½ p. 11 Sept. 1772.

His wife Elizth. Magill, extx. His daughter Rachell Magill. A debt due by John Reilly, Esq. His son Wm. Magill. His son John Magill. The house in which he lived [situation not mentioned].

Witnesses to Will and Memorial: Wm. Ker and Wm. Maddock, both Dublin, gents.

288, 575, 192803 Eliza. Magill (seal)

490 KAVANAGH, WILLIAM, Drunbrow, Co. Dublin.

25 Sept. 1772. Full 1 p. 30 Sept. 1772.

To be buried in the churchyard of St. Margarets.

My wife. Patrick Kavanagh my eldest son. Edward Kavanagh, my third son, £50 when out of his apprenticeship. Joseph Kavanagh my second son. To my son Thomas Kavanagh and Bridget Kavanagh and Mary Kavanagh my two daughters, £50 each when 21 years or on marriage. My daughter Margt. Kavanagh, my second daughter. To William Kavanagh, my son, £20 when 21 years. My son Joseph and Anthy. McMahon, Tubberbun, exors. To James Kavanagh for his support and maintenance for life the lands of Ednbingh to be in trust in the hands of my said son Joseph. Lands of Ballymun, Drumbrow [Dunbro] and Portmillock [Portmellick] and St. Margaret's. Edward Fitzharris to have the part of the house and garden he now lives in free during the lease of Drumbrow.

Witnesses: William Loughman, Chapelmidway, Anthy. McMahon, Tubberbun, both Co. Dublin, gents.

Memorial witnessed by: Wm. Loughman, Michael Smyth, Sublin, gent.

293, 10, 192948 Jos. Cavanagh (seal)

491 DODD, MARY, Newtown, Co. Dublin, widow.

3 Aug. 1767. Narrate ½ p. 22 May 1773.

To her daughter Mary Segrave, and to her daughter Bridget Carberry all her interest in lease of Newtown and Dunganstown, Co. Dublin, and all the substance and effects which belonged to her late husband, Patrick Dodd, equally between her said daughters. Thomas Segrave and James Carberry exors.

Witnesses: Rev. Patrick Grace, Skerrys, John Lenaghan, Beavertown, farmer, Patrick Boyle, Lusk, schoolmaster, all Co. Dublin.

Memorial witnessed by: John Lenaghan, James Barlow, Dublin, gent.

297, 549, 193139 James Carberry (seal)

492 DONNELLON, ANNE, then of Athenry, Co. Galway, spinster, daughter of John Donnellon, of Ballydonnellon, said Co., Esq. 4 March 1748. Narrate ¾ p. 26 Nov. 1772.

To be buried in Abbey of Kilconnell. Reciting that testatrix was entitled by Will of her father, said John Donnellon, deceased, to sum of £1,500 when 18 years, which sum was to be paid by his son and heir Malacky Donnellon, brother to testatrix. Reciting that she attained said age of 18 years on 20th day of Feb. preceeding the day of date of said Will. Her brother Anthony Donnellon. Her brother Edmd. Donnellon. Her brother Charles Donnellon. Her eldest brother said Malacky Donnellon. Her nurse tender Mary Corilly otherwise Coppinger. Her foster father Dens. Connor. To John Burke of Kilconnell, for him and the rest of his fraternity £30 for their good offices. Widow Anne Donnellon of Loughrea. Her sister Mary Donnellon. Honora Wall who was servant to her mother. Her uncle Robert French at Rasans, said Co., Esq., and her said brother Anthony Donnellon, exors.

Witnesses: John Lapdell, Domk. Lapdell, Robt. Broughton.

Memorial witnessed by: Thos. Kenny, Galway, gent., Dens. Kibrenagh, Loughuky, Co. Galway, writing master.

296, 25, 193788 Edmd. Donnellon (seal)
of Loughukey, Co. Galway, Esq., brother to testatrix.

493 ANDERSON, ROBERT, Little Booter Lane, Dublin.

27 Aug. 1768. Full 2 pp. 26 Nov. 1772.

To be interred in St. Andrew's Churchyard, Dublin. My wife Mary Anderson, exor. John Carmichael, Castle Street, Dublin, hosier. Jonathan Binns, Castle Street, Dublin, ironmonger, trustees and exors. My son John ,under 21 years. My daughter Thomasine. Two houses on ground in Mosse Street, Dublin, mortgaged to Hopkin Harris deceased. My house in Little Booter Lane in which I live.

Witnesses: Wm. Jordan, Wm. Mondel, both Dublin, gents., John Hays, same, painter.

Memorial witnessed by: Wm. Jordan, Stephen Malone, Dublin, woolcomber.

293, 55, 193795 John Carmichael (seal)

494 EDGEWORTH, ROBERT, Dublin, Esq.

12 Dec. 1772. Précis ½ p. 14 Jan. 1773.

His brother Usher Edgeworth. John Usher, Esq., Co. Wicklow, Christopher Usher, Co. Carlow, Esq., trustees and exors. His real estate in Ireland.

Witnesses: Richd. Williams, Dublin, jeweller, Love Theophilus Casson, Dublin, gent., William Williams, Dublin, public notary.

Memorial witnessed by: Richd. Williams, Wm. Glascock, Dublin, gent.

293, 120, 194310 John Usher (seal)

495 TRIQUET, JOHN PETER, Meath Street, Dublin, silk dyer.

4 Oct. 1771. Narrate 1¾ p. 16 Jan. 1773.

His two sisters Lucy Roberdeau and Susanna Lecras, both resident in London. A part of testator's effects for their children to be paid into hands of Mr. Isaac Roberdeau for use of said children. To Jno. Combs and his wife Margaret Combs who resided and dwelt in his dwelling house in Meath street, Dublin, until their daughter Mary Combs should arrive at the age of 21 years, his house and concerns at or near Stephen's Green, Dublin tenanted by Jno. Carden, Esq. To said Jno. Combs and Margt. Combs his lease of his said dwelling house in Meath Street. His friend Mark Bloxham and said Jno. Combs, exors.

Witnesses: Jno. Lennon, Dublin, silk dyer, Lewis Moore, Dublin, gent., George Cullen, Dublin, then apprentice to said Lewis Moore.

Memorial witnessed by: Lewis Moore, Geo. Reynolds, Dublin, apprentice to said Lewis Moore.

294, 192, 194340 John Combs (seal)

496 McCALLY, MARY, otherwise BRADSTREET, Willsbrook, Co. Longford, widow. 11 Aug. 1768. Narrate 1¼ p. 23 Jan. 1773.

Her grandson Thomas Wright. Her daughter Margaret Connor otherwise McCally otherwise Tramessea extx. Her grand-daughter Mary McCally daughter to her late son Simon Bradstreet McCally (under 21 years, unmarried). Her son-in-law James Wright. The children of her deceased daughter Euphemia Wright, otherwise McCally. Her daughter-in-law Catherine McCally. Her nephew Robert Richd. McCally, Esq. Her servant Jno. Brady.

Town and lands of Innestown otherwise Jonestown and other lands she held therewith in Co. Westmeath. Lower Killeen, Co. Longford. To Patrick Toole she bequeathed her interest in lands of Rath, Co. Westmeath.

Witnesses: Robert Richard McCally, Tully, Co. Longford, gent., Arthur Webb, Dublin, gent., attorney, Jno. Sheridan, Doctor of Physick, Co. Longford, David Reilly, gent., Co. Longford.

Memorial witnessed by: Thos. Digenan, servant to Michael Tramassea, Dublin, wine merchant, Sarah Nowlan, servant to said Michl. Tramassea.

294, 217, 194422 Margt. Tramassea (seal)

497 ELLIS, EDWARD, Dublin, Esq.
22 Jan. 1773. Narrate 3½ pp. 10 Feb. 1773.

His wife Mary Ellis. His son Edward Ellis. His grandson Francis Edward Ellis, the first and then the only son and child of his said son Edward Ellis. Testator wished said Francis Edward Ellis as soon as he attained the age of 8 years to be sent to some reputable public school and from thence sent to the University. Testator's brother-in-law Francis Whyte, Esq. had agreed to pay his nephew, testator's son Thomas Ellis an annuity. Said Thomas had one daughter Maria Ellis (unmarried). Francis Edgworth, Dublin, Esq., Rev. Singleton Harpur, Dublin, clerk, trustees.

Lands of Corlea and Bill[e]ady, Co. Monaghan, Lands of New-grange, Co. Meath, Bellfadock, Co. Meath, and Hermitage, Co. Fermanagh. Lands and tenements in town of Drogheda leased from the Corporation of Drogheda.

Witnesses: Joseph Ellis, Jno. Ellis, both of Dublin, cabinet makers, Alexr. Anderson, Dublin, gent.

Memorial witnessed by: Joseph Ellis, Joseph Griffith, Dublin, gent.

293, 177, 194741 Fras. Edgworth (seal)
Singleton Harpur (seal)

498 WHITE, RICHARD, BallymacEgan, Co. Tipperary, farmer.

4 Feb. 1744. Full 1¾ p. 30 April 1773.

My wife Ann White. To my son Richard White my interest in lands of BallymacEgan. My grand-daughter Ann Palmer, daughter of Francis Palmer, deceased. My daughter Ann Palmer. My son Joseph White. My two sons Joseph White and Richard White. My two daughters Sarah Palmer and Mary Palmer. Jonathan Harding, Derrykeel, King's Co., my wife Ann White and my son Richard White, exors.

Witnesses: William Harding, Jonathan Harding the younger, John Dann.

Jonathan Harding of Ballygaddy, King's Co., gent., maketh oath that he saw above named Richard White execute the Will, and saith that Jonathan Harding, Ann White and Richard White the exors. in said Will are dead. Sworn 24 April 1773 at Birr.

297, 419, 195633 Jona. Harding.

499 GILLYLAND, ALICE, parish of Newtown, Co. Down, spinster. 5 May 1756. Full 1 p. 12 May 1773.

My sister Margaret Morrison, parish of Newtown, widow. My nephew Archibald Morrison, exor. I am seized in fee of a third part of the tenement formerly in the possession of Widow Oliver and three quarters of a tenement formerly in possession of James Templeton, both on north side of the High Street of Newtown, Co. Down, and two acres of land near the highway leading from Newtown to Belfast (bounded by the park formerly Hugh Campbell's, the park formerly Nevin Caldwell's, and the park formerly Alexr. Gregg's) which I hold under the late Sir Robt. Colvill, Knt.

Witnesses: James Thompson, merchant, John Thompson, white smith, both of Newtown, James Chambers and William Shannon, both of Greengraves, parish of Newtown, farmers.

Memorial witnessed by: William Shannon, David Henderson, Belfast, Co. Antrim, stationer.

293, 379, 195952 Archibd. Morrison (seal)

500 COOPER, EXPERIENCE, late of Cooper's Hill, Queen's Co., but last of Dublin, widow. 18 Sept. 1769. Narrate 3 p. 7 June 1773.

Joshua Clibborne and Alexr. Jaffray, both Dublin, merchants, trustees. Her son Edward Cooper. Her daughter Lydia Clibborne, wife of Joshua Clibborne, son of Robert Clibborne. Her daughter Ann Barclay. Her third daughter Sarah Clibborne. Daughters Lydia and Sarah Clibborne, exors.

House in Meath Street, Dublin, held by lease from Bernard Brown deceased, and set by lease by her late brother Jonathan Strettle to the late John Newett and then occupied by his son Jonathan. Her house in Elbow Lane, Dublin, held by lease from Anthony Sharp, devised to her by her brother Jonathan Strettle deceased. Her ground, houses and tenements in Eustace Street, Dublin, lately occupied by Henry Barton deceased, and then by Francis Christian; her two houses in Cooke Street devised to her in last Will of her father Abell Strettell deceased, set to late Jno. Newett and occupied by his under tenants. Ground in Hanover Square held from Bernard Brown, deceased.

Witnesses: Thomas Jaffray, Dublin, gent., Robert Jaffray, Dublin, merchant, Richard Thwaites, Dublin, public notary.

Memorial witnessed by: Saml. Boursiquot, Dublin, public notary. Robt. Jeffray.

296, 279, 196369 Sarah Clibborne (seal)

501 FENNELL, JOHN, Shangunagh, Queen's Co., gent.

5 June 1765. Précis ¼ p. 22 July 1773.

To his eldest daughter Elizabeth Fennell, his lease of Ballylopeen, Co. Cork, under Lord Kingston.

[Names of witnesses to Will not recorded].

Memorial witnessed by: James Kearney, Newenham Lawless, both of Dublin, gents.

299, 21, 197014 Eliza. Fennell (seal)

502 KERBY, LAWRENCE, Dublin, chairman.

1 April 1772. Narrate ½ p. 24 July 1773.

" Hannah Kerby, Margaret Kerby and Mary Kerby his lawful wife and children " to divide equally between them profit rents of leases of 1766, 1767, 1770 [situation not mentioned]. Desires they will be careful of his mother and allow her 10/– per year.

Witnesses: Andrew Kerby, Dublin, gent., Richard Tagart, Dublin cordwainer.

Memorial witnessed by: Richard Tagart, Richard Henry Molloy.

293, 507, 197051 Hannah Kerby (seal)
(widow of testator)

503 ROWLEY, JAMES, James Street, Dublin, slater.

31 May 1772. Narrate ¾ p. 25 Sept. 1773.

His son John Rowley, and Elinor his [son's] wife exors. His grandson James Mackilwaine. His houses and concerns in James Street and Bason Lane held by lease under Sir Samuel Cooke, deceased. His holding in Duck Lane near Smithfield.

Witnesses: Robert Beven, Bason Lane, Dublin, gent., Peter Wilkinson, James Street, weaver, George Ledgwick, James Street, girt-weaver.

Memorial witnessed by: George Ledgwick, Michael Macabe, Dublin, gent.

298, 300, 197498 Elinor Rowley (seal)

504 KELLETT, WILLIAM, Derry, parish Kildrumfartan, Barony Castleraghan, Co. Cavan, Esq. 14 May 1773. Narrate ¾ p. 4 Oct. 1773.

His wife Susanna Kellett. His son Solomon Kellett. His son Thomas Kellett. His daughter Ann Kellett. His daughter Martha Kellett. Christopher Spinks the elder, and Charles Spinks and his [testator's] wife Susanna Kellett, exors. Lands of Mullaghmore and Aughnedrunk [Aghnadrung, Co. Cavan]. A sum to be raised after his father's death out of lands of Corroiloughan and Killekine, [? Co. Cavan].

Witnesses: Connor Maguire, Corlateran, farmer, Alexr. Spinks, Togher, mason, Mathew Maguire, Colateran, gent.

Memorial witnessed by: Mathew Maguire, Chr. Spinks the younger, Derry, Co. Cavan.

298, 342, 197607 Susanna Kellett (seal)

505 MOORE, JOHN, Rockfield, Co. Fermanagh, Esq.
28 Jan. 1762. Narrate ¾ p. 13 Nov. 1773.

His daughters Elizabeth and Lydia. John Dundass, son of James Dundass, Killmackbrack. Ralph Noble, Donagh, Esq., and James Dundass, Killmackbrack, exors. His town and lands of Rockfield and his freehold leases.

Witnesses: John Dundass, Carramore, Wm. Orniston, Mullyban, John Smyth, Donyhall, Co. Fermanagh, gent.

Memorial witnessed by: Wm. Orniston, John Dundass, Carramore.

295, 556, 198116 James Dundass (seal)

506 HOEY, HANNAH, Dublin, widow.

12 Dec. 1772. Précis ¼ p. 23 Dec. 1773.

Residue of her real and personal estate to her grand-daughter Elizabeth Sandys otherwise Ryves, wife of Nehemiah Sandys, Esq. Said Nehemiah Sandys and Mrs. Ann Mills exors.

Witnesses: John Thewless, Esq., Samuel Paterson and William Short, gent., all of Dublin.

Memorial witnessed by: Samuel Paterson, Hugh Berne, Dublin, gent.

299, 391, 198677 Nehemiah Sandys (seal)

507 SYDNEY, DUDLEY ALEXANDER SYDNEY COSBY, LORD, [Baron] Sydney of Leix, Stradbally, Queen's Co. 14 Dec. 1772, re-signed 18 Jan. 1774. Narrate 1 p. 1 Feb. 1774.

Sir Annesley Stewart, Dublin, Bart., Rt. Hon. William Pole, Ballyfin, Queen's Co., Rev. Peter Warburton, Garryhinch, King's Co., clerk, trustees. Phillips Cosby, Esq., Captain in H.M. Navy, son of said Lord Sydney's great uncle Col. Alexander Cosby. All money and other personal fortune he was entitled into in right of Mrs. Elizabeth Etkins otherwise Morgan otherwise Kenny otherwise Dodwell([1]). Manors, towns, lands tenements etc. in Baronies of Stradbally and Cullinagh or wheresoever else in Queen's Co., and in County of Roscommon.

Witnesses: John Collier, Dublin, gent., Francis Hutchinson, Dublin, Doctor in Physick, Thomas Ievers, Dublin, gent.

Witnesses to re-signing: George Watson, Maryborough, Queen's Co., Doctor in Physick, Michael Dodd, Stradbally, Queen's Co., gent., Benjamin Whitley, Diset, Queen's Co., gent.

Memorial witnessed by: John Macartney, Dublin, gent., Thomas Tothall, Dublin, gent.

299, 470, 199039 Phills. Cosby (seal)

([1]) Testator's aunt. She was sister of his mother Mary, daughter of Henry Dodwell.

508 CLARKE, GEORGE, Rath, King's Co., gent.

7 Jan. 1773. Narrate ½ p. 8 Feb. 1774.

His grandson John Clarke. His cousin Eusebuis Drought, Esq., Thomas Spunner and his son John Clarke exors. His interest in lands of Cloncheenogue in parish of Lusma[g]h, [King's Co.], in Phoolagh, Co. Galway and in lands of Clonkilly and Ballyrickardbegg in King's Co., with the Park near Birr held by Charles Melsop, and in tenements in Moore Park Street, Birr that he bought from widow Eaton.

Witnesses: Thos. Bernard the younger, Castletown, King's Co., Esq., John Whelan, Curraghmore, said Co., gent., Isaac Johns, servant to testator.

Memorial witnessed by: John Whelan, Henry Palmer, Bride Street, Dublin, gent.

298, 632, 199143 John Clarke (seal)
(an exor)

509 STOTHARD, COSSLET, Donagheleney, Co. Down, gent.

13 Sept. 1768. Full 1½ p. 11 March 1774.

Release dated 13 July 1765 made previous to my intermarriage with Margaret Montgomery, my late wife. My son Mathew Stothard. My son Cosslet Stothard. James Waddell, Springfield, Co. Down, trustee and guardian of my said sons. My brother John Stothard, gent. My sisters. My brother Mathew Stothard, exor. Town and lands of Banogh and Drumabruse, Co. Down.

Witnesses: Boleyn Douglass, gent., Terence Heyland, Dromore, Co. Down, gent., Richd. Workman, Dublin, gent.

Memorial witnessed by: Richd. Workman, Saml. Holmes, Dublin, gent.

299, 629, 199636 James Waddell (seal)

510 SPUNNER, WILLIAM, Loughkeen, Co. Tipperary, gent.

10 April 1754. Narrate 1 p. 15 March 1774.

His wife Sarah Spunner. Charles Spunner, son of testator. His son Robt. Spunner "£40 to be paid . . . . . after his arrival in this

Kingdom," in case of his non-return said money to be divided between said Charles and testator's daughter Margaret James or her husband John James. His son Reginald. His grand-daughter Sarah James. His son-in-law John Spunner of Realouges. His brother Chas. Spunner, his [testator's] wife and son Charles, exors. Lands of Loughkeen and Ballaghgare, Co. Tipperary.

Witnesses: Den. Dwyer, William Higgs, Wm. Eides.

Memorial witnessed by: Michael Macabe, Pat. Smyth, both Dublin, gents.

302, 198, 199713 Robert Spunner (seal)

511 BROWNE, DOMINICK, of Mayfield, but then of Kiltyculla, Co. Mayo, Esq. 20 Aug. 1771. Narrate 1½ p. 2 May 1774.

To his relation and friend George Fitzgerald, Turlagh, Co. Mayo, Esq., all his lands, tenements and hereditaments in counties of Mayo, Galway and Roscommon, and all his right, title and interest in the lands etc. " most fraduently obtained from him by James Browne the Attorney late of Kiltyculla." There might be some disputes in law " and some claims made by the then James Browne of Kiltycurra under the colour of the fraudulent agreements his grandfather James Browne Attorney, deceased invegled him into " . . . by his means said Dominick Browne " was kept in the utmost misery and distress." Testator desired his exor. said George Fitzgerald to prosecute and defend all causes wherein he was plaintiff or defendant in at the time of his decease, and to break through all the fraudulent agreements which he had been brought into by said James Browne the grandfather of the said James the younger, and by Jacob Browne deceased father of said James the younger.

Witnesses to Will and Memorial: Elizabeth Lyons, Henry Davett, Andrew Mitchell, all of Turlagh, Co. Mayo.

303, 142, 200400 George Fitzgerald (seal)

512 BEAGHAN, BRIDGET, Liffey Street, Dublin, widow.

3 Nov. 1772. Full ¾ p. 14 June 1774.

To be buried in St. James Churchyard, Dublin. To William Lyster, Abbey Street, county of city of Dublin, exor., house in Liffey Street now in possession of John Archdeacon and his undertenants.

Witnesses: Colley Grattan, Robert Sandys, gent., Thos. Bracken, clerk to William Lyster, Dublin, gent.

Memorial witnessed by: Robt. Sandys, Thomas Bracken.

305, 99, 200907 Willm. Lyster (seal)

513 ANDREWS, Rt. Hon. FRANCIS, Provost Trinity College, Dublin. Will [date not recorded] and codicil. Full 2½ pp. 27 June 1774.

My lands in Co. Antrim to my mother for life, subject to an annuity to Mrs. Hamilton. Miss Ann Hamilton, daughter of said Ann Hamilton. After decease of my mother said estate to Rt. Hon. Edmond Sexton Perry, Esq., Speaker of the House of Commons, and to Rt. Hon. Marcus Paterson, Esq., Chief Justice of the Common Pleas upon special trusts. £3,000 to be raised and paid to the Provost, Fellows and Scholars of Trinity College to be applied in erecting and furnishing an Observatory and other necessary Buildings for making Astronomical Observations, and the further annual sum of £250 for ever for the salaries of such professor of Astronomy and of such person skilful in taking astronomical observations and such other persons as the said Provost, Fellows and Scholas shall appoint. My leasehold interest in Co. Galway and my leasehold interest in Co. Meath now held by Wm. Gamble in trust for me. After decease of my mother, my leasehold interest in Co. Galway shall go to Robt. Gamble subject to an annuity of £100 to Geo. Gamble Esq., his brother, and my leasehold interest in Co. Meath to Wm. Gamble Esq., and Margaret his wife for life subject to an annuity to Mrs. Anne Norman, daughter of said Wm. Gamble. Busts, lustres, bookcases, my telescope and Globes etc. to said Provosts, Fellows and Scholars, and £400 to be distributed among poor people belonging to the College. £100 towards building the Blue Coat Hospital. My mother and Wm. Gamble, Esq., exors.

Codicil([1]): Books to Rt. Hon. Richard Rigby; my coloured prints to Miss Dolly Monroe.

---

(1) Codicil signed but apparently not witnessed. Wm. Gamble, sworn 22 June 1774, said that the codicil was the proper handwriting and signature of deceased who died 10th. inst.

Witnesses: Jno. Monk Mason, Wm. Montgomery, Vaunt Montgomery.

Memorial witnessed by: John Stephens, Dublin, gent., John Macabe, Dublin, gent.

301, 338, 201041 Wm. Gamble (seal)

514 WATSON, SAMUEL, Tullalast [Tullylost], Co. Kildare.
2 Sept. 1747. Full 1½ p. 20 June 1774.

My wife Sarah Watson. My eldest son Thos. Watson. My second son Samuel Watson. My daughters Ann and Margaret Watson. My daughter Mary Watson. Thos. Watson, Derrygarran, King's Co. and Jno. Stephenson, Rathangan, Co. Kildare, exors. Town and lands of Clonsast, King's Co.

Witnesses: Richd. Fayle, Samuel Neale, junr., Samuel Neale.

Memorial witnessed by: William Gun, Dublin, gent., John Bury, Dublin, public notary.

302, 491, 201067 Ann Russell (seal)
otherwise Watson, a legatee in said Will named

515 MEATH, JOHN, Loughlinstown, Co. Dublin, publican.
3 Sept. 1774. Précis ½ p. 20 Sept. 1774.

His wife Elizabeth Meath, extx. His son John. His son Simon. His son Patrick. His daughter Margaret McCulloh.

Witnesses: Edwd. Lyons, the waiter to testator, Fras. McNemee, Navan, Co. Meath, gent.

Memorial witnessed by: Fras. McNemee, Michael Macabe, Dublin, gent.

304, 268, 201762 Elizth. Meath (seal)

516 MARSHALL, ANTHONY, Drogheda, Alderman.
14 May 1764. Narrate 1 p. 12 Oct. 1774.

His wife Rebecca Marshall, exor. His brother John Marshall of St. Peter's, Dublin, exor. His brother-in-law John Partington

Vanhomrigh exor. To his cousin John Marshall £100 out of Rathcor in Cooley near Carlingford. The house next Laurence Gate, Drogheda, the parks and lease he had bought belonging to the Corporation of Drogheda; his meadow field at Lismanus, Co. Louth. His lands and profit rents in Louth and Drogheda.

Witnesses: Rev. Samuel Murray, Henrietta Street, Dublin, clerk. Christopher Jenney, Brabazon Park, Co. Louth, gent., Patk. McGauran, Drogheda, merchant.

Memorial witnessed by: Patk. McGauran, Christopher Abbott, Dublin, gent.

302, 546, 201902 Rebecca Marshall (seal)

517 DON[N]ALDSON, HUGH, late of Philadelphia, but then of Drumnasole, Co. Antrim, gent. 12 Oct. 1773. Précis ½ p. 2 Nov. 1774.

To Wm. Agnew, Kilwaghter, Hugh McCollum, Liminary, Esqrs., Wm. Burgess, Belfast, merchant, all in Co. Antrim, as trustees, the quarter land of Drumnasole, the half quarter land of Ballyvalligan, and all his houses and tenements in Larne and Glenarme, all in Co. Antrim.

Witnesses: Valentine Jones, Belfast, Co. Antrim, merchant, Robt. Harrison, Dublin, gent., Thomas Elder, Belfast, merchant.

Memorial witnessed by: Robt. Harrison, Samuel Ashmore, Belfast, merchant.

305, 294, 202036 Wm. Burgess (seal)

518 REA, DAVID, Belycreen, parish of Maghredrool, Co. Down, farmer. 2 Feb. 1754. Full 1 p. 7 Nov. 1774.

To be buried in the churchyard of Sa[i]ntfield. My two sons Mathew and Hugh Rea, exors. My last wife's children she had to me Debro Rea, Jas. Rea, Jane Rea and Robt. Rea. Wm. Ansle of Clough, overseer. Lands of Kelein belonging to me, now in possession of John and Robt. Grangar. The holding in Belycreen and Magherynock [Magheraknock] Mill and lands which I hold by lease under Mr. Onsley [? Ousley].

Witnesses: John Rea, Munlogh, Co. Down, farmer, David Rea, Belycreen, Co. Down, farmer, Saml. Rea, late of Belycreen, farmer, deceased.

Memorial witnessed by: David Rea, Thomas Compton, Lisburn, Co. Antrim, writing clerk.

302, 571, 202079 Debro Armstrong (seal)
her mark.
otherwise Rea now the wife of John Armstrong of Maghrenock, Co. Down, farmer.

519 HUGHES, FRANCIS ANNESLY, Dublin, Esq.

24 Sept. 1771. Full 4¼ pp. 29 Dec. 1774.

Mary Seayrs otherwise Hughes my wife, extx. My brother Thomas Hughes. My brothers and sisters. My sister Deborah Hughes. My nephew Francis Annesly Hughes, son of my brother John Hughes. My brother Paul Hughes. My friend Attiwell Wood, Esq., counsellor at law, trustee. My nephew Joshua Paul Barker, under 21 years. My dearly beloved Mary to give sum of money out of rents every year " to the person who shall be apparently entitled to the same . . . till his arrival at twenty one years . . . it being my desire that he shall be educated for and called to the Bar."

All my real estate. My real estate in Co. Tipperary. Whosoever shall become entitled to rents etc. of said real estate shall use the name of Francis Annesly Hughes, and shall live in Ireland at least 10 calendar months per year except during education. My house, garden and Demesne at Whitehall, Co. Dublin. My house in Chancery Lane, Dublin.

Witnesses: James Taylor, Dublin, Barrister at law, deceased, Andrew Hamilton, Dublin, gent., Josh. Hamilton, Dublin, notary public.

Memorial witnessed by: Wm. Costello, Dublin, gent.

306, 151, 202827 M. Hughes (seal)
(Mary Hughes widow)

520 DOMVILLE, REV. BENJAMIN, D.D., Vicar of St. Ann's. Dublin, formerly called Benjamin Barrington. 29 April 1769, Narrate 2 pp. 9 Feb. 1775.

His wife Anna Maria Domville. His aunt Elizth. Barrington. A deed of settlement signed by him 9 April then last past just before his marriage. His estate in Co. Galway purchased from John Digby. Lands and premises devised to him by his uncle William Domville, Esq. The dwelling house wherein Sir Compton Domville, Baronet, deceased, lately dwelt situate on the east side of Merrion Street and ground adjoining thereto lately purchased by him from George Darley of York Street, Dublin, stone cutter.

Witnesses: Gabriel Villeneuve, then of Clarendon Street, Dublin, Esq., William Woolsey, the stepson of said Gabriel Villeneuve, John Gelling, Dublin, gent.

Memorial witnessed by: John Gelling, John Tynan, servant to said Anna Maria Domville.

301, 662, 203293 Anna Maria Domville (seal)

521 BATEMAN, WILLIAM, George's Quay, Dublin, publican. 8 Apl. 1772. Précis, a few lines. 11 Feb. 1775.

To his wife A(l)lice Bateman (sole extx.) all real and personal estate(1).

Witnesses: John Priestly, Richd. Keane, Peter Dillon, all of Dublin, gents.

Memorial witnessed by: Peter Dillon, Edmond McCan, Dublin, gent.

301, 683, 203350 Allice Bateman (seal)

522 GRIERSON, ROBERT, Dublin, gent. 27 Dec. 1774. Précis ½ p. 13 Feb. 1775.

To Wm. Hale, Meath St., Dublin, silk weaver, his lease and farm of Mollinam otherwise Mollineam [Mullinam] and the seventeen acres

(1) Lease dated 1 July 1767 whereby James Hart of Maiden Lane, Dublin, silk weaver, demised to Wm. Bateman, a piece of ground in Maiden Lane and Wood Street for 40 years. This lease registered by Alice Bateman, exor. of said Wm., 11 Feb. 1775. Book 301, p. 682, memorial 203348.

called the Commons of the Lough, Co. Meath, held under George Lowther, Esq., and all other his real and personal estate. Said Wm. Hale and Richard Hale, Meath Street, ironmonger, exors.

Witnesses: Mark Bloxham, Dublin, tallow chandler, Festus Kelly, Dublin, shoemaker, Townly Ahmuty, Dublin, gent.

Memorial witnessed by: John Gelling, Dublin, gent., John Scallion, clerk to said John Gelling.

301, 684, 203357 Wm. Hale (seal)

523 CROWE, JAMES, Dublin, gent.

20 Aug. 1767. Narrate 2 pp. 20 March 1775.

His wife Mary Crowe. To his eldest son Robert Crowe lands of Nutfield otherwise Drumconora and all the other lands he purchased from trustees of Mrs. Leslie, and lands purchased from Chas. McDonnell Esq., (except the lands of Affogh and all the lands and tenements purchased from the Earl of Inchiquin except Cahermacunna [? Co. Clare] and except the tenements called Peter's Cell in the city of Limerick. Francis Upton and Henry Upton, Dublin, gent., trustees. His [testator's] son George [Crowe]. His daughter Elizabeth Crowe. His nephew James Crowe. His wife Mary Crowe, his sons Robert and George Crowe, Geo. Boleyn Whitney and Francis Upton, exors.

Lands of Frequin and Reneen and all other lands within the parish of Quin, Co. Clare: Affogh, Barony Tulla, purchased from Chas. McDonnell Esq., the two Cahirmacunnas purchased from the Earl of Inchiquin and Sir Lucius O'Brien, Bart., parks and field in Lifford near Ennis purchased from the representatives of Anthony Wolfe deceased.

Witnesses: Joseph Ridge, clerk of St. Peter's parish, Dublin. Thomas Connor, Dublin, clerk, Francis Sullivan, Dublin, gent., Attorney, Court of Exchequer in Ireland, since deceased.

Memorial witnessed by: Thomas Connor, Andrew Hehir, Dublin, gent.

301, 720, 203767 George Crowe (seal)

524 PALMER, POTTER, Clareen, King's Co., gent.
11 Jan. 1747. Full 1¾ p. 21 April 1775.

My wife Sarah Palmer. My eldest son Robert Palmer (a minor). My younger son Richard Palmer (under 21 years). My daughters Ann, Mary and Sarah Palmer (under 21 years and unmarried). My brother Robert Palmer and my friend James Ruddock, the younger, trustees, guardians of said children and exors. My freehold leases and interests.

Witnesses: Henry Palmer, Ballyegan, King's Co., Joseph Palmer, Derrinsollow, Co. Tipperary, Paul Palmer, Fortall, King's Co., gent.

Memorial witnessed by: Wm. Harding, ribband weaver, John Robinson, notary public, both of Dublin.

308, 135, 204019(1) Robert Palmer (seal)
(principal and residuary legatee).

525 LANGFORD, ABRAHAM, parish of St. Paul, Covent Garden, Middlesex, auctioneer. 30 Oct. 1773. Précis ½ p. 4 May 1775.

Residue of his estate to Robert Langford and James Duberly, trustees and exors. Said Will was proved in the Prerogative Court, Canterbury, and Prerogative Court, Ireland.

Witnesses: Morgan Thomas, Middle Temple, London, John Richards, clerk to said Abraham and Robert Langford, Wm. Barlow, clerk to said Morgan Thomas.

Memorial witnessed by: Morgan Thomas, J. Way.

308, 157, 204162 Robt. Langford (seal)
J. Duberly (seal)

526 DAWSON, ARTHUR, one of the Barons of H.M. Court of Exchequer in Ireland. 11 Aug. 1774. Full 2 pp. 8 May 1775.

My brother Rev. Joshua Dawson. The jointure settled upon my "daughter-[in-law] Ann Dawson(2) on her marriage with my late son John Dawson." My nephew Arthur Dawson, son of my late brother

(1) There is a mistake in the pagination of Book 308. The pages are numbered 1 to 143, then 135 onwards. Memorial 204019 will be found on p. 135 in the first sequence.

(2) Ann daughter of George Cuppaidge.

William Dawson, exor. My brother Charles Dawson. William Sharman and Luke Sterling, Dublin, Esqrs., trustees. £1,000 to Charles Dawson, now a Lieutenant in H.M.'s Sixty Second Regiment of Foot, to be applied to the purchase of a Company of Foot for him. £200 to each of the children of my brother Charles who shall be living at the time of his death. My honest servant Pat. Brolly. My servant John Lennon.

My lands and estate in Co. Cavan. My estate of Castle Dawson, Co. Londonderry, and my estate in Ormond Markett and the Pill in the city of Dublin, and my real estate elsewhere in Ireland.

Witnesses to Will and Memorial: William Dunn, Dublin, Esq., Samuel Plant, Dublin, gent., now cash keeper of the Bank kept by Messrs. Gleadow, Newcomen & Co., Daniel Malone, gent., clerk in said Bank.

303, 712, 204273 Arthur Dawson (seal)

527 TARLTON, WELDON, Mountmellick, Queen's Co.
6 April 1775. Narrate 1 p. 31 May 1775.

His wife Ann Tarlton extrx. His daughters Arabella, Elizabeth and Ann (under 21 and unmarried). His son Robert (under 21 years). His two sons Digby and John Tarlton, under 21 years. Wm. Humphreys, Dublin, merchant and John Humphreys, Dublin, gent., trustees. His wife and said Wm. Humphreys guardians to his said children. Lands of Mucklone, Queen's Co.

Witnesses: James Lewis Higgins, Mountmellick, gent., Samuel Strangman, Mountmellick, gent., Willcocks Robinson, Mountmellick, gent.

Memorial witnessed by: Willcocks Robinson, Allen Kelly, Portarlington, Queen's Co., gent.

309, 61, 204644 Ann Tarlton (seal)

528 MOLESWORTH, EDWARD, Bueno Retiro, Co. Dublin, Esq.
31 June 1765. Narrate 1 p. 16 June 1775.

Mary Molesworth, his wife, exor. His two sons Jno. and Robt. Molesworth. Testator's nephew Chas. Walker, Dublin, Esq., one of the Masters in Chancery, exor. . His brother Byse Molesworth, exor. His real estate.

Witnesses: Esther Grenan or Esther Gunning, Edward Roberts, both then of Bueno Retiro, servants of testator, Richard Thwaites, Dublin, Esq.

Memorial witnessed by: Jno. Doherty, Newton McMullen, Dublin, gent.

306, 581, 204836 Robt. Molesworth (seal)

529 MIDDLETON, LETTICE, otherwise VESEY, Dublin, widow.

9 June 1775. Narrate ½ p. 19 June 1775.

Her brother Jno. Theodore Vesey, Co. Galway, Esq. Frances Ward, daughter of testator's niece Jane Ward, Dublin, widow. Jno. Wm. Ward, son of said Jane. £100 to Danl. Mansergh, Athy, Co. Kildare. James Monaghan, her old servant. Robt. Flinn, a minor. Wm. Oates, Mary Oates. Mary Flynn. Robt. Atkins, Dublin, Esq., and said Jane Ward exors. Her estate in city of Dublin.

Witnesses: Wm. Atkins, Jno. Collis, Geo. Edkins, all of Dublin, gents.

Memorial witnessed by: Geo. Edkins, Letitia Vesey, Dublin, spinster.

306, 593, 204877 Jane Ward (seal)

530 McCRINDLE, THOMAS, Bellaghy, Co. Londonderry.

7 April 1769. Narrate ½ p. 28 June 1775.

His daughter Agnes Higgins. Fergus Kennedy and Martin Steel both now or lately of Bellaghy, exors. His freehold tenement in Bellaghy, No. 51, held under Wm. Conolly, Esq.

Witnesses: Andrew Brady, John Brady, John Spear, all of Bally-McCombs, Co. Londonderry, farmers.

Memorial witnessed by: John Brady, John Spotswood, Bellaghy, gent.

307, 459, 205019 Agnes Higgins (seal)
of Bellaghy, widow.

531 GILLMOR, HUGH, Anney McNeale, parish of Tullycorbet, Co. Monaghan. 23 July 1768. Narrate $\frac{3}{4}$ p. 1 July 1775.

His wife Elizabeth Gillmor. His son John Gillmor, exor. His son-in-law Thomas Logan, exor. His three sons Wm. Gillmor, Thos. Gillmor and James Gillmor. His youngest son James Gillmor. All his lands, goods and effects.

Witnesses: Francis McCleland, John Riddle, Wm. Riddle, all of parish of Tullycorbet, Co. Monaghan.

Memorial witnessed by: Francis McCleland, Saml. Swanzy, parish of Tullycorbet.

309, 156, 205079 Thos. Logan (seal)

532 DE LACHEROIS, SAMUEL, Hillden, Co. Antrim, Esq. 5 Sept. 1773. Full 2 pp. 3 July 1775.

My eldest son Daniel. Samuel Heron, Lisburn, Co. Antrim, gent., trustee. My second son Nicholas. My third son Samuel. My three sons exors. My daughter Judith, now the wife of John Smith, Lisburn, Co. Antrim, linen draper. My real estate in parishes of Cumber and Donaghadea, Co. Down to which I am entitled under Will of the late Countess Dowager of Mount Alexander.

Witnesses: Saumarez Dubourdieu, John Johnson, Saml. Heron.

Memorial witnessed by: John Johnson, Thos. Compton.

309, 157, 205089 Danl. De la Cherois (seal)

533 SHIRLEY, THOMAS, Gra[i]gudarrigg, Co. Tipperary, farmer. 7 March 1775. Narrate $\frac{1}{2}$ p. 6 July 1775.

His sister Betty Shirley, otherwise Mara. Thomas Lloyd, Cranagh, Esq., exor. His sister Sally Shirley, otherwise Keessan. His sister Mary Shirley, otherwise Mara. Lands of Graiguedarrigg.

Witnesses: Thomas Lloyd, farmer, John Farrell, woolcomber. Michael Kennedy, carpenter, all of parish of Killea, Co. Tipperary.

Memorial witnessed by: Thomas Lloyd, Michael Kennedy.

307, 486, 205147 Thomas Lloyd (seal) of Cranagh.

534 CORNYN, MARY, Dublin, widow.

29 Dec. 1774. Narrate 1 p. 7 July 1775.

Robt. Donnelly, Dublin, gent. Her cousin James Rainsford. Her cousin Henrietta Gruebear, widow, sister of said James Rainsford. George Rainsford, second son of said James Rainsford. Wm. Crowe, Dublin, gent. and Robt. Donnelly, exors.

Her house in Chancery Lane, Dublin, held under lease from Ann Pearson, widow of Alderman Pearson, deceased, and Mathew Pearson, Esq. Her estate on the Poddle and in New Row near the Poddle in manor and liberty of Thomas Court and Donore, Co. Dublin, held under lease from Edward Earl of Meath, deceased. Duncormicke and Leckan, Barony Bargie, Co. Wexford.

Witnesses: Rev. John Lyon, Dublin, D.D., curate of parish of St. Bridget, Dublin, Rev. Jno. Rowelen, D.D., vicar of parish of Santry, Co. Dublin, Adam Taitt, Exchequer Street, lately called Chequer Lane, Dublin, gent.

Memorial witnessed by: Robt. Jones, Dublin, gent., Jno. Johnston Darrah, clerk to said Wm. Crowe.

306, 662, 205155 Wm. Crowe (seal)
Robt. Donnelly (seal)

535 LLOYD, JOHN, Crannagh, Co. Tipperary.

12 July 1770. Narrate 2¼ pp. 8 July 1775.

John Lloyd, Gloster, King's Co. Esq., Wm. Lloyd, Dublin, Esq., Doctor of Physick, trustees. His eldest son John. His second son Thomas. His fourth son Richd. His fifth son Henry Lloyd Jesse. His sixth son Frederick. His third son George. His daughters Elizabeth and Deborah (under 21 years and unmarried) £3,000 each. His brother George Lloyd. His kinsman Thomas Lloyd Prince, Esq. His trustee and kinsman Wm. Lloyd, Esq., Doctor of Physick.

Lands of Crannagh and Garrymore, Lloydsborough otherwise Gortrone, Kill[a]wardy otherwise Killevardagh, Killduff, Skehanagh otherwise Skepane and Tinnekilly, parts of Killmacuddy as he was seized of called Simpson's lot, Knockantymannor, Buresnoe [Borrisnoe], Burralisheen, Ballyknockin, Drummin, Ballylahy, part of Killea, all in Barony Eliogarty and Ikerrin, Co. Tipperary. Lands of Gortnapishey and Mondayshole, Coolacullagh [? Coolaculla, Co. Tipperary] and Killclony [Kilclonagh, Co. Tipperary], Glenag[u]ile, Co. Tipperary by a freehold lease. Lands of Lissheen, Ballyerk, Co. Tipperary, and Lissdonoulty [? Lisdonowly, Co. Tipperary] otherwise Lissdonnelly and all other lands purchased by him from George Grace.

Witnesses: Roger Thompson, Dublin, merchant, Isaac Stoney, John Bradshaw, both Dublin, gents.

Memorial witnessed by: Roger Thompson, Jno. Pilkington, Dublin, gent.

310, 16, 205166 John Lloyd (seal)
(eldest son of testator)

536 BRABAZON, REVD. LUDLOW, Brabazon's Park, Co. Louth, clerk. 11 July 1755. Narrate ¾ p. 27 July 1775.

His sister Elizabeth Jenney. Christophilus Jenney, youngest son of his sister Elizabeth Jenney.

Lands of Balrobin, leased from John Ludlow, Esq. Lands of Sherriffs Park now called Brabazon's Park which he formerly held under Capt. Kelly but then leased from Alderman Richd. Dawson. Tithes of parish of Phillipstown Nugent, held from Dean and Chapter of Christ Church, Dublin, all in Co. Louth.

Witnesses: Richard Bolton, Thomas Bowers, Robert Draper.

Memorial witnessed by: Barry Colles, Dublin, Esq., Wm. Costello Dublin, gent.

308, 345, 205362 Christophs. Jenney (seal)

537 GRAVES, THOMAS, Castledawson, Co. Londonderry.

1 June 1775. Narrate 2 pp. 31 July 1775.

His wife Mary Graves, exor. His son Samuel Graves, exor. His brother Samuel Graves, Esq., Vice Admiral of the Blue, of Hunbury Fort, Devon, trustee. His daughter Jane Graves. His daughter Olivia, the widow of John Courtenay deceased. His daughter Sarah, the wife of Alexander Saunders. His grand-daughter Mary Saunders.

Money that he or his family have any right to under Will of his father-in-law, Mr. Neve[1]. Andrew Spotswood, Bellaghy, exor.

His freehold in townland of Aughrim, Moyola purchased from Wm. Porter, Annaghmore, Co. Londonderry, commonly called The Coppice Farm which he was entitled to under his father's Will as heir at law to said father and to his brother James deceased. Farm in townland of BallymacPeake commonly called the South Division, purchased from Wm. McPeake, farm of Mulloghbuoy purchased from James Verner, farm in Drumlamph purchased from Thomas and William Boney, his freehold in town of Castledawson purchased from William Steed, the son of James Steed of Castledawson, all in Barony Loughlinshollin, Co. Londonderry, and all other real and freehold estates. His chattle leases purchased from Ann Ward, administratrix of Francis Ward. The lease made to him by the Hon. Baron Dawson.

Witnesses: John Sheil, Castledawson, Co. Londonderry, John Garvan, Castledawson, John Heany, Castledawson.

Memorial witnessed by: John Sheil, John Garvan.

306, 698, 205385 Samuel Graves (seal)
son and heir of said testator.

538 CARY, EDWARD, Castlecarey, Co. Donegal, Esq.

18 May 1774. Narrate. 7 Aug. 1775.

Wife Ann Cary otherwise Benson. Settlement made on marriage of his eldest daughter Elizabeth Cary with Rev. Joseph Elwood. His daughter Ann Cary, her children by George Cary, Esq., deceased. His son-in-law Henry Cary and Susanna his wife, the testator's daughter. His daughters Rose Cary (spinster), Catherine Cary and Amelia Cary. His son George Cary. His grandson Lucius Cary, second son of George Cary of Redcastle, deceased. Money due by representatives of James Hamilton late of Ballynagarey, Co. Antrim, deceased. Exors. said wife Ann Cary and Edward Cary, Dungiven, Esq. His house and offices at Greencastle, half a ballyboe of land called Portaville. His leasehold interests in Co. Donegal.

(1) The Will of Thomas Neve, Ballyneill, dated 1739, mentions two daughters, one being Mary wife of Thomas Graves.

Witnesses: Thos. McKinney, Coolaneen, Co. Donegal, farmer, Mathew Murphy, Castlecary, gardener, John Maginnes, Castlecary, servant.

Memorial witnessed by: Richardson Williams, Dublin, gent., Henry Richardson, clerk to said Richardson Williams.

2054501 (1). Ann Cary (seal)

539 MITCHELL, ROBERT, Ballykealy, King's Co., gent.

2 June 1775. Narrate $1\frac{1}{4}$ p. 9 Aug. 1775.

His wife Mary Mitchell. His nephew Thos. Mitchell of Clondalla, only son of his brother Wm. Mitchell. His nephew Wm. Mitchell. His nephew Marlborough Mitchell. His nephew Robt. Mitchell, only son of his brother Andrew Mitchell. His sister Margaret Watkins. His sister Elizth. Bayly. His nephew Thos. Watkins. His nephew Thos. Mitchell eldest son of his brother. His sister Jane White. His said wife, his brother Andrew Mitchell and his nephew Thos. Mitchell, exors.

Lands of Ballykealy and his dwelling house. Lands of Parkmore, Cooloag and Galrush. Part of lands of Bolenarig [Boolinarig] containing the following, Foxberry, Ballynagooleen, Clonmeelan and Cush and part of Bolenecarrig known as the School lands, and lands called the Glinns.

Witnesses: Thos. Woods, Garbally, gent., Andrew Mitchell, Ardgauage, gent., Phebe Sharp, Bannagher, all in King's Co.

Memorial witnessed by: Michael Macabe, Wm. Kelly, Dublin, gents.

310, 60, 205476 Thos. Watkins (seal)

540 HATHORN, JOHN, Drogheda town, merchant, but then of Balbriggan, Co. Dublin. 23 Dec. 1770. Narrate 1 p. 28 Aug. 1775.

All his freehold leases to his wife and mother. His nephew Alexr. Schive, Balbriggan. The late Thomas Hathorn's children. His wife Hesther Hathorn (since married to John Paine of Balbriggan, gent.) and his mother Mary Hathorn and said Alexr. Schive, exors.

(1) This memorial was not transcribed. It will be found in Folio 686.

Witnesses: John Callin, Drogheda, merchant, Dennis McCarthy, Balbriggan, mariner, Robt. Rochfort, Balbriggan, yeoman.

Memorial witnessed by: Dennis McCarthy, Theobald Bermingham, Dublin, gent.

309, 273, 205647 Hesther Paine (seal)

541 HUMPHRY(S), JOHN, Dublin, Esq.

14 May 1775. Narrate 1 p. 27 Sept. 1775.

His nephew Richard Humphrys of Co. Kildare, clerk. His friend Robert Hamilton, Dublin, Esq., second son of Alexander Hamilton, late of said city, Esq., deceased, trustee. Thomas Humphrys of Kingston, Jamacia, planter. His nephew William Humphrys. Kinsman John Butler. Godson Henry Butler, third son of said John Butler. Mary the eldest daughter of said John Butler, then the wife of Benjamin Yeates, Dublin. Margaret Butler, spinster, second daughter of said John Butler. Sarah Butler, youngest daughter of said John Butler, aged about 6 years. His cousin John Butler of Dublin, Esq., and his nephew Richard Humphrys, exors. His real and personal estate in this Kingdom or Great Britain.

Witnesses: John Morris, Dublin, Esq., John Chambers, Dublin, timber merchant, James Stafford, Dublin, gent.

Memorial witnessed by: John Chambers, James Jackson.

304, 473, 205820 John Butler (seal)

542 RICHARDSON, PETER, Ballyrogan, Co. Wicklow, farmer.

28 March 1772. Précis ½ p. 10 Oct. 1775.

His wife Jane Richardson. His son William Richardson. Lands of Ballyrogan.

Witnesses: James Farrell, Arklow, carpenter. Robert Ansley, Crone, farmer. Maurice ——(1) Ballyrogan, farmer, all Co. Wicklow.

Memorial witnessed by: Michael Macabe, Wm. Farrell, Dublin.

304, 498, 205915 William Richardson (seal)

(1) The surname is left out of both memorial and transcript of memorial.

543 CANNING, STRATFORD, Dublin, Esq.

8 Oct. 1773. Précis ½ p. 11 Oct. 1775.

His second son Paul Canning, Esq., exor. Jno. Doherty, Dublin, gent., trustee. Lands of Tyannee otherwise Teanee, and Craigmore, Co. Londonderry. His estates in counties of Cavan and Kilkenny.

Witnesses: Hugh Dogherty, Jno. O'Donnell, Richd. Wilson (the younger), all of Dublin, gents.

Memorial witnessed by: Richd. Wilson, Newton McMollen, Dublin, gent.

310, 152, 205922 Paul Canning (seal)

544 CROZIER, JOHN, Drumash, Co. Tyrone.

18 April 1775. Narrate ¾ p. 14 Nov. 1775.

His wife Jane Crozier extx. His grandson James Crozier, son of his son Ralph Crozier. To Elrr. Bryden 2/6. To his son Ralph Crozier 2/6. To Richd. Crozier 2/6. To Elizabeth Brown 2/6. To Mary Metlen 2/6. To Ann Leard 2/6. His said children are not to have anything else.

Part of lands of Drumash, and part let to Robt. Brown. Rest of real and personal estate.

Witnesses: Rev. Jas. Pollock, Cavanamarra, James Irvine, Magheralough, Chas. Porter, Cardrumady, Thos. Beacon, Glassmullagh, all in Co. Tyrone.

Memorial witnessed by: Chas. Porter, Wm. Porter, Derry, Co. Tyrone.

309, 421, 206235 James Crozier (seal)

545 GRAHAM, THOMAS, Knockmanoul, Co. Fermanagh.

3 Jan. 1766. Précis ½ p. 14 Nov. 1775.

To his son James Graham his lands of Knockmanoul, held from Wm. Conolly, deceased, with the dwelling house etc.

Witnesses: John Toomath, Trory, Co. Fermanagh, Mathew Graham and John Graham, Knockmanoul.

Memorial witnessed by: John Toomath, David Cowan, Trelick, Co. Tyrone, gent.

309, 422, 206236 Jas. Graham (seal)

546 CARLETON, JOHN, Darlinghill, Co. Tipperary, Esq.

27 July 1772. Full 1½ p. 29 Dec. 1775.

My late father John Carleton. My brother Robert Carleton. My third brother Francis Carleton (under age). My six sisters, Frances Smythwick otherwise Carleton, Jane Carleton, Grace Carleton, Isabella Dixon otherwise Carleton, Anna Maria Carleton, and Rebecca Carleton. My brother Oliver Carleton. Francis Carleton, Cork, Ambrose Power, Baritstown, Co. Tipperary, and Hugh Carleton, Dublin, Esq., exors.

Lands etc. of Darlinghill alias Knockananama, Ballybeg, Quarter Cross, Clare, Burden's Grange alias Burden's Kill, houses etc. in town of Clonmell, and lands of Ballycarnane, all in Co. Tipperary.

Witnesses: Rev. Robert Watts, Carrick, Co. Tipperary, clerk, Thomas Newcomen, Dovehill, Co. Tipperary, Thomas Ryan, Clonmell, Co. Tipperary, merchant.

Memorial witnessed by: Thomas Ryan, Edmund English, Clonmell, gent.

308, 484, 206730 Jane Carleton (seal)

547 HENDERSON, GEORGE, Prussia Street, Dublin, gent.

29 Dec. 1775. Narrate ½ p. 29 Dec. 1775.

His wife Margaret Henderson, exor. with Chas Brown and Thos. Ewart, Dublin, bookbinders. Jas. Tomlin and Ann Tomlin, David Murray and Agneas Hill. His two houses on Lazers Hill in the possession of Jno. and Daniel Mooly. His other holdings devised to David Murray of Edinburgh [situation not mentioned].

Witnesses: Jno. Green, Jno. Hill, both Dublin, bookbinders, Willm. Willson, Dublin, gent.

Memorial witnessed by: William Willson.

310, 331, 206735

548 WAINHOUSE, JOSEPH, The Coomb, city of Dublin, weaver. 28 Dec. 1775. Précis ½ p. 3 Jan. 1776.

His eldest daughter Martha Paine. His son Josh. Wainhouse. His daughter Elizabeth Turner. His son Richd. Wainhouse. His four children. Wm. Paine and Joseph Wainhouse, exors.

Witnesses: Michl. Dowling and Jno. Chandler, both Dublin, weavers.

Memorial witnessed by: Patk. Smyth, Wm. Kelly, Dublin, gents.

310, 336, 206766 Josh. Wainhouse (seal)

549 FLEMING, THOMAS, Dolphin's Barn, parish of Crumlin, Co. Dublin. 26 Feb. 1774. Narrate ½ p. 16 Jan. 1776.

His wife Elizabeth, then enciente, extx. His sons Robert, Thomas and Adams Fleming (all under 21 years). Elizabeth Fleming, testator's daughter (under 21 years). His freehold leases in Dolphin's Barn and Crooked Staff, Co. Dublin, the house in Crooked Staff then possessed by Bartholomew Byrne. Two houses in Vicars Street formerly devised by Robert Adams.

Witnesses: Michael Heagarty, Walter Cusack, both Dublin, gents., Elizabeth Bourke.

Memorial witnessed by: Michael Macabe, Dublin, gent., Pat. Smith, Dublin, gent.

311, 60, 206850 Elizth. Fleming (seal)

550 KEATING, DANIEL, Dublin, grocer.
20 March 1773. Précis ¼ p. 16 Jan. 1776.

To his wife Elizth. Keating, extx. and his daughter Catherine Keating one half each of all his substance.

Witnesses: John Q[u]atermain, Dublin, gent., John Wilson, Dublin, silk weaver.

Memorial witnessed by: John Wilson, Martin Keating.

312, 13, 206856 Elizth. Keating (seal)
her mark

551 BEAUCHAMP, Richard, Narra[gh]more, Co. Kildare, clerk.
3 June 1772. Narrate. 24 Jan. 1776.

Wife Juliana, extx. George Carr and Francis Harvey, Dublin, Esqrs. Nephew John Beauchamp. His sister Margaret Colclough. His deceased sister Martha Harvey. His deceased sister Elinor Bagnall. Maurice Keating, Esq., his brother-in-law. Estates in Co. Carlow.

Witnesses: James Dunkin, Esq., Barrister at law, George Cheney and David Forrest, Dublin, gents.

Memorial witnessed by: James Dunkin, Edward Bradford, Dublin, gent.

206907([1]) Juliana Beauchamp (seal)

552 SWIFT, WILLIAM, late of Donnybrook, but formerly of city of Dublin, Counsellor at law. 1 Feb. 1769. Full 1 p. 17 Feb. 1776.

My wife Elizabeth Swift otherwise Longfield, extx., our children. She is to pay out such legacies as are bequeathed by the Will of the late Mrs. Helena Maria Bor.

My lands etc. in the County of Dublin, County of Catherlogh and County of city of Dublin and elsewhere.

Witnesses: Josh. Ivie, Dublin, gent., John Lawless, Dublin, gent., clerk to said Josh. Ivie, George Ivie, Dublin, gent., attorney.

Memorial witnessed by: Josh. Ivie, Michl. Swift, Dublin, attorney.

310, 438, 207221 Eliz. Swift (seal)
widow of testator.

([1]) This memorial was not transcribed. It will be found in Folio 691.

553 WHITE, JOHN, Castlebellingham, Co. Louth, Esq.

14 May 1767. Narrate ¾ p. 4 March 1776.

His nephew Henry Hughes, exor. His sister Jane Palmer. His niece Margt. Palmer. His niece Abigail Palmer. His nephew John Palmer. His nephew Henry Palmer. His sister Lucy Hughes. Small sums left to Bartholemew White, Molly Carroll, and poor of parish of Kilsaran. Alan Bellingham, Castlebellingham, exor.

His freehold interest in lands of Cannonstown, Barony Ferrard, Co. Louth, held by lease under Joseph Leeson, Esq. Priorstown, said Barony, Scogginstown, Barony Atherdee, Co. Louth. Messuage etc. in Castlebellingham. Lands in Drumiskin, Co. Lough, and the farm called the Spaw.

Witnesses: Patk. Finegan, merchant, Pat. Pouderly, carpenter, Denis Lyons, waiter, then all of Castlebellingham, aforesaid.

Memorial witnessed by: Michl. Macabe, Pat. Smith, both Dublin, gents.

313, 78, 207387 Henry Hughes (seal)

554 BURTON, WILLIAM, Blackford, Queen's Co., farmer.

4 Oct. 1765. Précis ¼ p. 20 March 1776.

To his son Robert Brophy, commonly called Robert Burton, all his leasehold interests [situation not mentioned].

Witnesses: Benj. Johnson, Dublin, gent., Rev. Raphael Walsh, Dean of Dromore, James Sheal, Ballykilcaven, Queen's Co.

Memorial witnessed by: Wm. Burton, Benedict Hamilton, Dublin, gent., Benj. Johnson.

308, 570, 207611 Robert Brophy Burton (seal)

555 JONES, RICHARD, George's Lane, Dublin, coachman.

1 May 1765. Narrate 1½ p. 27 April 1776.

His wife Frances Jones, exor. His sons John and Francis. His younger children Robt. and Sophia. His son-in-law Nichs. Grumly, exor.

His house then inhabited by him and the house inhabited by Mrs. Broadway, both in George's Lane. His freehold interests in George's Lane. His house in Grafton Street, another in Little Booter Lane held under Mrs. Loyd. Interest in Mrs. Broadway's house after his wife's death " to go to such of his children Richd. or Robert . . . as his said wife should think fit."(1).

Witnesses: Rev. John Lyon, Dublin, D.D. and curate of St. Bridget's in said city, Thomas Tudor, late of said city, one of the attorneys, deceased, John Greanger, Dublin, coachmaker.

Memorial witnessed by: Thos. Ferrall, Dublin, coachmaker, Thos. Darcy, Dublin, clerk to said John and Francis Jones.

313, 162, 207923 Frances Jones (seal)

556 PROCTOR, THOMAS, Dublin, cooper.

25 April 1776. Narrate ½ p. 21 May 1776.

His son-in-law James Rochfort, Dublin, and James Lambe of same, merchant, trustees and exors. His grandson Thomas Rochfort. His grand-daughter Elizabeth Fox, daughter of Alice Fox. His holding in Bray which is held by Sir William Montgomery, Baronet. Residue of his real and personal estate.

Witnesses: Thomas Hackett, Thomas Hutton, victualler, Thomas Downing, grocer, all of Dublin.

Memorial witnessed by: Thomas Hackett, Bartholomew O'Brien.

312, 184, 208016 James Rochfort (seal)

557 BRENNAN, CHRISTOPHER, Crossaghy, Co. Monaghan, farmer. 9 Aug. 1776. Narrate ½ p. 20 Aug. 1776.

His wife Catherine Brennan. Bryan Brennan, his son. His [testator's] children. Joseph McKittrick, Terence Duffy, Pholemy Conolly his son-in-law. His son-in-law Terence Duffy exor.

His lands and holdings in Crossaghy and lands of Crossmoare adjoining. Lands of Lemegoar [Lemgare], Clontibret and a tenement in town of Castleshane [Co. Monaghan].

(1) Richard is shown as eldest son in Betham's abstract of this Will. Another daughter Elizabeth, wife of . . . . O'Neill is included by Betham. (*Betham Will Pedigrees, Genealogical Office*).

Witnesses: Edwd. Carolan, Dromgavne, Co. Monaghan, farmer, Andrew McKittrick, Greaghnerogue, Francis Meey, same place, both Co. Monaghan, farmers, Archibald McKittrick, Dromisk, Co. Louth, dealer and yarn merchant.

Memorial witnessed by: Andrew McKittrick.

311, 233, 209213 Joseph McKittrick (seal)

558 STYLE, CATHERINE, wife of Wm. Style, parish of St. George, Hanover Sq., Westminster. 20 June 1754. Précis ½ p. 7 Sept. 1776.

Settlement(1) made previous to her marriage with Wm. Style. Her husband Wm. Style exor., " every part and parcel thereof unto her dear husband(2) Wm. Style."

Witnesses: Chas. Style, afterwards Sir Charles Style, of Wateringbury, Kent, Bart., since deceased, John Raymond, Inner Temple London, since deceased, Wm. Jenkin, parish of St. George, Hanover Square, since deceased.

Memorial witnessed by: John Stonehouse, Piccadilly, Middlesex, grocer, Mark Stephenson, Plough Street, Fetter Lane, Middlesex, gent.

313, 411, 209386 Wm. Style (seal)

559 CAPEL, Mrs. ELIZABETH, Cloghroe, Co. Cork. 25 June 1764. Full 1 p. 6 Nov. 1770.

My husband Josh. Capel and Richd. Meade, counsellor at law, trustees. The child I am now enceinte of. My daughter Mary Capel and my daughter Jane Capel (both under 21 years). My kinsman the said Richd. Meade. My real and personal estate.

(1) 209387. Agreement dated 9 April 1754 (27 Geo. 11) between Wm. Style, Maddock Street, parish of St. George, Hanover Square, Esq., youngest son of Sir Thomas Style, Wateringbury, Kent, Bart., of the 1st. part, Catherine Bateman of same parish, spinster, only surviving daughter of Charles Bateman, Esq., deceased, by Catherine Bateman, the then widow of said Charles Bateman, which said Catherine Bateman, party thereto, was one of the sisters of John Long Bateman, Esq., her late brother, deceased, of the 2nd part, and others in consideration of a marriage intended to be solemnized between said Wm. Style and Catherine Bateman, concerning lands in Co. Donegal.

(2) The transcript has the word " son " here, an error for " husband."

Witnesses: Henry Rugge, Cork, vintner, James Wherland, junr., said city, gent., since deceased, Wm. Heard, said city, public notary.

Memorial witnessed by: Henry Rugge, Wm. Heard.

315, 211, 209767 Josh. Capel (seal)

560 ROBSON, RACHEL, Antrim, Co. Antrim, widow of John Robson and daughter of John Robson, both late of Antrim, deceased. 30 Sept. 1766. Précis $\frac{1}{2}$ p. 6 Nov. 1776.

Her freehold estates [situation not mentioned] to James Lewis, Belfast, Co. Antrim, merchant and Alexander Anderson, Dublin, gent., trustees and exors.

Witnesses: Robert Simms, Belfast, tanner, Bryce Smith, Belfast, tanner, Andrew Orr, formerly of Belfast but now of Island of Madeira, merchant.

Memorial witnessed by: Chas. Lewis, merchant, Alexander Arthur, gent., both of Belfast.

317, 33, 209791 James Lewis (seal)

561 ARMSTRONG, WILLIAM, Mullygorie, Co. Fermanagh. 12 May 1761. Narrate $\frac{3}{4}$ p. 13 Nov. 1776.

Margaret Armstrong his wife. His son John Armstrong. His son Simon Armstrong. His son Robt. Armstrong. His son Wm. Armstrong. His daughter Margaret. His daughters Jean Armstrong and Ann Armstrong. His son John Armstrong and Simon Armstrong, James Montgomery of Carry and William Fausett, Moykeel, exors.

Mullygorie. Leases of Moykeel, of Shanmullagh and of Conoglass. Corn[a]cully, Carrickmasparrars [Carrickmacsparrow] and Mullaghmore [Co. Fermanagh]. Money in Hugh Montgomerie's hands.

Witnesses: William Miles, John Cathcart, Thos. Carson.

Memorial witnessed by: Wm. Miles, Charles Fausett.

316, 93, 209984 James Montgomery (seal)

562 RADFORD, BENJAMIN, Ballynecarigg, Co. Wexford, Esq.

8 April 1776. Full 2 pp. 19 Nov. 1776.

A deed of settlement 13 Sept. 1772 made between me and Elizabeth Radford otherwise Sandwith my wife, and Ebenezer Radford my son of the first part, Ebenezer Jacob of Bettyville and Bostocke Radford Jacob of Wexford, both Co. Wexford, of the second part, and Rev. Christopher Harvey and Rev. Joseph Miller of Wexford, of the third part. My wife Elizabeth Radford, exor. My now only daughter Anne Radford. My niece Rebecca Radford, daughter of my brother Ebenezer Radford. My son Ebenezer Radford. My grand-nephew John Jacob, eldest son of my nephew, the before named Ebenezer Jacob. My nephew Bostocke Radford, son of my brother Ebenezer Radford. Ebenezer Jacob, exor.

Witnesses: Mathew Keogh, River View, Esq., Nicholas Gray, Whiteford, Benjamin Wilson, Wexford, gent., all in Co. Wexford.

Memorial witnessed by: Benjamin Wilson, Robt. Piggott, Wexford, gent.

314, 47, 210104 Elizth. Radford (seal)

563 MURRAY, THOMAS, Ballineally, Co. Wicklow, farmer.

22 June 1765. Narrate ½ p. 26 Nov. 1776.

His wife Rose Murray, exor. His eldest son Wm. Murray, exor. His second son Paul Murray. His daughter Rose Murray (unmarried). His daughter Esther Commins, and his daughter Mary Lacy had already had their portions. Fifty Masses for his soul.

The farm of Balline Alley which he held from Christopher Fitzsimon, Esq. House and about 15 acres of land then in his possession in and about the town of Redcross.

Witnesses: Peter Murray, carpenter, Thos. Murray, farmer, Henry Masterson, breeches maker, all of Co. Wicklow.

Memorial witnessed by: Thos. Murray, Gerald Cotter, Dublin, writing clerk.

316, 119, 210196 William Murray (seal)

564 MURRAY, ROSE, Ballinvally, Co. Wicklow, widow of Thos. Murray, deceased. 13 Nov. 1775. Narrate ½ p. 26 Nov. 1776.

Her son Wm. Murray. Her daughter Mary Lacy. Her daughter Rose Macdonnell. Her daughter Ester Commins. Her grand-daughter Rose Commins. Thomas Murray of Sheepwalk and Maurice Byrne of Ballyrogan, exors.

Witnesses: Thos. Murray, farmer, Stephen Byrne, labourer, both of Co. Wicklow.

Memorial witnessed by: Thos. Murray, Gerald Cotter, Dublin, writing clerk.

316, 119, 210197 Willm. Murray (seal)

565 DUTTON, JAMES LENOX([1]), Sherborne, Co. Gloucester. 8 Sept. 1772. Codicil 25 June 1776. Narrate 20 pp. 22 Jan. 1777.

His wife Jane Dutton. His eldest son James Dutton. His second son William Dutton. His third son Ralph Dutton. His second daughter Mary wife of Thomas Master. His third daughter Frances Lambert wife of Charles Lambert. His fourth daughter Jane Dutton. His eldest daughter Ann Blackwell wife of Samuel Blackwell. Henry Duke of Beaufort and Rev. Peter Warburton, Garryhinch, Queen's Co., trustees.

His manors, messuages, lands, tenants and hereditaments in counties of Meath, Westmeath, Galway and King's Co. To said Samuel Blackwell, said Charles Lambert and said Thomas Master as trustees his lands etc. in Co. Meath except Tallaghanoge, Growtown and Rahinstown, purchased of the co-heiress of Justin late Earl of Fingall deceased, and other lands in Killbride and Robinstown, Co. Meath, purchased from representatives of Robert Longfield, and Tecroghan, Co. Meath purchased from Mr. Trench, persons who become intitled to possession of said estates to take surname of Naper and bear the Naper Arms unless they should become intitled to his mansion house or seat and estate of Sherborne. Codicil says his wife Jane then lately deceased. A lawsuit at issue between testator and the guardians of

([1]) James Lenox Naper of Loughcrew who assumed the name and Arms of Dutton.

the natural son of his late cousin Genl. Naper, deceased, for the recovery of lands, rents etc. in counties of Westmeath and Dublin, and city of Dublin.

Witnesses: Ja Carmichael, Saint Martins Street, Leicester Fields, Richard Thurston, Lincoln's Inn, Geo. Jones, Lincoln's Inn.

Codicil witnessed by: Joseph Twyning, Charles Gunning, William Burge.

Memorial witnessed by: Francis Adams, John D[e]labere.

314, 116, 210681 James Dutton (seal)

566 JOYANS, WALTER, Dublin, baker.

[Date not recorded]. Précis ¼ p. 27 Jan. 1777.

To his wife Charlotte Joyans all his lands and premises in Uttoxitier in Staffordshire then in possession of his brother Thomas Joyans.

Witnesses: John Rice, gent., Robert Shiel, publican, Charles Morgan, watchmaker, all of Dublin.

Memorial witnessed by: John Rice, Andrew Cunningham, Dublin, cabinet maker.

312, 528, 210736 Charlotte Joyans (seal)
her mark.

567 ECCLES, JOHN, Dublin, gent.

29 Jan. 1777. Full ½ p. 16 April 1777.

To be buried in St. Mark's churchyard with remains of my wife and father. David A[i]goin, Esq., Dublin, trustee(1). My daughter Grace Gilliard, wife of William Gilliard, Dublin.

Witnesses: Daniel Kinsilagh, Dublin, blockmaker, John Haughton, carver, John Crawford, Dublin, bargeman.

Memorial witnessed by: John Crawford, William Crookshank, Dublin, Esq.

316, 208, 211544 David A[i]goin (seal)

(1) In Index of Dublin Grants and Wills, 26th. *Report of Deputy Keeper of the Records Ireland* there is the entry of Aigoin, David and Ann Heywood, 1748, Marriage Licence.

568 BOTTOMS, JOHN, Tallagh, Co. Dublin, farmer.

7 March 1769. Narrate ½ p. 26 April 1777.

His wife Elizth. Bottoms alias Barnes. His nephew Samuel Bottoms.

Holdings of the lands of Whitestowne, Co. Dublin: William Dixon's, James Sinnott's, William Lennon's, Richard Jones and Peter Kane's holdings.

Witnesses: Richd. Hawkins, Newhall, Co. Dublin, farmer, John Maddock, Ballymana, said Co., farmer, William Hill, the Commons of Tallagh, said Co., nailer.

Memorial witnessed by: John Maddock.

313, 625, 211705 Elizth. Ferrall (seal)
said Elizth. Bottoms now the wife of Thomas Ferrall.

569 CLAXTON, ARTHUR, Palmerstown, Co. Kildare.

11 Dec. 1776. Précis ½ p. 29 April, 1777.

To his son Thos. Claxton (sole exor.) all his real estate, goods and chattles.

Witnesses: Thos. Allen, Palmerstown, Co. Kildare, farmer. Richd. Rawson, Palmerstown, shoemaker, Robert Allen, son of said Thos. Allen.

Memorial witnessed by: Richd. Rawson, Edward Fisher, Dublin, gent.

325, 2, 211785 Thos. Claxton (seal)

570 BAILIE, ANDREW THOMAS, Newry, Co. Down, merchant.

19 March 1769. Narrate 1 p. 6 May 1777.

His mother Margaret Kennedy wife of Dr. James Kennedy. His half brother Thomas Kennedy, her son, exor. His second half brother Robert Kennedy. His third half brother James Kennedy. His fourth half brother Nicholas Ward Kennedy. His half sisters Sarah Donaldson, Elizth. Kennedy and Rebecca Kennedy. Wm. Stewart,

Killymoon, Esq., Rev. Hugh Stewart, Ballymena, both Co. Tyrone, trustees. Clunivaddy otherwise Aghnagar and Sessiagh Donaghy otherwise Creeve, Co. Tyrone.

Witnesses: Arthur Johnston, Dublin, Esq., Rev. William Nevin, Downpatrick, Co. Down, Patrick Simpson Kennedy, Dublin, attorney at law.

Memorial witnessed by: Patrick Simpson Kennedy, Malcolm Kennedy, Dublin, attorney.

318, 97, 211876 Tho. Kennedy (seal)

571 PEXTON, HENRY, Dublin, gent.

16 Jan. 1777. Précis ½ p. 7 June 1777.

To his son-in-law Thomas Wilkinson in trust all his house and concerns in Pallace Street, Dublin.

Witnesses: James Groves, Dublin, gent., John Frankling, Dublin, coachmaker, Michael Mullery, Dublin, gent.

Memorial witnessed by: John Frankling, Alexr. Brennan, Dublin, gent.

311, 499, 212324 Thos. Wilkinson (seal)

572 REED (REID), ANN, Castle Street, Newry, Co. Down, widow.

12 Oct. 1776. Narrate 1½ p. 14 June 1777.

Her nephew George Smith. Her sister Catherine Winder. Her sister Mary Cannon. Her sister Margarett Baxter. Her niece Mary Markey otherwise Winder. Her niece Jane Davis, widow. Her grand-niece Ann Davis daughter to said Jane Davis. Her grand-niece Ann Montgomery, daughter to John Montgomery of Lisdrumgullion, Co. Armagh, merchant. Said John Montgomery and Hugh McDowell, both of Lisdrumgullion, Co. Armagh, gents., exors. Her freehold tenement in Castle St., Newry, shop and garden, (a garden held by John Ogle adjoining).

Witnesses: James Maxwell and William Searight, merchants, James Murdock, publican, all of Newry.

Memorial witnessed by: James Maxwell, William Bourke, Newry, gent.

319, 227, 212407 John Montgomery (seal)

573 McILWAIN, THOMAS, Belfast, merchant.
25 Feb. 1774. Narrate ½ p. 21 June 1777.

His wife. His daughter Mary McIlwain, Belfast, widow, and her three children Ann, Elizabeth and Rebecca McIlwain. His son Hugh McIlwain, Belfast, merchant, exor. His dwelling house wherein he then lived in Bridge Street, Belfast. His leasehold interest in Millfield in town of Belfast.

Witnesses: Joseph Stephenson, John Smyth, Henry Joy, all of Belfast, merchants.

Memorial witnessed by: Charles Dowdall, Dublin, grocer, Alexr. Arthur, Belfast, gent.

311, 535, 212507 Hu McIlwain (seal)

574 FORWARD, ELIZABETH, " otherwise called Smyth," Dublin, working milliner. 14 June 1777. Full 1½ p. 10 July 1777.

My father Mark Forward late of the city of Dublin, upholder, deceased, by his Will dated 30 Sept. 1761 devised his estate of Little Grange, Co. Louth in trust to permit his wife Martha Forward to receive the rents for her life, and after her death to the use of me and my sister Mary. Expectant on the death of my step-mother, the said Martha Forward, I am now entitled to the reversion of one moiety of said lands. My said sister Mary who was in like manner entitled to the other moiety having left this Kingdom several years ago. I have good reason to believe she is dead without issue. My friend Richd. Cox, Dublin, haberdasher, and his wife with whom I have lived (without receiving any kind of assistance from any of my relations or kindred). To said Richard Cox (exor.) my interest in said lands.

Witnesses: Francis Pelissior, Dublin, gent., clerk to Messrs. John Dawson & Co. Dublin, merchants, John Kelly, Dublin, goldsmith, Patrick Corbet, Dublin, gent.

Memorial witnessed by: Patrick Corbet, William Dawson, Dublin, merchant.

318, 151, 212855 Richard Cox (seal)

575 HORE, WILLIAM, "Killary," Co. Wicklow, farmer and brewer. 7 Aug. 1777. Full 1 p. 19 Aug. 1777.

My son Thos. Hore. To my son Joseph Hore, the coppice joining the Glinn of the Downs which I purchased from Richard Lambert. My son William Hore. My grandson Charles McDonald. My grandson Charles Hore, son of William Hore of Irishtown. Charles McDonald of Delgarry [? Delgany]. Robert Carefoot of Daumen.

Lands of Killinurry which I hold under Mr. Adare. Bills of Mr. La Touche. Sum due on a Kerry Bill of Mr. John Ball when recovered to be divided between my sons William Hore, Thos. Hore and Joseph Hore. Bond of James Bunn and Mrs. Elizabeth Siggens of Kindlestown. £3 to be disposed of to poor by Rev. Diggs Latouch. My son William Hore, Thomas Hore, Val Bourke and George Dickeson exors.

Witnesses: Thomas Fox, Kilmurry, farmer, George Walker, Kilmurry, farmer, George Dickeson, Ballsdonough, farmer, all in Co. Wicklow.

Memorial witnessed by: Thomas Fox, Wingfield Burton, clerk to John Lambert, Dublin, gent.

316, 358, 213119 William Hore (seal)

576 MILLS, JOHN, then of Rush, Co. Dublin.

4 May 1777. Précis ¾ p. 19 Sept. 1777.

Reciting settlement 21 Jan. 1760 made between Samuel Mills, the elder of Turnings, Co. Kildare, Esq., Margaret Mills, otherwise Bradford, wife of said Samuel, John Mills, eldest son of said Samuel, and James and Samuel Mills the younger two other sons of the said Samuel the elder, whereby the lands of Moyvally, Co. Kildare (about

700 acres) were granted to said John Mills on conditions therein mentioned. His wife Jane Mills otherwise Litton of Dublin. Rev. Brabston [Brabazon] Wye and Wm. Wye his brother, exors.

Witnesses: Rev. Brabazon Wye, Plunkett Ceary, Rush, Co. Dublin, weaver, Jane Gilfoyle, Dublin, wife of Michael Gilfoyle, late of Dublin.

Memorial witnessed by: Geo. Cullin, Dublin, attorney and Laurence Fowler, Dublin, his writing clerk.

314, 269, 213343 Jane Mills (seal)

577 FERIS, WILLIAM, the elder, Ballanakil [Ballynakill], parish of Clonmore, Co. Carlow, gent. 26 Aug. 1777. Narrate, part in full, ½ p. 29 Oct. 1777.

Eldest son Peter Feris. Eldest daughter Mary Feris. Second eldest son William Feris to whom testator had already made over all his lands by deed of lease and release. Youngest daughter Elizabeth Feris otherwise Holmes who has already had her share. My youngest son Joseph Feris. My wife Mary Feris, extx. Henry Hall, Clondaw, Co. Wexford, gent., exor.

Witnesses: Simon Barker, Wm. Barker, both Co. Carlow, farmers. Jervis Paul, said Co., farmer.

Memorial witnessed by: Simon Barker, Joseph Barker.

316, 412, 213573 William Feris (seal)

578 McDOWELL, JAMES, Derrynaughton, Co. Armagh, gent. 18 March 1777. Narrate 1 p. 6 Nov. 1777.

His wife Jane McDowell otherwise Cairnovan, exor. His son Cairnovan McDowell. His son John McDowell, exor. His daughter Ann McDowell.

His house etc. and lands of Derrynaught, parish Kildarton, (boundaries of his lands mentioned, George Cartney, Hugh Neilson, William Kidd, John Mallon and Mathew Bell have holdings adjoining) and turf bog in Derrynaught next adjoining Drumahee and Neternett.

Witnesses: Benjamin Bell, George Crozier, both Dublin, gents. Robert Sinclair, Markett Hill, Co. Armagh, surgeon.

Memorial witnessed by: Benjamin Bell, George Crozier.

324, 161, 213626 John McDowell (seal)

579 GRAHAM, JOHN, Gt. George's Street, Dublin.

22 Jan. 1770. Précis ½ p. 12 Nov. 1777.

To Graves Chamney, exor., Platten, Co. Meath, Esq., his real estate in Co. Meath and in town and country of the town of Drogheda for ever. To Mrs. Ann Mansell lands of Knock Island, Co. Meath, then set to Nicholas Hatch.

Witnesses: Theops. Casson, gent., John Williams, gent., William Williams, public notary, all of Dublin.

Memorial witnessed by: Thos. Chamney, Bullingate, Co. Wicklow, Esq., Christopher Abbott, junior, Dublin.

320, 98, 213771 Graves Chamney (seal)

580 MADDOCK, HENRY, Gilbertstown, Co. Meath, gent.

3 July 1773. Narrate ¾ p. 24 Jan. 1778.

His wife Elizabeth Maddock, exor. His son Jno. Maddock, exor. His daughter Kunning. His son-in-law Danl. Kunning, exor. His son Arthur Maddock. His sons Henry and Thomas.

Lands of Gilbertstown and Castlepole both in Co. Meath. Lease of Castlepole made by James Lennox Napper to him. His holdings in Church Minchal in Cheshire.

Witnesses: Geo. Armstrong, Edwd. Armstrong, Robt. Gartside, all of Dublin, merchants.

Memorial witnessed by: Geo. Armstrong, Francis McMahon, Dublin, gent.

315, 427, 214612 Jno. Maddock (seal)

581 STAFFORD, PATRICK, Four Court Marshalsea, Dublin, gent.

17 March 1777. Précis ½ p. 28 Jan. 1778.

To his wife Sidney Stafford otherwise Jackson otherwise Crowe all his real and personal estate. Said wife and Thos. O'Brien, Dublin, tobacconist, exors.

Witnesses: Anthony Keogh, Wm. O'Brien, Chas. Burnside, all Dublin, gents.

Memorial witnessed by: Anthy. Keogh, Cornelius Reilly.

316, 561, 214643 Sidney Stafford (seal)

582 WELSH, ANTHONY, Dublin, Esq.

18 July 1777. Codicil 17 Jan. 1778. Narrate 1½ p. 3 Feb. 1778.

His sister Frances Mabella Hall wife of Rowley Hall, Dublin, Esq. His cousin Faithfull Fortescue, Corderry, Co. Louth, Esq. Sir Roger Palmer, Ballyshannon, Co. Kildare, Bart. Roger Palmer Esq., eldest son of said Sir Roger Palmer Bart. His cousin Wm. Smith, Ralphsdale, Co. Westmeath, Esq. Francis Palmer, Castlelachen, Co. Mayo, Esq., brother to said Sir Roger Palmer, Bart. James Cummin, Killough, Co. Down, gent. Hugh Wilson, Dublin, barrister at law, No. 10 Clare Street, Dublin and George Crookshank, Esq., Bride Street, Dublin, trustees.

Lands of Ballynagross and Ballytrustan, Co. Down, and rents of Tullychin, Corbally, Carricknabb, Lower Islandmuck otherwise Han(n)amuck and Toulla otherwise Torrela and Upper Islandmuck otherwise Hanamuck and Clontibegg, all in Co. Down. Lands of Grangetown, Ballagh otherwise Spittlefield, Clonard otherwise Clooneard, Clonishell otherwise Clooneneshell, Killintagart, Ballina otherwise Grange, Sarcinstown [Sarsanstown], Raivcarroughter otherwide Farrnishock [? Farranistick], all in Co. Westmeath. Grangecam, Co. Down.

Witnesses: Geo. Surman, groom to the Earl of Clanbrassil, Dudley Trueman, Dundalk, Co. Louth, gent., Ralph Trueman, son to said Dudley Trueman.

Codicil: Geo. Crookshank, Dublin, gent., Caleb Jenkin, Dublin, bookseller, Jeremiah Bronson, apprentice to said Caleb Jenkin.

Memorial witnessed by: Dudley Trueman, Arthur Dunn.

315, 433, 214725 Faith Fortescue (seal)
Frances M. Hall (seal)

583 WARREN, JOSEPH, Galtrim, Co. Meath, Esq.

22 March 1773. Full 2 pp. 28 Feb. 1778.

My wife Frances Warren, exor. and guardian of children. My mother Mrs. Frances Warren, exor. Frances my eldest daughter(1). To Rev. Joseph Warren, Clontibritt, Co. Monaghan, exor., £200 for use of my niece Frances Warren, daughter of my brother Thos. Warren on marriage. My nephew Robert Powell, Dublin, exor. If I die without issue male or female my real and personal estate to exors. for use of the children of my sister Margaret Warren, and the children of William Powell, late of Thomas Street, share and share alike.

Lands of Galtrim, my house of Galtrim and the demesne containing about 34 acres.

Witnesses: William Lyster, Dublin, Esq., John Nelson, Thos. Bracken, said city, gents.

Memorial witnessed by: William Lyster, Thomas Bracken.

319, 372, 215060 Frans. Warren (seal)
(an exor.)

584 CORRY, SAMUEL, Dunmurry, Co. Fermanagh.

14 July 1769. Narrate ½ p. 19 March 1778.

His step father Michael Slack. To his uncle Johnston Anderson, and to his uncle John Betty and James Slack £5 each. His aunt Margery Corry. To his brother Wm. Corry's children his part of Drumsloe and Cra[g]han failing them to his brother Anthony Slack, failing whose heirs to his sister Jane Slack.

(1) Provision is made for younger children, but the testator had probably only the one child Frances.

Witnesses: Robert Anderson, Michael Slack, Drummurry, Jane Slack, daughter to said Michael Slack.

Memorial witnessed by: Robert Anderson, Johnston Hamilton, Enniskillen, Co. Fermanagh, gent.

316, 576, 215286 Michl. Slack (seal)

585 VIPONT, CHARLES, Jamestown, Co. Dublin, Esq.

25 Aug. 1777. Narrate 1 p. 4 April 1778.

Rev. Bigoe Henzell, Drogheda, (his kinsman), Graves Chamney, Platten and John Bayly, Shrubbs, Esq., trustees. Mrs. Mary Stiles, his housekeeper in Hampton Court, Co. Middlesex. Estate to Philip the son of the said Mary Stiles, when 21 years. Ann and Jane, the daughters of said Mary Stiles (under 21, unmarried). Rachel Watson, Summerhill, Co. Dublin, widow. His kinsman the said Bigoe Henzell, Mary Stiles and Wm. Faden, London, printer, exors. and guardians of said Philip, Anne and Jane. His real estate and leasehold interest in Cos. Dublin and Cavan, and real estate in Church Street and Francis Street, Dublin.

Witnesses: Gregory Byrne, James Archbold, Dublin, merchants, Matt. St. Leger, clerk to said Gregory Byrne.

Memorial witnessed by: Charles Abbott, the younger, Clement Moore, both of Dublin, gents.

323, 357, 215449 Bigoe Henzell (seal)

586 HATTON, JOHN, Ballymartin, Co. Wexford, Esq.

11 Nov. 1775. Narrate 1 p. 11 May 1778.

His wife Alice Hatton otherwise Coles exor. and guardian of children. His son Geo. Hatton, (under 21 years). His daughter Martha Hatton, (under 21 years).

His estate and lands of Ballynaclash, and Upper and Lower Ballyna, [? Co. Wexford].

Witnesses: Armstrong Brown, Killtown, Co. Wexford, Esq., Richard Bennett, Wexford, cabinetmaker, Paul Kenny, Killtown, servant of said Armstrong Brown.

Memorial witnessed by: Armstrong Brown, Richard Waddy, Dublin, gent.

321, 268, 215766 Alice Hatton (seal)

587 McDERMOTT, EDMOND, Emla, Co. Roscommon, Esq.

27 Oct. 1776. Précis ½ p. 3 June 1778.

Henry Sandford, Castlerea, Wm. Cary, Elphin, both Co. Roscommon, trustees.

Lands of Kiltul[t]oge, Castletran, Driminlogh, his acres in Annaghlogh and Brenabeg, Co. Roscommon.

Witnesses: Chas. Croghan, Donamon, Co. Roscommon, John Thewles, Dublin, Esq., Bernard Kelly, Mucklow, Co. Galway, gent.

Memorial witnessed by: John Thewles, Wm. Kelly, Dublin, gent.

319, 457, 216145 Dan. Kelly (seal)
an exor. named in said Will

588 GEOGHEGAN, DAVID, Donore, Co. Westmeath, Esq.

20 June 1778. Précis ¾ p. 1 July 1778.

Jno. Geoghegan, Attyblaney, King's Co., gent. His estate in the kingdom of Ireland or elsewhere to Roger Sheil, Clarmont, Co. Mayo, Owen Mooney, Doone, King's Co., trustees, for testator's grand-nephew Kedagh Geoghegan, Esq., (son of Kedagh Geoghegan, Esq., deceased) remainder to Jno. Geoghegan, Esq., testator's grand-nephew, Richard Nagle, testator's grand-npehew, John Kelly, gent., nephew of testator. Said Kedagh Geoghegan, Roger Sheill, Owen Mooney and Edwd. Bermingham, Kilfrylan, King's Co., Esq., and Denis Daly, Castle Daly, Co. Meath, exors.

Witnesses: Jno. Ardill, Dublin, gent., Josh. Bayly and Patk. Meara, two of said Jno. Ardill's clerks.

Memorial witnessed by: Jno. Ardill, Joseph Bayly.

323, 392, 216479 K. Geoghegan (seal)

589 WILMOT, ELINOR, Dublin, widow.

5 June 1777. Précis ½ p. 3 July 1778.

Her only daughter Elinor Millikin, her husband William Millikin. Mortgage on ground in Charles Street, Dublin, dated April 1754.

Witnesses: William Conway, John Annesley, sadler, Lewis Pollard, attorney, all of Dublin.

Memorial witnessed by: John Annesley, Michael Macabe, Dublin, gent.

319, 497, 216508 Elinor Millikin (seal)

590 BRADY, JOHN, Bellaghy, Co. Londonderry, farmer.

21 March 1778. Précis ½ p. 10 July 1778.

To his wife Jane Brady otherwise Moore, extx., all his goods and effects and remainder of purchase money owed by Richard Williams of Bellaghy, gent., due to testator for lands of Lisderry, Co. Fermanagh, sold to said Mr. Williams.

Witnesses: Henry Richardson, Dublin, Charles Conway, Monytroghan, Co. Londonderry, gent., Francis McQuead, Dublin, servant.

Memorial witnessed by: Henry Richardson, William Lenox, Dublin, gent.

327, 173, 216602 Jane Brady her mark (seal)

591 DONNELLY, ANNE, St. Nicholas Street, Dublin, widow.

19 Dec. 1772. Narrate 1 p. 30 July 1778.

Her daughters Jane Hindes and Susana Walsh, 5/- each. Her grand children Michael Hindes, John Hindes, Ann Hindes, Jane Hindes and Susana Hindes (under 21 years). Her son James Sheil, exor. Her grand-children John and James Hindes.

Witnesses: Laurence Johnston, Dublin, weaver, Samuel Peirce, Dublin, clerk to said James Sheil.

Memorial witnessed by: Samuel Peirce, Michl. Macabe, Dublin, gent.

316, 696, 216811 James Sheil (seal)

592 CALDWELL, ROBERT, Ballybogan, Co. Donegal, gent.

18 April 1774. Précis ¾ p. 11 Aug. 1778.

Benjamin Fenton, Strabane, Co. Tyrone, apothecary, Richd. Cowan, Lifford, Co. Donegal, Esq., trustees

Town and lands of Legnaneil and Gortindoragh, held in fee farm in manor of Lifford, and part of Ballybogan held under See of Derry, called Cames [Camus] then in occupation of Miles McTeher, Daniel McTeague and Wm. Kearney, and his third part of the corn mill on lands of Ballybogan aforesaid, and the holding occupied by the miller thereof.

Witnesses: Geo. Leathem, innkeeper, John Clarke, parish clerk, Robt. Smith, innkeeper, all of Lifford.

Memorial witnessed by: Robt. Smith, Samuel Shortt, Lifford, gent.

319, 546, 216927 Richd. Cowan (seal)

593 COGHRAN, JOHN, Edenmore, Co. Donegal, gent.

18 Nov. 1776. Narrate ½ p. 22 Sept. 1770.

His brother Zacherius Cochran, exor. All his estate in Edenmore in manor of Stranorlar, Co. Donegal, and all other his real and personal estate.

Witnesses: Gust. Henderson, Isaac Armstrong, Alexr. Purviance, all of Lifford, Co. Donegal, gents.

Memorial witnessed by: Gust. Henderson, Alexr. Purviance.

317, 237, 217191 Zachs. Coghran (seal)

594 SMITH, JAMES, Knocknagorm, parish of Garvagh, Co. Down.

18 Oct. 1778. Narrate, part in full, 1 p. 7 Nov. 1778.

My wife Jane, exor. My son-in-law Joseph McCracken, exor., a settlement made upon his intermarriage with my daughter Jane. Joseph Beck and his wife Elizabeth. To David Martin one shilling in right of his wife. My daughter Ann Smith (unmarried).

My lands bounded on one side by John Johnston and Patrick McGiveron.

Witnesses: James Moore, parish of Moyra, Co. Down, gent., John Sheperd, Dublin, gent.

Memorial witnessed by: James Moore, John Sheperd.

324, 462, 217509 James Smith [the testator]

595 GAMBLE, RICHARD, Cullenagh, parish Kilmeadow [Kilmeadan] Barony of Middle Third, Co. Waterford, gent. 31 Dec. 1764. Narrate ½ p. 17 Nov. 1778.

His eldest son Thomas Gamble. His son Richard Gamble. His son Robert Gamble. His son George Gamble. His daughter Mary Lyndon, her husband John Lyndon. His daughter Susanna Gamble, her husband Thomas Gamble.

Lands of Cullenagh held from Lord Doneraile, part of lands of Cullenagh held by his son Richard from him, part in possession of John Fling and David Fling.

Witnesses: Andrew Kearney, Benjamin Lyndon, John Gunston, all of Co. Waterford, gents.

Memorial witnessed by: Andrew Kearney, Thomas Cuthbert, Waterford, merchant.

321, 554, 217717 Richd. Gamble (seal)
son of testator.

596 DUNBAR, CHARLES, Blessington, Co. Wicklow, Esq. who died 13 Oct. 1778. 3 Oct. 1778. Full 3 pp. 24 Nov. 1778.

My wife Penelope Dunbar. Dillon Massy, Esq., and John Dillon Esq.

My lands, tenements and heritaments in counties of Wicklow and Kildare, (my intention is to continue my real estate in the family and blood of the late Primate Boyle), to the Earl of Hillsborough, Lord Fairford eldest son of said Earl, and in remainder to Lord Knapton, Lord Longford and the right heirs of late Primate Boyle. Theophilus Jones and Edmond Sexton Perry, trustees.

Witnesses: Irnham, Maria Irnham, Richard Dodd.

Memorial witnessed by: William Greene, William Street, Dublin, Esq., Rev. James Ford, Ballyhinch, Co. Down.

321, 572, 217848 Hillsborough (seal)

597 McDOWELL, JOHN, Derrynaught, Co. Armagh, gent.

25 Aug. 1778. Narrate ½ p. 27 Nov. 1778.

His mother Jane McDowell. His sister Ann McDowell. His estate in Derrynaught and all his other estates, freeholds, etc.

Witnesses: Rev. Geo. Ferguson, Magheravary, Robt. Publes, Hamilton's Bawn, linen draper, James McCartney, Dunnyram, gent., all in Co. Armagh.

Memorial witnessed by: James McCartney, Jno. Beatty, Eliza Hill, said Co. gent.

317, 336, 217910 Ann McDowell (seal)

598 HILL, ABRAHAM, Bray, Co. Wicklow.

19 Oct. 1775. Narrate ¾ p. 1 Dec. 1778.

To his wife Elizabeth Hill, sole extx., all his real and personal estate. To his reputed son William Hill one British shilling " to show him that he had remembrance that there was such a person."

Witnesses: Wm. Green, Esq., one of the clerks of H.M.'s Privy Council, Arthur Loughlin, Dublin, shoemaker, John Keough, Dublin, Esq.

Memorial witnessed by: John Keough, John Callaghan, Dublin, gent.

317, 346, 217938 Elizth Hill (seal)

599 McCANN, JOHN, Artane, parish of Coolock, Co. Dublin, land holder. 19 Jan. 1779. Full 1 p. 22 Jan. 1779.

To my friend John Crowe of Artane, the farm or lands about 12 acres, formerly held by . . . . Farrell and now in possession of John

Crowe, lying between the lands of Wm. Espinas, Esq., and those lands of . . . . Williams of Dublin, glass blower.

Witnesses: Laurence Murry, Donnecarney, farmer, John Brichell, Ballybough Bridge, Co. Dublin.

Memorial witnessed by: Laurence Murry, Wm. Dunphy.

317, 463, 218423 John Crowe (seal)

600 BYRNE, MICHAEL, Dirty Lane, county of city of Dublin, dairyman. 5 Sept. 1778. Précis ¼ p. 20 Feb. 1779.

To his wife Catherine extx., all his wordly substance.

Witnesses: Owen Reilly, gent., Nichs. Aylward, baker, both of Dublin.

Memorial witnessed by: Owen Reilly, Edwd. Smyth, Dublin, gent.

317, 534, 218806 Catherine Byrne (seal)
her mark

601 WHITE, FRANCIS, Redhills, Co. Cavan.

9 Jan. 1765. Narrate 10 pp. 20 Feb. 1779.

Testator's nephew the eldest and only son of testator's sister Anne White called Francis White (under 22 years). His said sister Anne White wife to John White, Esq. His nephew Francis Edgworth, the eldest son of his sister Sarah Edgworth alias White. Her daughter Ann White testator's niece (unmarried). Essex Edgworth second son of his sister Sarah Edgworth. Edward Ellis youngest son of testator's sister Mary Ellis alias White. Alexander Sanderson, Esq., of Castle Sanderson. Alexander Sanderson, Esq., of Drumcassidy, Rev. Francis Sander[son] his brother. Alexander Sanderson, Esq., Cloverhill, Co. Cavan and James Fleming, Esq., Killebandrick, trustees and exors. Alexander Cecil, testator's godson, eldest son to James Fleming aforesaid, Esq. To Elizabeth Smith alias White the testator's eldest sister an annuity in lieu of the interest payable to her for money left her by Will of testator's father. Mr. William Sanderson then living with testator.

His real estate in Co. Cavan which he had by right of birth and inheritance or by virtue of a deed perfected by him in 1742; the mansion house of Redhills. Persons inheriting his estates to use surname of White and bear arms of White of Redhills. Estate in Co. Tyrone called the manor of Ballynagrane. House in Jervis Street, Dublin.

Witnesses: Joseph Welsh, late of Tullymurphy, Co. Monaghan, gent., deceased, John Bell, Killinure, Thomas Armstrong, Redhills, both Co. Cavan.

2 Dec. 1769. Republished as his last Will and testament. Witnesses: Burton Tandy, Drunearn, Co. Cavan, gent., James Griffith, Cornapeast, Co. Monaghan, gent., said Thomas Armstrong, Redhills, Thomas Topham, Drumadoris, Co. Cavan, gent.

Codicil 16 Feb. 1765. Thomas Ellis his nephew eldest son of his sister Ellis. Witnesses: Said John Bell, Thomas Armstrong and Thomas Topham.

Codicil 2 Dec. 1769. Fourteen hundred pounds due to him upon Government Security for which he had debentures. Witnesses: Burton Tandy, James Griffith, Thomas Armstrong, Thomas Topham.

Codicil 27 April 1773. £300 deposited in hands of Rev. James Cottingham of Cavan, bond dated 7 Feb. 1773. Said sum to said trustees for the purpose of building a church near the town of Redhills on plot of ground bequeathed by testator for ever his intention being it should never be used as a burying place. Witnesses: said James Griffith, Thomas Topham.

Codicil 7 May 1774. Republished his said Will. Witnesses: James Griffith, Thomas Topham, Patrick Maguire, Redhills, Co Cavan, merchant. Said Francis White or any other person on whom his estate in Co. Cavan and Co. Tyrone are entailed, empowered to lease and demise any part of his said estates, house, demesne and lands of Redhills including Mullinavernog. By his Will appointed his cousin Alexander Sanderson of Castle Sanderson and heirs male to succeed to his real estate in failure of issue male of his nephews; by codicil revokes said appointment, his cousin Alexander Sanderson of Cloverhill and heirs male and in failure of them the issue male of testator's cousin James Sanderson, Esq., deceased, to inherit and after them in failure of issue male to issue male of testator's cousin, Alexander Sanderson, Esq., of Castle Sanderson, deceased. Witnesses: James Griffith, James [recte Thomas] Topham, Patrick Maguire.

Codicil 9 Nov. 1774. If owing to delay said church at Redhills not built within three years of testator's death the £300 to be used to establish a fund with the interest for charitable uses and relief of the poor for ever in Belturbet, Cavan and Ballyhaise [Co. Cavan]. Alexander Sanderson, Esq., to be joint exor. with Mr. William Sanderson. Witnesses: James Griffith, Thomas Topham.

Codicil 19 Jan. 1775. All residue to his exors. equally between them. Witnesses: Thomas Topham, Patrick Maguire.

Memorial witnessed by: James Griffith, Patrick Maguire.

318, 539, 218807 Alexr. Sanderson (seal)

602 LIGGAT, GEORGE, Tullyblety, parish Aghaloo, Co. Tyrone. 14 May 1754. Narrate 1 p. 20 Aug. 1779.

His wife Susanna Liggat. His son George Liggat. George Liggat son to testator's son William deceased. James Liggat son to William. His son David Liggat. His son Robert Liggat. His son Samuel Liggat. His son James Liggat. His son John Liggat. John Marshall his son-in-law. His son-in-law Joseph Craig. Thomas Motherwell, Glendavagh, Alexr. Brown, Drumcain and David Johnston of same, exors. His farm of Tullyblety.

Witnesses: Joseph Bell, Tullyblety, John Stell, Glendavagh, John Wilson, Rahaghy, all Co. Tyrone, farmers.

Memorial witnessed by: Joseph Bell, David Johnston, Callidon, Co. Tyrone, gent.

322, 377, 219419 Jno. Liggat his mark (seal)
John Liggat one of the sons and devisee in said Will named

603 POLLOCK, ANNE, Glassanera, parish of Billy, Co. Antrim, spinster. 29 April 1778. Narrate 1¼ p. 30 April 1779.

To be buried in the churchyard of Derrykeighan. £5 each to poor of parish of Billy and parish of Derrykeighan. Her nephew Rev. James Huey, Newtownards, Co. Down. Her nephew John Huey, Ballallaght, Co. Antrim. Her niece Jane Ferrier wife of John Ferrier,

Bellyclogh. Her niece Agnes Martin wife of William Martin, Ballymaris, her sons James Martin, John Martin and William Martin. Jane Huey wife of James Huey, Ballallaght. The children of John Johnston late of Muff, Co. Donegal, deceased. Her cousin John Cummin, parish of Killraghts, carpenter, his sister Mary Cummin, and his sister Mary Ann Cummin. Hugh Cummin of Toberbilly. Jane Cummin the mother of said John Cummin. Her cousin James Pollock, Diffrick, and his son Kennedy Pollock. Martha Hunter, wife of David Hunter of Toberdoney. Ann Laughlan, wife of Andrew Laughlan, Dervock. Ephraim Cummin, Toberbilly, her cousin. All residue of her estate to her nephew John Stuart, Ballynaris, Co. Antrim, gent. Said John Stuart exor.

Witnesses: James Glenn, Carroveagh, parish of Derrykeighan aforesaid, Patrick McMichael, Glassanera and Alexander Thomson, Maghrag, both in parish of Billy.

Memorial witnessed by: James Glenn, Patrick McMichael, Alexander Thomson([1]).

329, 256, 219486 John Stewart (seal)

604 WOLFE, RICHARD, Baronrath, Co. Kildare, Esq.

11 Dec. 1773. Codicil 15 Apr. 1774. Codicil 29th March 1779.

Full 4½ pp. 21 May 1779.

My daughters Elizabeth and Ann. My son William Standish Wolfe. My brothers the Rev. John Standish and Theobald Wolfe, Esq., trustees, exors. and guardians of my children until respectively aged 21 years.

My lands, tenements and hereditaments in counties of Kildare and Dublin and my freehold lease of lands of Bishops Court, and my chattell lease of lands of Baronrath, Co. Kildare.

First Codicil says daughter Ann hath lately intermarried with Robert French, Esq.

Second Codicil appoints son and Robert French my son-in-law and my brothers Thomas and Theobald exors.

Witnesses to Will and first codicil: Thomas Pleasants, James Braddish, John Carroll, attorneys at law, all of Dublin.

(1) They witness to the signing by John *Stuart*.

Witnesses to second codicil: Ann Bullen, Baronrath, Co. Kildare, widow, Francis Hutcheson, Dublin, Doctor of Physick, Mathew Milton, Clean, Co. Kildare, surgeon.

Memorial witnessed by: Robert French, William Street, Dublin, Esq., John Carroll, Dublin, gent.

329, 360, 219844 Theobald Wolfe (seal)
Dublin, Esq.

605 FRYER, CATHERINE, otherwise McCABE, widow of Jno. Fryer, Waterford city, slater, deceased.

16 April 1779. Précis ½ p. 31 May 1779.

Her only daughter Mary Gahan otherwise Fryer (extx.) wife of Edmond Gahan, Waterford, shopkeeper. Her only son Jno. Fryer of Waterford, farmer. Sum due to testatrix from Thomas Carew, Ballynamona, Co. Waterford.

Witnesses: Mathew Power, Waterford, gent., Maurice Power, Waterford, innholder.

Memorial witnessed by: Maurice Power, Valentine Kelly, Waterford, gent.

320, 516, 219915 Mary Gahan (seal)

606 EELS, THOMAS (1), Lahcen, parish Carrigallen, Co. Leitrim. [Date not recorded]. Narrate, part in full, 1 p. 31 July 1779.

The two children I have by Mary Farrell, Mary Eils and Elizabeth Eils (my two daughters). If Mary Farrell's child to be born is a son my estate to him.

His [testator's] cousin Richd. Gilpin. His cousin Wm. Gilpin. To Mary Farrell his house and garden etc. Capt. Robert Armstrong, and his exors. Richd. Gilpin, Teenoloy, parish Kildallen, Co. Cavan, and Jno. Timon, Kilashandra, Co. Cavan. to divide residue of his fortune among his legatees and friends.

(1) The testator is incorrectly listed in the Names Index of Grantors as "Eccles, Thomas." The surname in the original is Eels.

Witnesses: Rev. Arthur Richardson, Longfield, Jno. Kiernan, Drumhalry, Wm. Stodart, Brownhill, all Co. Leitrim.

Memorial witnessed by: Wm. Stodart. Jno. Reilly, Dublin, gent.

325, 323, 220690 John Timon (seal)
Richd. Gilpin his mark (seal)

607 EUSTACE, Rev. ALEXANDER, Swords, Co. Dublin, clerk.
14 March 1778. Full ½ p. 24 Sept. 1779.

To my nephew Chas. Eustace, Esq., (sole exor.) son of my late brother John Eustace, deceased, all my estate real and personal in and near Naas, Co. Kildare.

Debts owed by Chas. King Esq., and Thos. Cobbe, Esq., (bond in hands of Edmd. Kane, Esq.).

Witnesses: Fras. Gorman, Mark West, Saml. Gardiner.

Memorial witnessed by: Edwd. Cahill and George Cheney, both Dublin, gents., attorneys at law.

325, 366, 221017 Chas. Eustace (seal)

608 VIGORS, JOHN, Dublin.
6 Dec. 1773. Narrate 2¾ p. 5 Oct. 1779.

His wife Ann Vigors. His eldest son Nicholas Aylward Vigors. His second son Richard Vigors. His three younger children. Reciting that his brother Rev. Dean Bartholomew Vigors had demised to him a dwelling house, orchard and garden in Old Leighlin, and the fields known by the name of Coolgallis, Incihcorckeragh, Farnane, an acre at the old gate of Moneduffe and Acrantubrid, Co. Catherlogh and also demised to him part of lands of Moneduffe, Co. Catherlogh and that subsequent to these two demises and in consideration of testator's intermarriage with Ann Vigors otherwise Aylward the said Bartholomew Vigors covenanted to settle his several estates in countries of Wexford and Catherlogh on the testator for life. A sum due to Mary Dean widow secured by a mortgage executed by said Bartholomew Vigors and a judgment to be executed to Thomas Tench, Dublin, gent., as a trustee therein. A legacy of £600 bequeathed to said Ann by her father Nicholas Aylward. A sum paid to his sister Elinor Cliffe settled on her and charged on said lands by said Bartholomew Vigors. A jointure payable to Frances Vigors the widow of said Bartholomew Vigors for life. John Hely, Foulkescourt, Co. Kilkenny Esq., and said Thomas Tench trustees. Land and holding at Old Leighlin, and Parkbane, Co. Catherlogh, demised by Arabella King, widow; lands of Newtown otherwise Newland, Co. Kildare.

Witnesses: Wm. Patrickson, Thos. Patrickson both of Dublin, gents., Charles Costello, Dublin, writing clerk.

Memorial witnessed by: Thos. Patrickson, Wm. Cruise, Dublin, writing clerk.

330, 165, 221075 Jo. Hely (seal)

609 ANNESLEY, ISAAC, Celbridge, Co. Kildare, mason.
10 Nov. 1779. Précis ½ p. 18 Nov. 1779.

To his eldest daughter Mary Annesley his house, garden etc. in Celbridge, Co. Kildare, being a lease of three lives unrenewable. Land in the Reg Lane, Co. Kildare, being a lease of lives renewable for ever.

Witnesses: Richard Hinde, Hugh Henry, John Jacob, all of Dublin, gents.

Memorial witnessed by: John Jacob, Wm. Servant, cabinet-maker, Dublin.

334, 6, 221586 Mary Annesley (seal)

610 JACKSON, WILLIAM, Calverstown, Co. Kildare, wheelright.
1 Jan. 1779. Narrate ¾ p. 1 Dec. 1779.

His wife Ealse Jackson. His daughter Elizabeth Murphy otherwise Jackson. His daughter Hannah Fullard otherwise Jackson. His daughter Mary Lawler otherwise Jackson. His daughter Christian Toole otherwise Jackson. His daughter Sarah Karr otherwise Jackson. His three sons Wm. Jackson, David Jackson, and John Jackson. William Plowman, Gilbinstown, Co. Kildare, gent. and Edward Valentine, Randallstown, Co. Wicklow, exors.

Witnesses: William Jackson, Calverstown, Co. Kildare, weaver, Jacob Jackson, Spinans, Co. Wicklow, farmer, George Rawson, Calverstown, slater.

Memorial witnessed by: Jacob Jackson, Edward Smyth, Dublin, gent.

328, 473, 221775 David Jackson (seal)

611 TRIMLESTOWN, LORD, ROBERT BARNEWALL called Lord Trimlestown. 4 Dec. 1779. Précis ½ p. 14 Dec. 1779.

His wife Anna Maria Barnewall called Lady Trimlestown exor. To his son Joseph Barnewall exor. all his estate of inheritance and all other estate in manner or reported manor of Ro[e]buck, and Glanskeagh otherwise Clonskeagh, Co. Dublin, subject to charges thereon made by settlement on his marriage with his then present wife. His daughter Alicia Barnewall.

Witnesses: Tyrrell O'Reilly, Dublin, Esq., Elizabeth Harris, Primrose Hill, Co. Dublin, spinster, Thomas Dennis, gent., agent to testator.

Memorial witnessed by: Tyrell O'Reilly, Christopher Abbott, junior, Dublin, Esq.

330, 242, 221928 Joseph Barnewall (seal)
(The Hon. Joseph Barnewall)

612 NICHOLSON, EDWARD, formerly of Primrose Grange, Co. Sligo and late of Leinster Street, County of city of Dublin, Esq. 25 Nov. 1776. Full 1½ p. 20 Jan. 1780.

My three daughters: Emily Lhoyd otherwise Nicholson my eldest, Hariet Nicholson my second (exor.), and Mary Fortescue otherwise Nicholson my youngest.

My real estate in Co. Sligo and real and personal estate.

Witnesses: Wm. Lushington, Merrion Square, Dublin, Esq., Will Cary, Elphin, Co. Roscommon, Esq., Rev. Richard Bourne, Holles Street, Dublin, clerk.

Memorial witnessed by: Richard Bourne, Francis Gorman, Dublin, Esq.

334, 96, 222188 Hariet Nicholson (seal)

613 FITZGERALD, ROBERT UNIACK, Corkbegg, Co. Cork, Esq.
27 Oct. 1773. Précis 1 p. 28 Jan. 1780.

His wife Frances FitzGerald exor. John Lapp Judkin, Cashel, Co. Tipperary, Esq., trustee. His second son Thomas FitzGerald exor.

Seized in fee of lands of Cullintra, Fardistown, Ballyshelan. Tincurry, Treacestown, Youngstown, Dirr, Harveystown and Bally-hust, Co. Wexford which he purchased from William Wallis and his only son Barachiah Wallis both late of Ballycrenan, Co. Cork, Esqs.

Witnesses: Thos. Garde, William Garde, both of Dublin, gents., attorneys, Rev. John Lawless, Cloyne, Co. Cork, clerk.

Memorial witnessed by: Thomas Hodgson, John Hill, both Dublin, gents.

334, 125, 222291 Thos. FitzGerald (seal)

614 CUSACK, EDWARD, Dublin, Esq., only surviving son of Ann Cusack otherwise Donovan, late of said city, widow and relict of Adam Cusack late of Rathgarr otherwise Rathgarth, Co. Dublin, Esq., deceased. 3 June 1779. Codicil 10 July 1779. Full 5½ pp. 28 April 1780.

Francis Gorman, Dublin, Esq., exor. William Gorman, Esq. Robert Gorman, gent., youngest son of the said Francis Gorman, Miss Martha Gorman his youngest sister. My kinsman Captain Jeremiah Donovan, exor. Robert FitzGerald, Stephen's Green, Dublin, Esq., exor. My kinsman Cusack Green. Edward Cahill, Dublin, attorney at law. Wm. Whittingham, Dawson Street, Dublin, Esq. A mortgage due to Joseph Hone, junior, merchant. A bank note of Latouche and Sons payable to myself only for £1,000 sterling. Money owed by Rev. Dr. Carr and Henry Coulson, Esq.

My old acquaintance Daniel Jackman. My servant maid Ann Scott, spinster, her sister Bridget Scott, her sister Mary Scott. My old friend Thomas Hannigan, Bride Street, publican.

Golden Lane, Whitefryer Street, Dublin, Maiden Lane. Town and lands of Rathgarr otherwise Rathgarth lately in possession of

James Starkey deceased and now in possession of Owen Hogan attorney at law and his undertenants. Little Bray, Co. Dublin. I confirm the conveyance made by me of my estate in Co. Wexford to said Francis Gorman, part in possession of John Kean, miller, part lately in possession of Phillip Carr deceased and since of Denis Doyle and now of Henry Coulson, Esq., and his undertenants and part called the Booley late in possession of Thomas Toole and now of Samuel Percival, merchant, to the said Henry Coulson. Part agreed by John Cusack to be conveyed to Redmond Morris, Dublin. House and tenements in High Street, Dublin, formerly known by the name of King Charles Head. Wood Street and Oliver's Alley, Dublin. Lands of Kilmackabea, Co. Cork. Kilcoalman, Bruley, house, lands etc. of Bruley and all other my estates in said county and city of Cork. Houses in James Street, Back Lane, Corn Market and Butter Market, Dublin. I ratify conveyance made by me of my estate in Mount Tallant, Co. Dublin unto Wm. Flemming, Esq. My estate of town and lands of Bodinstown, Co. Kildare now in the possession of Thomas Wolfe, Esq., or his undertenants. Bellsarno and Black Ditch, Co. Meath. Farganstown, Ardmulchan and Johnstown, Co. Meath, now in possession of Robert Taaffe, Esq., or his undertenants.

Witnesses: Robert Allenson, attorney, Richard Echlin, notary public, Thomas Bond, attorney, all of Dublin.

Codicil mentions papers, title deeds etc. (which were by order of Court of Chancery, about the year 1728, lodged in hands of William Cooper, Esq., deceased then of said Court, and then came and remain in the hands of Doctor Charles Walker) concerned in a case wherein Jeremiah Donovan late of Little Bray, Co. Dublin, deceased, was plaintiff and Ann Cusack otherwise Donovan my late mother, deceased, was defendant. Desires to be buried in St. Peter's churchyard.

Codicil witnessed by: Richard Morgan, John Madden, Dublin and John Miller, Dublin, gent.

Memorial witnessed by: Richard Echlin, Wm. Morgan, John Madden.

333, 189, 223386

Francis Gorman (seal)
Jeremiah Donovan (seal)
Robt. FitzGerald (seal)

615 VIRAZEL, MARIE ANNE SARAH, Dublin, widow.

12 Oct. 1779. Précis ¾ p. 28 April 1780.

Her friend Thomas Bolger, Ship Street, Dublin, gent. Her real and personal estate. Her leasehold interests in King's Co. which by a deed executed by her daughter Mary Ann Wyer otherwise Virazel she was entitled to.

Witnesses: Francis Whyte Edgworth and John Eccles of Eccles Street, Dublin, Esqrs., Richard Gilliard, Philipstown, King's Co., gent.

Memorial witnessed by: Richard Gilliard, Bryan Moran, Dublin, clerk to said Thomas Bolger.

332, 97, 223410 Thomas Bolger (seal)

616 COX, MARY, late of parish of St. George, Hanover Square, spinster, but since lodging at Mr. Reguers at Chelsea. [Date not recorded]. Narrate 1 p. 10 May 1780.

To her schoolfellow Miss Ann Knowles as a mark of her great regard and esteem for her a yearly rent charge of £20 out of her real estate. Her lands, tenements and hereditaments in kingdom of Ireland. Her friend Charles Style of Wateringbury, Co. Kent, Esq., eldest son and heir of Sir Thomas Style of Wateringbury, Bart. Said Charles Style exor.

Witnesses: Leonard Martin, Chancery Lane, London, gent., Samuel Rossoan, Chelsea, Alexander Bland, clerk to said Leonard Martin.

Memorial witnessed by: Rev. Henry Irvine de Sales, Urry, Co. Bucks. D.D., Mark Stephenson, Plerle Court otherwise Lane, city of London.

330, 381, 223576 Robert Style (seal)

Rev. Robert Style, Wateringbury, exor. of his brother Sir Charles Style who proved said Will in the Prerogative Court of Canterbury.

617 CHENEY, JAMES, Co. Cork, gent.

9 Jan. 1775. Narrate 1½ p. 20 May 1780.

His four sons Doctor Andrew Francis Cheney, Oliver Cheney, James Cheney and Bradston Cheney. His sisters Catherine Bradston otherwise Cheney, Mary Cheney and Elizabeth Cheney. To his daughters Helena Cheney and Elizabeth Cheney, £800 each on their days of marriage. To his grand-daughter Elizabeth Cheney daughter of his son Oliver £400 on marriage. His brother Andrew Cheney deceased. His son James Cheney and Thomas Lucas, Richardfordstown, Co. Cork, gent., exors.

Lands of Macetown, Painstown, Polenewtown, Riggins and Corballis, Co. Meath. Town and lands of Mount Cheney otherwise Cloghanaspig and Knockastondon, Barony Ibane and Barryroe, Co. Cork.

Witnesses: John Jervois and Arthur Jervois, both Cork, Esqs., Jonas Travers, Dublin, gent.

Memorial witnessed by: Thomas Spring, Dublin, gent., John McGee, Dublin, writing clerk.

332, 136, 223706 James Cheney (seal)

618 MOILES, WILLIAM, Raheen, Queen's Co., gent.

28 Dec. 1773. Full 1 p. 22 June 1780.

My wife Catherine Moiles otherwise Lalor exor. My daughter Mary Egan otherwise Moiles. My eldest son Carter Joseph Moiles. My daughter Lucy Clare otherwise Moiles. My son James. My son Michael. My son William Moiles. My brother Thos. Moiles, Carran, exor.

Lands of Kileny, Queen's Co. and Morett said Co.

Witnesses: Thos. Mathews, Bryan McDonald, Laughlin Gorman.

Memorial witnessed by: Bryan McDonald, Geo. Phelan, Dublin, gent.

333, 298, 224273 Catherine Moiles (seal)

619 HUNT, Rev. JOHN, Clopooke, Queen's Co., clerk.

28 Feb. 1780. Narrate 2 pp. 14 July 1780.

His wife Olivia Hunt. His son John (under 21 years). His daughters Sarah and Olivia Hunt (unmarried). Miss Sarah Hankes. Miss Bell Hankes. His sister Hester Doran. His niece Bridget Lewes. His said wife, Denis George, Dublin, Counsellor at Law, and Rev. William Birney exors.

Lands of Tully. His farm of Clopook and Temeelavan. To Henry. Certain 2 acres of ground then in his possession rent free [situation not mentioned] and £3 yearly to be laid out in clothes for him by Thomas Henbery.

Witnesses: Tobias Purcell, Timrock, Queen's Co., Esq., Thomas Wright, Grenan, Queen's Co., farmer, Thomas Byrne, Mountmellick, farmer.

Memorial witnessed by: Tobias Purcell, Edward Smyth, Dublin, gent.

330, 493, 224543 William Birney (seal)

620 ROBINSON, JOHN, Mountmellick, Queen's Co., pumpborer.

12 Aug. 1760. Full(1). ¾ p. 14 Aug. 1780.

My wife. My son John Robinson. My two sons Wm. Robinson and Richard Robinson.

The dwelling house in the town of Mountmellick wherein I now live. Two dwelling houses in town of Mountmellick wherein Robert Harris the younger and Geo. Forster now live, a ground rent payable to Thomas Strangman.

Witnesses: William Mayrs, James Dury, both of Mountmellick, shoemakers, Wilcocks Robinson formerly of Mountmellick now of Dublin, gent.

Memorial witnessed by: Wilcocks Robinson, Jonathan Gatchell, Mountmellick, gent.

337, 31, 224780 Richard Robinson (seal)

---

(1) Not a complete copy; it is described as " A memorial . . . . in which are the following devises: "

621 STUART, ANTHONY, the elder, Dunmuckrum, Co. Donegal.

19 Dec. 1759. Précis ¾ p. 21 Aug. 1780.

His wife Ann Stuart. His three sons Robt. Stuart, Anthony Stuart, and John Stuart. Thos. Coome, Finner, and Mathew Scanlon, Ballyshannon, since deceased, exors. His farm of Dunmuck[r]um.

Witnesses: Francis Allingham and John Scanlon both of Ballyshannon, since deceased, Wm. Britton, Park, Co. Leitrim, farmer.

Memorial witnessed by: Wm. Britton, Moses Monk, Ballyshannon, wheelwright.

333, 365, 224863 Anthony Stuart (seal)
the younger son to testator.

622 BASIL, EDMOND, Newhouse, Buckinghamshire.

12 April 1779. Full 5¾ pp. 25 Aug. 1780.

My brother-in-law Saml. Hayes, Leicester Fields, Middlesex, Esq., and my friend Henry Boldero, London, banker, exors. and trustees. My brother George Basil. My sister Annie Basil. If said sister dies without issue attaining twenty-one years money to be transferred unto " such of the three children of the said Samuel Hayes by my late sister Mary his late wife as shall survive my said sister Annie." My friend William Hamilton, Esq., who now resides with me. Sarah Edwards who now resides with me. Money due to Robert Palk [? Pack] Esq., by mortgage.

My lands etc. in Co. Donegal. £1,000 invested at 6% by virtue of an Act of Parliament lately passed in Ireland; I have since nominated the lives of my said nephew and niece Saml. and Mary Hayes for £500 each; if they die without attaining 21 years or being married then to transfer the same to Frances their younger sister.

Witnesses: John Gawler, London, Esq., attorney at law, Thos. Harvey and Geo. Tilsley, gents., clerks to said John Gawler.

Memorial witnessed by: Wm. Glascock, Dublin, attorney at law, Edwd. Scriven, Dublin, clerk, an apprentice to said Wm. Glascock.

332, 365, 224883 Saml. Hayes (seal)

623 LONGFORD, WILLIAM, "near Donnebrook."
4 June 1776. Full 1½ p. 16 Nov. 1780.

My daughter Catherine Longford (under 21 years). My daughter Ann Longford (under 21 years). My daughter Elizabeth Fleming otherwise Longford. My daughter Elinor Moore otherwise Longford, her husband. My daughter Ann Gunning otherwise Longford, her husband. My son William Longford apprentice to George Simpson of Donnebrook. My son Michael Longford.

Seven acres of lands of Simons Court near Donnebrook which I have lately demised by lease to Joseph Madden, Donnebrook. John Smyth of or near Ballsbridge and George Simpson, Donnebrook, exors.

Witnesses: William Bolger, Dublin, gent., Robert Bolger and Richard Bolger, his sons.

Memorial witnessed by: William Bolger, Richard Bolger.

332, 476, 225622 William Longford (seal)

624 HIGGINBOTHAM, THOMAS, Ballintrure, parish of Donnoghmore, Co. Wicklow, farmer. 13 Aug. 1772. Narrate 1 p. 24 Nov. 1780.

His wife Abigail Higginbotham, extx. His eldest son Richard Higginbotham. Testator's youngest son Hawkshead Higginbotham.

His freehold lands, tenements and hereditaments on south and north side of Little Ballintrure road, Co. Wicklow. Part of Ballinacrow, Co. Wicklow, leased from Morley Saunders Pender, Esq.

Witnesses: Jacob Jackson, Spinans, Edward Valentine, Randalstown, Christr. Medcalf, Newtown, all Co. Wicklow.

Memorial witnessed by: Jacob Jackson, Joseph Jackson, Spinans, gent.

336, 458, 225769 Abigail Higginbotham (seal)

625 CUNINGHAM, HUGH, Randalstown, Co. Antrim, gent.
6 April 1780. Full 1¼ p. 1 Dec. 1780.

My wife Elizabeth exor. My daughter Sarah Elizabeth Cuningham and my son William John Cuningham to live with their mother and be maintained and educated by her with advice of John Kerr, Tannaghmore, gent. (exor.).

My real and personal estate. My lands in Tully, parish of Killead, Co. Antrim held under Hugh Henry, Dublin, Esq.

Witnesses: Francis Joy, gent., and Thomas Adams, both of Randallstown, Henry McCullock, Antrim, surgeon.

Memorial witnessed by: Thomas Adams, William Adams, Randallstown, merchant.

333, 540, 225866 Elizabeth Cuningham (seal)

626 JACKSON, Philip, Eyrecourt, Co. Galway, gent.

22 June 1765. Full ¾ p. 5 Dec. 1780.

My wife Mary Jackson. My grandson Philip Jackson, his father Henry Jackson. My son Charles Jackson. My grand-daughter Mary daughter to Henry Jackson. My grand-daughter Mary daughter to Charles Jackson. My son Henry Jackson.

The holding in Eyrecourt lately occupied by John Moore. The lower plot in the Soldier's Row [situation not mentioned]. Money in hands of Thomas Millbank.

Witnesses: Rev. George Gardner, clerk, Timothy Ward and John Bowker both of Eyrescourt, gents.

Memorial witnessed by: Hugh Concannon and Malachy Daly, both Dublin, gents.

332, 552, 225925 Philip Jackson (seal)

627 BYRN, CHARLES, Sleaty, Queen's Co., gent.

10 April 1765. Précis ½ p. 11 Dec. 1780.

Vere Ward, Hollymount, Queen's Co., gent., John Byrn, Leighlinbridge, Co. Carlow, gent., trustees. His daughter Ann Best.

His real estate in Queen's Co., Co. Carlow and Co. Kilkenny or elsewhere.

Witnesses: Vere Ward, junior, Hollymount, Queen's Co., gent., Lucy Nally, Hollymount, spinster, George Lemaria, Mooneenroe, Co Kilkenny, gent.

Memorial witnessed by: George Lemaria, Peter Feriss, Dublin, carpenter.

332, 571, 225994 Ann Best (seal)

628 SMITH, ROBERT, Moneystaghan, parish of Tamlaght, Co. Londonderry. [Date not recorded]. Précis ½ p. 29 Jan. 1781.

His son John, his son Robert. If they die without issue "his deed" [? of Moneystaghan] to Sarah Smith and her issue [? testator's daughter]. Arthur Hendry and Arabell Gilmore exors. His tenement and houses beyond the water.

Witnesses: Francis Smith, John Reed, Arthur Hendry.

Memorial witnessed by: Arthur Hendry, Henry McCann, Maghera-felt, Co. Londonderry.

335, 437, 226494 Robert Smith (seal)

629 VAN NOST, JOHN, Mecklenburgh Street, Dublin, statuary. 24 Oct. 1779. Précis ¾ p. 3 Feb. 1781.

His wife Ann Van Nost otherwise Armstrong, exor. His only sister Catherine Legross widow. His nephew Richard Lynd. His houses, lands, etc.

Witnesses: James Wilder, painter, Samuel Dickson, gent., Archibald Smith, gent., all of Mecklenburg Street.

Memorial witnessed by: James Wilder, Adw. Chalenor, King Street, Dublin, lead caster.

338, 145, 226588 Ann Van Nost (seal)

630 GREEN, GODFREY, Scart, liberties of Limerick, Esq. 1 Oct. 1777. Précis ½ p. 17 Feb. 1781.

To Francis Green, Grange, Co. Limerick and Caleb Powell, Limerick, Esq., trustees, lands of Garryduffe, otherwise Greenhills, Co. Tipperary.

Witnesses: Joseph Holland, Thomas Dickson, Samuel Maxwell, all of Limerick, gents.

Memorial witnessed by: Thomas Dickson, James Cooper, Cooper's Hill, Co. Limerick, gent.

340, 28, 226776 Francis Green (seal)

631 BAYLY, JOHN, Gowran, Co. Kilkenny, Esq.

25 Feb. 1772. Narrate ¾ p. 2 March 1781.

His wife Susannah Bayly otherwise Strettle extx. His eldest daughter Sarah Bayly. His youngest daughter Susannah Bayly. His son Robert Bayly. His real and personal estate.

Witnesses: Thos. Bayly, Newtown Barry, Co. Wexford, gent., attorney at law and since deceased, Peter Bayly and Wm. Bayly both of Dublin, attorneys at law.

Memorial witnessed by: Alexr. Jaffray, Dublin, merchant, Thos. Tench, Dublin, gent.

340, 56, 226929 Susannah Bayly (seal)

632 HANKS, JEREMIAH, the elder, Birr, King's Co.

9 April 1766. Full ¾ p. 3 March 1781.

My son Thomas Hanks. My daughter Ann Hanks. My daughter Sarah Hanks alias Philips (her brother Thomas Hanks). Jeremiah Davis my grandson, Elizabeth Davis my grand-daughter (under 21 years). My sons Thomas and Jeremiah Hanks exors.

My two freehold leases, Drumbane, [King's Co.], held from Sir Laurence Parsons and part Ballinderry, [Ballindarra, King's Co.], held from James Jackson.

Witnesses: Joseph Marshall, merchant, Gord. Buchanan, innkeeper, John Wilkinson, apothecary, all of Birr, King's Co.

Memorial witnessed by: John Wilkinson, Richd. Morgan.

335, 541, 226959 Jer. Hanks (seal)

633 HANKS, THOMAS, Birr, King's Co., maulster.

21 Feb. 1778. Full 1½ p. 3 March 1781.

My wife Elizabeth Hanks otherwise Thompson. My daughter Mary Ann Hanks (unmarried and under 21 years). My nephew Jeremiah Hanks son of Joseph Hanks. My brother Jeremiah Hanks. My four nephews: Jer. Hanks and Joseph Hanks, sons of Joseph Hanks, Jer. Hanks son of Jer. Hanks, and Jeremiah Morriss son of Thomas Morriss. My brother Joseph Hanks. My sister Elizabeth Sheppard. My sister Mary Morris(s). My nephew Jeremiah Hanks and my cousin Joseph Manly, junior, exors. My brothers Jeremiah Hanks and Thomas Morris trustees and guardians.

My holding under Edward Treacy on the Bridge. My freehold of Doumbaune, and freehold interest of the lands and houses of Doumbaune. Lands of Ballindarra held under James Jackson. The tanyard holding under Will Jones [situation not mentioned].

Witnesses: John Wilkinson, apothecary, Lawford Godfrey, gent., Thomas Dooly, tanner, all of Birr, King's Co.

Memorial witnessed by: John Wilkinson, Richard Morgan.

337, 254, 226960 Jer. Hanks (seal)

634 GRACE, GEORGE, Brittas, Co. Tipperary, Esq.

6 April 1768. Full 1¾ p. 10 March 1781.

Reciting that Oliver Grace late of Brittas, deceased, bequeathed his estates in Co. Tipperary to his eldest son John Grace, with remainder to the issue male of said John, remainder to Patrick Grace his second son for life with like remainder to Richard Grace and James Grace, his third and fourth sons for life, and failing issue male of said John, Patrick, Richard and James Grace said estates devised to his nephew George Grace and his heirs male. Reciting that said John, Patrick, Richard and James are dead, unmarried and without issue, " on whose death the said estate hath descended to the said George Grace " [the testator].

To my wife Martha Grace otherwise Clarke exor. £300 yearly and to my [younger] children by her £2,000 out of said estates pursuant to the power for that purpose given by the Will of my uncle the said Oliver Grace. My son George Grace. If said George dies under age of 21 years and without lawful issue all rights, estates and demands intended for him to such of his sisters as shall survive him. John Grace, son to Catherine Malby, and now or lately a Dragoon in Lord Drogheda's Light Horse.

I have a demand on estates of Howard Egan deceased in right of my former wife Mary Egan deceased; inheritance of Anamedle, Blane, Cahil and other lands in [Barony] of Upper Ormond, [Co. Tipperary] conveyed to me by said Mary Egan otherwise Carroll, and as agent or receiver of rents of estates and interests of said Howard (which account lies now before Chas. Walker one of the Masters of Chancery to be settled, there appears a large balance due to me). A charge of £60 per annum for ever due to me on estate and lands of Dennis O'Brien, attorney [situation not mentioned]. My holdings in or about the town of Clonmell.

Witnesses: James Fogerty, Castle Fogerty, Co. Tipperary, Esq., Patrick Larkin, Brittas, servant man, George Hayes, late of Ballinakill, cottier, both said County.

Memorial witnessed by: James Fogerty, Thos. Weston, Clonmell, Co. Tipperary, gent.

339, 81, 227038 Martha Grace (seal)

635 WRIGHT, ANDREW, Moywollen, Co. Londonderry, Esq.

30 Nov. 1775. Narrate 1 p. 14 March 1781.

His nephew Andrew Wright. His relation John Wright, Dungannon, Co. Tyrone, gent., exor. Samuel Wright, son of said John Wright. Rev. Chas. Caldwell, Rockspring, Archibald Hamilton, Moneymore, Esq., both Co. Londonderry, trustees.

His estate, title and interest in town and lands of Moywollen otherwise Moywolly, manor of Salters, Co. Londonderry.

Witnesses: Charles Caldwell, Ballendrum, junr., gent., Michael Johnston, innkeeper, Archd. Hamilton, junior, gent., both of Moneymore, all Co. Londonderry.

Memorial witnessed by: Michael Johnston, Archd. Hamilton, junior.

339, 89, 227079 John Wright (seal)

636 NEVIN, JOHN, Craigboy, Co. Down, gent.
18 Oct. 1776. Précis ¾ p. 10 May 1781.

John Holmes, junior, Belfast, merchant, Rev. James Cochran, Ballyobigan, Co. Down, exors. and trustees.

His real and personal estate in Scotland, in Ireland or elsewhere.

Witnesses: Willoughby Semple, Donaghadee, Co. Down, surgeon, Rev. John Adams, and Thomas Adams, farmer, both of Craigboy.

Memorial witnessed by: John Adams, Donaghadee, merchant, Alexander Arthur, Belfast, Co. Antrim, gent.

340, 163, 227670 John Holmes (seal)
Jas. Cochran (seal)

637 SANDERS, MARK, senior, Brabazon's Row, parish of St. Luke, Co. Dublin. 21 April 1781. Narrate ½ p. 17 May 1781.

His wife Hannah Sanders, extx. His daughter Ann Sanders. His grandson Mark Sanders, junior. His dwelling house in Brabazon Row. His freehold in Mutten Lane.

Witnesses: John Giball and James Giball both of Co. Dublin, skinners, Samuel Banks, Wardshill, Co. Dublin, gent.

Memorial witnessed by: John Gelling and Howard Dawker, both Dublin, gents.

341, 115, 227776 Hannah Sanders (seal)

638 DELANY, ANNA DOROTHY, Loughrea, Co. Galway, widow of Martin Delany formerly of Ballybrittas, Queen's Co., gent., deceased. 17 Dec. 1773. Narrate ¾ p. 1 June 1781.

Her daughter Frances Loftus otherwise Delany extx., wife of John Loftus of Loughrea, Co. Galway, Esq. Stephen FitzGerald, Ballythomas, Queen's Co., Esq., trustee.

Lands called Grennans, Casey's and Tuck's quarter and that part called Thos. Hall's in Barony Maryborough, Queen's Co., held by lease made by the late Periam Pole, Esq., to the late Martin Delany deceased for three lives of which there was then in being the said Anna Dorothea Delany and her brother-in-law Daniel Delany, Castletown, Queen's Co.

Witnesses:–FitzGerald, Strabow, Queen's Co., Esq., and Sarah FitzGerald, his wife, Daniel McEvoy, Mountrath, merchant.

Memorial witnessed by: Daniel McEvoy, Alexander FitzGerald, Ballybrittas, Esq.

338, 362, 227999 F. Loftus (seal)

639 PERSSE, ROBERT, Roxborough, Co. Galway.

2 Ap. 1779. Narrate 1½ p. 9 June 1781.

James Dennis, Esq., Chief Baron of the Court of Exchequer in Ireland and William Acton, Dublin, Esq., trustees.

His eldest son William Persse. His second son Parsons Persse exor. His youngest son Burton Persse, Sarah wife of said Burton Persse. Testator's grandson Robert St. George second son of Sir Richard St. George by testator's daughter Sarah St. George otherwise Persse. Edward Crofton, Moat, Co. Roscommon, Esq., exor.

Lands of Cahirniney otherwise Cahirning otherwise Cahirliny being part of lands of Iser[t]kelly, Co. Galway formerly part of estate of Sir William Scawen and purchased by testator from Mr. Ruck. His manors, towns, lands and hereditaments of Moyode, Crossderry otherwise Crossnadairy, Lissherrigg otherwise Licherigg [Lickerrig], Callagh, part of Clashnegammy otherwise Classganny [Clashagarry], Garrancoyle, Garryglass otherwise Cahirglass otherwise Caherowen, Cahirkinoonley [? Caherkinmonwee], Garrymore otherwise Bayle-dorragh, Cahenduff otherwise Cahanduff, Shanvally otherwise Bally-nebragh, Cahirkenny, Gortiory otherwise Gortihorky, Ballindoragh, Carronglass, Courhoor, Graige and lands of Ardnasaddan, Mongee otherwise Mung [? Munga], Ballyna, Tomkin otherwise Tomkeen, Lougheneal and Ballyglass in Co. Galway formerly estate of said Sir William Scawen and purchased by testator from the said Ruck.

Witnesses: Henry Persse, Ballylee, Co. Galway, Rev. Andrew

Cochran, clerk, then of Roxborough, said County but now of Omagh, Co. Tyrone, Michael Dillon, Roxborough, gent.

Memorial witnessed by: Henry Faircloth, Dublin, gent., John Cullen, Dublin gent.

342, 46, 228086 Burton Persse (seal)

640 LIPSETT, LEWIS the elder, Cashell Lipsett, parish of Kill-barron, Co. Donegal. 10 Aug. 1771. Narrate 1 p. 23 Jan. 1781.

His wife Hannah Lipsett. His son Lewis Lipsett the younger. Testator's three daughters, Anna Lipsett, Hannah and Rebecca Lipsett. His son Humphry Lipsett. His daughter Margaret Lipsett wife of Joseph Lipsett. John Menzies, Ballintrah, Francis Allingham, Ballyshannon exors.

One full and entire ballyboe of lands of Upper Cashell Lipsett with the dwelling house, gardens etc. One fourth part of a ballyboe of land of Lower Cashell Lipsett, Co. Donegal, then tenanted by Owen Dongan and John Quin.

Witnesses: Francis Allingham, schoolmaster, William Scott, publican, both of Ballyshannon, since deceased, John Menzies, Ballintra, merchant.

Memorial witnessed by: John Menzies, Lewis Lipsett, the younger.

337, 563, 228338 Hannah Lipsett (seal)

641 McNALLOW, CHARLES, Mary's Abbey, Dublin, grocer. 30 Nov. 1778. Full 2 pp. 26 July 1781.

To be buried in churchyard of Donnybrook near Dublin where I have a burying place as near to my dear brother as may be convenient. My wife Elizabeth McNallow and my natural son Chas. McNallow now an apprentice to Arthur Dunn, Dublin, attorney, to live together in my house in Mary's Abbey, my wife to carry on my business of a grocer in said house until son be sworn an attorney. A sum due to Fras. Lowndes, Finnstown, Co. Dublin, Esq. A sum deposited in my hands by John Jameson for safe keeping. My friends Fras. Lowndes and Patrick Corbett, Dublin, gent., exors.

Witnesses: John Alment, Mary's Abbey, optician, William Wrightson, Mary's Abbey, wigmaker, Patrick Corbet, Dublin.

Memorial witnessed by: John Alment, Gilbert Kilbee, junior, Dublin, gent.

339, 286, 228757 Fras. Lowndes (seal)

642 CORR, JAMES, Ballytobin, Co. Kilkenny, merchant.

23 Dec. 1775. Narrate ¾ p. 27 July 1781.

His brother Joseph Corr. Con. Phelan, Leighlinbridge, Co. Carlow, land surveyor, trustee and exor. Edmond Dowling, Leighlinbridge, Co. Carlow.

His freehold and leasehold lands, etc. which descended to him as heir-at-law to Josh. Fitzpatrick, Carlow, Doctor of Physick, deceased, in town and County of Carlow. Freehold and leasehold lands etc. of Loughteague, Queen's Co., the Earl of Upper Ossory landlord of said lands.

Witnesses: Robert Lawler, Carlow, weaver, Thomas Lawler, Carlow, weaver, James Lawler, Leighlinbridge, land surveyor.

Memorial witnessed by: Thomas Lawler, Archibald Armstrong, Dublin, Esq., attorney at law.

338, 459, 228778 Con. Phelan (seal)

643 DICKISON, STUART, Keeloganehay, Co. Westmeath, carpenter. 14 Feb. 1777. Narrate ¾ p. 21 Aug. 1781.

His wife Jane Dickison. His youngest daughter Ann Mitchell otherwise Dickison wife of John Mitchell of Keeloganehy, farmer. His son John Dickison, Stonehall. His son Stuart Dickison. His grand daughter Elizabeth Tolbert. "To John Downs in right of his wife Mary one shilling, and to his son Dickison(1), the like sum of one shilling." Sir Richard Levinge Bart., John Wilson and James Gibson exors.

(1) Probably testator's grandson Dickison Downs.

His former mansion dwelling house in Stonewall, Co. Westmeath. Lands of Larkinstown, Co. Westmeath.

Witnesses: Edmond Quin, Loghagar, farmer, John Wilson, Knockatee, farmer, Richd. Boyhan, Highpark, blacksmith, all Co. Westmeath.

Memorial witnessed by: John Wilson, Peter McDermott, Dublin, gent.

340, 302, 228995 Ann Mitchell (seal)
Ann Mitchell otherwise Dickison, daughter of testator.

644 MALIE, ANN, Dublin, spinster.

31 July 1781. Full 2 pp. 19 Sept. 1781.

My father Andrew Malie left to me by his last Will securities for money etc., now in the hands of James Ormsby Esq., one of the exors; if I married without consent of his exors. said securities etc. he gave to his brother Thos. Malie.

I give said personal estate to my uncle said Thos. Malie. To John Pentland, Mary's Abbey, Dublin, Esq., exor., houses and concerns on Usher's Quay, Dublin, devised to me by last Will of my aunt Alice Clarkson, deceased, and also my houses in Mary's Abbey, and Johnston's Alley, devised to me by my late aunt. Grizzel Pentland otherwise Cahill, the wife of said John Pentland. Miss Honora Pentland. My two houses in Castle Street, Dublin. My aunt Albinia Malie. My cousin Thos. Malie. My servant maid Sarah Stringer, Martha Stringer her sister, Mark Stringer brother to my said servant maid, Joseph Stringer father of my said servant maid. My man servant Robert Kinchelagh.

Witnesses: Arthur Dunn, Mary's Abbey, Dublin, attorney, Michael Hutchinson, Dame Street, Dublin, gunmaker, Gilbert Kilbee, Mary's Abbey, junior.

Memorial witnessed by: Arthur Dunn, Thos. Mooney, Dublin, writing clerk.

339, 383, 229175 John Pentland (seal)

645 GOFFE, GEORGE, Tomnafunshoge, Co. Wexford, farmer.

27 July 1781. Narrate ½ p. 24 Sept. 1781.

His eldest son Daniel Goffe and his son Jacob Goffe (both having already had their fortunes). All residue of real and personal estate to his son Joseph Goffe, exor.

Witnesses: John Stephens, Drimgold, Co. Wexford, farmer, John Stephens, Enniscorthy, gent., Samuel Ralph, Templeshannon, Co. Wexford, gent.

Memorial witnessed by: John Stephens of Drimgold, Wm. Sparrow Enniscorthy, victualler.

340, 322, 229195 Joseph Goffe (seal)

646 MALONE, JAMES, Ballyraggan, Co. Kildare, farmer.

27 Nov. 1780. Codicil 27 Dec. 1780. Narrate 1 p. 10 Oct. 1781. His younger son James Malone. His sons Joseph Malone and James Malone, exors. His daughter Sarah Malone. His daughter Mary Malone. His daughter Hannah Taylor. His daughter Susanna Grub. His daughter Abigail Fayle. The four children of his late daughter Elizabeth Dudley.

His freehold lease of lands of Ballybramhill, Co. Carlow, chargeable with £400 for the widow and children of the testator's late son Francis. His lands of Ballyraggan and Knockfield, Co. Kildare.

Witnesses to Will and Codicil: John Brown, Luke Brown, Michael Brown, all of Ballyraggan, Co. Kildare, farmers.

Memorial witnessed by: John Brown, Thos. Bolger, Dublin, gent.

339, 417, 229309 James Malone (seal)

647 LYNAM, JAMES, Moycashell, Co. Westmeath, farmer.

13 Jan. 1773. Narrate 1 p. 26 Oct. 1781.

His sister Ann Geoghan otherwise Lynam wife of James Geoghan of Kilbeggan, Co. Westmeath, said Ann and James exors.

Piece of ground in Kilbeggan, Co. Westmeath whereon are built two large slate houses held from Gustavus Lambert, Esq., and 7½ acres land thereunto belonging called Fury's Park. Land in parish of Kilbeggan called Carton's Park held from said Gustavus Lambert. His lease of Moycashell held from Andrew Armstrong, Esq., of Clara, King's Co.

Witnesses: Peter Norris, Dublin, gent., Bryan McLaughlin, Dublin, merchant and Mary McLaughlin, wife of said Bryan McLaughlin.

Memorial witnessed by: Talbot Falkner, Kilbeggan, gent., Thomas Lusk, Ardnaglew, Co. Westmeath, farmer.

341, 458, 229417 James Geoghan (seal)

648 EXHAM, MARGARET, Dublin, widow.

25 June 1781. Full 1½ p. 27 Oct. 1781.

My daughter Catherine Pritchett late of Dublin, spinster, deceased. My nephew Arthur Gambell, Dublin, grocer, residuary legatee and sole exor. My servant maid now living with me Bridget Mooney. Edward Brett eldest son of Robert Brett of Greek Street, Dublin, cabinet maker.

Witnesses: Ann Brett, Dublin, wife of Robert Brett of Greek Street, John O'Neill, Dublin, gent., Henry Harding, Dublin, gent., attorney at law.

Memorial witnessed by: John O'Neill, Daniel Murphy, Dublin.

343, 23, 229435 Arthur Gambell (seal)

649 KELLY, JAMES, Grafton Street, Dublin, grocer.

30 Nov. 1781. Full ½ p. 15 Dec. 1781.

£20 per annum to Elizabeth Kelly for life. £10 per annum to Elizabeth Field for her care and attention to me. My brother Thomas Kelly. William Smith, Dublin, saddler, exor.

My holding in Grafton Street. A bond from Sackvill Gardiner to James Kelly made over by me to George Kelly.

Witnesses: Sylvestr. Oliver Mathews, gent., Wm. Lennon, mariner, Richd. Purcell, coachmaker, all of Dublin.

Memorial witnessed by: Sylvester Oliver Mathews, Elizabeth Kelly, Dublin.

334, 104, 230174 Elizabeth Kelly (seal)
a devisee (her mark)

650 MEARS, BENJAMIN, Ballinderry, Co. Westmeath, distiller.

17 Oct. 1781. Narrate 1 p. 24 Dec. 1781.

His wife Mary Mears extx. His youngest daughter Frances Mears unmarried. His son Benjamin Mears. His daughter Catherine Mears.

Lease of Ralavana, rent paid to Peter Delamar, Esq. Lease of Ballinderry and house wherein the testator now lives and lands which he holds in partnership with John Pilsworth and John Gaynor of Ballinderry. The utensils belonging to the Distillery, the large still is to be sold.

Witnesses: Thomas Moore, Rathganny, Co. Westmeath, said Benjamin Mears the younger, Thomas Glenon, Multifarn[h]am.

Memorial witnessed by: Thomas Moore, Wm. Dunphy, Dublin, gent.

346, 47, 230287 Benjamin Mears (seal)

651 BEERS, JOSEPH, Ballymoney, Co. Antrim, surgeon.

29 Sept. 1781. Narrate ¾ p. 26 Jan. 1782.

His wife Elizabeth and his children. His sisters Hellen Cuppage otherwise Beers and Dorothy Beers. Exors. his wife Elizabeth, James Blair Shaw, of Doagh, and William Adair, Loughmore.

The quarter land of Lismoralty, parish of Derryke[ig]han, Grange of Drumtullagh, Co. Antrim, leased from Earl of Antrim.

Witnesses: Andrew Allison, Coleraine, Co. Antrim, surgeon, Detliff Orr, Ballymoney, Co. Antrim, ganger, Adam Catherwood, Ballymoney, Co. Antrim, merchant.

Memorial witnessed by: Detliff Orr, Adam Catherwood.

341, 533, 230523 Elizabeth Beers (seal)

652 DON(N), EDWARD, Thoronmoor, King's Co., farmer.
9 Nov. 1773. Full 1 p. 19 Feb. 1782.

My wife Neley Donn. My two sons Tom Donn and Paddy Donn. My son Mick Don (I have paid him all his portions and forten). Mick Donn and Morris Donn. My two daughters Catey Don and Poll Don. Lease of Thorin(moor).

Witnesses: Maurice (Morres) Donn his mark, Michael Dunn, Thomas Shortt.

Memorial witnessed by: Richd. Wm. Jackson, Robert Lannigan, both Dublin, gents., Samuel Aickin, Dublin, gent.

346, 130, 230937 Michael Dunn (seal)

653 SHAW, ANDREW, Millough, parish of Drombo, Co. Down.
18 Oct. 1780. Narrate 1 p. 11 Mar. 1782.

His son Samuel Shaw. His sons Andrew Shaw, John Shaw, Mathew Shaw, James Shaw and Wm. Shaw. His six sons. His daughter Janey Hoy or Shaw, William Hoy her husband. His daughters Mary Shaw and Ann Shaw. His grandson Andrew Hoy. Thomas Scott, Killeleagh and Samuel Shaw, son of his brother John Shaw, overseers.

His freehold estate in Ballanagarick [Ballynagarrick], parish of Drumbo, Co. Down (Thomas Hunter and John Walker, tenants). The large moss and other mosses. His farm of land in Melough, parish of Drumbo, Co. Down.

Witnesses: John Shaw, William Shaw, both of Co. Down, Joshua Shepard, Lisburn, Co. Antrim.

Memorial witnessed by: David McAnally, Lisburn, Co. Down, Joshua Shepard (of the profession of the people called Quakers).

344, 232, 231168 Andrew Shaw (seal)

654 BENTON, ELIZABETH, otherwise ROBERTS, otherwise COULSON. 29 June 1780. Précis ½ p. 3 April 1782.

To Othaniel Benton her husband £14 yearly issuing out of concerns in or near Har[o]ldscross, Co. Dublin.

Witnesses: William Roberts, Dublin, gent., Christr. Kelly, the Comb, liberties of said city, cordwainer, Edwd. Wade, Dublin, weaver.

Memorial witnessed by: Christr. Kelly, Owen O'Neil, Dublin, gent.

347, 119, 231347 Othnial Benton (seal)

655 CARY, TRISTRAM, Bushfield, Parish of Taughboyne, Co. Donegal. 20 May 1780. Narrate ½ p. 10 April 1782.

His son George Cary. His son John Cary. Rt. Hon. Edwd. Cary, Dungevin, Co. Londonderry, trustee.

His fee farm of Tirn, parish of Urney; lease of Rockfield, part of the lands of Altaskin in the See of Rapho, and his lease of Rushfield where he then lived, all in Co. Donegal.

Witnesses: Owens Colhoun, Carnamoyle, Robert McCarter, Carrigans, John Cox the younger and John Cox the elder, of Cloughfinn, gents., Robert McClintock, Dunmore, Esq., all in Co. Donegal.

Memorial witnessed by: John Cox the elder, aged 59 years and upwards, Thomas Chambers, Londonderry, merchant.

347, 128, 231393 Edwd. Cary (seal)

656 EDMUNSON, ANDREW, Tokenhouse Yard, London, merchant. 27 Jan. 1782. Narrate ½ p. 1 June 1782.

His brother, Robt. Edmunson, an infant. Constantine Sloper, Castlebar, and his brother-in-law Thomas Ellis of same, exors.

His dwelling houses, tenements etc. on the green in Castlebar, Co. Mayo, which he held jointly with his cousin Henry Sheridan, by lease.

Witnesses: J. Watkins, Througmorton Street, London, M. Quin, Watling Street, in said city, Jno. Griffin, Watling Street, clerk to said Mr. Quin.

Memorial witnessed by: Henry Sheridan, Castlebar, George Bingham, Antigua, both Co. Mayo, gents.

347, 243, 232083 Thos. Ellis (seal)

657 CARTHY, ANDREW, Naas, Co. Kildare, tanner.
23 Jan. 1781. Full ¾ p. 1 June 1782.

My wife Alice Carthy. My son Nicholas Carthy. My son Dennis Carthy. My son Richard Carthy. Thomas Fitzpatrick, Carnalway, Co. Kildare, exor. My estate and effects.

Witnesses: John Corbally, Naas, shopkeeper, Thos. Nowlan, Naas, chandler.

Memorial witnessed by: John Corbally, Wm. Kelly, Dublin, gent.

346, 321, 232088 Dennis Carthy (seal)

658 DRAKE, WILLIAM, Ballymacombs, parish of Ballyscullen, Co. Londonderry, 13 Nov. 1747. Precis ½ p. 10 June 1782.

To his daughter Jane Drake his goods, houses, lands and cattle.

Witnesses: John Godfrey; Richard Stafford and Francs. Judkin both of Ballymacombs.

Memorial witnessed by: John Godfree and John Brady both of Ballymacombs.

347, 255, 232219 Jane Drake her mark (seal)

659 JACKSON, THOMAS, the elder, formerly of Hollywell but now of Antrim, Co. Antrim. 22 Oct. 1772. Full 1¼ p. 27 June 1782.

My wife Rose Jackson. My son Thomas Jackson exor. My daughter Rose Jackson. My two grand-daughters Rose Clark and Elinor Clark. My son William Jackson exor.

My freehold lease of Hollywell. My lands of Ballynadrentagh [Co. Antrim].

Witnesses: William Holmes, Robert Young, Antrim, merchants, Hugh O'Neill, Antrim, linen draper.

Memorial witnessed by: William Holmes, Thomas Dawson, Carmoney, Co. Antrim, farmer.

348, 124, 232454 William Jackson (seal)

660 TRACTON, JAMES, LORD BARON, Tracton Abbey.

1 May 1782. Full, partly narrate, 8¼ pp. 4 July 1782.

His wife Elizabeth Baroness Tracton extx. Nephew John Swift to take surname of Dennis if he succeeds to testator's estates. My nephew Meade Swift (ditto), Thomas Swift his son by his present wife. Testator's cousin german William Bullen, Kinsale, to take surname of Dennis if he succeeds to testator's estates. Joseph Bullen eldest son of said William Bullen, (ditto). Thomas Bullen second son of said William Bullen, (ditto). His sister Frances Swift. Rev. Dr. Richard Pigott, Frances Kearney, Esq., of Barrettstown, trustees.

John Dennis, Dublin, attorney of the Exchequer, Joseph Bullen Dennis, eldest son of said John, Hawley Dennis, second son of said John, John Dennis, third son of said John Dennis the elder, James Dennis fourth son of said John Dennis the elder, Gabriel Dennis fifth son of said John Dennis the elder. Niece Judith Chetwynd.

His real and freehold estates in Counties of Cork and Kerry, and county of city of Cork. The two Lisnaheries, Ballinpierce, Upper and Lower Ballyduhig, Chetwine [Chetwynd], the Ballygarvans, Adamstown, Tulligbeg, Coolegeely and tenements in city of Cork held by representatives of Richard Harrison. His estates in Ballydahin, and Carrowkeal, [? Co. Cork]. His freeholds at Rathcormack; estate in town of Kinsale. His dwelling houses at Stephen's Green and Newtown and all his lands in Co. Dublin. His pew in [St.] Peter's Church. Lands of Dunleary. A rent charge payable to Alexander Pigott [? lands in Co. Kerry]. His house in Fleet Street, [? Dublin] where his said sister resides.

Witnesses: Richard Townsend, Hugh Carleton, William Tonson.

Memorial witnessed by: John Heard, Dublin, gent., Mathew Ryan, Dublin, counsellor at law.

346, 343, 232541 E. Tracton (seal)

661 FITZGERALD, MARY. This name appears in the Names Index of Grantors followed by the words " her Will," but, as will be seen from abstract 662, the memorial is of a deed transferring interests formerly devised by a Will.

348, 144, 232628

662 McCOM, MARY, Deed by way of a Will dated 10th June 1782. Narrate ½ p. 10 July 1782.

Reciting that 1 March 1781 Robert FitzGerald, Ranelagh Road, by Will devised to Mary McCom otherwise FitzGerald certain leasehold interests. Whereby said Mary McCom transferred to her husband Wm. McCom said premises so devised to her by said Will [situation not mentioned].

Witnesses: John Clark, Dublin gent., Benj. Moore, Dublin, gent.

Memorial witnessed by: John Clark.

348, 144, 232628 Mary McCom (seal)

663 VICARS, DANIEL, Ballyedmond, Queen's Co. 13 April 1781. Narrate 1½ p. 30 July 1782.

His son Richard Vicars. His daughter Mary Vicars and his daughter Frances Vicars; provision for them on marriage if with consent of their uncle Richard Gilborne, Peafield, Queen's Co., or their cousin german Potter Harman Gilborne; 5/- only if either of them should marry a Papist. His daughter Susanna had acted with disobedience.

His real and freehold, personal and other estate. His house at Ballyedmond.

Witnesses: Rev. Daniel Nowlan, Whiteswall, Co. Kilkenny, clerk, Richd. Gilborne, Peafield, Queen's Co., gent., Richd. Thompson, Dublin, attorney.

Memorial witnessed by: Richd. Thompson, Vicars Fisher, Castlegrogan, Queen's Co., gent.

345, 209, 232838 Richd. Vicars (seal)

664 FITZGERALD, GEORGE, Turlough, Co. Mayo. 16 March 1782. Full 2¼ pp. 4 Oct. 1782.

I annull a Will by me formerly made and deposited in hands of Archibald Noble my former attorney which he secreted.

My only daughter Elizabeth Fitzgerald now living with me a minor of very tender years is totally unprovided for. My eldest son George

Robert FitzGerald has made me lament the extent of the provision already made by me for him. My younger son Charles Lionel Fitz-Gerald. Hugh Brown, Co. Dublin Esq., and Sir Frederick Flood, Bart., trustees. Mrs. Elizabeth Lyons who has lived with me for many years, guardian of said daughter.

I am seized in fee of lands of Clooncough, Co. Roscommon and several lands in Co. Mayo by virtue of Will of Dominick Browne, Rahard, Esq., deceased. My estate of Turlough and Mohina, Co. Mayo of the reversion of which in fee I am seized expectant upon the decease of my son George Robert FitzGerald without issue male, an event likely to happen as he never had any issue male.

Witnesses: Thomas Lyster, Dublin, John Macartney, Dublin, Esq., James Groves, Dublin, gent.

Memorial witnessed by: Mathew Black, Dublin, gent., William Kean, Dublin, servant to Charles Lionel Fitzgerald.

344, 531, 233396 C. L. FitzGerald (seal)

665 UPTON, JOHN, Newtown of Greenoge, parish of Greenoge, Barony Ratoath, Co. Meath. 21 Jan. 1773. Full ½ p. 19 Oct. 1782.

My wife Julia Upton otherwise Gready exor. Mary Vanstan my grand-niece. Patt. Langan, Mathew Dowling, both of Greenoge, exors.

My estate or freehold interest in lands and holdings of Newtown of Greenoge aforesaid. I desire I may be buried in Killsallaghan.

Witnesses: James Langan, farmer, Nichs. Brien and Thos. Magee, tailors, all of Greenoge.

Memorial witnessed by: Thos. Magee, William Dunphy, Dublin gent.

348, 290, 233523 Julia Upton (seal)

666 THORN, EDWARD, Ballyhane, Co. Tipperary, gent.
28 Nov. 1778. Narrate 1 p. 13 Nov. 1782.

His wife. John Madder, New Port, clerk, Nicholas Smyth, Limerick, Esq., trustees. William Thorn his [testator's] eldest son. Testator's son Edward Thorn. £100 as a provision for five of his younger children to wit: £20 to his son John Thorn, £20 to his son Edward Thorn, £20 to his son Francis Thorn, £20 to his daughter Ann Thorn and £20 to his daughter Mary Ann Thorn. £30 to daughter Jane Thorn, £20 to his daughter Elinor Thorn, to be paid on marriage.

Ewer Ryan, Ballymakeogh, Richard Going, Birdhill, both Co. Tipperary, Esq., exors. Lands of Ballyhane, Co. Tipperary.

Witnesses: George Franklin, Ahane, liberties of Limerick, gent., Joseph Wilson, Craige, John Floyd, Birdhill, both Co. Tipperary farmers.

Memorial witnessed by: George Franklin, Patrick Connor, Limerick gent.

344, 563, 233885 William Thorn (seal)

667 KENNY, COURTNEY, Ballinrobe, Co. Mayo, gent. 25 July 1779. Précis ¾ p. 16 Nov. 1782.

His wife exor. His second son Courtney Kenny exor. His children.

All his freehold leases and interests in Co. Mayo lands are Ballisnehiney, Park P: Q: near the town of Ballinrobe, and leases in and about the town of Ballinrobe, Co. Mayo, Knockanotish and Cahernelecky.

Witnesses: Thos. Atkins, then of Ballinrobe, chirurgeon and apothecary but now of Edinburgh, Scotland, Andrew Clarke, Ballinrobe, attorney, Martin Richisson, Ballinrobe, gent.

Codicil witnessed by: Christr. Bowen, Hollymount, Co. Mayo, attorney, David Richisson.

Memorial witnessed by: David Courtney, John Cooke Courtney, Dublin, attorney.

349, 243, 233959 Courtney Kenny (seal) exor.

668 DOWNING, SAMUEL, Lemnaroy, parish of Termoneeny, Co. Londonderry. 31 March 1753. Narrate ¾ p. 23 Nov. 1782.

His wife Martha. His grandson. Testator's son Adam Downing. James Downing, Lemnaroy, John Downing, Ballynocker, William

Downing, Cabragh and Richard O'Cahan, Rocktown, exors. His house and lands.

Witnesses: Thomas Fawset and James Downing both of Lemnaroy, Bernard Downing, Rocktown, both Co. Londonderry.

Memorial witnessed by: Adam Downing, Lemnaroy, gent., Henry Richardson, Dublin, gent.

347, 442, 234070 Samuel Downing (seal) grandson of testator and a devisee named in said Will.

669 CULLIMORE, JOHN, Taghmon, Co. Wexford, gent.

1 Ap. 1779. Précis 1¼ p. 25 Nov. 1782.

His eldest son Josiah Martin Cullimore. His friend William Sparrow, Ballyannick, Co. Wexford, gent., trustee.

Town and lands of both Russellstown and Newtown, Co. Wexford. Moiety of town and lands of Crandaniel Little, Holmestown and part of Knockmullen called Porter's Knock, Great Ballymanane and part of Bunnarget, Co. Wexford held by lease. Freehold lands of Reedstown, Rathshillins, Rossenstown and part of Bunarget and Knockmullen, Co. Wexford. Freehold of lands of Taghmon and the customs of the fairs of Taghmon, Ballygoman and part of Barkstown, Co. Wexford, and reversion of said lands expectant on death of testator's uncle Josiah Martin. Lands of Clarestown and Sheastown, Co. Wexford, held under a lease of 999 years.

Witnesses: Walter Breen, Taghmon, Co. Wexford, merchant, John Griffin, Taghmon, Benjamin Wilson, both Wexford, gents.

Memorial witnessed by: James Howlen and Richd. Waddy both of Camden St., Co. Dublin, gent.

348, 387, 234125 Dan. Cullimore (seal)

670 CARR, ARTHUR, Ballaghhenry, Co. Down.

8 Apl. 1782. Narrate 1 p. 26 Nov. 1782.

His father Nicholas Carr, his brother William Carr and Owen Magarry exors. His wife Mary Gibbons otherwise Carr. To his eldest daughter Elizabeth Carr and his daughter Margt. Carr and his son William Carr, legacies when they are 21. His farm in Bryansford [? Co. Down].

Witnesses: Wm. Boyd, Aghlasnafinn, linen draper, Arthur Carr, junior, and Neice Fitzpatrick, farmer, both of the Ballagh, all in Co. Down.

Memorial witnessed by: Wm. Boyd and David Boyd, both of Aughlessnafin aforesaid.

345, 423, 234127 Arthur Carr (seal)

671 WILLIAMSON, GEORGE, Mullaghmore, Co. Meath, gent.

19 Nov. 1778. Full 1 p. 14 Dec. 1782.

To be interred in churchyard of Stabannon, Co. Louth with my ancestors. Wm. Wynne, Middletown, Co. Louth, Mark Cassidy, Derry, Co. Monaghan, gents., trustees and exors. My nephew George Williamson, under 21 years; his two sisters Mary and Agnes Williamson, under 21 years. My nephew Robert Williamson. My brother James Williamson. My brother Joseph Williamson.

My farms of land called Mullaghmore and my part of Largy, both Co. Meath.

Witnesses: Ralph Collier, Ballyhoe, Co. Meath, innkeeper, John Young, Meath Hill, Co. Meath, farmer, Thomas Higgins, Barley Hill, Co. Meath, farmer, Michael O'Brien, then of Mullaghmore, land surveyor.

Memorial witnessed by: Thos. Higgins, James Metcalf, Dublin, gent.

350, 139, 234364 George Williamson (seal)

672 BLAKE, CHARITY, Dublin, widow.

Codicil 11 March 1769. Narrate $\frac{3}{4}$ p. 1 Feb. 1783.

Annuls bequest by her former Will of her right of inheritance to lands of Lullymore, Lullybeg and Barnarane, Co. Kildare. Now devises said lands to her son Henry Blake, Lahinch, Co. Mayo, Esq., for life and to his issue male or female failing such issue to her cousin and friend John Annesley, Esq., Ballysax, Co. Kildare.

Witnesses: Thos. Brownrigg, Dublin, gent., Miles Jennings now of Dublin, servant, James Browne, also then of Dublin, gent.

Memorial witnessed by: Wynne Hillas, Henry Annesley, Miles Jennings.

345, 548, 234982 John Annesley (seal)
the legatee

673 CLIFFORD, HENRY, Great Gurtins, Co. Wexford, gent.
6 May 1781. Narrate $1\frac{1}{4}$ p. 8 Ap. 1783.

His wife Mary and her brother Edward Carty exors. and guardians of children. His eldest son Robert Clifford. His son William Clifford. His sons Wm. and Henry Clifford and his daughters Jane, Mary and Sarah Clifford all his children by his said then present wife Mary Slifford orse. Carty.

Town and lands of Ballyregan, Barony Forth, Co. Wexford. Houses etc. near West Gate of town of Wexford. Lands of Larestown. The house wherein he formerly lived in the Flesh Market of the town of Wexford and two houses in same street formerly held by John Reade and Patrick Carty.

Witnesses: Robert Elward, Haystown, Mathew Beahan, Johnstown and Robert Carty, junior, Leaghmolan, Co. Wexford, farmers.

Memorial witnessed by: Robert Allen, Latimerstown, Christian Wilson, Wexford town, both Co. Wexford, gents.

343, 233, 235859 Mary Clifford (seal)
an exor. and guardian.

674 CASTLETON, NATHANIEL, Margaret Street, parish of St. Mary le Bone, Co. Middlesex, Esq. 30 June 1778. Précis 1 p. 24 Apl. 1782.

His nephew Rev. Newdigate Poyntz, now of Tormaston, Co. Gloucester, clerk, and Rev. Francis Mapletoft now of Aynho, Co. Northampton, clerk, trustees and exors. All his real and personal estate in kingdoms of Great Britain and Ireland.

Witnessed by: Pierson Lloyd, said parish of St. Mary le Bone, Doctor of Divinity, Mathew Duane, Lincoln's Inn, Co. Middlesex, Esq., Hugh Smith clerk to said Mathew Duane.

Memorial witnessed by: Geo. Wilson, Hugh Smith, Warwick Court, parish of St. Andrew, Holborn, gent., late clerk to Mathew Duane.

353, 333, 235982 Newdigate Poyntz (seal)

675 MERVYN, ANN Dublin, widow and extx. of James Mervyn, formerly called James Richardson of Castlehill, Co. Tyrone, Esq. 12 Apl. 1764. Full 2¾ pp. 7 May 1783.

Reciting that whereas James Mervyn by Will dated 4 April 1753 devised to Andrew Knox, Prehen, Co. Londonderry, Esq., and William Wray, Ards, Co. Donegal Esq., the town and lands of Springtown, Aughnacarny otherwise Altnakerny McKay, Aughnacarny McKinley, Aghamintall, [Ahgamilkin], McKenna([1]), Corgagh, Carnamucklagh Black, Carnamucklagh Murphy, Dunscobe, Derrycloony, Dernasell, Derrydruman [Derrydrummond], Glencapog, Killridon [Kilruddan], Killycarnan, Lisgor[r]an, Cavan, Tully, Cullamore, Lisbane, Analochan, Ballygreenhill, Altnaveagh, Aghadara, Ballymacan, Corr, Callbell, Tullingar([1]) Derryclea, Aghadaragh, Lungs, Mullans, Mullaghmore-buchan, Ballyclagan [? Belnaclogh], Statmore [? Stratigore], Tamly-more [? Tamlagh], Caldrum, The Lough, Castle and Parks adjoining the town of Augher and Killaney, the corn mill of Augher, all his estate and interest in town of Augher and rents of Bellnageragh, and Killclay([2]), his moiety of the advowson of the Church of Ballynasagart, and the reversion of Castlehill after his wife's death, in Co. Tyrone, and his estate in manor of Favor Royal in said County and part of lands of Oughterard, Skreen, Glennon, Lisgannon [? Lisgorran], Lisnalloy, Sheergram [Sheerigrim], Gortrush, Mullaghbane, Clone-mullan, Munalboy Golan, the mill thereof, Camderry, Straduff, Cavanacre([1]), Gortmore, Kilmore, Lisnamallagh [? Lisnamaghery], Highland Hill, a tenement and park in Omagh formerly in possession of Rev. Mr. Maxwell, rent out of lands of Attaghmore, his moiety of mills of Omagh, and the Barley Park in Co. Tyrone, also his moiety of lands of Naul otherwise Snowtown, the mill of Naul, Baringtown otherwise Bedingtown([3]), Mooresides, Kenroestown, Dardistown,

([1]) See footnote to Abstract 133.
([2]) Doris [?Doras] is mentioned here in James Mervyn's Will. See abstract 133.
([3]) Compare with Abstract 133.

Clogherstown and Cloghan, Co. Meath in trust to the use of his daughter Letitia and her heirs, his said wife for life and after her death in default of issue of his said daughter to such one of his three brothers St. George, Galbraith and Erskine Richardson as his said wife Ann should think fit with remainder in tail mail and in default of issue in trust for such other of testator's two remaining brothers as she should appoint, and in default of issue for the remaining brother.

After determination of the said several estates so limited to the said Letitia and her issue male and female the said trustees to hold said lands in trust for use of said St. George Richardson failing whose issue to the use of said Galbraith Richards failing whose issue to the use of said Erskine Richardson.

Witnesses: Lieut. Thomas Bligh, Henry Irvine, Drogheda, Esq., Jemett McClintock, Dublin, gent.

Memorial witnessed by: Henry Irvine, Arthur Dunn, both Dublin, gents.

351, 260, 236101 William Richardson (seal)

Only son and heir of St. George Richardson Esq., deceased, one of the devisees in said Will named.

676 GARTLANY, HUGH, Cullenstown, parish of Darver, Co. Louth, farmer. 8 May 1783. Full 1¼ p. 31 May 1783.

To be buried in churchyard of Dromiskin, Co. Louth. My wife Madlin Gartlany. My son Nicholas Gartlany. My stepson John Gartlany. My stepson Patt Gartlany. My daughters Ann Gartlany otherwise Conry, Mary and Catherine. My daughter Rose. My daughter Margt., wife of Thomas Rooney of Peppardstown, Co. Louth. William M'Gawley, Rogerisk, and Owen Byrne, Rossmakea, said Co., exors. Lands of Cullenstown, held by lease.

Witnesses: John Shekelton, farmer, John Moran, schoolmaster, Patrick Newcome, farmer, all of Co. Louth.

Memorial witnessed by: Patrick Newcome, Wm. Dunphy, Dublin, gent.

354, 99, 236714 Nicholas Gartlany (seal)

677 DUNLAP, JOHN, Strabane, sadler.

10 Feb. 1780. Précis ½ p. 3 June 1782.

His wife. His son Gabriel. Bequests to Robt. Rutherford, Willm. Irwin. His son John then in America. Said William Irvine and Archibald Allen exors. Houses and premises in Strabane.

Witnesses: John Cooper, James O'Donnell, Gabriel Dunlap, all of Strabane, gents.

Memorial witnessed by: John Cooper, Anthony Griffith, Strabane, gent.

352, 95, 236767 William Irvine (seal)

678 BADCOCK, BENJAMIN, Templebarr, Co. Dublin, gunsmith.

9 April 1781. Narrate ½ p. 6 Aug. 1783.

My daughter Julia Woods otherwise Badcock wife of Ed. Woods hairdresser. James Flood, Templebarr, vintner, trustee and exor. James Flood, son of said James Flood.

House, tenement and premises on Temple Barr held by lease renewable for ever.

Witnesses: Charles Kellett, Templebarr, hatter, Christopher Carlile, Werburgh St., perukemaker, Daniel Bourne, of St. Patrick's Back Close, Co. Dublin, gent.

Memorial witnessed by: Daniel Bourne, Walter Bourne of St. Patrick's Back Close, clerk to said Daniel Bourne.

343, 473, 237632 James Flood (seal)

679 KELLY, JOHN, Galway.

2 June 1783. Narrate ¾ p. 3 Sept. 1783.

His wife Catherine Kelly otherwise Waldron. His daughter Susanna. His son Robert Kelly. Furniture in his house belonging to the widow of the late Hugh Montgomery of Galway. Half of his shirts left to his wife Catherine for the care of his grandson. Bartholomew Kelly and Wm. Smyth, Galway, exors. His holding in North and East suburbs of the town of Galway.

Witnesses: Fras. Burke, baker, and Fray Troy, stone cutter, both Galway, Bridget Kelly, spinster, Kentville, Co. Galway.

Memorial witnessed by: Patrick Little, Wm. Kelly, Dublin, gent.

355, 81, 237854 Barthw. Kelly (seal)

680 SOXSMITH, THOMAS, Hammond Lane, Dublin, merchant.
27 May 1783. Full ¾ p. 24 Oct. 1783.

My wife Mary Soxsmith extx. My brother Abraham Soxsmith, Kilnew, Co. Meath. My sister Elizabeth Callaghan otherwise Soxsmith 1/- and to each and every of her children the sum of 1/- likewise. My brother Wm. Soxsmith. My sister Esther Taaffe otherwise Soxsmith.

To be interred in churchyard of Julianstown, Co. Meath. My houses and concerns in Hammond Lane, Dublin.

Witnesses: Mathew Walsh, Bow Street, Dublin, gent., Geo. Eltum, Phraper Lane, Dublin, painter, John Butler, Bow Lane, baker.

Memorial witnessed by: Mathew Hagarty, Dublin, gent. Edwd. Hansard Petrey, Dublin gent.

357, 13, 238216 Mary Soxsmith (seal)

681 MILLTOWN, RT. HON. JOSEPH, EARL OF
10 Oct. 1783. Précis 3 p.p 7 Nov. 1783.

Confirms settlement made 18 Jan. 1768 made upon marriage with Elizabeth, Countess of Milltown(1), his then wife. His wife Elizabeth exor. Testator's eldest son Joseph, now Earl of Milltown, exor. The Hon. John Bourke trustee. Rt. Hon. John Ponsonby trustee. Testator's second son Brice Leeson. Testator's grandson Joseph Leeson. Testator's third son William. Testator's fourth son Robert. His brother-in-law Robert French, Esq., exor.

All his manors, messuages, houses, towns, lands, tenements and hereditaments in the Kingdom of Ireland. His house and demesne of Russborough otherwise Russellstown [Co. Wicklow], and all other his lands in the counties of Wicklow and Dublin which he purchased from John Graydon, Esq., deceased; and Humphreystown, Co. Wicklow, purchased from representatives of Nicholas Sherlock, Esq., deceased. The manor of Bormount, Co. Wexford and all other lands,

(1) Elizabeth French, testator's third wife.

Co. Wexford, which he purchased from Arthur Houghton, and lands of Ballymacdonaghfin, which he formerly purchased from Robert Birch, and lands etc. in Co. Meath purchased from said John Graydon, and lands in Co. Westmeath which he purchased from Thos. Magan, Esq., deceased. His dwellinghouse etc. on North side of St. Stephen's Green purchased from Hon. Richard Gore. The park of Pallice and lands etc. of Lowertownmore and other lands purchased from the Trustees appointed by Act of Parliament for the sale of estate of Maurice O'Connor a minor in King's Co. Lands of Quolins and Parsonstown, Co. Meath, etc. purchased from Rt. Hon. Thos. Connolly and his trustees. Lands in Co. Kilkenny purchased from Gervais Parker Bush, Esq. and lands purchased from Nehemiah Nixon Donnellan, Esq. Lands of Coombe, Co. Tipperary, lately purchased under the decree of Court of Chancery and formerly the estate of Thos. Parker, and other lands in Co. Tipperary. Lands of Rathmore, Call[i]agh[s]town and Killballbraigh, Co. Westmeath formerly the estate of Robt. late Earl of Belvedere which testator purchased under a decree of Court of Chancery. Lands of Banan and Pottaghane otherwise Bullaghane, King's Co. and Knockincosker otherwise Knock, and Cloneheige, Co. Westmeath, and other lands purchased from Rev. Lancelot Lowe. Lands of Plumersfarm, the Downs and Killickilawn, Co. Wicklow, and all other lands etc. purchased from Mathew Read, Esq., and Richd. Read his son. Lands of Ballyvolloe and Ballyroan, Co. Wexford and other lands purchased from the assignees of said Robert Birch a bankrupt. Lands of Clongawny purchased from the trustee for the sale of estate of said Maurice O'Connor, and also for the lands of Skreen formerly the estate of the said Earl of Belvedere, in Co. Meath. Also Fryarstown otherwise Ballynabraheen and testator's other lands in Co. Leitrim.

Witnesses: Charles [Agar], Lord Archbishop of Cashel, Theobd. Wolfe, Aungier St., Dublin, Esq., John Carroll, Golden Lane, Dublin, gent.

Memorial witnessed by: Francis Gorman, Stephen's Green, Dublin, Esq., John Carroll, Golden Lane, Dublin, gent.

Milltown (seal)
(Joseph now Earl of Milltown eldest son of testator).

355, 154, 238338

E. Milltown (seal)
(Elizabeth Countess Dowager of Milltown).

682 MOORE, JAMES, Ballydivity, Co. Antrim.

24 Dec. 1778. Full 6 pp. 11 Nov. 1783.

My only son James Moore. My sister Ann Hill, widow of Rev. John Hill late of Drumna, her three sons John, Charles and James, her daughters Mary Given wife of Wm. Givern, and Ann Edmiston wife of Hugh Edmiston. My nephew John Walker, his brothers James, Charles and Robert Walker, their sisters Mary Kithcart wife to Alexr. Kithcart, Sarah Hill wife to John Hill. My two nephews James and Robert Walker both of Glenleary, Co. Londonderry, farmers. My nephew Chas. Walker of Glenleary, Co. Londonderry, farmer. My nephew John Walker, Ballydivity, Barony Dunluce, Co. Antrim, gent. My son-in-law Jno. Stewart, Ballintoy, his only son James Stewart, my grandson (a minor). My grandson James Stewart only son of John Stewart of Ballintoy, Co. Antrim, Esq., if he should become seized of my real estate shall take and assume the surname of Moore. My nephew Chas. Hill, Drumna, Co. Antrim, linen draper, my nephew James Hill of same, linen draper. Margaret Poak otherwise Hamill wife of Wm. Hamill. Robt. Ogilby, Newtownlimavaddy, Co. Londonderry, Esq., M.D. John Hill, Hill[s]mount, Barony Toomb, Co. Antrim (my nephew), linen draper and Wm. Owens, Holestone, Co. Antrim, watchmaker, trustees. My son-in-law John Stewart, Ballintoy, Esq., Rev. William Lynd, Moyargit, Gospel minister, and John Huey, Ballyalaght, gent., all in Barony Cary, Co. Antrim, exors. Legacies to poor of parishes of Derrykeighan, and Billy.

The lands of North Ballydivity, Cluntice and Islandahoo which I hold from Earl of Antrim; lands of South Ballydivity, Carnfeog[ne] which I hold under the heirs of James Stewart, Esq., deceased, Upper Ballynaris and Ballyness leased from Earl of Antrim, all in Barony Dunluce, Co. Antrim. Frosses, Barony Kilconway, Co. Antrim held from Earl of Antrim, North Torcrum (ditto) in Grange of Killegan, Co. Antrim, Lissaniske, Barony Dunluce, Duncarbit, Drumchullen and Cullyveely (ditto) Barony Cary, all in Co. Antrim. Upper and Lower Moyargits, held from heirs of Hugh Boyd, Ballycastle, Co. Antrim, deceased. Upper Ballinlea, Barony Carey, Co. Antrim held from Earl of Antrim, Lisbel[la]nagroagh More, Barony Carey, Cloughhorr, Barony Dunluce both Co. Antrim (ditto). Ballymacklevennon [Co. Londonderry] in liberties of Coleraine which I hold from Mrs. Jennett Boyd, widow, deceased.

Witnesses: Wm. Martin, Ballynaris, parish Billy, Co. Antrim, farmer, James Martin, Ballynaris, Presbyterian teacher, commonly called a Probationer, John Martin, Ballynaris, bachelor.

Memorial witnessed by: Said Wm. Martin, James Martin and John Martin.

355, 170, 238479 John Hill (seal)

683 MOORE, JAMES, Ballydivity, Co. Antrim.

Codicil 10 Feb. 1781. Full 1¼ p. 11 Nov. 1783.

In former Will appointed as exors. John Stewart, Ballintoy, Co. Antrim, Esq., Rev. Wm. Lynd, Moyarget, Co. Antrim, preacher and John Huey, Ballyalaught, Co. Antrim, farmer. Revokes exorship of said Wm. Lynd and John Huey and appoints as exors. said John Stewart, Ballintoy, Richard Lloyd, Coleraine, Co. Londonderry, Esq., and Jackson Wray, Dowey, Co. Antrim, gent.

To my only son James Moore the younger all real and personal estate. Debt due by Randal Wm. Earl of Antrim who executed a mortgage deed to me, the rents etc. of lands which I hold under his Lordship in Baronies of Dunluce, Cary and Kilconway, Co. Antrim being a collateral security.

Witnesses: William Martin, Ballynaris, parish of Billy, Barony Dunluce, Co. Antrim, farmer, John Martin, Ballynaris aforesaid, bachelor, James Martin, Ballynaris aforesaid, Presbyterian teacher commonly called a Probationer.

Memorial witnessed by: William Martin, John Martin, James Martin.

356, 89, 238480 John Hill (seal)
a trustee in said Will.

684 MOORE, JAMES, of Ballydivity, Co. Antrim.

Postscript. 6 March 1781. Full ½ p. 11 Nov. 1783.

To my nephew John Walker the feather bed and bedclothes, bedstead and hangings that are now all upon the bed in the Blue Room on which he now sleeps, and to possess the said Blue Room for life provided he continues unmarried.

Witnesses: John Hood, parish of Deryaghy, Barony of Massereene, Co. Antrim, Ann Hill in Drumra in parish of Attoghel [? Drumramer, parish Ahoghill], Barony Toom, Co. Antrim, spinster, James Martin, Ballynaris, parish Billy, Barony Dunluce, Co. Antrim, Presbyterian teacher commonly called Probationer.

Memorial witnessed by: James Martin, John Hood.

356, 90, 238481 John Hill (seal)

685 BLOUNT, SAMUEL, London, gent.

20 Nov. 1783. Précis ½ p. 9 Dec. 1783.

To Sir Thos. Sewell, Knt., Master of the Rolls, trustee, lands of Ballybirrane, Fearthugh, Ballyglass, Ball[y]david, Pollaghmonemore, Lisnegunie, Dromackie and Ballyduff, all in Co. Tipperary.

Witnesses: John Thomas Atkinson, Chancery Lane, London, gent., Patrick Hart, clerk to Mr. Palmer of Chancery Lane, Robert Druce of Little Saint Thomas Apostle, London, packer.

Memorial witnessed by: John Palmer, Chancery Lane, gent., John Thomas Atkinson.

357, 999, 239002 Thos. Sewell (seal)

686 KEOGH, HONORA, Camlagh, Co. Roscommon, widow.

5 Apl. 1783. Narrate ¾ p. 17 Dec. 1783.

Her grandson Ignatius Keogh. Her grandson Collin Keogh and her grandson Anthony Keogh both under 21 years. Grand-daughters Ellis Naghten and Bell Naghten. Her daughter Bell. Her son Anthony Keogh and her nephew William Keogh exors.

Farms of Camlagh, Ballyduff and Clonkeen, Co. Roscommon, which were purchased by her from her son Anthony Keogh to be managed by her exors. for the use and better education of her said grandson Ignatius until 21 years.

Witnesses: Thos. Kelly, Dublin, gent., Dominick Kelly, Ballyglass, Co. Roscommon, Doctor of Physick, William Keogh, Camlagh, Co. Roscommon, gent.

Memorial witnessed by: James Hamilton, James Kelly.

352, 415, 239100 Anthony Keogh (seal)
son of testatrix

687 HIFFERNAN, MICHAEL, Camas, Co. Limerick.

10 Dec. 1779. Full 3 pp. 23 Dec. 1783.

To be privately interred in my family burying place at Newcastle, Co. Limerick.

My sister Mary Cantillon. My nephew Terence McMahon, Limerick, merchant, exor. James Cantillon, Castleroberts, Co. Limerick, gent., exor. My late brother John Hiffernan, deceased. My nephew John Hiffernan, gent., deceased. To my niece Elinor Cantillon now wife of Wm. Bourke, gent., Bridget Dwyer and Catherine Kennedy, widow, £200 each, and to my niece Elizabeth Herlihy £200. The two sons of my nephew John McMahon deceased. Bryan Sheehy's three children by my niece Mary McMahon. My natural children Thos. Hiffernan, Patrick Hiffernan, David Hiffernan, Elinor Hiffernan and Mary Hiffernan. My particular good friends Wm. Hiffernan, Derk, Co. Limerick and Thos. Prendergast, Dublin, Esq., trustees. £115 to poor of parishes of Newcastle, Monagay, Ballingarry, Killeady and Rathkeale, Co. Limerick. My cousins William Bluet, Patrick Bluet and John Bluet. My youngest natural son William Hiffernan by Mary Harding.

All my lands etc. in Counties of Limerick, Kildare, Dublin, County of the City of Dublin and in City of Dublin. Persons who come into possession of said lands to assume name of Hiffernan. Rathnascar, and Commons of Cleaghlish, Co. Limerick to be leased to my said natural son Wm. Hiffernan provided he takes the oath required by an Act of Parliament made seventeenth and eighteenth years of King George III entitled An Act for the relief of His Majesties subjects of this Kingdom professing the Popish religion.

Witnesses: James Walsh, Dublin, merchant, Stawell Webb, Dublin, attorney at law, Dennis Charles, Dublin, clerk to said Thos. Prendergast.

Memorial witnessed by: James Walsh, Edward Denroche, Dublin, clerk to said Thos. Prendergast.

358, 122, 239199 Thos. Prendergast (seal)

688 SISSON, JONATHAN, Dublin.

8 July 1776. Codicil 2 Feb. 1780. Full 4 pp. 12 March 1784.

My wife Catherine Sisson exor. My eldest son Wm. Sisson I have already provided for. My son Jonathan Sisson, the younger, having also already been provided for, (trustee). My son Jacob Sisson. My daughter Catherin Turner otherwise Sisson. My daughter Hannah Cooper otherwise Sisson. My son-in-law Timothy Turner, Dublin, Esq., trustee and exor. My daughter Sarah Sisson exor.

My house in Clare Street, No 2 now in occupation of Mrs. Forward. My two houses in Patrick St., wherein Mr. Kelly and Mr. Gordon now dwell. My house, coach house and stable in Merrion Square, Dublin which I hold under Lord FitzWilliam and now in tenancy or occupation of Lovett Ashe, Esq. Piece of ground in Park Street near Trinity College, Dublin, which I hold by lease from Thos. Manning with all dwelling houses, stables, etc. thereon. Deed dated 12 Nov. 1771, reciting deed of 9 Nov. 1771 whereby I demised to my said sons Jonathan and Jacob the dwelling house and premises which I hold under Mr. Vesey at Lucan, Co. Dublin, concerning rents of said lands.

Codicil about rent of £25 granted to Mercy Taylor, Dublin, widow, for life out of my houses No. 1, 2, and 3 Clare Street. A debt due to John Hewetson deceased. My holdings at Lucan on north side of River Liffey and all mills, coppers, lead, printing tables, etc. relating to the printing business by me left at Lucan.

Witnesses: Robert Corbet, Dublin, gent., Anthony Nowland, Dublin, grocer, Henrietta Nowland, wife of said Anthony Nowland.

Codicil witnessed by: William Jordan, Robert Baldwin, Dublin, scriveners.

Memorial witnessed by: Wm. Jordan, George Jordan, Dublin, writing clerk.

356, 281, 240181 Sarah Sisson (seal)

689 BUCHANAN, JOHN, Belfast Co. Antrim, merchant.

11 Oct. 1783. Full 1 p. 23 Apl. 1784.

William Legg, Malone, exor. James Carson. My Aunt Carson. To my Aunt Clark my mother's best rich flowered silk, her garnet hoop ring etc. My cousin William Clark. To Miss Legg my bay mare she is so fond of. An annuity to Lilly Money " should she be so foolish as to marry this annuity to stop." Benjamin Robinson's indentures may be given up to him.

All property of whatever kind. Profits arising from the tenements at the Market house.

Witnesses: Thomas Stewart, Esq., Patrick Sargason, yeoman, Benjamin Robinson, yeoman, all of Belfast.

Memorial witnessed by: Thomas Stewart, David Henderson, Belfast, stationer.

357, 303, 240616 William Legg (seal)

690 GOODWIN, NATHANIEL Dublin, brushmaker.
6 April 1768. Full ¾ p. 30 Apr. 1784.

My wordly substance to my wife Margaret Goodwin, extx. My brother John Goodwin. To Mary Sutton, John Sutton and Elizth. Kelly (wife of Edward Kelly) one shilling each.

Witnesses: Thomas Dease, writing clerk, Benjn. White, cordwainer, Wm. Tanner, gent., all of Dublin.

Memorial witnessed by: Benj. White, James Dunphy, Dublin, woodcarver and gilder.

354, 563, 240733 Margt. Goodwin (seal)

691 STEELE, MARY, Ballymacombs, parish Ballyscullin, Co. Londonderry, widow. 21 Jan. 1759. Précis ¾ p. 3 May 1784.

To her son James Sewright two parts of the holding of land then in his possession that was willed to her by her husband Andrew Sewright [situation not mentioned]. John Dickson. Martin Steel, Robert McMullan and Robert Steel, exors.

Witnesses: John Dickson, William Dickson, Bryan Mulhollan.

Memorial witnessed by: William Dickson, Ballymacombs, Co. Londonderry, Andrew Sewright, Ballymacombs, yeoman.

358, 320, 240745 James Sewright (seal)

692 MULLOCK, THOMAS, Dublin, notary public.
3 Feb. 1774. Narrate 2 pp. 12 May 1784.

Testator's eldest son Thos. Mullock, said Thomas's brothers Robt., Wm. and Jno. Mullock [testator's sons].

John Dawson Coates, Dublin, banker, his kinsman, the Rev. Geo. Reston, Dublin, clerk, and testator's nephew Rev. John Mullock, Bellair, King's Co. clerk. trustees.

Town and lands of Kilnegarnagh, Castlereagh, Derryckmore, Liss, Leymore Oughter, the kitchen of Leymore and Derrynavlirg, Bunkiran. Dwelling house in Skinner Row devised to testator by Hosea Coates, deceased.

Witnesses: Richd. Magan, Oliver Nelson, Thos. Coates.

Memorial witnessed by: Richd. Magan, Skinner's Row, Dublin, apothecary, Jno. Ardill, Dublin, gent.

355, 420, 241017 Thos. Mullock (seal)

693 SHERWOOD, RICHARD, Cork Abbey, Co. Dublin, gent.

4 May 1783. Précis ½ p. 24 May 1784.

His wife Mary Sherwood, said Mary Sherwood and John Sherwood exors. and guardians of his children.

His lands of Killahurlo, Co. Wicklow. The house and lands of Cork Abbey.

Witnesses: John Alment "optition," James Dowlan, brazier, Charles Bury, gent., all of Dublin.

Memorial witnessed by: John Alment, Charles McMahon, Dublin, gent.

356, 436, 241261 Mary Sherwood (seal)

694 BUSHELL, EDWARD, Ballyvaughan, Co. Tipperary, gent.

30 July 1778. Endorsement by widow 14 Sept. 1778. Narrate 2 pp. 12 June 1784.

His eldest son Edward Bushell, his second son James Bushell, under 21 years. His son John. His son Thomas. His son Robert. His son William. His daughter Mary Cooke otherwise Bushell. To his five daughters viz. Elizabeth, Judith, Ann, Ruth and Catherine £200 each provided they married Protestants. His sister Elizabeth Bushell otherwise Doran. His sister Mary Cahill otherwise Bushell.

His nephew John Sq[u]ibb Bushell son of his brother Sq[u]ibb Bushell deceased. His friends Wm. Hayes, Liseva, Esq., John Squibb, Foxes Den, gent, both Co. Tipperary, exors.

The farm of Ballyvaughan. The farm of Kilotlea commonly called Seven Acres. To his son John the interest of Johnstown otherwise Powerstown, [? Co. Tipperary] willed to him by testator's uncle Bushell deceased when 25 years of age. Lands of Lakepol part of the lands of Kiltinan [Co. Tipperary].

Witnesses: Joseph Strangeman, Two Mile Bridge, James Cave, Clonmell, James Roche, Ballyvaughan, all of Co. Tipperary, gents.

Endorsement 14 Sept. 1778. Said Elizabeth Bushell the widow of said testator confirms the said Will in all matters.

Witnesses to endorsement: Said James Cave, James Roche, John Hill, Dublin, gent.

Memorial witnessed by: James Cave, James Roche.

359, 120, 241476 Edwd. Bushell (seal)

695 COOTE, PRUDENCE, Dublin, widow.
15 July 1776. Précis ½ p. 12 June 1784.

Fredk. Trench, Woodlawn, Co. Galway, Esq., and her daughter Frances Boxwell, widow, trustees.

Her estate of Ballykittagh otherwise Ballykilty, Ballycronelch otherwise Ballycronclogh, and all her estate in Co. Wexford.

Witnesses: Rev. Dive Downs, Doctor in Divinity, John FitzGibbon, Esq., both of Donnybrook, Co. Dublin, Robt. Blakely, Dublin, attorney at law.

Memorial witnessed by: Robt. Harrison, Aungier Street, Dublin, gent., attorney of H.M.'s Court of Exchequer in Ireland, Peter Jackson, Dublin, Esq., attorney of H.M. Court of King's Bench in Ireland.

357, 417, 241500 Frances Boxwell (seal)

696 McKEAL, THOMAS, Saunders Court, Co. Wexford.
24 April 1784. Full 1 p. 9 July 1784.

My cousin Thos. McKeal, Dublin, now servant to Sir John Freke, Bart., Dublin, to be sole exor. and guardian of my only daughter

Mary McKeal, now about 10 years of age. £100 in hands of Arthur Earl of Arran and other sums lawfully due to me by wages to be used for her education. My wife Margt. McKeal. My sisters Mary and Bridget McKeal. My mother Mary McKeal of Castlegore, Co. Mayo, a sum to be paid to her by Henry Crummer of Castlegore. My brother Laurence McKeal, Grange, Co. Mayo.

Witnesses: William Thornton, Saunders Court, gent., Patrick Malone, servant to said Lord Arran.

Memorial witnessed by: Patk. Malone, William Dunphy, Dublin, gent.

359, 170, 241964 Thos. McKeal (seal)

697 BEGLEY, JOHN, The Mill Yard of Brides Alley, Dublin, publican. 3 Aug. 1784. Narrate ¾ p. 11 Aug. 1784.

His grandson John Begley, a minor under age of 4 years. Henry Singleton, Brabazon Street, Co. Dublin, currier, exor.

Dwelling house etc. on east side Patrick Street, Dublin, (bounding on north to Mr. Fearnsley's concerns, on east and south to Mr. Sweeny's concern and house, and on west to Ralph Warnells stall) testator being entitled to an annual rent of £7 5s. 0d. under Will of Miles Best deceased.

Witnesses: Owen Murtagh, Brides Alley, cabinet maker, John Roberts, Dublin, gent.

Memorial witnessed by: John Roberts, Wm. Dunphy, Dublin, gent.

360, 238, 242433 Henry Singleton (seal)

698 LIPSETT, LEWIS, Lower Cashell, Co. Donegal. 7 Feb. 1783. Narrate 1½ p. 19 Aug. 1784.

His wife. His son Thomas. His son John. His daughter, her uncles John and Francis Lipsett to give consent to her marriage. His son Edward.

His holding in the In land of said town of Cashell; his part of the Out Land of his said holding. The holding in Ballyshannon, known by the name of Thomas Lipsett's tenements.

Witnesses: Arthur Lipsett, Cashel, Alexr. Kelly, Ardeelan, David Johnston, Lurgan, Francis Gillgar, Ballyshannon all Co. Donegal, farmers.

Memorial witnessed by: Francis Gillgar, Michl. Hanly, Ballyshannon, gent.

358, 506, 242531 Francis Lipsett (seal)

699 DAWSON, MICHAEL, Harristown, parish Ballyboggan, Co. Meath. 25 Aug. 1784. Full ¾ p. 4 Sept. 1784.

My wife Nancy Dawson, and her children. My daughter Margaret Dawson. To my eldest son Roger Dawson " a child's part . . . . to be reserved for him untill the expiration of his time at his trade and then to be given to him to commence business for himself." My second eldest son Dennis Dawson to live with his mother Nancy until sent to business that will best agree with him to be considered by his uncle Patrick Dawson or his guardians. Said Patrick Dawson and Walter Hussey exors. and guardians of children.

My holding on lands of Harristown.

Witnesses: Thady Grehan, Ballybeggan, Co. Meath, parish priest, James Canavan, Gainhu, Patrick Canavan, Blackwater, both said Co., farmers.

Memorial witnessed by: James Canavan, Patrick Canavan.

358, 527, 242700 Ann Dawson (seal)

700 BAYLY, SUSANNA, Ballytore, Co. Kildare, widow of John Bayly late of Gowran, Co. Kilkenny, Esq., deceased.

21 July 1784. Narrate 2 pp. 2 Oct. 1784.

Robert Bayly then the youngest son of the said John Bayly and of testatrix, exor. Her son Clayton Bayly, a settlement executed on his marriage.

Reciting that said John Bayly was seized of lands in counties of Kildare and Dublin, and of lands of Donacomper, Old St. Wolstan's, New St. Wolstan's and other lands all situated in counties of Kildare and Dublin, and Parsonstown, New Bridge and part of St. Woolstanes and Cooldrina, also lands near the town of Carlow, Co. Catherlogh, and the small island in the River Barrow. Cabragh, Figott, and Rathenrick, Co. Meath.

Witnesses: George Dunbar, Greenbank, Co. Kildare, Robert Power, Powers Grove, Co. Kildare, Esq., William Cooper, Camden Street, Dublin, gent.

Memorial witnessed by: John Gelling, Dublin, gent., John Scallion, clerk to said John Gelling.

358, 550, 242945 Robert Bayly (seal)

701 BELL, ALEXANDER, Drumlough, parish Drumgarth, Co. Down, farmer. 15 Oct. 1784. Précis ½ p. 19 Oct. 1784.

His wife Jean Bell. William Bell and Joseph Morrow sons-in-law. Farm of land in Drumlough held under Lord Clanwilliam.

Witnesses to Will and memorial: Walter Robinson, Damully, lordship of Newry, Thomas Marshall, Achnarven, both Co. Down.

364, 64, 243078 Alexr. Bell (seal)

702 LESTER, CHARLES, Maryborough, Queen's Co., apothecary. 17 May 1763. Narrate 1 p. 22 Oct. 1784.

His daughter Sarah Lester, her brother Robert Lester, her sister Ann Lester, her brother Thos. His [testator's] son Charles Lester, Dundalk, exor.

His premises in Maryborough, a tenement in possession of William Atkinson.

Witnesses: Rev. James Jenkin, James Graves, William Lawler, all of Maryborough.

Memorial witnessed by: William Lawler, Wm. Budds, Maryborough.

363, 87, 243122 Sarah Dimond (seal)
Sarah Dimond otherwise Lester

703 ROCKINGHAM, CHARLES MARQUIS OF

4 Sept. 1764. Codicils 5 Dec. 1781 and 1 July 1782. Précis ¾ p. 29 Oct. 1784.

Concerning his real estate in Ireland [no details].

Witnesses: Edward Oates, Raw Marsh, Co. York, Esq., deceased, Thos. Smith, Bassingthorpe, Greasbrough, Co. York, yeoman, deceased, Jno. Cooke, Greasbrough aforesaid, yeoman.

First codicil witnessed by: Rt. Hon. George Cavendish, Wm. Bromfield, Conduit Street, parish of St. George, Hanover Square, Middlesex, Esq., Edwd. Barwell, Abington Street, parish of St. Margt. Westminster, Esq.

Second codicil witnessed by: Richard Warren, Sackville Street, parish of St. James, Middlesex, Doctor of Physick, James Swift, Putney, Co. Surrey, surgeon and apothecary, Rev. Walker King, Stratton Street, parish of St. George, aforesaid, clerk.

Memorial witnessed by: Thos. Douse, clerk to Lord Mansfield, Chas. Bowns, Banktop, near Barnsley, Yorkshire.

363, 93, 243163 Mansfield (seal)
(William Earl of Mansfield the surviving devisee in trust.)

704 STRAUCHAN, GEORGE, Lisnacrager [Lisnacrogher] parish of Skerry, Diocese of Connor, Co. Antrim. 9 March 1773. Narrate 1¾ p. 11 Nov. 1784.

His two sons James Strauchan and John Strauchan (exor.). His son Gordon Strauchan, exor. His son Mathew Strauchan. His son George Strauchan. His daughter Sarah Strauchan alias Glenn. His son James's daughter Ann Strauchan, and grandson George Strauchan son to James. To his son John's daughter Ann Strauchan £20, and if his son John should happen to have a son £20 to him also. His sister Jane Strauchan alias Willson. His nephew George Strauchan. Hugh Campbell and Robt. Campbell overseers.

Lands of Inshamp[h], [Co. Antrim], and his two flax mills. Lands of Clinty, [Co. Antrim]. A farm held under Lord Mountcashell. The moss of Lisnacrager [Lisnacrogher, Co. Antrim]. Lands in Lisnamurrican [Lisnamurrikin, Co. Antrim].

Witnesses: James McNaghten, Wm. McNaghten both of Ballyreagh, Saml. Strauchan, Lisnacrougher, Co. Antrim, gent.

Memorial witnessed by: Roger Casement, Michl. Harrison, both Ballymena, Co. Antrim, gents.

365, 114, 243515 John Strahan (seal)
Gordon Strahan (seal)

705 LEANY, WALTER, Baltrasna, parish Culmullin, Co. Meath.
25 Feb. 1782. Narrate ¾ p. 3 Dec. 1784.

His daughter Ann Leany and her husband Richard Plunkett. His son James Leany. His son John Leany. Christopher Leany and Maurice Coffey exors.

Witnesses: Maurice Coffey, Crosskeys, Co. Meath, land surveyor, Peter Meighan, Mullagh, Co. Meath, yeoman.

22 Oct. 1784 written at foot of said Will " To his son Michl. Leany who he did not [know] was living at the time he signed said Will" 5/-.

Witness: Maurice Coffey.

Memorial witnessed by: Maurice Coffey, Edwd. Smyth, Dublin, gent.

360, 401, 243993 John Leany (seal)

706 MILES, EDWARD, Ballyloughan, Co. Tipperary, gent.
13 Oct. 1778. Narrate ¾ p. 18 Dec. 1784.

His wife Mary Miles extx. His daughters Mary, Rebecca, Ann, Alice, Elizabeth and Catherine Miles. His sons Lawford, Henry, John, Edward and Robert Miles. His brother John Miles. Thomas Miles, Kellallyvaughan, John Miles, Rochestown, trustees and exors. His lands of Ballyloughan and Moonemore, Barony Iffa, Co. Tipperary.

Witnesses: Wm. Reymond, Mitchelstown, Co. Cork, gent., William Bagnell, Marlehill, Wm. Maher, Tibrea, both Co. Tipperary.

Memorial witnessed by: William Maher, John Nowlan, Clonmell, servant.

363, 250, 244229 Mary Miles (seal)
extx.

707 MULLIN, GEORGE, Grange Trevit, Co. Meath.

5 Jan. 1783. Full 1¼ p. 1 Feb. 1785.

My wife Sarah Miles. Deed made 22 July 1751, on account of the marriage of my only child Jane Mullin now Buckley wife of Anthony Buckley of Grange Trevit, farmer. Said Anthony Buckley exor.

My house and yard in Grafton Street [Dublin].

Witnesses: Thomas Bryan, John Cowley, John Buckley.

Memorial witnessed by: John Buckley, Wm. Dunphy, Dublin, gent.

362, 300, 244797 Anthony Buckley (seal)

708 VICARS, WILLIAM, Ballynakill, Co. Carlow, Esq.

29 Nov. 1784. Narrate 1½ p. 7 Feb. 1785.

His wife Ann Vicars, his eldest daughter Ann Vicars. His youngest dau. Elizabeth Jane Vicars. His worthy friend Willm. Burton, Burton Hall, Richard Vicars, senior, Levally, and John Bambrick, Maidenhead, Esqrs., exors. and with his said wife guardian of said children.

Town and lands of Ballycarney and Quinagh, Co. Carlow. Lease of Ballynakill, Co. Carlow. Derryfore, Clonticoe, Boolybeg, Clarbarracum and Ballyhen, Queen's Co., and Ballycollone, Co. Kildare.

Witnesses: Nicholas Warringford Vicars the younger, then of Levalley, Queen's Co., Esq., William Alexander, Carlow, surgeon, Benjm. Whiteace, Ballynakil, yeoman.

Memorial witnessed by: Stephen Goggin, Dublin, gent., James Elms servant to said William Burton.

365, 345, 244871 William Burton (seal)

709 CUMING, ANDREW, Lisbredan, Co. Down, gent.

14 Aug. codicil 15 Oct. 1783. Narrate 2 pp. 10 Feb. 1785.

His wife Elizh. Cuming exor. His present children. Ann Adair then of Carrickfergus. His son John Cuming. His second son William Cuming. His third son Robert Cuming. His fourth son Thomas

Cuming. His fifth son Andrew Cuming. His daughter Mary Cuming. His daughter Agnes Orr. Col. Robert McLeroth and John Todd, Toddstown, parish of Saintfield, Co. Down, gent., trustees and exors.

His freehold estate in Lisbredan.

Witnesses to Will and codicil: James Caldwell, Ballymiscam, Dissenting minister, John Boyde, Ballybeen, farmer, Robert Moore, Dundonald, schoolmaster, all in Co. Down.

Memorial witnessed by: James Caldwell, John Boyd.

366, 247, 244904

Elizh. Cuming (seal)
Wm. Cuming (seal)
Robert Cuming (seal)
Mary Cuming (seal)
Ann Orr (seal)
(Ann or Agnes Orr)

710 FOXALL, JOSEPH, Dublin, gent.
28 Aug. 1764. Narrate 1 p. 19 March 1785.

His wife Elinor Foxall extx. His two daughters Catherine and Constant Grace Foxall. The house in Mabot Street in which his son-in-law Gustavus Warner then dwelt; his daughter Jane Foxall wife of said Gustavus, her son Simon Warner. His son Joseph Foxall.

His house in Martin's Lane then in lease to William Becket. Ground on North Strand, Sir Quaile Somerville, Bart., lessor, then leased by him to Edwd. Chetham; his other houses in Mabot Street, all Dublin. His house wherein he then dwelt on the North Strand.

Witnesses: Edward Chetham, Toby Purcell, Robert Thompson, then all of Dublin, gents.

Memorial witnessed by: Toby Purcell, Gustavus Warner, junior, both Dublin, gents.

361, 459, 245503

Elinor Foxall (seal)

711 HENRY, MATHEW, Ballymoney, Diocese of Connor, Co. Antrim, innholder. 14 Dec. 1783. Full 3 pp. 11 April 1785.

My wife Margaret Henry extx. My eldest son Wm. Henry (under 21 years). My second son Robert Henry. My daughter Mary Ann

Henry (under 21 years, unmarried). Robert Gault, Alexr. Ramage, Mullans, exors.

That house in which the widow Boyd lives (adjoining the house of John Miller shoemaker in Main Street, Ballymoney), my house adjoining now in possession of Neal McCock, a malt kiln at rere. The house in which we now live and turnpike meadow. My holding at Whiskey Hall.

Witnesses: Robt. Kirk, Ballymoney, merchant, John Jordan, Ballymoney, yeoman, Geo. Hutcheson, Dublin, attorney.

Memorial witnessed by: Robert Kirk, John Jordon.

363, 554, 245746 Margt. Henry (seal)

712 HENRY, MATHEW, Ballymoney, Diocese of Connor, Co. Antrim, innholder. Codicil 22 Dec. 1783. Full ¾ p. 11 April 1785.

Empowers his children to sell or dispose of houses (mentioned in his Will) if they so wish.

Witnesses: Robert Kirk, Ballymoney, Co. Antrim, merchant, John Jordon, Ballymoney, yeoman, George Hutcheson, Dublin, attorney.

Memorial witnessed by: Robert Kirk, Allinson Campbell, Ballymoney, gent.

363, 554, 245747 Margt. Henry (seal)

713 COULSON, JOHN, Bellmount otherwise Ranaghan in parish of Dromully, Co. Fermanagh, Esq. 26 Oct. 1761. Full 3 pp. 26 Apl. 1785.

To be buried in church of Newtown Butler. My wife Sarah Coulson otherwise Stanford, her marriage settlement made 1719 by Luke Stanford, Esq., deceased. The law suit depending in the High Court of Chancery, wherein my wife and I and her son and others are plaintiffs and Bedley Stanford and others are defendants. My two sons Lieut. John Coulson (eldest) and Lancelot Coulson (second) and my daughter Irwine Coulson exors. My brother Henry Coulson deceased. Jane Coulson, eldest daughter to my brother Henry Coulson late of Newtown Butler, Co. Fermanagh. Abigail Coulson, second daughter to my brother Henry Coulson. Ennis and Nancy Coulson two daughters of my said brother Henry Coulson. A debt due by Michl. Ennis of Clones. Mrs. Sidney Crow, her husband. Edwd. McCaffrey.

Lands of Mullaghmore and Dugerry [Doogary], Co. Cavan; Beleek and Cloaghmore, Co. Donegall (Lord William Connolly lessor), Drumeroe [Drumroo], Drumallen, Sheeny, Ennis, Doocarin [Doocharn], Carnmore and Magherareigh, all in Co. Fermanagh; Coreavaghan and Colman, Co. Monaghan. Loughgallygreen [Loughkillygreen] and Kilturk, Co. Fermanagh. Bellmount formerly called Ranaghan and Gortgawen, Co. Fermanagh, (Nicholas Ward, Esq., deceased, lessor).

Witnesses: James Noble, Thomas Noble, Christopher Crow.

Memorial witnessed by: Henry Palmer and Daniel Thompson, Birr, King's Co., William Langton, Dublin, merchant.

368, 54, 245997 Irwine Cuffe (seal)
in said Will named

714 FRAYNE, RICHARD, Ballydicken, Co. Wexford, gent.
13 Oct. 1783. Narrate 1 p. 3 May 1785.

His wife Sarah Frayne. His eldest son Michael Frayne already provided for. His third son Walter Frayne exor. Farm and lands of Ballydicken, Co. Wexford.

Witnesses: Abraham Tate, Castlebridge, parish clerk, David Malone, Ballydicken, miller, Thomas Magra, Tikillen, farmer, all Co. Wexford.

Memorial witnessed by: David Malone, Benjn. Wilson, Wexford, gent.

358, 618, 246135 Walter Frayne (seal)

715 McADAM, PHILIP, Gortoher, Co. Clare, gent.
29 July 1782. Précis ½ p. 3 May 1785.

His wife Catherine McAdam. His younger children. Capt. Thos. Hobson, Fairyhill, Co. Clare and Rev. John Dickson, Knockdrommassell, Co. Limerick, clerk, exors.

Lands of Upper Gortato[g]her, Co. Clare in possession of James Nash and his under tenants. Coulvicknalira said county.

Witnesses: James Nash David, Parteen, Co. Clare, gent., James Nash John, Limerick, gent., Henry Sargent, Limerick, gent.

Memorial witnessed by: James Nash David, John Dickson, Dublin, attorney.

361, 503, 246145 Catherine McAdam (seal)

716 MORRIS, WILLIAM, Waterford, Esq.

22 Aug. 1782. Narrate 1 p. 4 May 1785.

His son Benj. Morris. Ann Morris otherwise Sheppard wife of said Benj. Morris, a settlement dated 5th April 1774 made on their marriage. His son William Morris, Esq. His son George Morris.

His house etc. on St. John's Hill, parish of St. John Without, liberties of city of Waterford. The old tan yards etc. and his dwelling house, and the malt mill which was then a forge or cellar with rooms over it, and house adjoining, all in Trinity parish Without, in county of city of Waterford, and houses etc. held under the Mayor, Sheriffs and citizens of Waterford. Town and lands of Kilmeadan, Co. Waterford. His houses etc. in the county of city of Kilkenny held under the late Duke of Ormonde. Lands of Ballylongmore, Barony of Gaultier, Co. Waterford. Lands of Ardagal, Queen's Co. Bayly's and Conduit Lane in Waterford, held under Viscount Enniskillen. Lands of Carrickbegg, Co. Waterford and Noard otherwise Nuard, Co. Tipperary. Garrythomas, Barony Kells, Co. Kilkenny. A parcel of ground on which did formerly stand a tan yard in the possession of widow Marshall and afterwards a waste piece of ground in possession of Edmd. Ryan, cooper, and Alderman Benjamin Norris son of Alderman John Norris, deceased and his undertenants in West Barron Strand Street, St. Patrick's parish, Waterford. Ground on the Quay at East End of the Custom House in Trinity parish, Waterford on which a large building hath been lately erected and added to said Custom house. Two houses in Milk Lane, Waterford set to Thos. Walsh.

Witnesses: Mathias Anderson, Waterford, wine cooper, Theodore Cooke and Robt. Cooke, Waterford, Esqrs.

Memorial witnessed by: Theodore Cooke, Rev. John Cooke, Waterford, clerk.

365, 518, 246175 George Morris (seal)

717 BLAKE, THOMAS, Furbough, Co. Galway, Esq.

11 Feb. 1760. Narrate $\frac{3}{4}$ p. 13 May 1785.

His father Francis Blake, Furrabough, Esq., then lately deceased. His cousin John Blake, Ballymanagh. Andrew, John Blake's only son; failing whose heirs male testator's lands etc. to Dominick Blake, Fartigare, Co. Galway, Esq., "and according to the last Will of Andrew Oge Blake formerly of town of Galway merchant." Walter Taylor, Castle Taylor, Thomas French, Muckullin, Mark Lynch, Barna, all Co. Galway, Esqrs, exors. His real estate in Co. Galway and lands, houses and mills etc. in town and county of the town of Galway.

Witnesses: Stephen Egan, Galway, Esq., M.D., Mathew Joice, same, Esq., M.D., Timothy McDonoh, late of Loughrea, Co. Galway, servant man.

Memorial witnessed by: Stephen Egan, James Quin, Galway, merchant.

364, 397, 246312 John Blake (seal)

of Summerhill, Co. Galway, Esq. eldest son of Andrew Blake late of Ballymanagh, Co. Galway, Esq. deceased, who was the eldest son of John Blake of Ballymanagh, aforesaid deceased who was the devisee named in said Will.

718 FORRESTER, ROBERT, Cloverhill, Co. Londonderry, Esq.

21 May 1784. Narrate $1\frac{1}{4}$ p. 18 June 1785.

His son William Forrester exor. Jane Forrester [wife of said Wm.] testator's daughter-in-law. His sister Martha. His son Anthony. His son Arthur.

Rent due to Robt. Alexander for the heirs of the late Mr. Dupre deceased. Neal McPeake.

His freehold lease of Drumrammer, parish of Drumachose, Co. Londonderry, held under Earl of Tyrone; of Mobue, parish of Errigal,

Co. Londonderry held under Earl of Tyrone. His furniture at Cloverhill. Sheep etc. at Culbane [? Co. Antrim].

Witnesses: Rev. Clotworthy Soden, Kilcronaghan, Rev. Ezekiel Brown, Maghera, Saml. McDowell, Maghera, all Co. Londonderry.

Memorial witnessed by: Saml. McDowell, William O'Scullion, Bellaghy, Co. Londonderry, clerk.

369, 148, 246757 Will. Forrester (seal)

719 MORRIS, ANDREW, Mulane, Co. Wexford, farmer.

11 March 1780. Narrate 2¼ pp. 13 June 1785.

His wife Susanna Morris, his two sons Stearne Morris (eldest) and Francis Morris exors. His four sons, Stearne and Francis Morris in part provided for, John insane, and Andrew. His four daughters Susanna, Alice, Elizabeth and Mary, said Elizabeth and Mary were already provided for.

Lands of Aughullen, Co. Wexford, Mrs. Margt. Bauman and John Bauman, Esq., lessors. Lands of Pallis called the Custodium lands of Pallis held by two several leases under Henry Monck and John Grogan. Mullanegrath, the Glebe lands of Kilnure leased from Rev. Abraham Symes.

Witnesses: Roger West, Dublin, gent., Mathew Redmond, Rawpierce, Co. Wexford, farmer, Patt. Ryan, of said place, farmer.

Memorial witnessed by: Patt. Ryan, J. J. Ashenhurst.

367, 227, 246788 Francs. Morris (seal)

720 COLLES, BARRY, Dublin, gent.

21 Jan. 1783. Narrate 1¾ p. 16 June 1785.

His daughter Susanna Meredith exor. His grandson Joshua Paul Meredith. His grandson Barry Colles Meredith, his eldest son Joshua Colles Meredith, John Eastwood Meredith second son of his said grandson, Edwd. Meredith third son of his grandson, Charles Meredith fourth son of his said grandson, Barry Colles Meredith fifth son of his said grandson.

John White Esq., and Henry Betagh, gent., trustees. Wm. Costello, Mary Isabella Costello. Peter Crossan.

Lotts and buildings on West side of St. Stephen's Green. Four tenements in Michael's Lane, and five in Borr Court all in county of city of Dublin. Lands of Greenoge, Co. Meath, Derrooly and Taully-mirahan [Tullymorerahan] and Clonegown in King's Co. Pelletstown, Co. Dublin. Kilcollan, Madleen, Timokeny and lands in Co. Kilkenny. Derrycooley, King's Co. to his said grandson Joshua Paul Meredith upon the trusts concerning same by the Will of Robert Reading, Esq., deceased.

Witnesses: John Brownrigg, Dublin, gent., then clerk to John Wheeler, gent., attorney at law, Dudley Davis, Dublin, then clerk to said John Wheeler and afterwards clerk to said Barry Colles, George Warren, Dublin, gent., attorney at law.

Memorial witnessed by: Dudley Davis, Joseph Cavanagh, Dublin, clerk to said Mr. Wheeler.

369, 173, 246827 John White (seal)
Sus. Meredith (seal)

721 GAYNOR, JOHN, Cole Alley, Meath Street, Dublin, mariner.

23 June 1785. Narrate 1 p. 28 June 1785.

To be interred in churchyard of St. Michan's, Dublin. His wife Mary Gaynor otherwise Collins extx. His daughters by his former wife, Catherine Gaynor and Ann Gaynor.

Witnesses: Martin FitzGerald, Dublin, carpenter. Edward Biker, Dublin, weaver. John Callaghan, Dublin, gent.

Memorial witnessed by: Martin Fitzgerald, John Callaghan.

367, 266, 247019 John Gaynor (seal)
the testator.

722 MAGUSTY, MARGARET, Londonderry, widow.

10 March 1768. Narrate $1\frac{3}{4}$ p. 7 July 1785.

William Reynolds, Thomas Venables and Thomas Ledlie, all of Londonderry, trustees and exors. Her daughter Elizabeth Balfour otherwise Magusty.

Her two houses in Pump Street, Londonderry. Seventy five perches which belonged to the tenement formerly belonging to Joseph Merrison and in her own and her undertenants possession on south side of road leading to Lifford.

Witnesses: Mathew Rutherford, merchant, Sarah Johnston, spinster and John Coningham, merchant, all of Londonderry.

Memorial witnessed by: Mathew Rutherford, James Davis, Stafford Street, Dublin, gent.

367, 289, 247119 Elizabeth Balfour (seal)

723 MOSS, JACOB, Mary Street, Dublin, cabinet maker.
23 Aug. 1784. Narrate 1¼ p. 10 Aug. 1785.

To his wife Mary Ann Moss otherwise Murphy one British shilling only. Reciting lease dated 12 Aug. 1782 whereby Precious Clarke, Dublin, merchant, demised to testator a house etc. on South side of Fleet Street, parish of St. Mark, Dublin, now set by testator to Francis Bourke, victualler. Testator at expense of £300 built a new house and concerns on said premises which he set to John Bouhier [? Bouchier] of College Street, confectioner. Rents of these two houses to be divided amongst his mother Elizabeth Hogan, extx. and his three children Cath. Moss, Patrick Moss and Elizabeth Moss.

Witnesses: Wm. Flood, Dublin, sailmaker, Richd. Supple, Dublin, publican, John Nugent, hairdresser, Dublin.

Memorial witnessed by: John Nugent, Patrick Little, Dublin, gent.

376, 8, 247548 Elizabeth Hogan (seal)
her mark.

724 RICHEY, NATHAN, the elder, Goosedub, parish and county of Antrim, farmer. 15 Sept. 1784. Full 2½ pp. 16 Sept. 1785.

My wife Sarah Richey. My son Nathan Richey exor. My son John (£10 when he shall come in person to receive it and not until then). My son Patrick. My son James. My son-in-law Josias Campbell. My grandson John Campbell. My son Wm. Richey exor. My daughters Isabella, Sarah and Margaret, Sarah and Margaret to be kept about the house for two years after my decease without any charge. My grandson John Fisher Richey son of James Richey. My farm, denominations of my said farm to son Wm., the Cloverfield, the Bierfield, the Broadfield, the field called the Stripe and the 23 acres next Calside. My good friend Rev. John Rankeen of Antrim.

Witnesses: Rev. John Rankeen, Dissenting minister, Robt. Young, post master, Robt. Young, junior, linen draper, all of Antrim.

374, 60, 247846 Nath. Richey (seal)

725 SCHAW, CHARLOTT, Little Queen Anne Street, parish of St. Marlebone, Middlesex. 25 July 1776. Narrate 1½ p. 38 Sept. 1785.

Her daughter Elizabeth Schaw, her daughter Charlotte Schaw. To her grand-daughter Frances Charlotte Schaw daughter of her son Frederick Bridges, £2,000 when 21 or on marriage. Her son John Bridges Schaw. All real estate in England and Ireland.

Witnesses: Henry Townley Ward, Henrietta Street, parish of St. Paul, Middlesex, gent., Robert Shaw and James Phillips, clerks to said Mr. Ward.

Memorial witnessed by: Henry Townley Ward, Benedict Hamilton, Dublin, gent.

369, 381, 248029 Charlotte Schaw (seal)
the daughter of testatrix

726 FRENCH, THOMAS, Moycullen, Co. Galway, Esq.
31 March 1783. Narrate 2¼ pp. 21 Nov. 1785.

His wife Ann French extx. His brother Peter French. Christopher St. George, Tyrone, Co. Galway and Patrick French, Bushy Park, Galway, Esq., trustees.

Legacies to Miss Catherine O'Flaherty, Mary Geoghegan otherwise Lynch widow of Chas. Geoghegan, Galway, merchant, deceased, Elinor Skerrett otherwise Daly widow of Eneas Daly, Foxford, Co. Mayo, gent., deceased, Mary McDonagh, otherwise Blake wife of Robert McDonagh, Galway, cabinet maker, Pierce Lynch late of

Dangin, Co. Galway but now of Galway, gent., Mary Lynch spinster, one of the daughters of said Pierce Lynch, George Lynch late of Ternaduane but then of Tuam, Go. Calway, gent., Patrick Flaherty, sadler, son of Francis Flaherty late of Moycullen, aforesaid, gent., deceased. Anne Mannin his wife's maid servant. Edmd. Tierney his man servant. Arthur French, French Park formerly called Dungar, Co. Roscommon, Esq.

His real estate in Co. Galway. His dwelling house and demesne of Moycullen. Lands of Atheemahon and Allenspark then held by Thomas Hynde, Kilclogan then held by Nicholas Mullowny, Gortachory then held by Laurence King and partners, Portdaragh held by Edmd. Scarrell, Esq. Curry and Fly Island.

Witnesses: Oliver Martyn, John Kirwan Anthony, and John Kergan, all of Galway, gents.

Memorial witnessed by: John Kergan, Michl. French, Claregalway Castle, Co. Galway, Esq.

375, 60, 248726 Patt. French (seal)

INDEX OF NAMES

Numbers refer to the number of the Abstract.

The names of **Testators** appear in heavier type.

A surname appearing in the Index does not necessarily appear also in the relevant Abstract. See *Introduction* page iii.

"N" refers to a name in a footnote.

Numbers refer to the number of the Abstract.

In cases where the modern spelling of a townland has been inserted within square brackets in the text the entry is indexed under the modern form and the alternative spelling as a cross reference.

www.ingramcontent.com/pod-product-compliance
Lightning Source LLC
Chambersburg PA
CBHW060128280326
41932CB00012B/1458